Popular Culture and Political Economic Thought

Popular Culture and Political Economic Thought

Fables of Commonwealth

Thomas Strychacz

LEXINGTON BOOKS
Lanham • Boulder • New York • London

Published by Lexington Books
An imprint of The Rowman & Littlefield Publishing Group, Inc.
4501 Forbes Boulevard, Suite 200, Lanham, Maryland 20706
www.rowman.com

86-90 Paul Street, London EC2A 4NE

British Library Cataloguing in Publication Information Available

Library of Congress Cataloging-in-Publication Data

Names: Strychacz, Thomas F., author.
Title: Popular culture and political economic thought : fables of commonwealth / Thomas Strychacz.
Description: Lanham : Lexington Books, 2023. | Includes bibliographical references and index.
Identifiers: LCCN 2022048542 (print) | LCCN 2022048543 (ebook) | ISBN 9781793633965 (cloth) | ISBN 9781793633972 (epub)
Subjects: LCSH: Economics in popular culture.
Classification: LCC HB71 .S8437 2023 (print) | LCC HB71 (ebook) | DDC 330--dc23/eng/20221212
LC record available at https://lccn.loc.gov/2022048542
LC ebook record available at https://lccn.loc.gov/2022048543

Contents

Preface

The impetus for this book came from several directions. One was a surprise. While trying to kickstart the introduction to *Kitchen Economics: Women's Regionalist Fiction and Political Economy* (2020), a book about the relationship of late-nineteenth century women writers to political economic discourses, I found myself preoccupied with contemporary works and events. For a summer or two it seemed plausible to introduce the likes of Sarah Orne Jewett and Mary Wilkins Freeman with Andy Weir's *The Martian*, and later on with an account of Michelle Obama's kitchen garden on the White House lawn. I was wrong. But I realized eventually that my intuition was right—just in reverse. The discursive formations of nineteenth-century political economy I was writing about—the narratives, the models, the strategies—were to be discovered everywhere in the landscapes of today's popular culture. So, this book is a sort of sequel to *Kitchen Economics*. It argues that older modes of political economic thought, which began to disappear from the disciplinary study of economics during the late-nineteenth century rise of neoclassicism, still demand our attention if we are to understand popular characterizations of "the economic." The second vector for this book was a shock: the inexorable onset of eco-crisis, which compelled me to see that understanding popular characterizations of "the economic" has never been more urgent. Faced with catastrophic climate change, we need new economic models, new ways of thinking about popular representations of economics, and a newly and *differently* engaged scholarship. If there is an emergent discourse on "the common good"—a sentiment that, I will argue, the Great Recession has done much to foster—it will have to make its presence felt through the powerful fables of popular culture.

As ever, there are too many people to thank individually for their contributions to this book. Judith Lakamper, Acquisitions Editor at Lexington Books, inspired me to start putting these ideas together—that was the third vector for this book, in fact. Kudos to the anonymous readers who tendered excellent advice on this manuscript, *Kitchen Economics*, and the two previously published articles that have made their way into this book. Particular thanks to Kathryn Reiss for her excellent feedback and to Kim Magowan for her generous and scrupulous reading of the finished manuscript—and to both for their unstinting support. I have two final dedications. One is to my institution. I began writing this book at Mills College; I finished it at Mills College at Northeastern, after the "merger" of the two institutions. I dedicate this book in part to the 150-year history of Mills College and to its students, who have never failed to inspire me over the 34 years of my tenure there. I also dedicate this book to my grandchildren, Lydia, Isla, Madeline, and Sylas. If there is a point to scholarship in an age of eco-crisis, then surely it must be to look to the future we hope our children will inhabit.

Introduction

Economic Fabling in an Age of Eco-Crisis

At the UN Climate Action summit in September 2019, young climate activist Greta Thunberg launched a ferocious attack on global capitalism's indifference to impending ecocatastrophe. "We are in the beginning of a mass extinction," she said, "and all you can talk about is money and fairy tales of eternal economic growth. How dare you!" She went on to note that the world's "CO_2 budget"—the planet's reserve before a potentially irreversible tipping point—would be entirely gone within eight and a half years.[1] A few months later, in January 2020, US Treasury secretary Steve Mnuchin combatted Thunberg's assaults by joking, "After she goes and studies economics in college she can come back and explain that to us." Mnuchin's argument exhibits a perfectly circular logic. The disciplinary study of neoclassical, or mainstream, economics in colleges concerns itself with the functioning of capitalist market economies. As twentieth-century economist Lionel Robbins famously put it, economics is the science of markets that "studies human behavior as a relationship between ends and scarce means which have alternative uses"; in Susan F. Feiner's succinct rewording, its provenance is the "allocation of scarce resources to the infinity of human wants."[2] Therefore studying economics in college could not "explain" the radical challenge to capitalism's over-exploitation of resources that Thunberg advocates. It could barely countenance the possibility, so central to green economics, that humans are not, or do not have to be, creatures of infinite wants. And a self-professed science of markets could hardly countenance the possibility that the only solution to eco-crisis might be to dramatically transform capitalist markets or abandon them altogether.

The fact that the head of the US Treasury found it necessary to insist, however patronizingly, on the privilege of neoclassical economics suggests another tipping point: a growing awareness that the legitimacy of its formal knowledge systems might be coming into serious question. The academic discipline of economics has of course long recognized the pertinence of heterodox approaches—the feminist critique of the concept of Economic Man as the paradigmatic economic agent is one important example.[3] And it has never proceeded in lockstep over the question of whether it truly offers a "science" of markets. In 2003 Tony Lawson observed that many economists acknowledge that "modern economics mostly fails to illuminate the world in which we live and, indeed, is in a state of disarray."[4] That its privilege has begun to require acknowledgement, rationalization, and enforcement by no less than the head of the Treasury, however, points to a disarray no longer confined to academic papers and conferences. In part, that new public scrutiny is a consequence of the relentlessly increasing threat of climate change. In part it is a consequence of the Great Recession, which caused economic knowledge systems to come under formidable challenge. Mainstream economists claiming scientific rigor and politicians enacting economic policies that purported to follow best economic practices led to the near collapse of the US financial system and the global economy. By 2009, the failure of "economics" as theory and in practice seemed writ large on Wall Street.

Like Mnuchin's mocking rebuff to Thunberg, post-recessionary assessments of and solutions to economic failure approximated a tone of confidence. They were entrenched in the idiom and logic that economists understand—GDP, quantitative easing, liquidity, leverage, credit spreads, and unemployment rates. The 2008 Troubled Asset Relief Program and the 2009 American Recovery and Reinvestment Act put nearly two trillion dollars toward restoring liquidity to credit markets and stimulating the economy. Further political legislation in 2009 enacted the federal "Home Affordable Modification Program," which, in an effort to keep (some) people in their homes, crunched numbers, interest rates, and credit scores for mortgage holders deemed worthy of having their monthly payments reduced. In the absence of convincing alternatives, the logic of these forms of analysis could not be quite resisted. Yet they could hardly be taken as laying to rest growing instabilities in economic knowledge systems. As Annie McClanahan observes in her important study of the rhetoric of debt during the Great Recession, our historical conjuncture is marked by a sense of a "terminal crisis" in centuries-long practices of capitalist accumulation, bringing about a "crisis subjectivity," a "demystified condition of radical percipience and canny knowing" whose signs are everywhere visible in cultural realms.[5] The signature neoliberal faith that markets are able to solve all earthly problems has dissolved into a "*crisis of market magic*," in John Clarke's resonant phrase. Its authority remains, but "as elements, fragments, or traces rather than a coherent and cohering project."[6]

Some ten years later, the issue Mnuchin faced, and upon which Thunberg seized, is that our eco-crisis is chronic, worsening, and exacerbated by the very tactics that "ended" the Great Recession: stimulating the economy places ever-greater stress on global ecosystems. Scientists can chart now with some degree of certainty the calamitous effects of climate change. So, to some extent, can economists. A study published in January 2020 by the world's central banks warns that GDP across the globe might plunge by 25% if nothing is done to combat climate change.[7] Another study (September 2020) prepared by a bipartisan committee of the US government warned that the "cascading effects" of climate change pose a "major risk to the stability of the US financial system and to its ability to sustain the American economy."[8] Worse, the outcome of that eco-crisis cannot be analyzed by conventional economic means. As well-known neoclassical economist Kenneth Arrow observes in an article entitled "Are We Consuming Too Much?": "Nonlinearities in ecosystem dynamics imply the presence of serious downside risks related to the loss of natural capital."[9] Arrow means that an ecosystem does not function, and cannot be modeled, like an economic system. Economists can, and do, model the economic effects of (say) a carbon tax into a distant future. But the risks of using up "natural capital" such as Thunberg's CO_2 budget in the next eight years are unquantifiable. No one can predict the consequences of a nonlinearity—an abrupt rupture in our global eco-system. This suggests that the reports cited above are best-case scenarios since all of them, dire as they are, rely on the assumption that our ecosystem will continue to behave in linear, predictable, and non-chaotic ways.

One effect of the Great Recession and of the scientific near-certainty about forthcoming environmental crises—major drivers of today's "radical percipience"—has been to generate a complex discourse of economic fabling. The Wall Street traders making a market in arcane financial products prior to the Great Recession were "fantasists" running a "fictitious Ponzi scheme."[10] To Thunberg, Mnuchin and other world leaders are selling "fairy tales," pretense ("how dare you pretend"), and science fiction ("technologies that barely exist"). To the Treasury boss, Thunberg's lack of a formal education makes a sham of her economic explanations. And though Thunberg does marshal facts and statistics—CO_2 levels, forecasts of rising global temperature—her most incendiary moments arise from emotive appeals drawn from an appropriately apocalyptic register. Googling Thunberg's UN speech brings to the front of the queue not statistics but "how dare you," "we will never forgive you," and "you have stolen my dreams." There are reasons for this beyond the fact that "how dare you" makes for potent gifs and memes—which it does and has. Such statements evoke and activate the attention of a mass audience attuned to the enormous power of similarly iconic moments saturating the cultural landscape. "You have stolen my dreams and my childhood," she accuses the conference attendees, reaching back into a potent narrative arcana to cast world leaders as fairy-tale stealers of children and babies, dream snatchers, Gothic body snatchers, perhaps crosscut with more recent graphic novels such as Neil Gaiman's *The Sandman* (1989–96). The uncompromising role of the younger generation—"We will not forgive you"—likewise calls on contemporary revenge drama. We might think of Inigo Montoya's long quest for revenge in *The Princess Bride* (1987) ("You killed my father. Prepare to die!") or, still more obviously, Lord Voldemort's vicious assaults on J. K. Rowling's ever-more resilient Harry Potter. "Don't you turn your back on me, Harry Potter! I want you to look at me when I kill you!" shrieks Voldemort at the end of the movie adaptation of *Harry Potter and the Goblet of Fire* (2005).

Thunberg's portentous warning that the "eyes of all future generations are upon you" also evokes multiple contexts. She may well be referencing Tom Paine's *Common Sense* (1776), which constantly frames the soon-to-be American Republic in terms of the backward glance that posterity is sure to bestow on a glorious revolutionary moment. The names of politicians who put into place merely temporary measures, for example, "will be remembered by future generations with detestation." But Paine shares the stage with other more recent popular myths concerning watchers from the future: George Washington's song "History Has Its Eyes on You" in Lin-Manuel Miranda's *Hamilton* (2015), or the end of *Star Wars: Return of the Jedi* (1983), where Luke Skywalker, receives the ghostly approbation of Yoda, Obi-Wan Kenobi, and that transformed and somehow-sanctified architect of mass extinction, Darth Vader. We might also look to Aragorn's coronation promise to the assembled crowd in *The Return of the King* (2003): "This day does not belong to one man but to all. Let us together rebuild this world." One can therefore see Mnuchin's point. Against the precise mathematical formulations of mainstream economics Thunberg sketches in an amorphous array of mythic moments that are, in themselves, of dubious economic insight or significance. One might never guess from the backward glance that *Hamilton* turns on the revolutionary moment that Alexander Hamilton was the foremost architect of US capitalism or that Washington had slaves. Partly because it is so vague and selective about the history it incorporates, however, "History Has Its Eyes on You" leverages a formidable emotional power. Thunberg's genius is to appropriate the floating power of a mass cultural disposition—any number of transcendent betrayals, angry denunciations, world (re)buildings, and heroic redemptions dramatized before the evaluating and accusing or ratifying gaze of posterity—and focus it on a specific historical crisis.

A cultural conjuncture at which the combined energies of *Common Sense*, *Hamilton*, and *Harry Potter* have come to seem an effective response to the fantasies of economic science (fiction) affords immense opportunities for thinking critically and theoretically about today's economic discourses. On the one hand, the chronic and even "terminal" crises generated by current levels of capital accumulation and resource depletion suggest that the kind of confidence Mnuchin expresses in economic disciplines will increasingly read like bravado, bluff, or fairy tale. On the other hand, the charges Mnuchin brings against Thunberg—that her comments are non-rigorous, trivial—are powerful. They are in fact characteristic of the attitude of economists to what David F. Ruccio and Jack Amariglio call "economic talk" or "everyday economics" outside the academy. Inquirers situated within the discipline tend to read those forms as the "modern-day equivalent of a Bakhtinian carnival"; they seem ungrounded, amorphous, possessing a sort of magical thinking, an "erratic shamanism" consonant with an "ersatz economics."[11] To economists schooled in the rigor of mathematical modeling, and in models that pose individuals as abstract entities within market forces, popular economic thinking is implausibly "replete with accounts that are historical and anthropomorphic, moral tales that have heroes and villains."[12]

Ruccio and Amariglio are among a number of scholars who argue that acknowledging the complexity and cogency of popular thinking about economic matters can bring about a "new knowledge of economics."[13] Our historical conjuncture has certainly underscored the need and prepared the conditions for the emergence of such formations. John Clarke contends that a crisis of market magic may even be "fertile ground for the construction of new popular political imaginaries."[14] One can be, and should be, skeptical about its extent and efficacy. Still, a sense of growing emergency shows how desperately we need new accounts of the potential of the popular imaginary to introduce or facilitate a new politics. That need impels my approach to cultural studies and to this book's analyses of popular economic thought in a variety of written fictions, graphic novels, adventure travelogues, animated movies, popular TV shows, and more. Though I have not limited this study to the post-Recessionary era, nor to mass-market popular culture, its center of gravity remains the formations that contribute toward today's attempts to represent, or somehow resolve—or somehow evade—the emergence of new "crisis subjectivities" while faith in neoliberal ideologies slowly erodes. In the schema of this book, the Recession-era novel (and movie) *The Martian* and post-Recessionary animated movies bookend events and works as diverse as Michelle Obama's planting a kitchen garden on the White House lawn during the first year of Barack Obama's presidency, Octavia Butler's *Dawn*, Dr. Seuss's *How the Grinch Stole Christmas!*, the groundbreaking TV Reality show *Survivor*, the equally groundbreaking online game *FarmVille*, a painting by Norman Rockwell, and Himalayan adventure literature. Like Thunberg, these analyses look to the past but open to the future.

The primary focus of this book is to examine a particular mode of economic fabling: the ways in which popular culture has co-opted, and adapted, what used to be commonplace narratives of political economy, by which I mean the traditional domain of pre-modern and Enlightenment thinkers such as Plato, Thomas More, John Locke, Thomas Hobbes, Baron de Montesquieu, and Jean Jacques Rousseau, later revised by classical economists such as Adam Smith, Thomas Malthus, and John Stuart Mill to address the conditions of market society.[15] Though the field of political economy post–Adam Smith set out to create a body of formal knowledge—David Ricardo and his disciples, in particular, were focused on deriving "irrevocable and universal" laws of economic behavior—the discipline was open to narrative exposition, to stories drawn from and about history, to "moral tales that have heroes and villains," to narrative models, and even to what would now seem a nonchalant reliance on anecdote, hearsay, and fable.[16] Building "large narrative structures" that joined "economic issues to political, social, and psychological concerns," it created a "wide canvas on which political economists once created pictures of social existence and discussed the relations that defined the way their world worked."[17] Political economists had the ability to "range freely across the economic and the non-economic, to incorporate the social and the psychological into their analyses, to move from historical narrative to theoretical discourse without apology."[18]

Deploying narrative exposition as method, political economists also developed core narratives detailing the logic of their enterprise. Persuasive fictions about the supposedly natural progression of human civilizations or the natural characteristics of homo economicus—"arguments about what the nature of man is or should be"[19]—underwrote political economic "laws" and constituted their claims to truth. Those claims must be considered perilous ones. The concept of homo economicus was, and still is, riddled with assumptions about the sanctity of gender and class differences and the "fact" of White racial superiority; it constructs a "distinctly androcentric and Western perspective on selfhood and individual agency."[20] And accounts of the development of human societies underwrote the imperialist and colonial ideologies that afforded European nations and the United States their claim on "civilization." Nonetheless, the fact that political economists set out to make the guiding assumptions that structured their formal schemas, models, and narratives a constitutive part of their arguments has prompted some heterodox scholars of economics to revive political economy as a mode of analysis to pose against the century-long domination of neoclassicism. Feminist economists Marilyn Power, Ellen Mutari, and Deborah M. Figart, for example, prefer the term "feminist political economy" to "feminist economics" on the grounds that the mode of inquiry fashioned by classical economics has always considered "community well-being a valid subject for economic interrogation."[21] The concept of political economy reminds us that "Economics is not an abstract notion; it does not exist without people."[22] Part of that progressive work entails restoring a cogent sense of how narrativity might reformulate the abstractions of economics—how, as feminist economic historians Diana Strassman and Livia Polanyi argue, "reconceptualizing economic practice as storytelling may further feminist efforts to transform economic knowledge and practice."[23] In part that reconceptualization urges us to consider the bedrock "facts" upon which neoclassical economists build their analyses—that humans are creatures of infinite wants, for example, or that the ultimate good of market capitalism can be assumed—as a set of master narratives that requires scrutiny. In part it invites economists to restore a sense of lived, historically situated social relations to the abstractions of mainstream economics, and thus to historicize its claims to universality and ideological neutrality.

In this study I trace the continuing relevance of three central narratives from political economic thought. The first is stadialism, or stages theory, a model of history and society to which nineteenth-century thinkers granted virtually unanimous consent. Stadialism was a complex description of how societies evolve—and how they *should* evolve—in stages over time, generally understood in terms of a linear and progressive movement from savagery (characterized by hunting and gathering), barbarism (settled agriculture) and civilization (commercialism, industrialism, and market economies). The second is the political economic mode that Catherine Gallagher terms "bioeconomics"—the tendency among classical political economists to focus on "interconnections among populations, the food supply, modes of production and exchange, and their impact on life forms" in order to bestow economic significance on narratives about food production, distribution, and consumption.[24] The third is a discourse on commonwealth, to which political economic thought gravitated, of which neoclassical economists have little to say, but which exists as an insistent if diffuse and disorganized concern throughout the works of popular culture. It is here that "community well-being" becomes a valid subject for representation, if not "economic interrogation."

Though attuned to the self-interested behavior of individuals in the marketplace, political economists were intellectually drawn to interpreting economic activity as the product of interdependent members of a social group. As John Stuart Mill observed in his introductory remarks to *Principles of Political Economy* (1848), the discipline focused on the "nature of Wealth, and the laws of its production and distribution," including the "operation of all the causes by which the condition of mankind, or of any society of human beings, in respect of this universal object of human desire, is made prosperous or the reverse."[25] The laws of production and distribution might be susceptible to formal analysis. But for Mill the concept of "Wealth" cannot be reduced to metrics of the bottom line: the amount of raw resources utilized or wages paid, the number of commodities produced, and, above all, the circulation of money capital. "Wealth" anchors the concept of capital in materialities—labor, tools, and the resources involved in the productive process—and in their consequences for the "condition of mankind." It means asking the question of what resources and capital are *for*; it requires broad narratives about what constitutes a prosperous and equitable society. In considering how a healthy polity might organize a productive distribution of resources and wealth for the common good, classical economists raised the sort of wide-ranging questions that the academic discipline of neoclassical economics is ill-equipped to handle, but which popular discourses retain in fragmentary form.

In keeping with the logic that popular culture has kept alive key formations of pre-neoclassical economic thought, I have included analyses of some earlier works in the ensuing chapters. In fact, I find British author Harriet Martineau's 1832 popularization of political economic principles in "Life in the Wilds" indispensable for theorizing the twentieth and twenty-first century fantasy of living "wild" in a "state of nature," which is supposed to represent the arche of economic practices at the origin of human civilizations. Martineau's fable of economic origins resonates in many of the works I analyze in this book: the adventure travel literature of the Himalayas, *Survivor*, *Dawn*, *Firefly*, and even, in Chapter 1, the novel that in many ways epitomizes the logic of neoclassicism, Andy Weir's *The Martian* (2011). In *The Martian*, Mark Watney's potato farming on Mars evokes the paradigmatic economic figure of *homo economicus*, the self-interested, maximizing agent who constantly prioritizes competing choices in order to allocate scarce resources rationally. NASA's Earth, conversely, is a fantastic world of "unlimited funding" where, overturning two centuries of (neo)classical economic principle, "every human being has a basic instinct to help each other out."[26] Historicizing the novel's confused attempts to reconcile homo economicus with a workable concept of the common good, this chapter examines other prominent documents of the recessionary era—the US government's official Report on the financial crisis, Occupy Wall Street's Declaration, and indeed the attempts by both Thunberg and Mnuchin in their debate to leverage a "we" who they say support them, and for whom they speak—all of which manifest the same yearning for, and the same difficulty with imagining, a coherent sense of commonwealth.

Chapter 2 returns to Earth "farms" real and virtual, all of which attempt to generate a radically different idiom in which to respond to the material and ideological crises of the recessionary era. In 2009, during the brutal early days of the Great Recession, Michelle Obama began an organic kitchen garden on the White House's South Lawn. An act of self-conscious political theater directed toward representing economic value in new ways, it modeled social and environmental relationships through the symbolic actions of breaking ground in an orderly fashion, and of producing and distributing goods through unalienated labor. As many vaguely recognized at the time, the Obamas' kitchen garden looked back to, and deployed, earlier models of classical economic thought. Here I align the Obamas' "farming" with the well-known passage in Hector Crèvecoeur's *Letters from an American Farmer* (1782) where the American farmer ploughs his field, and in the process creates an exemplary discourse on (new) nation building and the republican virtues that should attend it. The Obamas'—and Crèvecoeur's—efforts find a surprising complement in the online farm-management games that followed the phenomenal success of *FarmVille*. These games foreground what Weir's novel and the Obamas in their garden lack: a primer, or tutorial, introducing players to the joys of trading goods in the marketplace. But as these games invite players to build their fabulous worlds, they also typically delineate a model of sociality and value not wholly commensurate with the bedrock assumptions of capitalism.

The next section of this book examines stadialism, or stages theory, a complex account of how human societies evolve toward civilization. A multitude of anthropological, political, linguistic, political, and economic principles were marshalled to explain this logic. Assuming that humans were fundamentally motivated to exchange goods with each other, stadialists argued that the historical process was shaped by the efficiencies accruing to a division of labor, to a competitive market system presided over by the civilizing effect of capital, and to labor-saving technologies. To political economists, an analysis of how markets function was underwritten by an assured sense of how economic practices began, why market systems came to prominence—and, not incidentally, why certain nations reaped the benefit of them. Martineau's "Life in the Wilds," which I employ in Chapter 3 as an exemplary stadial narrative, sets out to address precisely these questions, using a group of Britons in South Africa as a representative colony to plot what Martineau calls the "many stages" of economic development. Aligning first principles of political economy with the British "civilizing mission" to South Africa, the story teaches the logic of stadialism along with the logic of empire. In the process it also asserts Martineau's privilege as the history-teller, the one who can recount the entire process by virtue of looking back from the end of history, the acme of what that process has produced. This too is part of the stadial imagination in popular culture.

Testifying to the continued power of the stadial trope are many other popular TV shows whose fables of "living wild" introduce characters, and viewers, to what purports to be authentic and universal economic behavior. One obvious example is British survivalist Bear Grylls's many shows (*Man Vs. Wild* [2006–11], *Running Wild with Bear Grylls* [2014–present], *You Vs. Wild* [2019–present]). Chapter 3 concludes, though, by examining the first season of long-running Reality TV show *Survivor*, which follows the stadial script in almost every respect, and indeed extends it into what the show seems to consider the last stage of history in its quest for a "new society": one of simulacra and electronic mediation. As many scholars have shown, *Survivor* stages a neo-colonial narrative of how US-inspired capitalism incorporates the "wild" countries of the world into a web of simulacra. But I argue that the success of the show lies elsewhere. By allowing a number of partial, contradictory, and even bewildering counter-narratives to invade its domain, it constructs a sort of melancholic stadialism. It longs for Martineau's confidence in what her schema of history shows: that history has shape and meaning, and that economic activity undertaken by individuals can nonetheless build a community of interests. *Survivor* fumbles toward the notion that neoclassical economics needs a telos beyond the figure of the solitary competitive individual, which the show otherwise undoubtedly promotes.

Chapter 4 extends this inquiry into latter-day constructions of stadial models with analyses of Octavia Butler's *Dawn* and Nalo Hopkinson's *Midnight Robber*, which read like disturbing versions of *Survivor* and Martineau: both novels take small groups of humans to "the wilds" in order to re-imagine the process whereby human societies develop from primal origins. Prominent Afrofuturists, Butler and Hopkinson write with a conscious sense of the history of colonialism and its accompanying narratives about how civilizations develop with growing economic efficiency—and about the racial or national superiority those narratives have always implied. Both novels problematize stages theory, though in unexpected ways. In *Dawn*, stadialism turns out to be an accurate description of the shape of human history. But here, stadialism turns out to lack its meliorative logic. When the humans on board the alien Oankali ship are forced to rehearse the stages of human evolution, starting with hunting and gathering, it begins to appear that more efficient ways to compete for scarce resources has led—and may lead again—to more efficient means of dominating other humans and the Earth. *Midnight Robber* raises a similar possibility. With one eye on the colonial nightmares visited on the Caribbean in Earth's history, the novel restages a familiar account of small human societies on New Half-Way Tree evolving toward an ever-greater domination of the planet. At the end of the novel the enigmatic AI, Granny Nanny, poses the very question that Martineau implied in 1832: does the super-consciousness privileged to look back over the entire course of human history have the power to change its repetitive patterns, or, since it represents the final stage of that evolution, merely confirm them?

Like *Dawn* and *Midnight Robber*, Joss Whedon's TV series *Firefly* and the capstone movie *Serenity* (2005) bring us to another fresh-start scenario after humans have fled a "used-up" Earth to a new solar system. The series focuses on issues that preoccupied pre-neoclassical economists: how human societies deploy physical and money capital to evolve, and the limits, if any, to capital accumulation. I pursue these abstract questions in Chapter 5 by locating *Firefly* within two crucial moments of US history where the debate over capital accumulation and allocation has surfaced most powerfully. One is the late-nineteenth-century Populist challenge to Northeastern money powers. The other is our own age of looming ecocatastrophe, which insists with increasing urgency on the importance of placing limits to capital-generation and resource-usage. Whedon's "space western" follows economist Kenneth Boulding's well-known distinction between the "cowboy economy," in which physical capital is sacrificed to profits (money capital), and the "spaceman economy," which makes the preservation of physical capital paramount because there is no way to manufacture more of it.[27] The movie *Serenity*, however, implies yet another shift: Whedon's plot arc ends here in a postmodern crypto-commonwealth where the hoarding of precious capital stock is replaced by investments in symbolic capital. *Serenity* implies that a world of dwindling resources might be replaceable by, in today's parlance, the "Internet of Things."

In the final section of this book I focus on "bioeconomic" discourses wherein "bodily well-being and . . . economic circulation are frequently articulated both through and against each other."[28] Stages theory always embraced bioeconomic reasoning, which underpinned the idea, for example, that early humans had to break away from hunting and gathering in order to develop more robust economies based on agriculture that allowed "civilized" pursuits such as the arts to emerge. And metaphors of eating and drinking have been used for millennia to address the health of the individual body and of the commonwealth, conceived of as a Body Politic, to which it contributes. Classical political economy incorporated bioeconomic narratives about food production and distribution to explain its economic principles. In Henry George's *Progress and Poverty* (1879), for example, his influential call for a progressive land tax, George argues that the "social organism secretes, as it were, the necessary amount of capital just as the human organism in a healthy condition secretes the requisite fat."[29] Like that of many other nineteenth-century political economists, George's organicist logic suggests the importance of a (social) body in healthy equilibrium. The Body Politic should and indeed *must* produce just enough capital for its needs if the model is that of the limited capacities of the human body.

Chapter 6 charts the bioeconomic significances of feasts, which surface with great regularity in popular culture as an index to accords about the nature of commonwealth—or to represent yearnings for it. I begin with the feast that the United States consciously uses to articulate key American social and political values: Thanksgiving. Representations of families and extended families arranged around the Thanksgiving table—which were so popular in the late nineteenth century as to constitute an entire genre—invoke complex narratives about how resources are supposed to be used and shared in an ideal economy. Norman Rockwell's famous painting "Freedom from Want" (1943), for example, stages an idealized American family, presided over by grandfather, around the turkey at the Thanksgiving table. Such feasts typically invest heavily in political iconography. But they also aim to extend a symbolic invitation to viewers and readers to join with the represented participants in defining principles of commonwealth. Sharing a feast that is sufficient but not excessive shows how resources should be distributed to perpetuate an equitable and prosperous society. I bracket Rockwell's painting with Joy Harjo's twenty-first-century poem "Perhaps the World Ends Here," and two late-nineteenth century stories by Mary Wilkins Freeman, "A Thanksgiving Thief" (1892) and the children's story "Thankful" (1890). Though these works certainly challenge aspects of Rockwell's vision—above all the representation of gender roles that has grandfather in charge of the table's symbolic economy—they do not so much overthrow Rockwell's work as supplement it, directing the feast-fable toward a more unsettling, but perhaps more satisfying, sense of commonwealth. I end this chapter with a discussion of an oblique version of the Thanksgiving celebration in the iconic feasts of *How the Grinch Stole Christmas!* (1957) as they morph from Dr. Seuss's book to the first animated movie and thence to twenty-first century re-imaginings.

Chapter 7 turns from feast to deprivation. Prominent in the accounts of trekking, mountaineering, and exploration that make up the literature of Himalayan adventure travel are complex descriptions of food consumption: the shock of new, or wrong, or no, food, changes in appetite, climbers' rations, menus designed to optimize performance, and much more. Focusing on several recent works, such as Jon Krakauer's well-known *Into Thin Air* (1997), but also looking at earlier works in the historical record, this chapter makes three main claims. First, descriptions of food consumption in these works signify within a bioeconomic idiom to construct a broad discourse on consumption and consumerism. Second, these accounts typically employ scenes of food deprivation to pose a challenge to Western discourses and practices of over-consumption. Third, the strategic moves enabling this challenge are "orientalist" (in Edward Said's sense of the term) insofar as they manifest a functional difference between the Western adventurer's experience of deprivation and the subsistence economies and foodways of the Himalayan region. The effect of these discourses is not in the end to cancel the adventurer's indebtedness to money economies—though these writers typically downplay the extent to which their high adventures are encumbered by money or logistics—but to allow a bioeconomic discourse to represent, and thus elide, their orientation toward US (and British) economic organization and the global capitalism of which it is part. Indeed, these stories of deprivation almost invariably end with a communal feast and a return to the symbolic realm of the feast fable.

The various threads of this book coalesce in the final chapter's analysis of animated movies. In Chapter 8, I read these movies as today's beast fables, where talking animals (or objects) impart moral and economic wisdom. Fables have long functioned to voice a variety of often marginalized political and economic views. As Annabel Patterson shows, Aesop's "The Belly and the Members" has been used for centuries to deconstruct hegemonic representations of the polity by making the interdependent biological functions of the body into political metaphor—to make the body signify the body politic.[30] Rooted in ancient traditions, contemporary beast fables employ bioeconomic and stadial strategies to restore political economic principles. The survival of the Stone Age family in the two *The Croods* (2013, 2020) movies maps neatly onto stages theory; in the *Ice Age* (2002–2016) franchise, Scrat's bedeviled pursuit of acorns acts to reinstate the importance of capital stock, a physical manifestation of the resources humans need to survive. I refer to these movies—and in a sense *Over the Hedge* (2006)—as paleo polities. Contextualized by the contemporary fascination for all things Paleolithic, as figured in the Paleo diet and in much popular archeology, paleo polities once more return us to origins, uncovering the authentic relations of production, distribution, and consumption supposedly existing between humans and the environment at the "dawn" of human sociality. Their counter-modern impulses pose alternatives to what Paleo diet advocates explicitly label a sick society, or body politic, metaphorized in the poor diet and health of today's human bodies. In situating their characters in vast unpopulated spaces without markets, these movies also raise an issue of tremendous contemporary importance to global economies: the fate of the "commons," or more precisely common pool resources such as water and air, amid the escalating draw-down of all global resources. As funny and raucous as it is, *The Croods: A New Age*, the most recent work considered in this book, turns its Stone Age "tragedy of the commons" on the water wars of the actual and symbolic home of animation—Hollywood and Southern California.

These introductory remarks about the economic-fantastic in popular works raise two issues that require broader theorization: the fraught concept of "commonwealth," and the relationship of "the popular" to the conditions of its making in the mechanisms of capitalist production. Neoclassical economics, as we shall see in Chapter 1, engineered its rise by eliding the practice of narrativization and the explanatory frameworks of nineteenth-century political economy. Making the study of economics coterminous with the rational choices individuals (or individual firms) are supposed to make in the marketplace in order to maximize their utility sidesteps questions that had preoccupied classical economists: why and how markets emerge, how economies change over time and through history, how humans adjudicate between self-interest and social relations, what constitutes true "Wealth," and how capital accumulation contributes to a prosperous commonwealth. The Great Recession and eco-crises make those questions newly consequential, though they are, in terms of Mnuchin's favored source of knowledge, "economics in college," unanswerable. Economists produce an array of competing explanations and solutions for market dysfunction. But the logic and methodologies of economics disbar them from extending those explanations and solutions to social dysfunction at a time when the question of how the economy fails to contribute to the common good—to commonwealth—is being experienced as an existential threat by hundreds of millions of people around the globe. In these days of eco-crisis, market failures no longer seem an issue that markets are able to resolve. At best, "economics" addresses the problem with neat, though suspect, circularity: the common good can be achieved by making market capitalism function more efficiently because the common good can only be understood as the aggregation of choices that individuals exercise in the market.

An exemplary instance is Jean Tirole's recent *Economics for the Common Good* (2017), probably the most successful attempt by a noted (Nobel Prize–winning) economist to make mainstream economic thought relevant to our most intransigent global problems. Tirole begins by noting that in the wake of the financial crisis the ideological valence of market economies has achieved only a "partial victory" because the "pursuit of the common good" has been sacrificed to the "ineptitude of our leaders in coping with climate change," various forms of wealth inequality, and geopolitical instability.[31] What follows is a lucid exposition of the aptitudes of economic thinking for "eliminating some of the arbitrariness inherent in defining the common good"; in fact economic reasoning "does not prejudge solutions and has no criteria other than the collective interest."[32] It helps, for example, in understanding the "extent of inequality" and analyzing the "effects of redistributive policies." This inquiry into inequality, however, merely leads to the point where "we can begin to make choices about the kind of society we want." "On this," Tirole admits poignantly, "an economist has little to say, except as an ordinary citizen."[33] The point is that Tirole's economic analysis can be held to not "prejudge" solutions for the common good only from within the matrix of market capitalism. "Choices about the kind of society we want" follow quite explicitly *from* an analysis grounded in today's actual market economies. No alternative starting points for conceiving of the common good are available. The problem with capitalism, after all, is deemed to be the fault of individuals (the "ineptitude of our leaders") rather than a structural defect.

This is not to discard Tirole's analysis; perhaps his call for carbon taxes, helping poorer nations to achieve eco-goals, and solving the free rider problem, is for now as good as action on climate change is likely to get.[34] But *Economics for the Common Good* allows us to draw some broader conclusions, which I explore at greater length in Chapter 1. Tirole's lengthy work is one of a number of efforts to demarcate and address a collective "we" that began to be articulated with striking urgency during and after the years of the Great Recession. His work stands alongside alternative attempts to theorize "the common" and "the collective" from Marxist and poststructuralist perspectives, such as Jeremy Gilbert's *Common Ground: Democracy and Collectivity in an Age of Individualism* (2013) and Antonio Negri and Michael Hardt's *Commonwealth* (2009). Hardt and Negri's concept of the "multitude" begins, in a sense, where Tirole's analysis abruptly ends—with the "Wealth" of the "ordinary citizen," the significance of which is, to Tirole, unthinkable outside of market relations, but which earlier formations of political economy were drawn to analyze in terms other than money capital. To Hardt and Negri, in fact, "wealth" connotes various sorts of wealth, including knowledge, affect, and expertise, generated, held, and wielded in common. Yet, as Jeremy Gilbert observes, the hegemony of neoliberal capitalism has promoted an anti-democratic "atomised, fragmented, and commodified culture" within which "all collectivities are inherently impotent."[35] Tirole's monologic approach—it is entirely self-consistent yet entirely unable to engage with any interpretation of the common good not generated by its own logic—testifies to the lack of a shared discourse within which to debate such issues. In one respect, therefore, it makes sense to conceive of today's discourse on commonwealth merely in negative terms, to mark its absence or incoherence, to mourn its loss as something about which our society "has little to say," or which can be addressed only piecemeal or as a sort of oneiric utopianism.

This study pursues two alternative ways of thinking through the problematic of commonwealth. One is to think of fable as a *strategy* we might use to think the future trajectory of human history into the popular works of the last half century. Fables are generally understood in one of two ways: either a fiction so obviously fabricated that it seems wholly out of step with anything we take for real, so that it is "just a fable"; or a fiction that comes to us, like Aesop's fables, with a moral in tow, so that it is reduced to a single, self-evident meaning. But the obviously fabricated nature of the fable is precisely where its potential lies. It can function like Bertolt Brecht's *Verfremdungseffekt* (or *V-effekt*)—an act of staging the seemingly natural and universal practices of routine life in such a way as to alienate them from and illuminate the conditions of their making. Terry Eagleton, in his important gloss on Brecht's dramatic theories, argues that the point of the dramatic gest is to represent "routine social behavior" in "contrivedly hollow ways" and thus to foreground "its lack . . . its suppression of material conditions and historical possibilities."[36] Fictions that are overtly "out of step" with what we consider real can point to the hollowness of that "real"—all that it erases in its fabrication of what seems natural and universal—and thus to the presence of alternative possibilities.

I associate Brecht's theories of social performance with Walter Benjamin and Michel de Certeau's pioneering inquiries into the rhetoric and practices of popular culture. All, in a sense, make a virtue of piecemeal analyses. Benjamin's Arcades project and de Certeau's *The Practice of Everyday Life* (1980) both generate fragmentary "street" narratives that remind us of alternatives to capitalist hegemony—to Wall Street, as it were. De Certeau's dialectical perspective on the city is paradigmatic. The panoramic view from the top of a skyscraper, whence the structures of urban capitalist life seem monumental and unchangeable, gives way in de Certeau's account to the ductile, capricious experiences of the city-wanderer. The streets are a place for roaming curiously or anxiously, for flânerie, for cruising, for having multiform encounters with the Other, for protesting, for speaking idiomatically and vulgarly, for acting illicitly, for creating unlikely assemblies and indeterminate assemblages. It is a place open to the graffiti artist and to the art of the bricoleur. From alleyways one can see into the "back stories" far removed from the official, public, commercial displays of the arcades and main avenues. The "street" is also, of course, a place more myth than reality, a fabulous realm that can never live up to its billing as a byword for the collective. Yet as an edgy, ironic, unstable concept, everyday street-wandering is in keeping with the economic fabling—with the *V-effekt*—I want to examine in this book. My opening discussion of Thunberg's rhetoric follows this protocol: in its assault on the "panorama" of capitalist malfeasance it incorporates pieces of the popular, picked up from the commercial displays of works like *The Princess Bride* and *The Lord of the Rings*—works that, in and of themselves, could hardly be considered radical—and powerfully reconstructs them in free-form assemblages.

The very strangeness of thinking "economically" in terms of growing potatoes on Mars, or eating Roast Beast in *The Grinch*, or a human society beginning again in the "wilds" of an alien spaceship, or cartoon animals talking about property rights and the commons, confuses and distances the seeming stability of economic discourses both then and now. First, it refuses a *mere* return to classical political economic narratives. Martineau's "Life in the Wilds" conforms structurally to *Survivor*'s story about individuals in a "new society" evolving under the tutelage of competitive self-interest toward the marketplace that awaits them—a million dollars for the winner. But *Survivor* cannot simply be taken at face value, as if its absurd staging of a group of Americans in a contrivedly fabulous realm had no bearing on its ideological significances and on its differences from Martineau. Second, economic fabling exposes what neoclassical economic assumptions lack: the material conditions and historical possibilities that a knowledge system mesmerized by market metrics overlooks. For all that *Survivor* wears its neoliberal and neocolonial heart on its sleeve—for all that its producers can take over a tropical island belonging to another nation as if it were the symbolic property of the United States—season one puts into play a debate about competitive individualism that mainstream economics, which assumes the "fact" that humans are naturally competitive creatures, cannot. Third, we live at a historical moment when popular fables—stories with a moral in tow—jibe with overtly political calls made by Green economists for an uncompromisable moral bottom line. As Diana Schumacher puts it, Green economics celebrates the "*transcendence of moral values*."[37] Counterintuitively, fables can exercise surprisingly powerful effects by tapping into a present day desire to embrace holism and determinate solutions: stories with a clear moral ("Save the Earth!") to set against a regime of abstraction.

The opportunities popular culture affords for "making economics strange" should not, however, be understood wholly in terms of the critical disposition one brings to interpretation, as if the legitimacy of Thunberg's rhetorical seizure of Aragorn's "Let us together rebuild this world" were merely contingent on one specific convergence of sociopolitical forces. Such fragments imply the presence of a political unconscious, a realm of awareness neither panoramic nor street-level but *subterranean*, which may be articulated precisely in the irrational, the fabulous, the piecemeal. The most convincing case for the purposes of this book has been made by Lawrence Buell, who builds on Marxist scholar Fredric Jameson's work to advance the notion of an "environmental unconscious." Our embeddedness within the natural world, our reliance on it for every moment of our human physical, emotional, creative, and social existences, is what constitutes for Buell the very ground of "our," though the effect of centuries of capitalist hegemony has been to alienate that orientation, thrusting it into an unconscious realm marked by the "impossibility of individual or collective perception coming to full consciousness." Yet an environmental unconscious has also to be seen as "potential: as a residual capacity . . . to awake to fuller apprehension of physical environment and one's interdependence with it."[38] Buell notes that an environmental unconscious "both links individuals to and differentiates them from groups," and argues, furthermore, that it affirms the realm of the imagination as "having a cogency if not also an authority not exhausted by formal reasoning." Finally, it motivates change, since it "affords a basis and incentive for efforts to raise unconsciousness to conscious awareness and articulacy."[39] It is in fact an "enabling ground condition" that stages the complex crises that capitalist practices and mainstream economics cannot resolve, while allowing for the emergence of fractured forms of collective awareness within imaginative domains.[40] It establishes nothing so concrete as a discourse—rather a locus, multiform and malleable, that remains perpetually open to diverse constructions of the collective. Buell's work implies that bricolage is one way to unleash the latent transformative energies at work in an environmental unconscious, arguably more powerfully today under the "terminal" anxieties of eco-crisis than ever before.

Though this book is not "about" the effects of an environmental unconscious, I have found the concept invaluable for establishing a potential ground of critique in the economic fabling of popular works. To begin with, the concept challenges influential postmodern inquiries into "everyday economics," to which I have already referred.[41] A "new knowledge" of economics situated in a popular carnivalization does indeed confront neoclassicism's privilege as the official center of that discourse. But since it favors decentering all truth claims, it also prohibits interpreters from securing any ground for adjudicating among the "existing diversity of economic representations" on offer. Adding new ones will not make for "better economic theory or better economic policy," argues David Ruccio, since no single theory can be "judged to be superior to others because its particular representation better reflects the existing facts, or can be used to predict the future trajectory of the facts."[42] Absent determinate truths, economic conflicts have to be studied as no more than competing stories or fables—the "absurd fictions" of neoclassical economics on one side, an ungrounded carnival of popular ideas on the other.[43] To conceive of economic fabling this way is to grant it an astonishing cultural reach while necessarily delimiting any explanatory power to which it may want to lay claim, since in effect *all* discourses about economics are equally cogent—or equally shamanistic—constructions of existing facts.

As my introductory remarks about Thunberg's insurgent rhetoric imply, comprehending the discursive shapes of the popular economic knowledge systems that saturate our cultural landscape is a matter not just of interest but of great urgency. *Pace* Ruccio, the "future trajectory of the facts" is, for the first time in history, known—if not in precise detail, then in enough detail to transform conjecture about the future into scientifically verifiable facts about the deleterious effects of climate change, even in best-case scenarios. Eco-crisis thrusts *our present* into history in the sense that we can look back on its (in)actions from the vantage point of what we are reasonably certain will be their consequences. Under the auspices of worsening climate crises and the disruptions to global economies we know are coming, the possibility begins to emerge that there may be no robust academic institutions to pay scholars to pay attention to our culture and history, no Econ 101 for a future Thunberg to take. Indeed, the cost of not confronting economic practices and discourses geared toward eventually overwhelming the earth's natural resources is the possibility of having no more human history to tell. In a useful popular idiom, we would in fact "be history." Studies of our cultural moment must begin to consider our interpretations of the past and of today's cultural artifacts as a function of the future that is already settling into the here and now, present in the mainstream economic fantasy that humans can continue to use up resources at an accelerating rate forever or that market forces can solve the problem, and present in the fantasy that no economic theory can be adjudged superior to any other. In that respect, it is incumbent on us to fashion a transformative, an efficacious, discourse out of popular economic thought.

The concept of an environmental unconscious also implies that popular works possess latent, unexpected capacities that cannot be determined solely by their position within the marketplace. Here I adopt a relatively unorthodox position in the long debate over whether popular mass market productions can leverage any sort of effective resistance to the commercial circumstances of their making. John Storey notes that the trajectory of cultural studies over the past half century has been to "deny that [the] culture of everyday life is little more than a degraded landscape of commercial and ideological manipulation, imposed from above in order to make profit and secure social control." Far from being "cultural dupes," people "make culture from the repertoire of commodities supplied by the culture industries."[44] By the mid-1990s, summarizes David Morley, cultural studies favored the notions that the "audience is active" (though not necessarily powerful) and that "media content is always 'polysemic' or open to interpretation," disposing scholars toward readings that emphasize conflict, contradiction, and irresolution.[45] The preponderance of such readings nonetheless emphasizes the ability of market forces to coerce popular works into compliance with their protocols. Refusing the argument that mass culture is no more than "sheer manipulation, sheer commercial brainwashing, and empty distraction by . . . multinational corporations," as Fredric Jameson puts it, does not preclude the presence of complex containment strategies: an "optical illusion of social harmony," for example, may convey corporate power by promising utopian collectivities realized through the "fantasy bribe" of seductive consumerist dreamworlds to which all would like to belong.[46] As Tony Tremblay argues, ideology might be thought to compel consumers most effectively by means of fantasy and pleasure. To "watch pleasurably" is to "submit willingly to the power of ideology, a power that, when misrecognized or looked at awry, appears as safe as it is familiar"—a move so powerful that Tremblay observes, quoting Slavoj Žižek, "*stepping out of (what we perceive as) ideology is the very form of our enslavement to it*."[47]

This book puts pressure on these normative approaches to the relationship of popular productions to market hegemony. Consider the critical responses to *Wall*E* (2008), the mass-market Pixar movie to which most scholarly attention has been drawn. Its opening thirty minutes depict a ruined ecosphere, a "literal apocalypse of trash" linked uncompromisingly to over-consumption and corporate malfeasance, which leads Christopher Todd Anderson to read it as the sign of a mass audience's "ambivalence" about consumerism, Sabine LeBel as an "important site of eco-criticism" (even though it does not foster an "ideal environmental politics of waste"), and Alexa Weik von Mossner as a "scathing critique of American-style consumerism capitalism."[48] Yet most scholarly responses—including those I have just cited—agree that *Wall*E* cannot escape its allegiance to "commercial cultural industries, which historically have both exemplified and rationalized the imperatives of consumerism," so that even in its marketing of a "popular anti-consumerism" it "ultimately aligns with the cultural values of the contemporary capitalist system that perpetuates and promotes ecological crisis."[49] That alignment makes for a "truly disturbing" disconnect between the "film's message and the structural conditions of its production, distribution, and consumption."[50] For most others, the movie's message merely sabotages itself. To Maria Bose, Pixar's attempts to establish its "corporate responsibility" over against its parent company, Disney, crumble into promoting "movement toward 'better' modes of consumption" at the end of the movie when humans return to Earth[51]; Michelle Yates also notes that the "film's narrative structure" returns viewers to an "Edenic recovery narrative" celebrating labor and commodity form, in the process abandoning what was "seemingly" its "dystopian, postapocalyptic vision of what will happen if humans continue to consume and waste at their current rate."[52] Scholarly inquiries typically lament the fact that this provocative satire of a world wrecked by consumerism and corporate greed has made "mega-millions" for Pixar/Disney.

Beginning with the structuring conditions of the marketplace possesses what appears to be an impeccable interpretive logic. Given that *Wall*E* was successfully marketed—it earned over half a billion dollars worldwide—it seems self-evident that, in the final analysis, the one truly relevant question about the movie is how its producers managed, and made profitable, its dystopian vision of the consequences of over-consumption. A critique "seemingly," it can be none other than a ruse of power, the narrative that generates it necessarily articulating strategies to manage its own (self-)critical or irreverent energies. In the case of *Wall*E*, scholars typically reference the movie's conclusion, where the humans returning to an Earth now ripe for restoration signals an optimistic "recovery narrative" prompting viewers to forget the wreckage of the long opening sequence. I concur with this sense that the movie's conclusion—as the credits roll humans labor in fields to rebuild a green Earth—"walks back" the formidable satire of the opening. But deriving meaning from *Wall*E* need not conform to the experience offered upon completing the act of viewing when one's backward glance can grasp the story as a totality. It is possible—some have done so—to "misrecognize" the first thirty minutes as a "scathing critique of consumerism and environmental degradation" and somehow to keep that alive through the cheer of the conclusion, if only by deliberately choosing to foster this "beloved" movie as a site of eco-criticism, as LeBel says, rather than "poisoning its hopeful message."[53]

There are in fact at least two historicizing moves one can make to disconcert the notion that interpretations of *Wall*E* must be grounded in the imperatives of the marketplace. The first, as Kylie and Brett R. Caraway argue, is that the movie is one of many animated features to represent an "underlying crisis in capitalism," whether one understands that as a "struggle to come to terms with ecological destabilization" or as one more instance of the effects of the Great Recession.[54] This analysis is consistent with Buell's proposition that meaning can be mobilized within an environmental unconscious and with McClanahan's point that we live in an era of crisis subjectivities. If the "imperatives" of consumerism are *themselves* riven by contradiction—if they speak imperatively, but dialogically—then we may inquire whether the movie's conclusion can ever be brought into any sort of comfortable rapprochement with its opening sequence. The second is to consider the reception of the movie within a horizon extending well beyond the years of its production and release and beyond any single viewing of it. An age of eco-crisis raises questions about which aspects of *Wall*E* will come to seem pertinent to emerging discourses about environmental sustainability and collective action as the urgency of an "end-times" scenario grows. Like Thunberg mobilizing the force of "History Has Its Eyes on You" despite what *Hamilton* overlooks in the historical record, Wall*E's lonely struggle to right a wrecked Earth may come to seem politically efficacious, even if we believe now that the movie's narrative arc ultimately circles back to the conditions of its making in the marketplace. Put more precisely, an act of interpretation that grasps the movie piecemeal—that "cherry picks" the remarkable opening sequence and "forgets" the ending, or that looks to future possibilities of doing so—implies and constructs a different discourse on consumerism than one that coordinates the movie's meanings with its conclusion.

The logic of this position suggests we cannot know the ends to which *Wall*E* might be put—how the movie might be seized upon, reconstructed, and re-signified as it is situated within competing discourses. It also suggests, by contrast, that narrative-arc approaches that insist on grasping the movie's totality play a *necessary* role in establishing the marketplace as the ultimate ground of interpretation: if the meanings of popular works are held to "ultimately" resolve in the corporate marketplace that produced them, narratives must effect closure. There can be no loose ends, no "back stories," no environmental unconscious, nothing to trouble the closed logic of a work that is "popular because it is ideological, and because it is ideological, it is popular," as Tremblay puts it.[55] Fable, pleasure, nostalgia, fantasy, dreamscapes, stories of renewal, representations of labor and collective action, emotional identification, even discordance itself, all in the final analysis support capitalist ideologies. It is worth noting that such analyses cannot be gainsaid, for any attempt to do so reduces to the suspicion that one is submitting willingly, or thoughtlessly, to the power of ideology. Such attempts can only map, as Žižek says, the "*very form of our enslavement to it.*"

Though subsequent chapters of this book certainly acknowledge the effect and reach of market forces, I resist the urge to pin interpretation to the structuring "imperatives" of production on the grounds that such a stance capitulates too easily to the ideological regime of capitalism. It is the discursive counterpart of microeconomic accounts of the rational agent. The closed logic of mainstream economics justifies the most irrational-seeming of choices on the basis either that it is rational to the individual making the decision, that the individual failed to make the normative decision, or that all decision-making invokes rational choice as an ideal to which individuals aspire. All behaviors in the market can therefore be understood ultimately to confirm the logic of maximizing utility. Critiques of the popular oriented toward market production likewise exercise an iron grip on popular works by reducing all to market functions: if works must be ideological to be popular, then analyses of such works must in the final analysis be studies of the complex machinations of corporate hegemony, and analyses of audience responses must in the final analysis be studies of how they submit to fantasy. An economics grounded in rational choice and cultural critiques of consumerist dreamworlds—in which the critic alone possesses a rational and critical perspective—are both hypostatized by their own logic: both are mesmerized by, and construct, market hegemony as a totalizing force.

I take inspiration here from what I consider the most persuasive recent approach to the art of the popular: Judith Halberstam's appraisal of the queer potentialities of animated movies in *The Queer Art of Failure* (2011). What Halberstam calls "Pixarvolt," a term for the harnessing of political revolt to the creativity of animated movies, underpins a quest for "low theory and counterknowledge in the realm of popular culture and in relation to queer lives, gender, and sexuality."[56] Though I do not adopt Halberstam's positionality within a queer discourse, and though animated movies are not my entire focus, the concept of Pixarvolt speaks to the kind of strangely defamiliarizing energies I want to claim for some of these works and to the unfamiliar interpretive posture critics might need to adopt at this moment of eco-crisis. In Halberstam's view, for example, *Over the Hedge*, an animated movie where food-foraging talking beasts satirize the empty consumerism of suburbanites, offers "more in the way of a vision of collective action than most independent films and critical theory put together." One can see the limits to such a paean—my own reading of the movie in Chapter 8 shows some of the ways it constrains its own calls to collective action. And Halberstam does not extend Pixarvolt energies to all works in the popular arena, including *Wall*E*, where the romance between Wall*E and Eve and the return of a "bloated humanity" to Earth overturn its early "fantastic rejection of commodity fetishism," its early "narrative of hope."[57]

But Halberstam's sense that some popular works require "low theory" deserves elucidation and emphasis, for it re-structures the potential relationships between scholarly inquiries and the materials of popular culture. Criticisms of the "culture industry" are indubitably accurate. They are also in several senses circular, even tautological. Produced to make money, all mass market works must in some way validate the basic imperatives of the market. So must criticisms of them. Critical interventions into the realm of popular culture are similarly enmeshed within a capitalist machinery—the "criticism industry" so to speak—that funds the articles and books, the institutions within which careers are advanced, the movies downloaded, and the leisure to watch and write about them. Like *Wall*E*, those interventions construct a critique of capitalism that grants authority to its imperatives; they too market a popular anti-consumerism. But what looks like complicity within a capitalist matrix can be transformed into grounds for collective action. The crucial feature of Halberstam's approach is that it allows room for *Over the Hedge* to create a powerful narrative of collective action *even though* it made tens of millions for DreamWorks Animation. That move has important ramifications. Most importantly, anti-consumerist sentiment does not have to be understood as the fealty a popular work owes to its making within the culture industry; it is no longer obligatory to read its critical energies as a function of how movie-makers *market* popular critical energies. It would even be possible to argue that the "mega-millions" Pixar made from *Wall*E* were collected from millions of viewers responding to its "narrative of hope," or what LeBel calls its "hopeful message"—in which case its "fantastic rejection" of consumerism might live on beyond its alleged overturn at the end of the movie. Too, Halberstam's move repositions the work and value of the critic. If the pursuit of "low theory" implies looking *to* Pixarvolt energies for inspiration, then scholars must start thinking of their work in terms of its participation in a tremendously diverse spectrum of cultural productions, ranging all the way from Pixar to academic studies of popular culture, from the culture industry to the critical industry.

To be sure, Halberstam's claims for the priority of popular works over theory are fabulous ones—perhaps even ridiculously utopian. But those claims, like the popular movies to which they refer, create a Brechtian gest, a disturbing and singular challenge to hegemonic economic discourses as much as to the normative ways scholars think through the relationship of popular culture to capitalism. Suggestions that theory may have to follow the lead of *Over the Hedge* glimpse the "back story," as it were, a "vision of collective action" that most critical responses overlook, but which is entirely consistent with Buell's notion of an environmental unconscious whose authority is "not exhausted by formal reasoning." In this book I want to at least broach the possibility that the most useful approaches to our age of crisis might lie in the realm of popular works such as *The Croods: A New Age*, or *The Martian*, or *Wall*E*—or National Geographic's TV series *Mars* (2016–2018), which oddly but effectively melds science fiction (settling Mars) with a caustic appraisal of the looming disaster of contemporary climate change. In *Mars*, the documentary evidence of the breaking up of the Arctic ice pack in our world (in 2016) sits very uneasily with the uplifting story of breaking ground on Mars for a near-future (in 2033) colonization of the planet. For all its contrivances—it glosses over how Lukrum Corporation monetizes its presence on Mars, for example, and seems unwilling to show what climate change in 2016 has wrought on the Earth of 2033—it is, like *The Martian*, and *Wall*E*, by turns poignant, incisive, fabulous, and ridiculous. It also comes with a moral in tow—Save the Earth!—that might be considered its bottom line, and thus another relatively powerful voice for embedding new economic knowledge systems in the realm of the popular.

NOTES

1. Greta Thunberg, Speech at the UN, www.npr.org/2019/09/23/763452863/transcript-greta-thunbergs-speech-at-the-u-n-climate-action-summit, September 23, 2019, n.p.
2. Lionel Robbins, *An Essay on the Nature and Significance of Economic Science* (1932; reprint London: Macmillan, 1945), 16; Susan F. Feiner, "A Portrait of *Homo Economicus* as A Young Man," in *The New Economic Criticism: Studies at the Intersection of Literature and Economics*, eds. Mark Osteen and Martha Woodmansee (New York: Routledge, 1999), 194.
3. For incisive feminist critiques of the concept of Economic Man, see Julie A. Nelson, *Feminism, Objectivity, and Economics* (New York: Routledge, 1996); Gillian J. Hewitson, *Feminist Economics: Interrogating the Masculinity of Rational Economic Man* (Cheltenham, UK: Edward Elgar, 1999); *Toward A Feminist Philosophy of Economics,* eds. Drucilla K. Barker and Edith Kuiper (New York: Routledge, 2003); Drucilla K. Barker and Susan F. Feiner, *Liberating Economics: Feminist Perspectives on Families, Work, and Globalization* (Ann Arbor: University of Michigan Press, 2004).
4. Tony Lawson, *Reorienting Economics* (New York: Routledge, 2003), 75.
5. Annie McClanahan, *Dead Pledges: Debt, Crisis, and Twenty-First-Century Culture* (Stanford: Stanford University Press, 2017), 15, 18.

6. John Clarke, "After Neo-Liberalism? Markets, States, and the Reinvention of Public Welfare," *Cultural Studies* 24, no. 3 (2010): 383, 391, doi.org/10.1080/09502381003750310.

7. Jack Ewing, "How Climate Change Could Cause Financial Meltdown." *San Francisco Chronicle*, January 25, 2020, D3. The organization cited in this article is the Bank for International Settlements.

8. Matt Egan, "US Report Warns Climate Change Could Create Economic Chaos," CNN Business. www.cnn.com/2020/09/09/business/climate-change-economy-cftc-report/index.html.

9. Kenneth Arrow et al, "Are We Consuming Too Much?" *Journal of Economic Perspectives*, Vol. 18, no. 3 (Summer 2004): 168, doi: 10.1257/0895330042162377.

10. Michael Lewis, *The Big Short: Inside the Doomsday Machine* (New York: Norton, 2010), 227, 158.

11. Jack Amariglio and David F. Ruccio, "The Transgressive Knowledge of 'Ersatz' Economics," in *What do Economists Know? New Economics of Knowledge, New Knowledge of Economics*, ed. Robert F. Garnett (New York: Routledge, 1999), 3, 26, 23, ProQuest Ebook Central.

12. Amariglio and Ruccio, "Transgressive Knowledge," 26.

13. I take the phrase "new knowledge of economics" from Robert F. Garnett's edited volume *What do Economists Know?: New Economics of Knowledge, New Knowledge of Economics* (1999).

14. Clarke, "After Neo-Liberalism?," 384. Clarke notes—presciently, it appears—that this reconstruction need not occur under the aegis of a progressive politics.

15. Here and in subsequent chapters I use versions of some paragraphs from *Kitchen Economics: Women's Regionalist Fiction and Political Economy* (Alabama: University of Alabama Press, 2020) to set up my inquiry into the discourses of political economy.

16. William Tabb, *Reconstructing Political Economy: The Great Divide in Economic Thought* (New York: Routledge, 1999), 53.

17. Claudia C. Klaver, *A/Moral Economics: Classical Political Economy and Cultural Authority in Nineteenth-Century England* (Columbus: Ohio State University Press, 2003), xxiv; Tabb, *Reconstructing Political Economy*, 6.

18. Ben Fine and Dimitris Milonakis, *From Political Economy to Economics: Method, the Social and the Historical in the Evolution of Economic Theory* (New York: Routledge, 2009), 2. For other important works seeking to revise neoclassical economic thought by looking to older models of political economy, see William Tabb, *Reconstructing Political Economy: The Great Divide in Economic Thought* (1999); Geoffrey M. Hodgson, *How Economics Forgot History: The Problem of Historical Specificity in Social Science* (New York: Routledge, 2001); Ben Fine, *Social Capital versus Social Theory: Political Economy and Social Science at the Turn of the Millennium* (New York: Routledge, 2001); Ben Fine and Dimitris Milonakis, *From Economics Imperialism to Freakonomics: The Shifting Boundary Between Economics and other Social Sciences* (New York: Routledge, 2009); and Ben Fine and Dimitris Milonakis, *From Political Economy to Economics: Method, the Social and the Historical in the Evolution of Economic Theory* (New York: Routledge, 2009).

19. Howard Horwitz, *By the Law of Nature: Form and Value in Nineteenth-Century America* (New York: Oxford University Press, 1991), 127.

20. Diana Strassman, "Not a Free Market: The Rhetoric of Disciplinary Authority in Economics," in *Beyond Economic Man: Feminist Theory and Economics*, eds. Marianne A. Ferber and Julie A. Nelson (Chicago: University of Chicago, 1993), 55.

21. Marilyn Power, Ellen Mutari, and Deborah M. Figart, "Beyond Markets: Wage Setting and the Methodology of Feminist Political Economy," in Barker and Kuiper, eds, *Toward a Feminist*, 83, 71.

22. Drucilla K. Barker and Edith Kuiper, "Introduction: Sketching the Contours of a Feminist Philosophy of Economics," in *Toward a Feminist*, eds. Barker and Kuiper, 3.

23. Diana Strassmann and Livia Polanyi, "The Economist as Storyteller: What the Texts Reveal," in *Out of the Margin: Feminist Perspectives on Economics*, eds. Susan Feiner, Edith Kuiper, Notburga Ott, Jolande Sap, Zafiris Tzannatos (New York: Routledge, 1995), 94.

24. Catherine Gallagher, *The Body Economic: Life, Death, and Sensation in Political Economy and the Victorian Novel* (Princeton: Princeton University Press, 2006), 3.

25. John Stuart Mill, *Principles of Political Economy* (London: John W. Parker, 1848; New York: Augustus M. Kelley, 1987), 13.

26. Andy Weir, *The Martian* (2011; reprint New York: Crown, 2014), 368–69.

27. The phrase "used up" is taken from the voiceover prologue to the TV shows, repeated in the history lesson that begins *Serenity*.

28. Gallagher, *Body Economic*, 46.

29. Henry George, *Progress and Poverty* (1879; reprint London: Kegan Paul, 1883), 77.

30. Annabel Patterson, *Fables of Power: Aesopian Writing and Political History* (Durham: Duke University Press, 1991), 4.

31. Jean Tirole, *Economics for the Common Good*, trans. Steven Rendall (Princeton: Princeton University Press, 2017), 1.

32. Tirole, 2, 4.

33. Tirole, 57.

34. The "free rider" issue is that some nations may forego costly measures to ameliorate climate change once they see other nations taking the lead in doing so.

35. Jeremy Gilbert, *Common Ground: Democracy and Collectivity in an Age of Individualism* (London: Pluto Press, 2013), viii, ix, ProQuest Ebook Central.

36. Terry Eagleton, "Brecht and Rhetoric," *New Literary History* 16, no. 3 (Spring 1985): 633, doi.org/10.2307/468845.

37. Quoted in Molly Scott Cato, *Green Economics: An Introduction to Theory, Policy and Practice* (London; Sterling, VA: Earthscan, 2009), 24.

38. Lawrence Buell, *Writing for an Endangered World: Literature, Culture, and Environment in the U.S. and Beyond* (Cambridge: Harvard University Press, 2001), 22, ProQuest Ebook Central.

39. Buell, 26.

40. Buell, 22.

41. For postmodern inquiries into economics, see *Postmodernism, Economics and Knowledge*, eds. Stephen E. Cullenberg, Jack Amariglio, and David F. Ruccio (New York: Routledge, 2001); David F. Ruccio and Jack Amariglio, *Postmodern Moments in Modern Economics* (Princeton: Princeton University Press, 2003); and *Economic Representations: Academic and Everyday*, ed. David F. Ruccio (New York: Routledge, 2008). These inquiries owe much to groundbreaking studies of the rhetorical basis of economic analysis, especially Deirdre McCloskey's *The Rhetoric of Economics* (1985) and *Knowledge and Persuasion in Economics* (1994), and Arjo Klamer's *The Consequences of Economic Rhetoric* (1988).

42. Ruccio, *Economic Representations*, 6.

43. Lawson, *Reorienting Economics*, 18.

44. John Storey, *Culture and Power in Cultural Studies: The Politics of Signification* (Edinburgh: Edinburgh University Press, 2010), 53.

45. David Morley, "Theories of Consumption in Media Studies," in *Acknowledging Consumption*, ed. Daniel Miller (London: Taylor and Francis, 1995), 305, ProQuest Ebook Central.

46. Jameson, *Signatures of the Visible* (New York: Routledge, 1990), 21, 26.

47. Tony Tremblay, "Reading the 'Real' in Survivor: Unearthing the Republican Roots in Reality Narrative," *Topia: Canadian Journal of Cultural Studies* 9 (2003): 63, doi:10.3138/topia.9.47.

48. David S. Whitley, *The Idea of Nature in Disney Animation* (Aldershot, Hampshire, Burlington, VT; Ashgate, 2008), 146; Christopher Todd Anderson, "Post-Apocalyptic Nostalgia: *WALL-E*, Garbage, and American Ambivalence toward Manufactured Goods," *Literature Interpretation Theory* 23 (2012), doi.org/10.1080/10436928.2012.703598; Sabine LeBel, "Notes on Cool: The Temporal Politics of Friendly Monsters and the E-Waste Aesthetic," *NANO: New American Notes Online* 7 (June 2015), n.p., www.proquest.com/scholarly-journals/notes-on-cool-temporal-politics-friendly-monsters/docview/2326835642/se-2; Alexa Weik Von Mossner, "Love in the Times of Ecocide: Environmental Trauma and Comic Relief in Andrew Stanton's *Wall-E*," in *Eco-Trauma Cinema*, ed. Anil Narine (New York: Routledge, 2015), 171.

49. Hugh McNaughtan, "Distinctive Consumption and Popular Anti-Consumerism: The Case of *Wall*E*." *Journal of Media & Cultural Studies* 26, no. 5 (June 2012), doi.org/10.1080/10304312.2012.664116; Michelle Yates, "Labor as 'Nature,' Nature as Labor: 'Stay the Course' of Capitalism in *Wall-E*'s Edenic Recovery Narrative," *ISLE* 22, no. 3 (Summer 2015): 527, doi.org/10.1093/isle/isu124. Robin L. Murray and Joseph K. Heumann also speak to the movie's "total immersion in an anti-environmental consumer market." *Ecology and Popular Film: Cinema on the Edge* (Albany: SUNY Press, 2009), 6.

50. Kelly Gates, "New Media Addiction," *Television and New Media* 10, no. 1 (2009): 58, doi.org/10.1177/1527476408325106.

51. Maria Bose, "Immaterial Thoughts: Brand Value, Environmental Sustainability, and *Wall-E*,"

Criticism 59, no. 2 (2017): 264, doi.org/10.13110/criticism.59.2.0247.

52. Yates, "Labor as 'Nature,'" 527.

53. LeBel, "Notes on Cool," n.p.

54. Kylie Caraway & Brett R. Caraway, "Representing Ecological Crises in Children's Media: An Analysis of *The Lorax* and *Wall-E*," *Environmental Communication* 14, no. 5 (2020): 695, doi.org/10.1080/17524032.2019.1710226. The authors consider that *Wall*E* attempts to maintain the status quo, though it responds to a "crisis that is increasingly difficult to contain or obscure" (695).

55. Tremblay, "Reading the 'Real,'" 62.

56. Judith Halberstam, *The Queer Art of Failure* (Durham: Duke University Press, 2011), 19.

57. Halberstam, *Queer Art of Failure*, 22.

Chapter One

The Political Economy of Potato Farming on Mars in Andy Weir's *The Martian*

The extraordinary success arc of Andy Weir's survival epic, *The Martian* (2011), which rose from self-published obscurity to the *New York Times*' bestseller list and thence to a major motion picture directed by Ridley Scott (2015), owes something to the pertinacity with which it addresses contemporary economic problems and to the curious resistance it puts up to resolving them.[1] A sci-fi version of Daniel Defoe's *Robinson Crusoe* (1719), Weir's book reads like a Robinsonade for the Great Recession. Like many victims of the 2008 financial and economic crisis and its long-lasting aftershocks, Mark Watney finds himself unhomed, abandoned, forced to make do with scant resources, ineluctably insecure. As the novel begins his chances are virtually zero. His "home," the Hab, a pressurized dome, is designed to last thirty-one days. If it breaches, Watney remarks, "I'll just kind of explode."[2] Since his stock of food amounts to twelve potatoes and nowhere-near-enough packaged food to last until any possible rescue, he knows that even if the Hab lasts he will "eventually run out of food and starve to death" (7) anyway. Unlike many real-world victims of financial catastrophe, however, Watney succeeds in his endeavors. With postmodern panache, the novel offers a mash-up of solutions to the problem of surviving under the duress of reduced circumstances. Watney weds high-tech miracle-making (he burns rocket fuel to produce water!) to the decidedly grimy business of potato farming. Though Mars compels him to count calories in a near-starvation diet, he is later stunned to realize that, with the full panoply of NASA technologies on tap, the "cost for my survival must have been hundreds of millions of dollars" (368). It is as though Weir cannot quite decide which set of strategies to recommend to the Recession's survivors: an investment in visionary technologies or a return to the old Jeffersonian dream of a nation of yeomen farmers; absolute self-sufficiency or a faith that "every human being has a basic instinct to help each other out" (368–69); an austerity regime or a US stimulus-sized package for the benefit of each and every person.

Positioning the novel within a cultural history of the Recession presents one immediate problem: it seems lugubrious to claim that *The Martian* addresses the realm of "the economic" at all. Is it not a book in which money and markets either cannot exist (on Mars) or do not seem pertinent (to profligate NASA on Earth)? Is not its superbly fuzzy logic, its smorgasbord of solutions, opposed to the rigorous economic analysis and hard-headed decisions that, arguably, prevented the Great Recession from becoming another Great Depression?[3] Perhaps the success of Weir's book rests on the way in which *traces* of rational economic thinking leverage feel-good, even euphoric, flights of fancy.[4] Moments of Mark Watney's battle against scarcity and a hostile environment sound like Microeconomics 101: "I had 400 plants, probably averaging 5 potatoes each: 2000 taters. At 150 calories each, I'll need to eat 10 per sol [a Mars day] to survive. That means they'll last me 200 sols" (171). Reinvesting (i.e., replanting) some of those potatoes will bring him another tranche of time. But pragmatic "Farmer Mark" (22) is aware that in the end his project is "not sustainable" (20). The sour Malthusian logic of Mars means that it would be "kind of pointless to continue the trend" (17): he cannot grow potatoes fast enough on his tiny plot of arable land to keep him alive beyond a second planting. It makes sense to ask whether the wild and fabulous *deus ex machina* ending—Watney lifting off into space with the nose cone of his rocket ripped off and covered by a tarpaulin, while his rescuers set off a bomb in their spacecraft to alter course—is an attempt to circumvent the novel's own grim logic of returns diminishing to zero. Or perhaps it is to head off the possibility that one might think Weir is seriously advocating potato farming as a *pro tem* solution to economic crisis.

Laura Brown affords a useful approach to Weir's fabling in her concept of the "cultural fable," a cultural narrative comprising a "set of related figures that have a distinctive structure," which is "generated collectively in many texts over a period of time"; a cultural fable "can be said to tell a story whose protagonist is an emanation of contemporary experience and whose action reflects an imaginative negotiation with that experience."[5] Brown introduces the eighteenth-century Lady Credit as an example, a figure that associates constructions of the female body with a "powerfully realized . . . cultural expression of fluctuation and excess, distinctive aspects of the experience of modernity."[6] Like the figure of Lady Credit who functioned to parlay anxieties about an emerging modernity in the eighteenth century, today's cultural fable of the abandoned/rescued astronaut—a feature of many recent popular films such as *Apollo 13* (1995), *Lost in Space* (1998), and *Gravity* (2013)—seems an equally distinctive representation of the experiences of postmodernity.

"Unhomed," the term I used earlier to describe Mark Watney's condition, is Homi K. Bhabha's way of enunciating the peculiar new architectures of postcolonial space, which he defines as the "realm of the *beyond*," subject to the "estranging sense of the relocation of the home and the world.[7] One has a home but is never quite *at* home. It is therefore possible to think of *The Martian* as a politically efficacious fable wherein Watney's experience introduces millions of US victims of the housing bust to an exponentially larger postcolonial experience of being "unhomed"—and then aligns all of them with the materially obsolete but psychologically compelling American mythos of self-reliance.

One reason for *The Martian*'s great popularity is that its fabling advances a set of creative and even brilliant symbolic solutions to the troubles roiling the world's post-recessionary economies. Its oddest conceit—potato farming on Mars—represents Watney as homo economicus, or Economic Man, and backs that representation with dramatic intensity: he cannot deviate for a second from his commitment to self-interested, logical, and efficient decision-making if he is to survive. Watney is a rational agent par excellence and from dire necessity. Yet the novel accommodates alternative economic strategies. The other end of its ideological arc takes us to a fabulous version of Earth where, under the aegis of an organization (NASA) whose "funding was limitless" (146), human lives need not be monetized, competition for resources seems largely immaterial, decisions between competing options rarely need to be made, and where, according to Watney's final words, the true "basic instinct" of human beings is a benevolent impulse to "help each other out" (368–69). Feel-good fabling on Earth upends Adam Smith's famous statement in *The Wealth of Nations* (1776) that "It is not from the benevolence of the butcher, the brewer, or the baker that we expect our dinner but from their regard to their self-interest"; this is the logic that has ever since underpinned the link between homo economicus and the marketplace, where self-interested agents exercise their prerogatives.[8] Nowhere is Weir's science fiction more fantastic and compelling than in the ideological conundrum that governs it: his representation of homo economicus cannot be reconciled with a market economy, while a money economy on Earth seems subject to a wholly irrational exuberance.[9]

I examine this puzzling dynamic by historicizing it. The novel renders into cultural fable some of the contradictions in twenty-first century-public discourses about what "economics" is and does. It particularly raised in the shadows of the cultural imagination a problematic that hegemonic economic discourses could barely name, let alone address, which is how a nation in crisis might think of its prosperity in terms of a community of interests—how it might vest "economics" in a discourse about commonwealth. *The Martian* is very much of its time. Its attempts to construct a persuasively rational agent, its attempts to assert a caring body politic, its wild swings between rigorous analysis and the fabulous—all are replicated in other public documents of the time as writers strove, with more-or-less lack of success, to restore to coherence older concepts of commonwealth. I shall pay particular attention here to the US government's official, and Occupy Wall Street's unofficial, responses to the crisis. But this broad cultural struggle to represent economic issues in terms of the common good needs to be contextualized historically: it is rooted in the important late-nineteenth-century shift away from "political economy" to neoclassical, or mainstream, economics, the hegemony of which powerfully foreclosed certain aspects of political economic discourse—among them any persuasive, publicly shared concept of commonwealth. By making the question of Watney's survival matter to "billions of people" and by raising the question of what broader value his survival implies—by trying, in short, to make his survival meaningful in terms of the common good—the novel sets out to recuperate a political economic idiom, an older *style* of representing economic knowledge, still emotionally persuasive in some recess of the political unconscious. The novel's economic fabling—its attempt to reunite homo economicus with a "help each other out" philosophy—remains hesitant. At best it is, in terms of the novel's own powerful metaphor, duct-taped together. Yet the cultural topography of today's discursive fault-lines in how "economic" materials signify, or might be made to signify, helps to explain how the political economy of potato farming on Mars might be thought "politically efficacious," or how a fable, and everyday economics, might count as "real" economic analysis or practice.

Political economy, John Stuart Mill observed in his introductory remarks to *Principles of Political Economy* (1848), was the discipline that studied the "nature of Wealth, and the laws of its production and distribution."[10] Though the concept of "Wealth" implied much more than money capital, as I noted in the Introduction and as this book will elaborate, the field of political economy post-Adam Smith coalesced around a number of "laws" that are still widely accepted in mainstream economics: first, humans act rationally to maximize the utility of their limited means; second, nature is miserly, so that resources are always scarce; third, the fact of scarce resources entails competition between economic agents; fourth, economic agents desire to accumulate wealth while avoiding the pain or disutility of labor; fifth, competitive markets reveal the aggregated operations of self-interested actions; and sixth, markets produce the best allocation of resources and the best method for accumulating wealth on the grounds of their superior efficiency. Political economists certainly set out to formalize such concepts. David Ricardo was a central figure here, he and his disciples focused on deriving laws of economic behavior such as the "law of diminishing returns, the law of population growth, the law of wages, the law of capital accumulation, the law of rent, and the law of markets."[11] Neoclassical economic thought largely incorporated these principles as self-evident, preferring to formalize the "laws" rather than debate the issue of, say, whether humans are naturally competitive.

By the 1870s, an emerging neoclassical economics was beginning to undertake the "desocialisation and dehistoricisation of the dismal science."[12] The rise of neoclassical economic thought within newly professionalizing departments of universities set out to empty the concept of a civil society of "much of the earlier social, institutional, cultural, and historical content that it was initially thought to embody."[13] In constituting itself as a distinct field of knowledge, neoclassical economics began to organize around the belief that "economics" could be studied and practiced with minimal regard to broad questions about what constituted a commonwealth. Alfred Marshall, one of the founders of neoclassical economics, wrote: "The nation used to be called 'the Body Politic.' So long as this phrase was in common use, men thought of the interests of the whole nation when they used the word 'Political'; and then 'Political Economy' served well enough as a name for the science."[14] Marshall's point is that what used to be the case no longer makes sense to the study of economics in its contemporary guise; the practice and study of "economics" was shifting away from normative assumptions about how to achieve the common good, or, as Marshall puts it, away from the "interests of the whole nation." The new science of economics, Marshall argued, must abandon the holistic but necessarily vague principles that political economy embraced in order to better understand the choices individuals make when trying to maximize the utility of their limited means in the marketplace.

In constituting a distinct field of knowledge, neoclassical economists continued to privilege the classical economic principles that competitive markets reveal the aggregated operations of self-interested desire and produce the best allocation of resources on the grounds of superior efficiency. But they narrowed them into a "science" of markets. Aspects of this transformation are of great consequence to how economics came to be understood and practiced from the early twentieth century. Focusing solely on market behaviors allowed the new "science" to quantify its insights. Though one cannot measure or quantify desire in the abstract, nor account for why individuals have certain preferences, the choices they make *in the market* can be quantified by virtue of a commodity's price, affording consumers a precise way to evaluate their options and businesses a precise way to evaluate changes in supply and demand. On that basis, economists could begin to consider their work a "pure," mathematically based science—indeed, the "only truly rigorous and scientific discipline across the social sciences."[15]

In another important extension of classical economic thought, markets began to be conceptualized as the primary constraint on human desires. Classical economists were prepared to consider humans capable of controlling their insatiable wants. For neoclassicists, what constrained human desire was not the ability of individuals to control themselves, nor an absolute limit to the total capital or resources available, but the effects of comparative utility in the marketplace. Individuals were thought of as rational economic agents constantly making subjective choices between various goods on offer. Economists began to study how individuals allocate value differentially and subjectively rather than absolutely; they granted a "new prominence to the causes that govern the relative exchange values of different things," as Marshall put it.[16] That meant that the value of a good was no longer determined by a labor theory of value—by the costs of labor required to produce and distribute it. Instead, value is thought to inhere in a good in the degree to which an individual's desire for that good exceeds its availability. Market value is, essentially, the aggregate of subjective choices made by numbers of individuals.

This single-minded focus on the "*mechanics of utility and self-interest*" favored methodological individualism[17]: analysis would proceed as though all economic laws could be derived from the "economic decisions of an individual in isolation."[18] It favored "isolated, individual decision making in an austere, putatively universally applicable context," where the "universal" context was the supposition that markets have penetrated human life to the extent that all wants have to be represented in and by them.[19] Self-interested action by individuals seeking the most efficient ways to optimize their good "was to become not only a component part of economic life in civil society but rather its only component."[20] It is no figure of speech to say that neoclassical economists reconceptualized homo economicus as a latter-day Robinson Crusoe. They turned (and still turn) obsessively to the story, William S. Kern observes, to model a new economic paradigm: the "isolated Crusoe, with given resources, tastes and technologies, secluded from social influences . . . provides a perfect setting for the application of the newly developed neoclassical tools."[21]

A space age Robinson Crusoe shipwrecked on Mars, the most isolated human being in history and in the solar system, Watney gravitates immediately and, it would seem, necessarily, to neoclassical principles defining how humans make rational decisions given the fact of scarce resources. His food will last only 300 days, or 400 with rationing (11); rescue is at least four years away. But Mars proves to be the perfect laboratory for testing out terrestrial neoclassical economics. For earthling economists, rationality, efficiency, self-interested behavior, and theories of value and cost are *ceteris paribus* scenarios. They are held to be true "all other things being equal." For example, economists proceed on the universalizing assumption that humans are selfish beings, screening out, for the sake of the model, circumstances that might seem to perturb it. On Mars there seem to be no perturbing circumstances; all other things are already equal because they constitute the unchanging limits within which Watney must work. He has no other self to consider, care for, or compete with; no supplemental resources come his way; and, as he notes at one point, his potatoes "grew even better than I had expected" because "Mars has no insects, parasites, or blights to deal with, and the Hab maintains perfect growing temperature and moisture at all times" (71). The environment allows near-perfect maximizing behavior. And maximizing behavior, for him, is no theory; it determines every movement he makes. Virtually every page of the novel describes him weighing the utility of his actions and thinking through how to perform them most efficiently.

Watney approaches survival in a manner familiar from the pages of any contemporary microeconomics textbook. Paul A. Samuelson and William D. Nordhaus's popular *Economics*—first published in 1948 and still, more than 18 editions on, a required text for many college economics courses—provides an almost exactly analogous example in the figure of Farmer Smith, who wants, the authors posit, to maximize the output on his farm. What, they ask, is the most efficient combination of added land or labor that will allow him to maximize his production, given the fact that the Farmer has limited resources? Farmer Smith discovers that after a period of increased production the utility, or value, of adding one more laborer is marked by a logic of diminishing returns. Since each unit of labor has less capital to work with as the number of laborers increases, the "marginal cost of output will rise because the extra output produced by each extra labor unit is going down."[22] At some point, in other words, the marginal cost of securing an additional laborer will outweigh the value of what the laborer helps to produce. The same holds true for the marginal cost of adding more land: after experiencing an initial burst of extra productivity, the costs associated with farming subsequent acres begin to grow and profitability decreases. Put differently, the incentive Farmer Smith experiences to keep adding land or labor decreases over time. Farmer Smith's goal—a quantifiable goal, Samuelson and Nordhaus point out—is to find the point of equilibrium where the combination of just the right amounts of land and labor maximizes his utility and thus his profitability.

The constraints on the political economy of potato farming on Mars of course seem different. "Farmer Mark" cannot add another laborer, cannot develop arable land beyond the Hab and two tents, and does not seek monetary gain. But to survive he employs the very same terrestrial logic to profit (or derive maximal utility) from his limited resources. He must, for example, obey the same laws of marginal utility. He plants twelve potatoes in an effort to bolster his meager supply of packaged food, which he knows will run out in 400 days. Like Farmer Smith, he expects to witness an initial rapid increase in his supply of potatoes. In Watney's first scenario, twelve potatoes, about a day's worth of food, will grow to become 76 days' worth (17). In his second scenario, he calculates he might grow enough potatoes to last another three years until rescue (20) by expanding his farm: placing soil in two tents, on two lab tables and five bunks would increase his arable land from 92 to 126 square meters. But the marginal value of growing more potatoes always diminishes in this novel. In his first scenario, replanting potatoes over the first 76 days after the first crop will not deliver an equivalent harvest since he must eat many of them to survive. A second planting might "tide me over for another 15" (17); after that, it is "kind of pointless to continue the trend" (17). The second scenario, in which Watney hopes that his last potato will have as much utility as the first (i.e., that the potatoes will last until he is rescued) threatens to buck that trend, until, of course, the explosive decompression that devastates his farm. The narrative effectively insists that the second scenario conform to the first-scenario logic of diminishing returns and rising marginal costs: by Sol 122, after the accident, the utility of trying to grow more potatoes has suddenly plunged to zero.

The novel, however, seems unable to extend its celebration of maximizing behavior—its microeconomic obsession with an individual devoted to efficient and rational decision-making in the face of scarce resources—to terrestrial economies. The good of Watney's survival turns out to be priceless, as his back-of-the-envelope "hundreds of millions of dollars" suggests: it is the one inexact calculation he makes in the novel, and necessarily so. His rescue carries a determinate *total* cost. But because there is no amount, no last dollar, that NASA is unwilling to pay, there is no *marginal* cost to his survival. It is worth considering in some detail how this scenario is at odds with neoclassical economic theory. In Preston R. McAfee and Tracy R. Lewis's *Introduction to Economic Analysis* (2009), for example, the authors note that converting opportunity costs into dollars can be controversial, and nowhere more so in "valuing human life": "How much is your life worth? Can it be converted into dollars?" The answer seems to be yes: if one purchases, or refuses to buy, a $400 airbag that will reduce the chance of death by 0.01 percent, one has implicitly established the marginal value of one's life (in terms of the utility of the airbag in a crash) at four million dollars (400 x 100 x 100).[23] The same logic and set of calculations cannot be applied to *The Martian* since NASA never monetizes the cost of Watney's survival. Since the organization never sets a price on its protective mechanisms, the value of his life must logically be infinite. Put another way, the sort of dilemmas Farmer Smith and Farmer Mark face in deciding between alternative uses for scarce resources—more land or more labor; growing potatoes in two rovers or using one of them for transportation (19)—are meaningless to NASA. The organization diverts resources to rescuing a human life without pondering the alternative uses to which the money might be put. It instantly sacrifices the "good" of other scientific projects, for example, on Watney's behalf.

The novel, in short, sets up incompatible economic domains: Mars, where Watney abides by the strictest neoclassical economic logic but without money or markets, and Earth, where NASA has access to so much money that economic principles seem to collapse. The novel's most complex attempt to address the puzzling abandonment of neoclassical economic principles on Earth occurs during the launch of the Chinese ship that has been repurposed to carry rescue materiel as part of a trade-off that will compel the Americans to put a Chinese astronaut on Mars. Mourning the loss of the scientific experiment he and "countless other researchers, scientists, and engineers" (254) have been preparing for four years, Chinese scientist Zhu Tao argues that the rescue "operation is a net loss for mankind's knowledge," since the "beautiful probe" will now "never fly"; the State Council "won't fund another booster like that." In reply, Venkat Kapoor, the American director of Mars operations, reaffirm the value of one individual's life: being rescued is a "net gain for Mark Watney" (254). The scene seems designed to score some conventional political points for the United States over their Socialist opponent: a well-funded NASA triumphs over a miserly State Council; the value of the individual trumps the needs of the abstract masses. Yet Zhu Tao's muted reply to Kapoor, "Mmm" (254), turns out to be a surprisingly troubling riposte within the economic ideologies of the novel. He introduces the precise neoclassical principles that NASA overrides. He invites Kapoor, and us, to consider seriously, for the only time in the novel, the possibility that scarce terrestrial funding might be allocated differently because other goods make valid competing claims. Positioning his argument with Kapoor on the rhetorical terrain of cost-benefit analysis—net loss considered against net gain—Zhu Tao reminds us of how far NASA has strayed from the guiding tenets and theoretical underpinnings of market capitalism by proceeding as if one person's life has infinite value.

That perplexing "Mmm" is vague enough to thrust the possibility that the rescue costs "too much" into the realm of the unthinkable, or at least into the realm of State Communism, but skeptical enough to invite readers to pursue other questions: why does the novel have so much trouble bridging the gap between the rigorously rational economies necessary for survival on Mars and the sky-is-the-limit fable on Earth? This disjunction, I argue, is generated by, and in part negotiates, the historical fact of the Great Recession and the economic discourses associated with it. Weir began to write *The Martian* in 2009, months after the puncturing of the housing/mortgage bubble in the United States brought about the near collapse of financial markets worldwide. The subsequent bailouts of venerable US financial and manufacturing institutions—Bear Stearns in March 2008, Fannie Mae and Freddie Mac in early September 2008, and then, after the September demise of Lehman Brothers, AIG, Citigroup, General Motors, and many others—was long, tortuous, and mind-bogglingly expensive. The October 2008 Troubled Asset Relief Program (TARP) pledged over 700 billion dollars to restore liquidity to the credit markets; the American Recovery and Reinvestment Act (ARRA), or the Recovery Act, which followed in 2009, aimed to provide a stimulus to the economy of over 800 billion dollars. The socioeconomic impact on the United States was nonetheless severe; the financial crisis led directly to a "real economy" recession. In November 2008, over 800,000 jobs disappeared. Between May 2007 and October 2009 over 7.5 million people lost their jobs; nearly two million families lost their homes to foreclosure in 2008 and 2009 alone.[24]

At the core of the crisis, explains Alan S. Blinder, former Vice Chair of the Federal Reserve, was a "fragile house of financial cards" built on subprime mortgages: the "intricate but precarious construction was based on asset-price bubbles, exaggerated by irresponsible leverage, encouraged by crazy compensation schemes and excessive complexity, and aided and abetted by embarrassingly bad underwriting standards, dismal performances by the statistical rating agencies, and lax financial regulation."[25] New investment vehicles such as mortgage backed securities (MBSs) packaged up subprime mortgage loans from different geographical regions in order (theoretically) to lessen risk. But MBSs were also "designed to default."[26] They were bets on house prices continuing to rise so that house owners could refinance their debt before it became too onerous. A mountain of debt, moreover, could be leveraged into new assets; indeed, "often leverage was piled on top of leverage."[27] (Leverage is the technical term for the ratio of debt to equity. If one borrows ten times the value of one's assets to invest it anew, one is leveraged in the ratio of 10:1.) This had disastrous results when falling house prices began to undermine the notional value of such assets. At the time of the collapse and fire sale of Bear Stearns on March 16, 2008, *The Economist* noted, Merrill Lynch, "the most leveraged," had "$1 trillion in assets . . . teetering on around $30 billion of equity."[28] A few months later, Merrill Lynch, its stock price plummeting, sold itself to Bank of America. By the end of 2008, writes Andrew Ross Sorkin, the much-touted idea that "American-style financial engineering was the global gold standard, was officially dead."[29]

As Blinder's "house of cards" summary hints, explanations of the financial crisis typically cite a sort of economic fabulism: the Wall Street traders making a "market in this fantasy stuff" were "fantasists" running a "fictitious Ponzi scheme"[30]; "having drunk the Kool-Aid," they were gambling in an "orgy of irresponsible risk taking."[31] Nor is this merely a retrospective view. A special nine-page report in *The Economist* at the height of the crisis in

September 2008—"Wall Street's Bad Dream"—begins by citing the "unreal air" to the carnage of the past fortnight.[32] An article in the *New York Times* three days after the demise of Lehman Brothers quoted one analyst (Glenn Schorr) as saying "It's all confidence, it's not reality," because the "increase in risk premiums investors are demanding on debt . . . now operate almost entirely detached from underlying fact."[33] The greater problem, others insist, was that there *was* no "underlying fact": credit markets in the middle of September 2008 threatened to dry up entirely because no one truly knew the market value of the esoteric financial instruments that comprised the "assets" of so many companies. Those instruments created "opacity—or maybe utter confusion."[34] "Some of the complexities of some of the instruments that were going into CDOs [Collateralized Debt Obligations]," said Alan Greenspan, former Chair of the Federal Reserve, "bewilders me."[35] Magical thinking hardly begins to describe the situation. The collapse of Lehman Brothers, says Lawrence G. McDonald, came about from "accounting sleight-of-hand, witchery, trickery, sorcery, or skullduggery. Now you see it, now you don't."[36]

One consequence of the financial crisis, as these comments imply, was to place under scrutiny the basic assumptions of mainstream economics. For some, the financial crisis amounted to a critique of the very principles of neoclassical economic thought. For example, it seemed to undermine one cornerstone of mainstream economics, the Efficient Market Hypothesis (EMH), which holds that markets are perfectly efficient because they price in all relevant information, and individuals therefore have perfect information at their disposal to make rational, and calculable, decisions. Jeff Madrick argues in *Seven Bad Ideas* (2014) that the Great Recession, among other recent financial disturbances, demolished this notion.[37] Had the concept of the EMH functioned correctly, markets would have begun pricing in the increased risks to derivatives based on subprime mortgages as soon as the housing market began to contract in late 2005. More typically, assessments of the economic crisis took the form of commentators arguing that traders in a new age of greed failed to observe the bedrock principles of economic thought. "America's financial markets," observed Joseph Stiglitz, "had failed to perform their essential societal functions of managing risk, allocating capital, and mobilizing savings while keeping transaction costs low"; by acting as if (or even believing that) housing prices could go up forever, they had simply ignored the central doctrine of economics since Adam Smith that "Resources are scarce."[38] From this perspective, the collapse of a mountain of bad debt did not indicate the failure of mainstream economics so much as the validation of the principles underpinning it; it meant the *resurgence* of homo economicus and the universal truths he is supposed to represent. That logic left its clear mark on the political scene. Austerity politics in Germany and

Great Britain, for example, focused on returning macroeconomic policies to the microeconomic "laws" about rationally allocating scarce resources that (are supposed to) undergird them.

The Martian writes in miniature the enormous political and economic efforts to overcome the financial crisis. It structures the symbolic terrain of Mars in such a way that every facet of Watney's struggle to survive invokes and seeks imaginative redemption for the clashing debates about how best to return economies to prosperity. The "hundreds of millions" his emergency rescue costs are given freely amid the unconditional support of billions of people; there is no conflict of wills or ideological perspectives. And this recipient of largesse, unlike the CEOs of major financial companies in 2008, makes no money from it. Indeed, his austere lifestyle and pragmatic calculations seem an exemplary response to a recession-era United States haunted by the legacy of "crazy" financial schemes and empty excess: too much credit and debt, too much complexity, too little regulation, too little productive allocation of resources. By making a lack of resources the driver of all his plans, the novel recuperates the concept of scarcity at the heart of classical and neoclassical theories about homo economicus's rational, maximizing behavior. The benefits are demonstrable. When Watney's fragile housing bubble (the Hab) ruptures, he quite literally loses his house and farm. But it proves to be no house of cards. He restores his house (and thus lives to return home) by dint of properly assessing and managing his resources. Planned economizing is vital: breakfasts featuring "a morning potato and Vicodin" (315) and "nothin' tea" (318) (hot water with nothing in it) get him to the point of rescue. His predicament shapes a plot dedicated to the political economy of austerity and to the economic logic of scarce resources that underpins it.

Arid Mars, however, always threatens Watney with a regime of *excessive* austerity: he needs more potatoes and an increased water supply to irrigate them since, early in the novel, he finds himself "250 liters short of my 250-liter goal" (20). Solving liquidity crises on Mars resonates oddly with the 2008 financial crisis, in which illiquidity became a cornerstone problem and key metaphor as declining house prices began to erode the value of securitized subprime mortgage loans, and banks, fearing that they were undercapitalized, resorted to hoarding their capital. "Ample 'liquidity' encouraged the lax lending that led to bad mortgage debts," *The Economist* observed in "When the rivers run dry" (March 2008), "and a sudden dearth of it helped to precipitate the crisis."[39] The metaphor continued to compel writers as the crisis deepened. On September 16, 2008, one day after the collapse of Lehman Brothers, Joe Nocera referred to the sudden seizing up of credit markets by observing that "As mortgage derivatives became increasingly toxic, they also became increasingly illiquid."[40] TARP's main function was to restore liquidity to the markets, which it did, though it took years for toxic assets to be unwound and their values resolved. Watney works in similar ways: to irrigate his farm he transforms his toxic assets (rocket fuel) into water. As if to demonstrate its perfect command over processes of liquidity, the novel concludes by having Watney electrolyze his remaining water (and urine) to turn it back into rocket fuel! Watney's wizard engineering, in fact, always stands in imaginative counterpoint to frozen, illiquid markets and the fabulous but empty "securities" offered by the financial engineers: farming keeps him alive in an insecure environment; *his* vehicles work. And, for him, leverage achieves determinate, productive ends: when his rovers get upended in a sandy gully, he uses scientific principle and leverage to right them. "I had Archimedes on my side" (316), he observes.

Failed financial engineering and institutional malfeasance on such unrepentant display in the years preceding and following the financial crisis helps, moreover, to explain the novel's odd lack of concern with NASA's profligacy. Unable to imagine a financial system that works for the benefit of ordinary people—and perhaps a functioning government—the novel fashions out of the displaced and reordered material of the crisis a sort of grand-scale fable of what might have been. Money, at the heart of the (financial) disaster, is thrust to the very periphery of the novel. It is still "crazy money," an ever-burgeoning amount, incalculably large, but here it plays a productive rather than socially destructive role. It permits rigorous science, elaborate systems, and cutting-edge technologies, the success of which first displaces and then erases the fact of real-world financial "sciences" that misfired disastrously. Moreover, freeing NASA from the logic of market forces is a crucial step toward allowing the institution to represent ethical considerations. Like the TARP and ARRA programs, the novel's NASA spends hundreds of millions in emergency rescue money—recovery is its goal too—but it does so out of concern for one human being rather than for the stability of the financial system. And though stabilizing the financial system (arguably) did little for the millions who were subsequently dispossessed of their homes, NASA devotes its energies and expertise to bringing one individual home; an entire organization acknowledges the gravity of just one person being abandoned. Home, in fact, has become a mythos, an entire planet, and everyone on this planet is committed to bringing the traveler back to it. In the novel's confabulation of history, those who presided over the unhoming of millions of families—Wall Street companies, mortgage brokers, and the US government and its agencies—are nowhere to be found.

That erasure of market history and market orthodoxy from the two worlds of *The Martian* produces diverse effects. It frees the novel to generate constructive symbolic solutions to the crises of the Great Recession. On Mars, homo economicus, the economizing, wholly rational, wholly self-interested agent, returns to first principles, posing the political economy of potato farming against a terrestrial history of dizzying financial excess; on Earth, NASA's generosity toward one individual stands in profound contrast to a bailout that disregarded the "little guys" in favor of an abstract financial system. These solutions, however, fail to correlate with each other or with any broader political economic strategy, largely because the novel lacks precisely what neoclassical economic thought assumes: a logical connection between the maximizing behavior of humans (the choices individuals make in the face of scarce resources) and the free market that governs the efficient allocation of resources by aggregating choices and providing a neutral and consistent mechanism (pricing systems) for adjudicating value. That lack presents an interpretive dilemma for readers. The novel's economic fabling precludes it from speaking to, or issuing a critique of, *real* markets and economies. Yet its detailed representation of maximizing behavior on Mars suggests another possibility: the novel represents symbolically the historical moment at which the free market system of the United States, by virtue of seeming to have gone haywire, no longer functions as a logical counterpart for or conclusion to the maximizing behavior individuals continue to exhibit. Inefficient, opaque, irrational, and fabulously exuberant markets, that is, invalidate the sequence of logical steps that should lead from homo economicus to the free market. And so, the novel envisages and celebrates the first without being able to make it signify in the context of the second.

The issue I want to address at greater length, however, is not the novel's reticence about markets so much as its frail and fuzzy efforts to conceive of commonwealth. Alfred Marshall, we saw, associated the rise of neoclassical economics with the end of shared concerns about the "Body Politic." *The Martian* attempts to disagree: Watney's concluding moral, "every human being has a basic instinct to help each other out," certainly advances a concept of human solidarity and, in that respect, promises a return to political economy, where the "interests of the whole nation," or for that matter the whole planet, might come into play.[41] The statement threatens the very telos of mainstream economics, which accepts as its bottom line the self-interested behavior of participants in market economies. But Watney's statement cannot be broadened from a generic sense of human solidarity to political economy. It actually *defies* his experience on Mars, the significance of which has to do with the actions undertaken by a completely isolated individual. And terrestrial activities simply turn the concept of the common good on its head. The entire economic output of the globe, it seems, is put at the service of one person—the one person, moreover, who demonstrates more conclusively than anyone else in the novel that the basic instinct of a human being is to help *himself* out. The novel here requires multiple aporias: a philosophy of the common good is dedicated to keeping alive the principles of homo economicus in the solar system's most isolated person, while homo economicus, flaunting his grasp of fundamental economic principles, strives to escape the planet and end his isolation forever.

But if the novel sabotages the neoclassical paradigm of homo economicus that it has so compellingly built up on Mars, it must also be said that it emerges from a historical moment that put on dramatic display the collapse of any universal agreement about or discourse on economics. The financial crisis presented a compelling need for an economic analysis that could be broadened to a consideration of commonwealth: what were the collective economic interests of the entire nation? The attempts to answer this question by many groups and individuals—the federal government, the mass media, think tanks, scholars, and progressive political movements—failed. It was not merely a breakdown of communication between economic camps (e.g., Friedmanians versus Keynesians) or finding that professional economic analysis speaks a jargon and employs a mathematical idiom incomprehensible to most people. The broader issue is that the very concept of commonwealth—the question of how to speak to and of the common good in contemporary economic terms—proved elusive *even when it was articulated as a legitimate goal.* The clash between Greta Thunberg and Steve Mnuchin, which I examine in the Introduction, is a case in point. Mnuchin's joke—Thunberg will have to study economics in college to "explain [her analysis] to us"—invokes an "us" consistent with college-educated economists who hold the explanatory keys that the rest of "us" would do well to respect. Thunberg makes a rhetorical claim on at least two constituencies: the "we" who face mass extinction, which is to say everyone, and the "we" who "will never forgive" dilatory inaction, specified at the end of the speech as "the young people" who are "starting to understand your betrayal."[42] Such fluid positions in the Thunberg-Mnuchin debate imply the lack of any convincing idiom in which to articulate a sense of the common good that a collective "we" could share.

Also exemplary is the document that more than any other would seem positioned to describe the national significance of the economic catastrophe: the US government's official interpretation of the crisis, the Financial Crisis Inquiry Commission Report of 2011, which was published almost simultaneously with *The Martian*. The Report marshals facts and apportions responsibility in an uncompromising way. Its lucid, no-nonsense prose style supports its consistent rhetorical commitment to bringing all Americans on board: "Like so many Americans"[43]; "We encourage the American people to join us" (xv); "To help our fellow citizens better understand this crisis" (xv). At a few points that rhetoric lays claim to a body politic finally united in its economic understanding and actions: "as a nation," the writers argue, "we must also accept responsibility for what we permitted to occur. Collectively, but certainly not unanimously, we acquiesced to or embraced a system, a set of policies and actions, that gave rise to our present predicament" (xxiii). But the rest of this lengthy document (633 pages) displaces or belies that exalted "we." The commissioners argue, for example, that the "captains of finance and the public stewards of our financial system . . . failed to question, understand, and manage evolving risks within a system essential to the well-being of the American public" (xvii). But if the captains of finance and the public stewards charged with understanding and managing the system could not in fact do so, who composes the collective "we" that permitted these pernicious errors to occur?

This dilemma ramifies through the entire document. On the one hand, the commissioners insist that the forthcoming crisis was perfectly legible. "Everyone in the whole world knew that the mortgage bubble was there," says Richard Breeden, former chairman of the Securities and Exchange Commission: it "wasn't hidden. . . . It wasn't out on Mars or Pluto or somewhere" (4). Economist Dean Baker observes that the critical errors were "absolute public knowledge" (23). The commissioners weigh in with similar remarks: "it soon became apparent that what had looked like newfound wealth was a mirage based on borrowed money" (7). But their next paragraph upends this confidence about what is "apparent," since, in this brave new world of "newfangled mortgage securities" (xxiv), "it wasn't even clear anymore who the lender was. The mortgages would be packaged, sliced, repackaged, insured, and sold as incomprehensibly complicated debt securities" (7). Moreover, "leverage was often hidden" (xx); in the financial system "transparency was not required or desired" (xx); and key components of the "shadow banking system" were "hidden from view" (xx). New types of mortgages ended up "confounding consumers who didn't examine the fine print, baffling conscientious borrowers who tried to puzzle out their implications" (7). Even the so-called experts were confounded. Key policy makers "did not have a clear grasp of the financial system they were charged with overseeing [and] lacked a full understanding of the risks and interconnections in the financial markets" (xxi). Still more harmful for their thesis that "everyone in the whole world knew," the commissioners admit that many of those most heavily involved in structuring arcane financial instruments somehow did not understand them. These traders, economists, and executives may have been "certifiable lunatics," as hedge fund manager Steve Eisman put it, but "Everyone really did believe that things were going to be okay" (194).

This contradictory exposition of "absolute public knowledge"—everyone in the whole world knew disaster was coming/everyone believed that things were okay—undermines the commission's fantasy of a collective body whose knowledge is supposed to be substantial enough to assert a *common* ownership or responsibility for what "we" permitted to occur. That collectivity could not be responsible if we are to believe the Report's accusations about an entire shadow banking system devising "incomprehensibly complicated" financial instruments, or if we accept the possibility that even the "experts" in the years leading up to 2008 knew much less than the Commission later found.[44] Indeed, the collective "we" used by "the Commission" to refer to itself turns out to be a fable. The Report was disavowed by four of its ten members. Writing at the end of the report, the first dissenting group identifies macroeconomic issues (global capital flows and risk repricing [421]) as the drivers of crisis; the second dissenting group blames politics (US government housing policy over two administrations [444]). The point here is not to adjudicate among these perspectives but to observe that *having to adjudicate* demonstrates the egregiousness of the Commission's own claims about a united body politic. One may not agree with Peter J. Wallison's statement in the second dissent that the majority opinion is a "just so story" (444), that is, a children's fable, about the financial crisis rather than an analysis of its causes; but it certainly characterizes the (majority) Report's claim that it secures a common ground upon which economic analyses might be established.

The concept of commonwealth proves just as elusive in another prominent public economic document of 2011, the Declaration of the Occupation of New York City by Occupy Wall Street (September 29, 2011). On the face of it, the Declaration has no such problem as the Report in constituting its imagined commons. Its rhetorical claim on "we" is unrelenting: "we gather together in solidarity"; "We write so that all people who feel wronged by the corporate forces of the world can know that we are your allies"; "As one people, united"; "the future of the human race requires the cooperation of its members"; "To the people of the world." Its readers are urged to "generate solutions accessible to everyone." "We" is specified variously here: as the New York City General Assembly occupying Wall Street; its potential allies; the human race; one people; and those wronged by corporate forces. "We," that is, references an actual body, currently gathered together, which writes in anticipation of solidarity with a much larger *imagined* body, not yet a collective, and not yet aware of its common cause with Occupy. What holds together this somewhat amorphous alliance is not, in fact, one definition of "we" but the ensuing list of economic, social, and environmental problems—foreclosures, bailouts, ecological degradation, outsourcing, discrimination, and much more—for which "They" are responsible. "They" performs much of the rhetorical heavy lifting in this document. The Declaration's sense of "one people, united" is firmed up and locked into place through its assertion that *we* are definitively not *they*.

One consequence of depending on a concept of "they" to constitute "we" is that the document affords a detailed exposition of corporate malfeasance around the globe but has virtually nothing to say about what socioeconomic principles a newly formed global alliance might stand for and put into practice. Nor can those principles be deduced from what "they" do wrong, for the items on the list are rooted in different economic provenances. It is not clear, for example, whether the document's aims are truly revolutionary, contemplating a moment in which the power to formulate economic policies passes from the 1 percent ("corporate forces") to the 99 percent (those wronged by global capitalism), or merely reformist. The solution to the problem that "They have continuously sought to strip employees of the right to negotiate for better pay and safer working conditions" might be, for example, stronger unions, where restoring a right to negotiate for better pay assumes the continuing presence of an asymmetric structure of power. But reforms such as these also jibe uneasily with the document's representation of the perils of globalization. It is certainly of concern that "They" have "consistently outsourced labor and used that outsourcing as leverage to cut workers' healthcare and pay," and stronger labor unions with more negotiating power might indeed be one answer. But this assumes "we" are thinking of the United States. It does not necessarily follow that outsourcing labor from the United States to China or India or Vietnam is detrimental to the economies and to the lives of workers (the 99%) of *these* countries; many proponents of globalization have in fact argued that global economic forces in the twenty-first century favor emerging-market workers in the short run and everyone, including the (perhaps temporarily) unemployed workers in richer countries, in the long run. This is not to argue that the Declaration is mistaken about global asymmetries of wealth and power. But it lacks a concept of commonwealth framed in a broad enough perspective to connect the unemployed in the United States to workers in other countries, and thus to demystify what appear to be the benefits accruing to the recipients of outsourced US labor.

In this respect, the Declaration's most important statement is the footnote that follows its final complaint: "*These grievances are not all-inclusive*." There are at least two reasons why the Declaration demands this footnote. It intimates that the list of grievances could go on and on, since the crimes of global capitalism are endless. Less obviously, the footnote allows that there is no all-inclusive statement of economic principle that we (or at least the 99%) might adopt to understand what is *generating* these striking instances of grievance. Put another way, the document's emphasis on enumerating instances covers for the fact that the body politic, the "we" on whose behalf the Declaration purports to speak, is no more than an eloquent fable, unable to address the issue of how outsourcing connects to colonialism, or how strong unions connect to the beneficiaries of globalization in other countries, or how, for that matter, illegal foreclosures in the United States connect to the "unhomed" in other nations across a postcolonial world. A never-ending list of grievances points ultimately to the presence of many different collectives of "we," many of whom are, consciously or not, in competition with each other.

The Martian's final paean to every human's "basic instinct to help each other out," and the bottom line be damned, thus has an excellent pedigree in the swirling economic arguments of its time. It fits neatly into the Declaration's "one people, united" and vaguely into the Commission's "we," and with about as much bearing on real economic conditions.[45] It also reminds us of one other important voice at this time: Barack Obama, campaigning for the presidency at the height of the crisis in 2008, and again in 2012, who clearly touched a nerve when he argued that "you're on your own economics" does not work.[46] He was speaking at a historical moment that was cruelly exposing the material and discursive pretensions of once-compelling mainstream economic dogmas—the preeminence of the isolated economic agent; the fact of perfectly efficient markets within which homo economicus could put his rational, maximizing behaviors to work; even the notion that the market capitalist system was essential, as the Report put it, "to the economic well-being of our nation" (xxii). The Report and the Declaration represent that historical moment in rhetorical terms. They, too, tap a widespread cultural yearning for, and betray anxieties about losing, the concept of a body politic wherein economic solutions for the commonwealth might be proposed; they too try to lay claim to a public discourse able to represent economics in different ways than "you're on your own."

The Martian participates in that same constellation of cultural anxieties, and with great symbolic power. It sets out to restore through the political economy of potato farming on Mars nothing less than the very legitimacy of homo economicus, dramatizing a compelling "on your own" scenario before evoking a fabulous "we" to collapse, or ameliorate, its own logic. Yet as ridiculous as the novel's assertion of a community of interests might seem at its crisis-filled, post-recessionary historical moment, it does, after all, leave traces in the narrative's *emotional* register as our desire to see Watney rescued (something he cannot in fact achieve alone) builds to a crescendo. The novel's implied economic discourses seem destined to inhabit different worlds forever. That may be its virtue. To the extent that it finds a form capable of holding together confused and contradictory discourses—at least, representing them in the same narrative—it accepts and for a precarious moment solves a challenge in ways that few other works of the Great Recession can claim.

NOTES

1. This chapter is derived, in part, from an article first published in *Science Fiction Studies* 44, no. 1 (2017): 1–20.

2. Andy Weir, *The Martian* (2011; reprint New York: Crown, 2014), 7. Subsequent references to this work are cited parenthetically in the text. *The Martian* was originally serialized on Weir's blog before appearing in book form in 2014.

3. Alan S. Blinder, for example, argues that by 2011, the effects of the government's "financial-market policies" were that "real GDP was about 6 percent higher, the unemployment rate was nearly 3 percentage points lower, and 4.8 million more Americans were employed" than if nothing had been done. *After the Music Stopped: The Financial Crisis, the Response, and the Work Ahead* (New York: Penguin, 2013), 209.

4. My argument about economic life on Mars accords with Jane Elliott's thoughtful study of the "microeconomic imagination" in recent cultural work, by which she means that neoliberal economic principles such as "methodological individualism, rational allocation, [and] utility maximization" appear, but have become "unmoored from the market focus of economics as a discipline." *The Microeconomic Mode: Political Subjectivity in Contemporary Popular Aesthetics* (New York: Columbia University Press, 2018), 9–10.

5. Laura Brown, *Fables of Modernity: Literature and Culture in the English Eighteenth Century* (Cornell: Cornell University Press, 2001), 1–3.

6. Brown, *Fables of Modernity*, 114.

7. Homi K. Bhabha, *The Location of Culture* (1994; reprint New York: Routledge, 2007), 1, 13. Emphasis in the original.

8. Adam Smith, *The Wealth of Nations* (1776; reprint, New York: Bantam Books, 2003), 23–24.

9. "Irrational exuberance" refers to Robert Shiller's well-known book on the dot-com boom, *Irrational Exuberance* (Princeton University Press, 2000), which he updated in 2005 to include the emerging housing bubble.

10. John Stuart Mill, *Principles of Political Economy* (London: John W. Parker, 1848; New York: Augustus M. Kelley, 1987), 13.

11. William Tabb, *Reconstructing Political Economy: The Great Divide in Economic Thought* (London; New York: Routledge, 1999), 53.

12. Ben Fine and Dimitris Milonakis, *From Political Economy to Economics: Method, the Social and the Historical in the Evolution of Economic Theory* (New York: Routledge, 2009), 1.

13. Murray Milgate and Shannon C. Stimson, *After Adam Smith: A Century of Transformation in Politics and Political Economy* (Princeton: Princeton University Press, 2009), 6.

14. Quoted in Charles E. Staley, *A History of Economic Thought from Aristotle to Arrow* (Oxford: Basil Blackwell, 1989), 133–34.

15. Ben Fine and Dimitris Milonakis, *From Economics to Freakonomics: The Shifting Boundary Between Economics and other Social Sciences* (New York: Routledge, 2009), 134.

16. Alfred Marshall, *Principles of Economics* (New York: Macmillan, 1891), 5.

17. William Stanley Jevons, *The Theory of Political Economy* (1871; reprint New York: Kelley & Millman, 1957), 21.

18. William S. Kern, "Robinson Crusoe and the Economists," in *Robinson Crusoe's Economic Man: A Construction and Deconstruction*, eds. Ulla Grapard and Gillian Hewitson (New York: Routledge, 1999), 62.
19. Milgate and Stimson, *After Adam Smith*, 5–6.
20. Milgate and Stimson, *After Adam Smith*, 6.
21. Kern, "Robinson Crusoe," 66.
22. Paul A. Samuelson and William D. Nordhaus, *Economics* (1948; reprint New York: McGraw-Hill, 2005), 131.
23. McAfee, R. Preston, and Tracy R. Lewis, *Introduction to Economic Analysis*, Open Textbook Library, 2009: 9, https://open.umn.edu/opentextbooks/textbooks/47.
24. David B. Grusky, Bruce Western, and Christopher Wimer, eds., *The Great Recession* (New York: Russell Sage Foundation, 2011), 4.
25. Blinder, *After the Music*, 84.
26. Blinder, *After the Music*, 70.
27. Blinder, *After the Music*, 55.
28. "What Went Wrong—Wall Street's Crisis," *The Economist* 386 (March 22, 2008).
29. Andrew Ross Sorkin, *Too Big to Fail: The Inside Story of How Wall Street and Washington Fought to Save the Financial System from Crisis—and Themselves* (New York: Viking, 2009), 3.
30. Michel Lewis, *The Big Short: Inside the Doomsday Machine* (New York: Norton, 2010), 186, 227, 158.
31. Blinder, *After the Music*, 72, 83.
32. Wall Street's Bad Dream," *The Economist* 388 (September 18, 2008), https://www-economist-com.ezproxy.neu.edu/finance-and-economics/2008/09/18/wall-streets-bad-dream.
33. Ben White and Eric Dash, "As Fears Grow, Wall St. Titans See Shares Fall," *New York Times*, September 18, 2008, A1, A33.
34. Blinder, *After the Music*, 76.
35. Quoted in Sorkin, *Too Big to Fail*, 90.
36. Lawrence G. McDonald, with Patrick Robinson, *A Colossal Failure of Common Sense: The Inside Story of the Collapse of Lehman Brothers* (New York: Crown Business, 2009), 221.
37. Jeff Madrick, *Seven Bad Ideas: How Mainstream Economists Have Damaged America and the World* (New York: Alfred A. Knopf, 2014), 138–63. Yves Smith also levels an assault on economic models, which constitute "Potemkin science, all façade and no substance." *Econned: How Unenlightened Self Interest Undermined Democracy and Corrupted Capitalism* (New York: Palgrave Macmillan, 2010), 19.
38. Joseph E. Stiglitz, *Freefall: America, Free Markets, and the Sinking of the World Economy* (New York: Norton, 2010), 7, 38.
39. "When the Rivers Run Dry; Economics Focus." *The Economist* 386 (March 8, 2008), www-economist-com.ezproxy.neu.edu/search?q=march+2008+when+the+rivers+run+dry.
40. Joe Nocera, "On Wall Street as on Main Street, a Problem of Denial," *New York Times*, September 16, 2008, A25.

41. Alfred Marshall, quoted in Charles E. Staley, *A History of Economic Thought from Aristotle to Arrow* (Oxford: Basil Blackwell, 1989), 133.

42. Greta Thunberg's Speech at the UN, September 23, 2019, n.p., www.npr.org/2019/09/23/763452863/transcript-greta-thunbergs-speech-at-the-u-n-climate-action-summit.

43. Financial Crisis Inquiry Commission. *The Financial Crisis Inquiry Report*, January 2011, xvi, fcic-static.law.stanford.edu/cdn_media/fcic-reports/fcic_final_report_full.pdf. Subsequent references to this work are cited parenthetically in the text.

44. One of the cornerstones of Peter J. Wallison's dissent is in fact the argument that the majority commission's report relies on hindsight and that focusing on what people knew in 2006 would have led to a very different analysis.

45. Six years after the Obama administration's "Home Affordable Modification Program" was launched in 2009, banks had modified 887,001 of around 4 million distressed loans—about 28%. Gretchen Morgenson, "Slack Lifeline for Drowning Homeowners," *New York Times*, August 2, 2015, 1, 5.

46. "Obama: 'You're on Your Own' Economics Doesn't Work," *Real Clear Politics*, 30 March, 2012, n.p., www.realclearpolitics.com/video/2012/03/30/obama_youre_on_your_own_economics_doesnt_work.html.

Chapter Two

Virtual Commonwealths of the Great Recession

The Obamas' Garden and Farm Management Games

In *The Martian*, we saw in Chapter 1, Andy Weir projects a fabulous concept of commonwealth without material or theoretical basis. The novel presents a near-flawless account of neoclassical economics while touting the wholly un-economic principle that humans have a basic instinct to help each other out; and it depicts a world full of people dedicated to bringing one man home while, as the book was published, millions of people around the globe were losing homes and jobs to an ugly recession. This chapter considers two other representations of commonwealth during the recession years: the Obamas' 2009 garden "farm" at the White House (inspired and run by Michelle Obama) and online farm management games, which sprang to popularity with the advent of *FarmVille* (2009). In one sense both sketch an economy more fabulous than Mark Watney's, for while potato farming on Mars dwindles toward zero, the Obamas' garden and farm management games promise a vision of productivity based on, as *Funky Bay* puts it, "plant one, harvest two." These representations of commonwealth could certainly lay claim to cultural prominence. *FarmVille* prompted the development of massive new gaming communities on the social media platform of Facebook. And President Obama came to power in 2009 under the unusual double burden of fulfilling the conventional duties of a president and shoring up an economy on the verge of collapse. In fact, Michelle Obama's garden/farm offers a striking counterpoint to the Obama administration's economic successes. It constructs an idealized commonwealth based on older political economic narratives reframed in complex ways by postmodern cultural formations, including feminist approaches to the concept of utopia.

In the spring of 2009, at the dawn of a new US presidency, First Lady Michelle Obama broke ground for an organic kitchen garden on the White House's South Lawn. A beehive followed. Commentators instantly recognized the Obamas' salute to environmentalism and healthy food movements. But that only begins to reveal the possible political and cultural implications of what was in many respects a symbolic tour de force. Its timing was auspicious. Barack Obama became president during the brutal early days of the Great Recession, when the bailout of banks and financial houses, of car and insurance companies, was drawing national attention to an economy bloated on throwaway credit and excessive debt, dedicated to fast and vast profits for a few, and driven by house-of-cards financial instruments whose labyrinthine complexities and occulted abstractions not even their creators seemed to understand. The economic crisis of 2008 was in great measure a crisis of lost or alienated value. The book value of trillions of dollars of assets worldwide disappeared or became indeterminate. With it, at least for a while, went the markets' and governments' faith in the epistemological claims of a discipline—economics—whose arcana of demand curves and computer algorithms, whose glib faith in efficient markets, seemed suddenly irrelevant. Economic value and the truth-claims of economics seemed to vanish into the same abyss.

We can therefore see why Michelle Obama and the president, who had campaigned on bringing "you're on your own economics" to an end, would be drawn to a different mode of representing economics. In her later book-length account of the garden, *American Grown* (2012), Michelle Obama explicitly claimed a broadly communal reach to their 2009 symbolic enterprise: she wanted to begin a "conversation about the food we eat, the lives we lead, and how all of that affects our children."[1] Transporting the collective imagination from the muck of Wall Street to the dirt from which nutritious products grow, the Obamas' kitchen garden put alternative social, epistemological, and narrative principles toward what Michelle Obama touted as the prospect of a "healthier nation."[2] The garden recommended dietary restrictions to an obese body politic fueled by "skyrocketing childhood obesity rates," while implicitly censuring corporate excess and congressional economies running on "pork."[3] Here, curatorial responsibilities for slow, natural, sustainable growth replaced computer-generated "flash" transactions on the stock market; here, value arose out of the persistent application of labor to the land; scale and process were comprehensible; goods produced were to be visible and tangible, and their worth would be recognized instantly by the body. The promise of a head of lettuce, raw, universally identifiable, stood against the "cooked" books and failed epistemologies of Wall Street, all the more so because the garden was to be pesticide-free and market-free.[4] And Michelle Obama made sure to emphasize the collective nature of the enterprise—that it spoke to a tradition of community gardening. She invited children from the local Bancroft Elementary to help and addressed them about "actually experiencing the joys of your work."[5] That "actually" is telling. It speaks to something now lost or at least lacking in a society where even those who still had jobs found their labor alienating. The garden predicted a renaissance for the joys of shared labor. And since this land was symbolically congruent with the birth of the United States, perhaps the garden was even supposed to adumbrate, to quote Thomas Paine in *Common Sense*, a "seed-time of Continental union" for a newly productive, pesticide-free American politics.[6]

Contemporary commentators glimpsed the fact that there were symbolic historical dimensions to the Obamas' little parable of independent, labor-intensive, market-free food production. Writers in the *New York Times* and the *Guardian* immediately noted that the garden seemed to be a salute to World War II victory gardens.[7] Andrea Wulf went further back in time, observing that it allowed Barack Obama to claim his place in a lineage of Founding Fathers who happened to be garden wizards: she cites George Washington's desire to garden at Mount Vernon as a reason for not pursuing a third term and enthuses over Jefferson's 250 varieties of vegetables at Monticello.[8] To be sure, that lineage is rooted in a national imaginary. Wulf's sanitized version of history neglects to mention the fact that these Founding Fathers used slave labor in their gardens and fields. That oversight was reproduced by almost every other commentator at the time, including Michele Obama herself in *American Grown* when she celebrates Thomas Jefferson's horticultural experiments at the White House and Monticello.[9] Melissa Harris-Lacewell in her blog "The Kitchen Table" was one of the few to attempt to revise this White male–oriented political narrative.[10] Hailing the garden as Michelle Obama's initiative, Harris-Lacewell points to a formidable body of Black feminist work connecting the political sphere to garden work, domestic economy, and artistic innovation. Citing Alice Walker's *In Search of Our Mothers' Gardens* (1983) as inspiration, she notes the multifaceted significance of gardens to African American women: a place where material bodies and families might be nurtured, where a creative outlet might be found for the "artistic genius" otherwise denied expression, and where a community of women engaged in similar activities might ultimately form a symbolic and literary tradition. From this heritage Harris-Lacewell quickly grasped the utopian possibilities of the Obamas' garden. It is a "perfect political symbol for our country in this moment" that "manifests and makes concrete these black feminist tradition[s] in such an inclusive and fully American way" by configuring the "vegetable garden [as] a symbol of self-reliance" and by ensuring that, as the economy declines, "something will grow."[11]

As Harris-Lacewell hints, there are other "fully American" garden sites where economic value might be attributed to the fact that "something will grow." The Obamas' garden does indeed self-consciously recall the victory gardens of WWII—Michele Obama notes early in *American Grown* that her mother's family had a victory garden.[12] It also looks back vaguely to the communes of the sixties, quietly to late-nineteenth-century agrarian populism, powerfully to Thoreau's experiments in self-reliance at Walden, mythically to the New World garden, and politically to Thomas Jefferson, whose celebration of the independent American yeoman farmer and the land he farms as the guarantee of economic security and political rights echoes through the political iconography being produced on the South Lawn. Those instances might be extended into still earlier times through what Timothy Sweet calls the tradition of the American georgic: an enduring cultural formation, derived formally from Virgil's *Georgics*, that builds metaphoric relationships between the landscape, its transformation by human work, and concepts of political economy. Sweet traces the tradition back to Stephen Parmenius's 1583 letter about a voyage to Newfoundland, when Europeans were forced to confront the implications of breaking (what they wanted to imagine as) fallow ground and utilizing its productions. New transnational economic systems and, as a corollary, new theories of political economy, arose. No one seems to have interpreted the Obamas' groundbreaking in terms of a georgic tradition. But a broader historical framework, both mythos and economic discourse, stands behind the representational strategy the Obamas' garden employs to compose narratives about utility, production, and economic well-being.

One *locus classicus* for grasping the economic implications of the Obamas' garden is the work of the eighteenth-century French Physiocrats, often considered the first scientifically oriented school of economic thought. Led by François Quesnay and including the Marquis de Mirabeau and Anne-Robert-Jacques Turgot, the Physiocrats' celebration of agriculture as the economic driver of a nation profoundly shaped the post-Revolutionary embrace of agrarian democracy in the United States. The "leading assumption of the Physiocrats' theoretical system," observes Ronald L. Meek, was that "agriculture was the supreme occupation."[13] The reason, as Turgot argues, is that the "earth was ever the first and the only source of all riches; it is that which by cultivation produces all revenue; it is that which has afforded the first fund for advances, anterior to all cultivation."[14] Land is "primary in the scale of wants," as Meek puts it; moreover, unlike the "sterile" capital generated by manufacturing, whose profits were held to be illusory, it "alone yielded a disposable surplus over necessary cost."[15] The land, in short, produces the original stock of capital (the "first fund for advances") upon which humans depended for their subsistence prior to the harvesting of the first crops. Inverting Watney's experience on Mars, the cultivation of it allows capital to replenish itself the shape of seeds and newborn livestock. The initial cost of a herd of sheep is conceivably the only capital outlay incurred by the farmer if the herd's natural increase generates both monetary income and still more sheep. In contrast, a clothing manufacturer must make constant purchases of wool; wool cannot grow more wool. Agricultural pursuits could therefore be identified with the natural order. This is not to deny the presence of markets and capital flows. Quesnay's 1758 *tableau économique*, which illustrated the flow of capital from agriculture to the sterile classes (landowners and manufacturers), is generally acknowledged to be the first scientific attempts to model the processes of a national economy. But the process whereby capital circulates through a society originates in the earth's produce and seems to be underpinned by the fruitfulness of the earth and the unvarying cycles of the seasons.

Such principles were of great importance to what Marianne Johnson calls the "American Physiocrats"—writers and politicians such as Thomas Jefferson, Ben Franklin, and Hector St. John de Crèvecoeur—who worked to outline, Manuela Albertone observes, a "politico-economic vision centred on the farmer as a politically active and economically dynamic producer working in the setting of commercial agriculture, and an extended decentralized participatory democracy aimed at defending the rights of the Confederation's thirteen member states."[16] As Jefferson wrote to John Jay, "Cultivators of the earth are the most valuable citizens. They are the most vigorous, the most independent, the most virtuous, & they are tied to their country & wedded to it's liberty & interests by the most lasting bonds."[17] That paradigm of a republican nation built on the simple virtues accruing to the farmer working the land was, as Elizabeth Hewitt argues, already out of step with post-Revolutionary economic realities—Jeffersonians, for example, were committed to opening up global markets for agricultural produce. Yet the mythos of an agrarian democracy provided for late-eighteenth-century Americans the "very regularity and simplicity that the new economic world had already begun to shatter with its increasingly specialized labor market and mediated supply chains."[18] As importantly, Hewitt notes, it has continued to be enshrined in a "populist national history that sees the rise of finance and commercial capitalism as a betrayal of democracy."[19]

We can gain insight into the economic implications of the Obamas' kitchen garden by reading it as a reprise of the symbolic language of key works of the "American Physiocrats." Crèvecoeur's *Letters from an American Farmer* (1782), for example, launches his inquiry into the political economy of America at another moment of crisis and potential revolution, the years leading up to the War of Independence. Crèvecoeur's rhetorical strategies offer a primer for understanding the Obamas' moves. If the installation of an apiary on the White House lawn can be explained in terms of a pragmatic salute to the natural order—a fertile garden requires fertilizing bees—it also invokes a long-standing tradition of making bee-colonies signify socioeconomic roles. In Letter II, Crèvecoeur celebrates "My bees [who] above any other tenants of my farm, attract my attention and respect."[20] Our "kingbirds are the destroyers of those industrious insects," Crèvecoeur adds, though "on the other hand, these birds preserve our fields from the depredation of crows" (30). Crèvecoeur draws here on Virgil's famous meditation on bee-husbandry as a metaphor for commonwealth in *Georgics IV*. Virgil applauds the "tiny citizens" (l.198) of the hive who labor as one body and, "remembering the winter to come/undergo labour, storing their gains for all" (l.156)—but who also in times of strife "lift the leader on their shoulders and expose their bodies/in war" (l.218).[21]

Virgil's applause for the bees' industry, communal laboring, a willingness to "pass their life under the might of the law" (l.165), and devotion to a military cause, all find their way into Crèvecoeur's parable of industrious life on an American farm. His complex allegory invokes pre-War political rhetoric. The king(bird) who protects the fields from the depredations of others reminds us of the promises of British rule—"she has protected us, say some," writes Tom Paine in *Common Sense* (1776) a few years later—and of American attacks on a sovereign power consuming and destroying the colonies' prosperity.[22] If the fable of the kingbird and the bees hints that natural law rationalizes current political strife, since "nothing exists but what has its enemy" (30), it also acknowledges the likelihood that the bees will live up to their warlike propensities when "new leaders command the early swarms" (l.15). With their tip of the hat to Virgil, Crèvecoeur's bees and the Obamas' apiary offer a meditation on the function of industrious workers, new leaders, and old principles within a polity under threat. The lazily unproductive Wall Street fat cats who shadow the entire scene on the South Lawn occupy the place of Crèvecoeur's king(bird) devouring his colony of workers, though with one key reversal: unlike the kingbird, the fat cats are *contra naturam*, swallowing far more than the 171 bees the kingbird is capable of ingesting.

The Obamas' groundbreaking finds other symbolic correlatives in Crèvecoeur. Elsewhere in Letter II, the American farmer describes the act of ploughing the fields with his son while his wife sits sewing, and watching, under a tree. "Often when I plough my low ground, I place my little boy on a chair which screws to the beam of the plough," writes the farmer, adding: "its motion and that of the horses pleases him; he is perfectly happy and begins to chat," while the "odiferous furrow exhilarates his spirits, and seems to do the child a great deal of good, for he looks more blooming since I had adopted that practice" (28). The historical and sociopolitical meanings of the farmer's activities are never far from this symbolic narrative, which transforms "low ground" into a stage upon which socioeconomic roles and stories about history can be performed, aiding Crèvecoeur in establishing a patriarchal pedagogy that articulates property relations through the application of disciplined, healthy labor to the land. His goal, to begin with, is to cultivate food *and* a human being, his son, for whom ploughing offers a range of benefits: bodily health, mental exercise, emotional uplift, the companionship and wisdom of his father, and a tutorial in the virtues of hard work and self-discipline displayed in the "straightness of [his] furrows" (24). Straight furrows imply the most efficient employment of space, allowing the maximum number of plants to thrive without being crowded; they model the ideal development of the child, and by extension a nation of children, and by further extension the uncrowded, orderly nation of knowledgeable farmers to come. In sum, the scene offers an object lesson to the farmer's heir(s) in the "bright idea of property, of exclusive right, of independence," which is held, following Jefferson, to have "established all our rights" (27).

Crèvecoeur integrates that pedagogy into complicated plots of historical progress as the farmer describes how the work of many enhances the value of the land over time. The American farmer here has inherited from his father, who converted this "formerly rude soil" into a "pleasant farm"; the farmer's son on the beam of the plough will in turn inherit a farm improved by constant labor. The regular back-and-forth motion of the plough urges us to read labor and its benefits in terms of an investment in the inexorable certainties of nature: land and the boy both bloom because the plough's path obeys, and replicates, the natural, cyclical progress of the seasons. And the plough's motion underpins other lessons about history. The land can symbolize a smooth and progressive enhancement of the family's property rights because "America," as the farmer famously states in his "What is an American?" meditation in Letter III, represents "new principles" (56): it marks a rupture in the age-old sequence of despotic polities. Through his little boy, Crèvecoeur's farmer celebrates the virtues this young colony will require when fathered not by a king but by rough-hewn though enlightened farmers. The plough upon which the boy rides performs a crucial role in this fable of enlightenment since it, too, represents a rupture—the moment when new technologies, and the new social forms to which it gives rise, consign to oblivion earlier stages of human sociality. Merely an implication here, this story of civilization unfolding around the plough is brought to completion in Letter XII when the American farmer, driven from his land by the impending Revolutionary war, and desiring to live in a Native American village, brings along with him new technologies to improve the lot of his (so to speak) grateful rescuers.

Letter XII complicates but does not erase the new model of social relationships that the American farmer begins to chart in Letter II, which constellates a number of symbolic helpers around the figure of the (White) "American" riding the plough. The American farmer places his wife in the shade of the trees next to his field, from where she can praise his industry, and in the home, where she spins, darns, makes mead, and, in bringing the farmer his egg, inspires him to make use of her domestic labor *and* to underscore the gender roles it implies: the egg transposes her metaphorically into a "gentle useful hen leading her chickens with a care and vigilance which speaks shame to many women" (29). The farmer mentions in passing his "tolerably faithful and healthy negroes" (25), whose condition of being the farmer's "property" underpins a connection between marketplace and "free" land problematic enough to force Crèvecoeur to banish it to the extreme margins of the text: their presence and labor somewhere on the farm is never described. We need to add back to this idyllic scene of the American farmer ploughing with his son a sense of how the productivity of his wife and slaves enables his labor and the future it shapes; rhetorically speaking, his ability to generalize from his work to a concept of "our" rights can only be maintained by quietly disavowing or rescripting the labor of others. In Dana D. Nelson's useful term, a sense of "national manhood" emerges out of the constellation of relationships the farmer imagines in Letter II: the regular actions of the plough unite the cultivation and capitalization of the land to the disciplinary regimes of a not-so-imaginary polity, a White American farmer at its head, supported "freely" by his wife, silently by his "faithful negroes" in the field, and rhetorically by a metaphoric transposition of his property into "our" rights.[23]

The presence of children on the White House lawn in 2009 being introduced to the joys of healthful labor remind us of the enduring capacity of the topoi that invest Crèvecoeur's *Letters* to represent political economic material in a coherent way. In both Crèvecoeur's and the Obamas' scenes, the metaphor of cultivating an undifferentiated area of dirt works metonymically to create a story, or "plot," of production. It transforms dirt into a "plot of land." And, recouping older discourses of land husbandry, it translates a plot of land into symbolic meaning by organizing the activities undertaken there into a narrative about how polities are created, governed, and reproduced. Its formal strategies and rhetorical structures replicate Crèvecoeur's. It announces a break, or rupture—"new principles" of being American. It promises that business will no longer be conducted as usual in the "Old World." Michelle Obama works alongside the children to model the sharing of responsibility, labor, and produce; a lettuce leaf someone will eventually eat represents tangible material value; the labor to produce it is thereby made worthwhile. And, like Crèvecoeur, the garden renews what is traditional, but also looks to posterity—a healthier future for American children, as Michelle Obama stated at the time and later made the key thematic of *American Grown.* At a moment during the Great Recession when it seemed "economics" could no longer be trusted to provide an accurate analysis and convincing solutions, the Obamas' model commonwealth constructed a riposte to economic crisis by laying claim to an eighteenth- and nineteenth-century *style* of representing economic activities, facts, and experiences, which twentieth century mainstream economics has not entirely erased. The formal characteristics of the discourse governing Crèvecoeur's *Letters*—as well as specific topoi such as breaking ground, communal laboring, the child in the garden, the gesture toward posterity—are still legible in the pedagogy of the Obamas' garden.

More precisely, those meanings can be *made* legible. The kaleidoscopic responses to the kitchen garden in 2009 shows that what could have been a relatively straightforward narrative setting out new relationships between humans, the economy, and the land quickly dissolved into an array of fractured gestures, glimpses of plot lines, and fuzzy histories. Though the *Washington Post* optimistically placed the garden at the "symbolic crossroads of a range of contemporary societal issues," mostly "child nutrition and health," no one made a concerted effort to enforce this new "economics." President Obama did not display a lasting interest. Apart from a minor fracas with Big Ag—the Mid-America CropLife Association (MACA), representing multinationals such as Dow, Montsanto, and DuPont, pleaded with the First Lady to use pesticides as was "conventional" in the United States—the Obamas' model commonwealth made a disappointingly poor showing on the national stage.[24] It certainly failed to make consequential changes to "economics" or to the US economy. It is therefore worth asking how such a "perfect political symbol" failed to signify to so many people. From the point of view of the president's political iconographers, there was no doubt that the garden's symbolic power could be misconstrued. The symbolic terrain the Obamas had to negotiate was indeed tricky if they were to superimpose a new world order—the new racial and gender roles produced by the first Black president and First Lady of the United States—onto the mythos of the New World garden, governed by White men, that Crèvecoeur imagines in Letter II. At such an economically fraught moment in the nation's history, it was possible that the public would view gardening, even kitchen gardening, as the pursuit of leisured elites.[25] Washington's and Jefferson's gardens, for example, fit this invidious association of gardening with upper class status. Some commentators at the time took that path, referencing an ongoing debate about whether organic food and gardening were the "preserves of the elite."[26] One critic writing in the Green Hell Blog savaged the Obamas "hornswoggling" people into "growing fancy vegetables" in order to "feed [their] exotic palate," while excoriating any pretensions they might have had to setting up a market-free environment: the Obamas were getting "free veggies" while "White House employees and children [were] doing all the work" and taxpayers were footing the bill.[27]

The fact that this argument so easily harnesses the residual republicanism that continues to play such an important part in the political rhetoric and cultural imaginary of the United States was doubtless not lost on PR people in 2009. Michelle Obama, for example, seemed to be anxiously referencing the dilemma of how to represent the industry of those who labor for the powerful when she insisted that her youthful conscripts from the local school should celebrate their own independent labor ("the joys of your work").[28] Market-free could not be allowed to imply "free" (forced or unpaid) labor. Crèvecoeur's confidently hierarchical map of gendered and racial social relations also failed to sit well with the Obamas' garden, though not necessarily in predictable ways. That Michelle Obama commanded a public discourse and was hardly going to sit knitting under a shady tree praising the straightness of her husband's furrows may have supported the Obamas' "new principles" of what makes an American. But to have Michelle Obama gathering children to her symbolic leadership—having them, metaphorically speaking, ride her plough—threatened the posture of masculine strength that Barack Obama needed to project so early in the first Black male presidency, with the new constructions of national manhood it would bring still fluid and unsettled.

A more fundamental reason why the narratives investing the garden with symbolic meaning could be so easily discounted is that they are not congruent with mainstream economic discourses in the early twenty-first century. Nick Greene wrote in *The Telegraph* that "Taxpayers will be relieved to hear that after a week of controversy surrounding federally funded, multi-million-dollar executive bonuses, the garden will only cost approximately $200."[29] Greene is being ironic. Nonetheless his comment is, and in several senses, on the money. He evokes a context within which the garden signifies as a quite profound response to economic crisis. But the excessive sums of money at stake are precisely what structure that context: a $200 garden does not matter in a financial sense to taxpayers responsible for paying failed CEOs multi-million-dollar bonuses, and therefore it cannot meaningfully "matter" within an ideological horizon where vast sums define the economic situation. The garden did indeed articulate an alternative economic idiom of frugality and self-sufficiency. The problem, as Nick Greene and the political iconographers at the White House were aware, was that the president was tasked with *expanding* the economy. The day after Michelle Obama broke ground he delivered an address (March 21, 2009) in which he laid out his plans to "jumpstart the economy," setting out a "vision of America where growth is not based on real estate bubbles or overleveraged banks."[30] But the "growth" he had in mind was a "firm foundation of investments in energy, education, and health care," not the slow business of growing vegetables. Professional economists, not gardeners, were responsible for handling the Great Recession over the next years. It was managed not by going market-free but by flooding American financial markets with money ["the stimulus," the American Recovery and Reinvestment Act of 2009], and the actions of the Federal Reserve [Quantitative Easing I and II]); by austerity measures in Great

Britain and Europe; by new regulations governing the amount of capital banks need to hold; and so on.

Perhaps worse, President Obama ran the risk of having people perceive the garden as a piece of *practical* advice to the swelling ranks of the unemployed—Why not plant vegetables and feed yourself?—rather than a broad-spectrum gesture toward republican virtues of self-sufficiency. MACA's letter to the Obamas, which was released to the media, shows why and in what terms this was a risk. "We live in a very different world than that of our grandparents," pronounced MACA, adding "If Americans were still required to farm to support their family's basic food and fibre needs, would the US have been leaders in the advancement of science, communication, education, medicine, transportation and the arts?" MACA's compelling meta-narrative of benevolent economic development—today, an "average farmer produces enough food to feed 144 Americans who are living longer lives than many of their ancestors"—reveals an underpinning plot of modernity. "Technology in agriculture" frees most Americans to work in technology (science, transportation); and it immerses Americans in new social technologies not dreamed of in the age of "our grandparents."[31] The implication is that the sort of organic gardening Michelle Obama promotes would push Americans back to a premodern age—Crèvecoeur's age, in fact, of oxen and ploughs. In essence, President Obama's speech emphasizing "investments in energy, education, and health care," promising economic growth and a better future, concurred with MACA's argument.

From this perspective, the Obamas' garden seems less a "symbolic crossroads" than testimony to the problematic of postmodern signifying strategies. It is photo-op Jeffersonianism, more camera than soil, more political theater starring imaginary yeomen than a serious call to be more self-sufficient, more strategic marketing than a serious recommendation to abandon the supermarket. It is more *sign of* a desire to resurrect faith in productivity and value, *sign of* authenticity, than a manifesto of how to achieve those benefits. As millions more Americans lost their jobs while the vegetables slowly grew, and as those with and without jobs began to recognize the extent of their indebtedness to others, the garden's ability to purvey symbolic narratives about self-sufficient labor must have seemed less and less compelling to the President's PR managers. Indeed, one of the more potent discourses that might have translated the political economy of the garden into specific economic language and recommendations—ecofeminism—may have been ideologically ruled out by the political cost of associating it with Barack Obama's already tenuous hold on ideologies of national manhood. His route to masculine authority lay in donning the mantle of homo economicus, not *femina economica.* Michelle Obama herself refrained from aggressively pursuing the critique of Big Ag her own garden implied. She used terms such as fresh rather than organic, nutritious rather than green; her brief, as it developed over the next several years, was to get fresh food into "food deserts" rather than dwelling on the arguably greater problem of the "desertification" of prime agricultural land through over-farming and the indiscriminate use of pesticides.

The public record of responses to the Obamas' garden shows that its vivid acts of symbol-making constructed in the cultural imaginary, at best, a fragmentary polity—a generalized, sliding, temporary point of opposition to the mayhem of Wall Street. It nonetheless kept alive, and demonstrated the viability of, an alternative to what looked to be an increasingly threadbare, even collapsing, neoclassical economic order. In part, it did so by following and richly restoring an older political economic script. As Crèvecoeur demonstrates, a narrative of ground-breaking and cultivation can model the very discourse of political economy. It relates disciplined effort to the health and wealth of individual and state; it designs a story of origins out of which the values of a polity begin to emerge. It scripts a narrative about commensality; leaders who work alongside a coalition of the willing; authentic value that inheres in material form; and value produced through useful labor outside of the market. It builds meaning out of productive relationships between humans and the soil in the sense of respecting the ecosystems upon which we depend, but also in the Physiocrats' sense that the land's ability to renew its resources year by year is the guarantor of economic value and a nation's wealth. That logic of renewability leverages stories of growth into powerful narratives about posterity. The American Farmer's boy blooming on the plough and Michelle Obama's corps of schoolchildren about to experience the joy of laboring in a garden both exploit a metaphoric transposition from growing crops, to growing children, to growing polities.

But the Obamas' garden also incorporates crucial *new* "new principles." To begin with, the Obamas' story of breaking new ground cannot be pushed far without having to confront the contradictions of their command of historical narratives. *Their* garden represents the United States' difference from itself—from its own history of racism and slavery. One cannot pretend, in short, that the Obamas in symbolically claiming the mantle of the Founding Fathers (and First Ladies) could have *been* one of them, and the attempts made by commentators to conflate a twenty-first century garden with those created by Washington and Jefferson (even Eleanor Roosevelt) quickly run up against the intransigence of actual historical contexts. In that respect, we might read the Obamas' restoration of the political economic idioms of the Physiocrats and Crèvecoeur in reverse. Though it is Crèvecoeur who articulates the relationship between breaking ground and political beginnings—the "bright idea of property, of exclusive right" establishing "all our rights"—the Obamas can lay better claim to "our rights" within a model commonwealth. Crèvecoeur's "our" functions not to name a collectivity but to mark a difference from those (for example his slaves) who do not belong to it. The Obamas' garden/farm wrests that "our" into a new configuration, in part merely by taking charge of the act of configuring it.

The Obamas, moreover, use the symbolic terrain of the White House to rescript key elements of political economic narratives. Orderly furrows on the American Farmer's fields metaphorize the orderly legal processes that grant him right to the land. But the Obamas do not own the land at the White House; their "right" of tenure is temporary. Generations of Presidents and First Ladies have of course used that fact to sketch on this symbolic canvas some sense of their administration's priorities.[32] In important ways Michelle Obama did the opposite. While the first Obama administration strove to restore faith in property rights and relations, Michelle Obama redesigned the concept of commonwealth to exclude the notion of an "exclusive right" to land as a necessary, indeed foundational, component in the formation of orderly psyches and social relations, healthy bodies, and body politics. She devises in the interstices of an older political economic narrative a new model of commonwealth—hesitant, understated, and fabulous, to be sure, but compelling to the extent that we recognize the kind of economic modelling that precedes it.

That odd and provisional formation can be theorized in terms of what some feminist scholars, wary of the inclination of utopias toward stable totalities, think of as a "process model of utopia," where an ideal society is an "ongoing task rather than a resting place."[33] By these lights, "utopia as *telos* is replaced by utopia as *strategic deployment*," creating not a "stable, utopian distance *from* ideology, but rather an "internal distance *between* the various positions that the subject is called upon to occupy, which can defamiliarize dominant norms and create opportunities for agency."[34] Michelle Obama is ideally placed to imagine commonwealth as process in light of the fact that tenure at the White House enforces impermanence. If that critical activity seems particularly problematic in the case of the Obamas, who were charged with upholding so many aspects of US ideology, it does suggest ways in which the garden/farm can generate momentary gaps and interruptions in dominant narratives that may outlast its, and Michelle Obama's, physical presence at the White House. In that respect, the Obamas' garden is not beset by contradictions so much as affording an insight into contradictory discourses on commonwealth in the twenty-first century.

While the Obamas' first crops were ripening on the White House lawn, Zynga brought to Facebook a game that was to transform social media and online gaming: *FarmVille* (2009).[35] Its great success—for two years it was the most popular game on the internet, receiving upward of 30 million users a day—gave rise to an entire ecology of imitations: *FarmVille 2: Country Escape* (2012), which is the version available in 2021, *Farm Up* (2012),

Stardew Valley (2016), *Tiny Pig* (2017), *Big Farm: Mobile Harvest* (2017), *Funky Bay* (2018), *My Grandfather's Farm* (2018), *Funky Bay: Farm and Adventure* (2021), and dozens more. Most reproduce key elements of *FarmVille*'s schema: gamers are supplied a relatively empty plot of land and, by careful management, proceed to plant and reap ever-richer harvests, acquire Farm Cash and Coin (or similar currency) with which to purchase tools and other labor-saving devices, expand, customize, and beautify the farm, and reach out to other gamers to trade for or gift farming needs. The game has caught the attention of scholars in sociology and psychology for the questions it poses about new forms of online sociality[36]; management and business studies have taken interest in the game's emphasis on managerial skills[37]; media and marketing studies have done likewise for the game's exploitation of new social media networks.[38] Game theory—how individuals "game" a world, finding more efficient ways to succeed—has also occupied a wide range of economically oriented inquiries. The farm-management game phenomenon stands as an important guide to the sudden and startling emergence of new monetary, and psychic, online economies.

I begin my investigation into the cultural environs of the farm-management game with what seems to be a contradiction: game developers usually begin by representing their virtual terrains as explicitly counter-modern. In the backstory that introduces players to the world of *Stardew Valley*, a grandfather confesses that "I'd lost sight of what mattered most in life . . . real connections with other people and nature."[39] His farm, the "place I truly belong," has transformed his life, and will transform the life of his descendants, for, the grandfather predicts, there "will come a day when you feel crushed by the burden of modern life . . . and your bright spirit will fade before a growing emptiness." Grandfather is prescient: the in-game avatars, to whom grandfather deeds the old farm, are trapped in a soulless office at Joja Corporation. The more perfunctory opening of *Funky Bay* rehearses the same material: the "old office routine" trapping a young couple with "All that work!" (a pile of legal documents) yields within a few seconds to their trip in a VW bus to the island of Funky Bay where, in the first level of the game, they (while lying in hammocks!) invite players to help them transform the old farm. Dozens of games embrace this cultural fable of an older generation passing on the family farm in some unspecified rural locale to escapees from the "Big City Blues" (*Country Friends* [2015]). That these games are oriented toward markets—in their symbolic narration, as we shall see, and in their predilection for persuading players to part with real cash to upgrade their farms—suggests that their counter-modern aspects do little more than market a hazy nostalgia for what Lee-Ann Sutherland calls "idyllic rurality" (351), still governed by a Jeffersonian fantasy of agrarian self-sufficiency. As Alenda Y. Chang argues in her insightful essay on *FarmVille*, guiding players to an "agricultural utopia" means overlooking problems of modern farming systems in the United States: the threats to ecologies posed by monoculture and overuse of pesticides, as well as the often difficult and underpaid conditions of farm labor. Chang is certainly correct. Nonetheless, these games tend to leverage a complex political economy that is not wholly compatible with neoclassical paradigms and the market systems they support.

The games' agrarian mythos is powerful and complex. The extraordinary success of *FarmVille* might be understood in terms of its serendipitous launch at a historical moment when the "burden of modern life" meant that so many, in losing their homes, were experiencing the "place I truly belong" as a life-changing dilemma. Farm-management games testify to what the Obamas's garden tried to exploit: the existence of a longing for alternative, "authentic," and meaningful economic significances oriented toward commonwealth. Several levels into *FarmVille*, after establishing the farm, players of online versions are able to visit other farms, invite visits, give gifts, help out on other people's farms, ask for needed implements or resources, and so on. These games insist that farming is a cooperative enterprise and often include subsidiary stories that enhance a sense of sociality. In *Stardew Valley*, for example, the mayor invites arriving players to "introduce yourself" to the townspeople, who would "appreciate that." Ted Friedman argues that the flip side of *FarmVille*'s "somewhat sleazy" business model—urging players to exchange real dollars for progress while inviting other friends into the game's ecology—is a "utopian gift economy of the game's mechanics" demonstrating an "inchoate desire" for a world in which collaboration and sharing replaces competitive acquisition.[40] Friedman overstates his case for a "new techno-pastoralism."[41] Nonetheless it is worth pursuing the relationships between *FarmVille* and the Obamas' garden. Both bring together a loosely connected group of people to break ground, produce sustenance, and model socioeconomic relations. Unlike Michelle Obama's experiment at the White House, farm management games set about demonstrating how capitalist relations emerge to foster sociality. Yet they also complicate their narratives in line with older debates about the true nature of "capital."

Unlike the Obamas's garden, all farm-management games come with a primer—a tutorial introducing players to the principles and rules of the game, usually doubling, much more quietly, as an introduction to economic principles. The phone app version of *FarmVille 2* opens with a young cartoon guide who offers advice and waits cheerfully (and with a frisson of impatience) for the gamer to consult the Quest Book containing small tasks, to click on the appropriate box, and move forward to the next level. But what logic guides the guide? To what body of knowledge and set of practices, to what order of operations, are new players introduced? These questions are all the more important because these games offer near-infinite permutations of a simple ruleset. What players learn in the first few minutes must offer a template attractive and capacious enough to configure possibly years of future game play. And that pedagogy must seem natural: it must align with and confirm what players already know or intuit about how economies work.

After arriving at one's new farm, typically in the form of an avatar, several events almost inevitably follow. Players are granted what in-game text and descriptions of the game usually call empty land; *Ranch Rush* (2011), for example, provides new gamers with "three acres of empty land." In fact, the land one buys or inherits is never empty but "fallen into disrepair" (*Harvest Moon* [1996]), or a "ruined farm" (*Farm Up* [2012]), or perhaps a "failed nursery" (*Ranch Rush*), so that the goal is always to "*rebuild* the old farm" (my italics; *Funky Bay: Farm and Adventure*) by planting and harvesting crops, and thereby making enough money to pay for improvements. In *FarmVille 2*, players get to refurbish the dilapidated farmhouse and barn within the first few minutes. The logic of these games is to begin *in medias res*. The rustic farmhouse, ruined barn, and detritus from previous farming efforts; the monetary system (Farm Coin or the like); a small plot of prepared land from which one can immediately start planting, watering, and harvesting crops; the presence of neighbors and neighborhoods on the periphery of the inherited plot of land—all show that one comes to the site of "empty" land within a preexisting social and economic context. Inheriting the family farm and arriving there to find a small amount of farm currency waiting obviates any questions players might have about whether these fictive societies respect capitalist principles. Once the game begins, players are swiftly reintroduced to markets and the importance of exchange. The computer version of *FarmVille 2* has a market stand, the phone version a market board, where players can click to sell produce. Earning Farm Coin (in *FarmVille*) through such sales allows players to purchase labor-saving devices (a tractor, a biplane), which will, over time, expand acreage and increase profits.

It would therefore certainly be true to say that the counter-modern gestures of these games are thoroughly enmeshed with the ideologies and practices of market capitalism. Most offer free downloads but are "freemium" games, offering special, premium features for real cash. *Stardew Valley*, frequently lauded for being designed and created by one person, and which builds an overt anti-corporatist stance into its in-game narratives, must be purchased. In every case, games stake players with a plot of land and some form of currency—coins and keys for speeding up play in the present edition of *FarmVille*—prior to the player's first moves. Game play itself is narrowly focused on selling and buying the many virtual commodities on display. In *FarmVille*, bouncy dollar signs surround the player's empty plot of land, inviting the player's click. The first crop goes up for sale immediately—there is no option to, say, preserve that crop for one's own consumption, as one might have to if one were to set up a real farm on unused land, or to receive gifts and resources from others, which can be a feature of later play. Players are therefore invited to acknowledge the hegemony of the marketplace; one cannot in fact otherwise begin, or continue, the game. And though new crops and commodities appear in the game, one's experience of the game as it unfolds depends on a mandatory return to the marketplace. In this respect the game conforms to what Umberto Eco anatomized as a key response to the massive disruptions experienced by people living in capitalist societies: a "narrative of redundance," which functions by organizing new information within a plot that keeps circling back to the same starting point.[42] The marketplace works to create a redundant narrative in farm-management games. Whatever new commodities, crops, storylines, or experiences appear in the game can only be achieved by players (re)stocking the market with Farm Coin (or real cash) and then (re)turning to the market to put them into play. The marketplace is the site where all *FarmVille* stories begin.

That said, the markets peculiar to farm-management games are not wholly consistent with neoclassical economic thought. To begin with: in positing the fantasy of an "empty" space that must be filled, or a once-productive site that now requires restoration, these games sketch in a sense of how economies unfold in time. That is not to say that the games invoke an actual historical record—all take place in an oneiric realm of which one can say only that the style of farming is neither sharecropping nor Big Ag—but they do invoke historicity in the sense that they represent farm-building and economy-building as a process. Like neoclassical economic thought, these games assume a marketplace as the cornerstone of economic production; but, to the extent that they position the marketplace within an articulated model of emerging sociality, they evoke classical economic models. Neoclassical economics accepts the market as a given; economics is defined *as* the science of market behaviors. So though mainstream economics can, if necessary, articulate its logical foundations—that humans desire to maximize their utility, for instance, or that market capitalism is the most efficient economic system—it no longer needs to do so. Classical economics, by contrast, still found it necessary to inquire into how markets evolved and why markets were in fact the most efficient way of exchanging goods.

From Adam Smith to the advent of neoclassicism at the end of the nineteenth century, one model accounting for the advent of markets broadly held sway. The *locus classicus* for this model is Smith's *The Wealth of Nations*, which begins by foregrounding the reciprocal relationship between the division of labor and the propensity of humans to "truck, barter, and exchange."[43] The desire to trade propels the need for a more efficient production of tradeable commodities; the division of labor allows commodities to be produced more efficiently. Without that propensity to exchange, "every man must have procured to himself every necessary and conveniency of life which he wanted"—and in fact does so in that "early and rude state of society which precedes both the accumulation of stock and the appropriation of land," and which still exists in such "desert" [sparsely populated] lands as the Highlands of Scotland, where "every farmer must be butcher, baker, and brewer for his own family."[44] Responsible for every task, even those for which they have no aptitude, farmers in "rude" societies are master of none. "Civilized and thriving nations" harness the division of labor to increase efficiency and the "quantity of capital stock," and thus improve the value of the land and the well-being of the people living on it.[45] The process of clearing land, for example, will be more rapid if a farmer enters into trade to acquire an axe rather than having to make it from scratch, especially if the farmer has no aptitude for the task.

As this example implies, the narrative of early economic relations emphasized by political economists was governed by important distinctions between wealth, capital, and money. The Physiocrats argued that the only true wealth was generated by the land; all else was derived from the land's produce. Later economists moved away from this stance without abandoning a distinction between capital and true wealth. J. S. Mill defines capital as the "accumulated stock of the produce of labor" that can be put to the service of producing more wealth.[46] Buildings, machines, tools, food—all that is set aside from profits in order to become "saved wealth devoted to reproduction"—function as capital.[47] The reproduction of capital is vital in another sense: hoarded, unused capital is in fact no longer capital because it has abrogated its generative functions. In these scenarios, money is merely a convenient means of exchanging goods. A person can therefore possess capital without having any money: an axe made from scratch is capital even though it cost its maker nothing. Capital, too, can come in different forms. An axe lasting for years is an example of fixed capital; circulating capital refers to wealth, such as food, that must be constantly renewed. In a nod to older models of wealth creation, Mill observes that the "most permanent of all kinds of fixed capital" is that which is employed "in giving increased productiveness to a natural agent, such as land."[48]

This model whereby the value of "desert" land is enhanced by capital investment and the division of labor became commonplace in the nineteenth century. But political economists contested the extent to which land, once ground has been broken, can continue to accumulate value. Adam Smith noted that improved land—once all land has become private property—will accrue an unearned added value. The logic, worked out more fully by David Ricardo in *Principles of Political Economy and Taxation* (1817), is that in a particular area the best (most fertile or best positioned) agricultural land will be appropriated first. If population pressure leads to increased demand, subsequent parcels of poorer land brought under cultivation will require more labor and capital investment, producing more costly crops. The total market price of that crop thus rising, the value of the crop currently being grown on the most fertile land increases. Tenants farming the best land will pay more to lease it, and landowners gain an unearned increment—economic rent—without any action undertaken on their part. The overarching logic, however, is one of diminishing returns. Since ever-poorer tracts of land must be taken under cultivation over time, the marginal costs of adding agricultural land keep rising. But already cultivated lands cannot be made more productive forever. In fact, the rate of increase of productivity on a particular plot of land will begin to tail off over time. At stake here for Ricardo is a crucial distinction: "Rent . . . is a creation of value, but not a creation of wealth; it adds nothing to the resources of a country."[49] The financial gain falling to those who own better quality land, in short, must be distinguished from the material benefits—the "necessaries, conveniences, and enjoyments of the society"—conceivably shared by all.[50]

Political economists of the American school tended to disagree with the premise that the rate of wealth creation diminished over time. In *Principles of Social Science* (1858), for example, Henry Charles Carey constructs what begins as a familiar narrative concerning the "Occupation of the Earth." The "first cultivator, the Robinson Crusoe of his day. . . . works alone," but with increasing capital—a stick to place seeds deeper, an axe to clear land more rapidly—"his condition is improved" and he "is enabled to clear other lands."[51] With the division of labor, the "supply of food increases rapidly, and with it the power of accumulation"; with more food, a growing population finds "an increase in the power of living in connection with each other."[52] Thus, Carey concludes, "are their labors rendered more productive and the facilities of commerce augmented . . . accompanied by constant increase of numbers, wealth, prosperity, and happiness."[53] Reversing the assumption of diminishing returns, Carey argues that there is a "constantly increasing return to labor."[54] Thinking of capital wealth as money helped to make this proposition seem self-evident. William Graham Sumner, a late-nineteenth-century apologist for laissez faire capitalism, argues that the first accumulation of capital "is slow, but as it proceeds the accumulation becomes rapid in a high ratio."[55] Capitalists' efforts generate "millions more of wealth, many-fold greater than their own."[56]

Henry George's *Progress and Poverty* (1879) follows a Ricardian distinction between value and wealth to Carey-like conclusions. Inveighing against the principle of rent on the basis that an ever-larger proportion of a nation's wealth goes to idle landowners, George at one crucial juncture returns to the classic model of a single inhabitant arriving at uninhabited land: "Here, let us imagine, is an unbounded savannah."[57] That inhabitant must perforce accomplish every task by himself. And because he must be "his own blacksmith, wagonmaker, carpenter, and cobbler," George argues that "though nature is prolific, the man is poor."[58] The man is also poor in time: one person performing all the manifold functions of subsisting and producing goods on the farm makes for a labor-intensive existence. But as soon as more occupants arrive on the land, the "wonderfully multiplying efficiency" of the division of labor means that its "productive powers" are "equivalent to the multiplication of its original fertility by the hundred fold and the thousand fold."[59] Efficiencies accrue to people who settle near each other, leading eventually to an urban center where the highly developed infrastructure and benefits of intellectual and cultural stimulation bestow ever-increasing added value on subsequent exchanges. Though the fundamental nature of the land owned by the single original inhabitant may not change—in fact its productivity may well decrease—its locational advantage must increase. For that reason, George, Jeffrey Sklansky argues, "reconceive[s] land itself as a potentially limitless social resource"—as long as social wealth is not misconceived in terms of (monetary) value.[60]

Farm management games reprise many of the opening moves of the classic political economic model. To begin with, players are responsible for every operation on their "desert" land, and thus the first levels are labor-intensive; it requires a great deal of time and effort to sustain a few rote activities. Acquiring capital stock creates efficiencies and allows players to initiate a value chain. A windmill purchased from the General Store within the first few levels of *FarmVille 2*, for example, allows the player to start milling flour and soon (if desired) to bake and sell cakes. Purchasing farm vehicles, explain Angela Morales and Kyle Morland in *FarmVille for Dummies* (2011), helps "speed up farming by decreasing the amount of manual labor you have to invest in common tasks," so that "Clicking an open area with a basic tractor . . . plows four plots of land instead of the usual one."[61] More expensive vehicles afford exponential gains. The Combine is the "ultimate *FarmVille* vehicle" since "With a single click" one can "quickly harvest, plow, and reseed a 2x2 area of 4 plots [of the] farm."[62] After a few levels, moreover, online games urge players to activate the "power of living in connection with each other," as Carey puts it, by reaching out to neighbors in order to tend their crops or have them tend one's own, or to exchange needed tools. Exchanges with neighbors also help *FarmVille* players level up, which is one of the very few ways to acquire Farm Cash without spending US dollars. Capital investment increases the rate at which capital is acquired over time. As Heinrich Söbke explains in his fascinating account of how to use limited *FarmVille* resources in the most productive manner, leveling up with the help of neighbors allows him to purchase Belted Cows, the "most lucrative animal," which in turn helps him produce more Farm Coins: "at the beginning it took 10 days to buy one Belted Cow, currently it takes 15 minutes of work a day to harvest the amount of Farm Coins necessary to buy 40 of them."[63]

Such games therefore rough out a well-rehearsed classical narrative of capital formation. A sole player on *FarmVille*'s virtual "unbounded savannah" learns how to acquire capital stock and harness the resources offered by neighbors to enact a division of labor, increase efficiency, and open up an ever-enlarging marketplace of commodities. Acquisition of capital advances, as Sumner predicted, at first slowly but then in a "many-fold greater" way as time goes by. A message in one of the early levels of *Funky Bay* proclaims: "Simple farm math: plant one, harvest two." Dedicated players like Söbke can accelerate that simple ratio in later levels. In many respects, then, farm management games seem to abide by a fantasy whereby the farm economy merely continues to expand. It is the kind of fantasy social world that led to the Great Recession, where it seemed house and land prices would simply continue to rise for ever, but it is also in general accord with late-nineteenth-century theorizing that proposed no limit to capital gains.

Nonetheless, several strikingly odd features of farm-game economies need to be recognized. Importantly, they typically dispense with neoclassical doctrines of increasing disutility. Two strategies are instrumental. First, unlike Mars, where Mark Watney recognizes that his arable land will produce less and less over time, *FarmVille* and similar games continue to produce with undiminished vigor. Production can be sped up in *FarmVille 2* by, for instance, purchasing keys. Moreover, all land on the farm is equally productive. Pace *Ricardo*, no area within farm-game territories offers positional advantage. The first version of *FarmVille* reveals the importance of this principle in the figure of the avatar-farmer whose function, at the start of the game, was to carry out a player's commands. By virtue of moving so slowly—*Dummies* refers to the avatar's movements as one of the "biggest time sinks in all of *FarmVille*" (50)—the avatar increased the utility of nearby land in comparison to land further away, and thus incorporated into the game a concept of relative value. The solution, which *Dummies* advocates as the very first tip for new farmers, is to block the avatar from moving, which permits the player to perform the actions instead. One consequence is to speed up production. Another, more important for our purposes, is to place the entire virtual space of the farm under the immediate scrutiny of the player, making every area of the farm equal in utility and value. Subsequent land expansions in *FarmVille* possess the same capacity as the first plot placed under cultivation.

The second strategy of farm management games is to place a firm cap on the number of levels players may reach and assets they may acquire. Söbke, for example, cannot acquire Belted Cows indefinitely; the first version of *FarmVille* allowed a maximum of five dairy farms, each holding forty cows.[64] As of 2019, *FarmVille 2* players were limited to six beehives and 499 levels.[65] There are obvious practical reasons for caps, given that companies redesign each level to open new rewards. But in the context of "Agricultural Economics 101" there are major economic issues at stake as well. Neoclassical economic models posit continuous change over time within an infinite matrix. In macroeconomic terms, for example, economists examine the nation's annual inflation rate without concerning themselves about what sort of economy there might be to inflate if there are in fact catastrophic climate changes. There is no reason to assume the economy will do anything but continue to inflate or deflate. Microeconomic analysis, too, looks to marginal change, not finitude. There is a sense in which the law of diminishing marginal utility contemplates the possibility that desire for a particular good might approach zero. It is the last unit of a commodity a consumer would want to acquire. But economists make the assumption that consumers choose from a basket, or bundle, of commodities. The concept of the "last" unit assumes that a consumer with limited resources has chosen to put those resources toward other priorities or desires. On a real farm, for example, a farmer's desire for beehives will tail off over time; the marginal utility of beehives to this farmer will be determined by the last beehive purchased. But economic analysis concerns itself with measuring the farmer's declining desire for beehives *comparatively*. It begins with the assumption that the farmer has limited resources and must therefore, over time, weigh whether to invest in more beehives when the farm also requires seeds or cows or additional plots of land. Put differently, the farmer's beehives possess an *ordinal* utility—their value cannot be determined in absolute terms, but only in relation to other utilities.

Farm management games do in fact offer players a wide range of options for building their agricultural environments. In *FarmVille*, for example, one could choose to invest in livestock, or crops, or decorations, or vehicles, or limited-edition items, and much more, which meant that in actual play gamers were presumably always facing issues of comparative choice. In practice, *Dummies* claims, "players tend to fall into one of a few broad categories," or "Farming Personalities": the "Breeder" (collecting animal offspring), The "Leveler" (collecting XP, or experience, points), the "Functional Farmer" (collecting "ample fields of prosperous crops"), and several more.[66] The fact that the game makes it possible to go "all in" on one experience may be one reason these games use price increases to effect a crude approximation of diminishing marginal utility. The six beehives allowed in *Country Escape* cost, in order: 40K Coins; 40K Coins; 5 keys; 10 Keys; 50 Keys; 75 keys.[67] Since the fourth beehive costs twice as much as the third, and the sixth 15 times as much—and since keys are difficult to obtain without spending real dollars—players find it more and more difficult (costly) to secure beehives.[68] Cost, then, mimics the concept of diminishing returns.

Yet one cannot build a seventh beehive—or reach the 421th level in 2018, or expand one's farm in *FarmVille* beyond the Grand Plantation (676 plots of land).[69] The sixth beehive, or the 676th plot of land, is in fact the very last players can acquire. They therefore possess a *cardinal* utility—their utility as the last beehive or plot is not relative to the desire to acquire anything else, nor relative to the amount of Coin or Cash or keys one has amassed. Put another way, one does not choose to pass over a seventh beehive; the rules of the game have already voided that possibility. To some extent, one can explain the logic of such caps in practical terms. It would seem odd to crowd a farm with (say) half a million beehives. Here the virtual space of online games seems to match up with real agricultural terrain. On the other hand, there is no logical reason why one might not have 12 beehives or a 677th plot of land. Such limits in the games are arbitrary. Being arbitrary, they direct attention toward the alternative economic principles found on the virtual farm. In particular, the logic of caps suggests an economy that limits capital in two ways: it limits the amount of capital one can acquire, and it harnesses the concept of capital to what eighteenth- and nineteenth-century economists thought of as "true wealth."

Though farm-management games introduce players immediately to the marketplace, so that one *must* exchange farm goods for Coin and thereafter be urged to exchange real dollars for Cash or keys, the caps built into these games make a concerted effort to exclude, or diminish, the one form of capital that has no limit: money. Among the ten farming personalities *Dummies* describes, none is a profiteer. The description of the "Functional Farmer" helps to explain why: "Farm expansion is a key concern for these farmers, who maximize their profit by growing as many crops as quickly as possible."[70] As economically defensible as this sounds, the authors actually point to the problematic of "maximizing profit" in these games: growing as many crops as quickly as possible constrains the profits that could otherwise be made were it possible to invest Coins in other venues such as financial markets. If it were possible to invest Coins in a cryptocurrency during one of its astonishing surges in value, for instance, there would be no way to predict, or constrain, the fortunes that might be made. But in these games, money produces money only via working capital and the produce of that capital. It limits capital-production to bees and Belted Cows.

Simple farm math—"plant one, harvest two"—ensures that players always have a mechanism to increase profits, since farm produce is always exchangeable for money. The converse is equally important: the mechanism of the game ensures that Coin and Cash can only be exchanged for farm produce or for tools to speed its production. In that respect, games cannot contemplate infinite expansion. Farm games thus stage a key physiocratic distinction between "sterile" and "productive" capital and *insist* that players invest money in productive pursuits. Because there are no banks, finance systems, mortgages, or credit, players are constrained from making money "grow" from money. They are likewise constrained from falling into debt. Here, the obsession of farm management games with inheriting land from an older generation makes sense in terms of their ideological alignment with the mythos of agrarian democracy: a small-market, debt-free, commonsensical economy prior to the rise of industrial and consumer capitalism. Yet these games cannot be understood entirely in terms of nostalgia. Players are after all charged with restoring the broken down or underutilized farms of the past. In so doing, they are constantly invited to renew scenarios that both limit capital accumulation and define their "wealth" in terms that are more familiar to political economic models of capital formation. The virtual farms people carry with them into streets and offices and onto public transportation are in that respect similar to the provisional, provocative meanings Michelle Obama manages to grow on the White House lawn.

NOTES

1. Michelle Obama, *American Grown: The Story of the White House Kitchen Garden and Gardens Across America* (New York: Crown, 2012), 9.
2. Obama, *American Grown*, 19.
3. Obama, *American Grown*, 9.
4. The seeds and materials cost $200 but the produce was not for sale; it wound up being used in the White House kitchens and local charities. Melissa Harris-Lacewell, "Michelle Obama's Garden" in "The Kitchen Table: Conversations Between Melissa Harris-Lacewell and Yolanda Pierce," n.p., princetonprofs.blogspot.com/2009/03/michelle-obamas-garden.html.
5. Marian Burros, "Obamas to Plant Vegetable Garden at White House," *New York Times*, March 20, 2009, www.nytimes.com/2009/03/20/dining/20garden.html.
6. Thomas Paine, *Common Sense* (Philadelphia: W. and T. Bradford, 1776; Project Gutenberg), n.p., www.gutenberg.org/ebooks/147.
7. Burros, "Obamas to Plant"; Megan Mulligan, "Michelle Obama to Create an Organic 'Victory' Garden at the White House," *The Guardian*, March 20, 2009, www.theguardian.com/world/2009/mar/20/michelle-obama-garden.
8. Andrea Wulf, "Politics in Spades: Why the Obama Veg Patch Matters," *The Guardian*, March 23, 2009, www.theguardian.com/lifeandstyle/2009/mar/24/gardens-michelle-obama.

9. Obama, *American Grown*, 24–26. In 2019 the Wikipedia entry on the Obamas' garden also detailed the early gardening presidents—and still neglected to mention that they (apart from John Adams) owned slaves.

10. Another was Eddie Gehman-Kohan, author of the blog *Obama Foodarama*, who called for placing the garden in its "historic/racial history aspect." obamafoodorama.blogspot.com/2009/03/white-house-kitchen-garden-intersection.html. en.wikipedia.org/wiki/White_House_Vegetable_Garden.

11. Harris-Lacewell, "Michelle Obama's Garden," n.p.

12. Obama, *American Grown*, 13.

13. Ronald L. Meek, *The Economics of Physiocracy: Essays and Translations* (1962; reprint New York: Routledge, 2003), 20.

14. Quoted in Warren J. Samuels and Stephen G. Medema, *A History of Economic Thought: A Reader* (New York: Routledge, 2013), 117.

15. Meek, *Economics of Physiocracy*, 20.

16. Marianne Johnson, "'More Native than French': American Physiocrats and Their Political Economy," *History of Economic Ideas*, X, 1, (2002), www.jstor.org/stable/23723148; Manuela Albertone, *National Identity and the Agrarian Republic: The Transatlantic Commerce of Ideas between America and France (1750–1830)* (New York: Routledge, 2016), 15. Albertone is arguing for a stronger influence of French thought on the United States than allowed by Johnson and most other writers.

17. Letter to John Jay; quoted in *Thomas Jefferson: Political Writings*, eds. Joyce Appleby and Terence Ball (New York: Cambridge University Press, 1999), 549.

18. Elizabeth Hewitt, *Speculative Fictions: Explaining the Economy in the Early United States* (Oxford: Oxford University Press, 2020), 6

19. Hewitt, *Speculative Fictions*, 2

20. Hector St. Jean de Crèvecoeur, *Letters from an American Farmer* (London: Davies and Davis, 1782; New York: Fox, Duffield, 1904), 29. Subsequent references to this work are cited parenthetically in the text.

21. Virgil, *Georgic IV*, translated by A.S. Kline, 2001, www.poetryintranslation.com/PITBR/Latin/VirgilGeorgicsIV.php#anchor_Toc534524378. Line numbers are approximate since Kline's refer to the original Latin.

22. Tom Paine, *Common Sense*, n.p.

23. Dana D. Nelson, *National Manhood: Capitalist Citizenship and the Imagined Fraternity of White Men* (Durham: Duke University Press, 1998).

24. Reported in "Michelle Obama's Organic Garden Angers US Farming Companies," *The Telegraph*, April 23, 2009, www.telegraph.co.uk/news/worldnews/michelle-obama/5204434/Michelle-Obamas-organic-garden-angers-US-farming-companies.html.

25. Michelle Obama tries to counter this aura of elitism in *American Grown* by emphasizing in word and photo the efficacy of community gardening and the contributions of common people.

26. "Vegetable Garden will be Installed on White House Grounds," *Washington Post*, March 20, 2009, www.washingtonpost.com/wpdyn/content/article/2009/03/19/AR2009031902886.html.

27. "Michelle Obama's Political Gardening," Green Hell Blog, March 20, 2009, n.p., greenhellblog.com/2009/03/20/michelle-obamas-political-gardening/.

28. "Politics in Spades: Why the Obama Veg Patch Matters," *The Guardian*, March 23, 2009, www.guardian.co.uk/lifeandstyle/2009/mar/24/gardens-michelle-obama.

29. "Michelle Obama Digs Kitchen Garden at White House," *The Telegraph*, March 20, 2009, www.telegraph.co.uk/news/worldnews/michelle-obama/5023654/Michelle-Obama-digs-kitchen-garden-at-White-House.html.

30. www.whitehouse.gov/the_press_office/Weekly-Address-President-Obama-to-Focus-on-Budget-Priorities-Next-Week.

31. Mid-America CropLife Association, "MACA Letter to White House about Organic Garden," (March 31, 2009), n. p., www.croplife.com/crop-inputs/maca-letter-to-white-house-about-organic-garden/.

32. Turgot would doubtless have consigned Melania Trump to the realm of the "sterile classes" for leaving her indelible mark on the White House gardens in the shape of a new tennis pavilion.

33. Erin McKenna, *The Task of Utopia. A Pragmatist and Feminist Perspective* (Oxford: Rowman and Littlefield, 2001), 3.

34. Jennifer Burwell. *Notes on Nowhere: Feminism, Utopian Logic, and Social Transformation* (Minneapolis: University of Minnesota Press, 1997), 107, 29–30.

35. *FarmVille* was preceded by similar games such as Harvest Moon and Happy Farm; its breakthrough importance was to wed the game to the burgeoning social media empire of Facebook.

36. See, for example, Chris Lewis, Noah Wardrip-Fruin, and Jim Whitehead, "Motivational Game Design Patterns of 'Ville Games," *Proceedings of the International Conference on the Foundations of Digital Games,* May 29, 2012: 172–79, dl.acm.org/doi/abs/10.1145/2282338.2282373.

37. See, for example, Ivan G. Guardiola, Susan L. Murray, Elizabeth A. Cudney, "Using Social Networking Game to Teach Operations Research and Management Science Fundamental Concepts," Proceedings of the ASEE Annual Conference and Exposition (2011, Vancouver, BC, Canada), American Society for Engineering Education, June 2011, scholarsmine.mst.edu/engman_syseng_facwork/294/.

38. See, for example, Ralf Terlutter and Michael L. Capella, "The Gamification of Advertising: Analysis and Research Directions of In-Game Advertising, Advergames, and Advertising in Social Network Games," *Journal of Advertising* 42, no. 2–3 (2013): 95–112, www.tandfonline.com/doi/abs/10.1080/00913367.2013.774610.

39. Quoted in Lee-Ann Sutherland, "The "Desk-Chair Countryside': Affect, Authenticity, and the Rural Idyll in a Farming Computer Game," *Journal of Rural Studies* 78 (August 2020): 354, doi.org/10.1016/j.jrurstud.2020.05.002.

40. Ted Friedman, "FarmVille: The Garden in the Machine," December 08, 2010, 1, www.academia.edu/12516321/Farmville_The_Garden_in_the_Machine.

41. Friedman, *FarmVille*, 1.

42. Umberto Eco, "The Myth of Superman," *Diacritics* 2, no. 1 (Spring 1972): 21.

43. Adam Smith, *The Wealth of Nations* (1776; reprint, New York: Bantam Books, 2003), 22.

44. Smith, *Wealth of Nations*, 25, 27.

45. Smith, *Wealth of Nations*, 2, 3.

46. John Stuart Mill, *Principles of Political Economy* (London: John W. Parker, 1848; New York: Augustus M. Kelley, 1987), 76.

47. Mill, *Principles*, 76–77.

48. Mill, *Principles*, 109.

49. David Ricardo, *Principles of Political Economy and Taxation* (London: John Murray, 1817; New York: Prometheus Books, 1996), 279.

50. Ricardo, *Principles*, 279.

51. Henry Charles Carey, *Principles of Social Science* (Philadelphia: J.B. Lippincott, 1858), 96, 97, 98.

52. Carey, *Principles*, 100, 102.

53. Carey, *Principles*, 103.

54. Carey, *Principles*, 103.

55. William Graham Sumner, *What Social Classes Owe to Each Other* (New York: Harper, 1883; New Haven: Yale University Press, 1934), 77.

56. Sumner, *What Social Classes*, 173.

57. Henry George, *Progress and Poverty* (1879; reprint London: Kegan Paul 1883), 212.

58. George, *Progress*, 212.

59. George, *Progress*, 216–17.

60. Jeffrey Sklansky, *The Soul's Economy: Market Society and Selfhood in American Thought, 1820–1920* (Chapel Hill: University of North Carolina Press, 2002), 122.

61. Angela Morales and Kyle Orland, *FarmVille for Dummies* (Hoboken, NJ: Wiley, 2011), 104.

62. Morales, *FarmVille*, 108.

63. Heinrich Söbke, "Gaming a Non-Game? A Long Term (Self) Experiment about *FarmVille*," n.p., www.researchgate.net/profile/Heinrich-Soebke/publication/274373986

64. FarmVille Wiki: Belted Cow, n.p., farmville.fandom.com/wiki/Belted_Cow.

65. FarmVille Wiki: Beehive, n.p., farmvillecountryescape.fandom.com/wiki/Beehive; FarmVille 2 Wiki: Levels, n.p., farmville2.fandom.com/wiki/Levels.

66. Morales, *FarmVille*, 235–37.

67. FarmVille Wiki: Beehive.

68. Reaching new levels with XP (experience points) in *FarmVille* exploited the same logic. Levels 35–70 required 10K XP; 100K after level 101. Reaching the (then) top level of 999 would require 91,300,000 XP. Morales, *FarmVille*, 144.

69. Morales, *FarmVille*, 101.

70. Morales, *FarmVille*, 235.

Chapter Three

Life in the Wilds

Plots of Polity in Harriet Martineau and Survivor

At a turning point in the history of economics, Adam Smith in *The Wealth of Nations* (1776) developed what he called the human propensity to "truck, barter, and exchange" into a description of the rational, competitive, self-interested economic agent, from whom he extrapolated a theory of how resources get distributed in a market economy: "It is not from the benevolence of the butcher, the brewer, or the baker that we expect our dinner but from their regard to their self-interest."[1] Smith's logic underpins a still broader account of social structure and, ultimately, a theory of how societies change through history. Self-interest urges humans wishing to exploit their talents and skills toward a division of labor, which makes itself felt by a widening discrepancy between a "rude state of society," in which "every man must have procured to himself every necessary and conveniency of life which he wanted," and those countries in which the efficiencies of the division of labor promote the "highest degree of industry and improvement."[2] A division of labor presides over the economic efficiencies of capital accumulation. More efficient production marks a crucial step beyond subsistence. Amassing a "general stock" beyond the requirements of "immediate consumption" frees humans from a hand-to-mouth existence.[3] From this stock a nation derives revenues and, reinvesting them, gradually grows its capital; this creates the possibility of commonwealth and allows civilization to emerge.

Smith, like most political economists until the end of the nineteenth century, followed the logic of stadialism, or stages theory, a metahistorical narrative of the order and progress of civilizations based on changes in the mode of subsistence. Classical political economy usually described a three- or four-stage process, plotting the evolution of societies from hunting and gathering (savagery) to pastoralism and settled agriculture (barbarism) and thence to commercial and market economies (civilization). Each stage was held to be characterized by growing specialization and increasing capital accumulation, and each corresponded with typical social and economic forms, which nineteenth-century social scientists elaborated in complex ways: language sophistication, technology, systems of religion, art, architectural styles, urbanism, gender roles, and familial, social, and political organization were all invoked on a regular basis. Acquiring a concept of private property was thought to be axiomatic for societies making the step to civilization. As political economist Henry Wood wrote in 1894, "*the condition of civilization or barbarism among nations is in proportion to the security and inviolability of individual property rights.*"[4] Given that systems of exchange seem foreordained, the final stage of "civilization" was considered the first to embrace fully the natural proclivities of humans toward exchange, self-interest, competition, acquisition, and the first to enshrine principles of contract and private property conducive to civil society.

As this summary suggests, stadialism was less a single idea than a persuasive, massively particularized cultural fable composed of an entire web of interlocking ideas. Ronald L. Meek has shown that stages theory was of crucial significance to the development of all the human sciences from the second half of the eighteenth century to the end of the nineteenth century.[5] It was also of great consequence to semi-formal and popular economic literatures of the nineteenth century. Stages theory was advanced to show how human civilizations should evolve, to describe how actual societies have evolved, and to show how and why some have failed to do so. Among its many effects, it underwrote a variety of narratives about imperialism, race, and national character. It afforded a putatively scientific way to categorize, and place at the apex of a hierarchy of civilization, such forms of social privilege as White masculinity, the imperial sway of European nations, and the supremacy of Anglo-Saxon and Anglo-American political ideals and economic power.[6] Though it is rarely recognized today as a meaningful account of historical or economic processes, the formal features and cultural implications of the stadial model are endemic to popular productions throughout the twentieth and twenty-first centuries. This chapter demonstrates how the first season of *Survivor* adapts stadial principles by recapitulating the unfolding of human history in the moves the show's protagonists make to "survive" on a supposedly deserted island. As Harriet Martineau's formal articulation of the concept in "Life in the Wilds" demonstrates, however, the exposition of a linear process is actually encoded within a recursive structure.

Though formally articulated as a sequence in which one stage necessarily follows another toward the inevitable-seeming denouement of a civilized polity, stadialism ramified through the cultural realm as a coordinating logic. It can be described as a *plot of polity* in at least three ways. First, each stage contributes to, and is secured by, the entire metanarrative to which it belongs. Since each stage carries with it a stable sense of how it stands in relation to every other stage, the narrative may be entered at any point and, crucially, reconstructed from a single stage. Any part of the structure may "speak for" another. Pastoralism (herding), for example, is more than a description of a human activity; it is a clarification of the schema that makes the description possible. Pastoralism is a stage *of*; the stage that led *to*. Second, a plot of polity mystifies its formulaic qualities—the sense in which its form and significance is already known—by adopting the ruse that it conforms to the shape of narratives that disclose how events are causally linked only after the plot has been apprehended as a whole. Pastoralists, that is, were in no position to understand the plot. Civilized nations could claim the knowledge of what it took to move from one stage to the next because, and only because, they had reached the standpoint of the final stage. Stadialism understood "civilization" in line with a nation's expertise in the long and arduous process of *becoming* a civilization that must have preceded it. Third, a plot of polity told from the standpoint of the end of history ensures that the narrative must always "come right." *Having been achieved*, civilization guaranteed the inevitability and coherence of the organizing narrative from which it was said to derive.

These principles are on full display in "Life in the Wilds," the first story in Harriet Martineau's very influential *Illustrations of Political Economy* (1832–34), the nine-volume work of short stories that was meant to "convey the leading truths of Political Economy, as soundly, as systematically" as possible so that when the "leading principles come out in order, one after another they [will be] so clear, so indisputable, so apparently familiar" as to illuminate and persuade anyone.[7] "Life in the Wilds" sets out those "leading principles" of political economy in terms of the British "civilizing mission" to South Africa. This long story teaches the logic of stadialism along with the logic of empire as she describes a South African British colony putting itself back on its feet in the aftermath of an attack by Bushmen "savages" (4), which leaves a small British colony destitute of everything but its knowledge, imagination, resourcefulness, and capacity for hard work. Out of its engrossing accounts of scavenging for honey, making platters out of slate, and fabricating bows and arrows from scratch, the story proceeds to detail the colony's (re)discovery of economic principles—division of labor, supply and demand, efficiencies of scale—and the meaning of true wealth and value, which the story ascribes to the power of labor. As Mr. Stone, the community's teacher and Martineau's foremost expert on political economy, notes: "There is no wealth without labour; and labour must be applied before the commonest productions can become wealth" (24). In fact, it is the need to theorize labor as the first principle of political economy that determines the story's locale, for, as Martineau remarks in her Preface, there is no such thing in Britain anymore as "Labour uncombined with Capital" (xvi). To chart labor "proceeding through many stages to a perfect union with Capital" (xvi–xvii) requires a shift to the colonial periphery—though the narrative describes the implacable return of the colonial center in every activity the colonists undertake and in every "natural" principle of political economy adduced to explain it.

For Martineau, the "many stages" of economic development are embedded in the stadialist model of history and society to which nineteenth-century thinkers granted virtually unanimous consent. "Life in the Wilds" takes its representative colony on a rapid-fire tour through barbarism, to pastoralism, to feudalism, and finally to civilization—this last stage anticipated in the final chapter when a wagonload of modern implements finally makes its way through from Cape Town. The sudden arrival of advanced technology from afar acknowledges the exigencies of the plot: having lost everything, the colony could not realistically develop the technology to make (say) a needle in a few months. But it also underscores the circular logic of Martineau's purportedly linear story of evolving civilization. The colony has two representative roles. Reduced to sleeping in caves and subsisting on hunting and gathering in the days after the attack, the colonists replay an ostensibly universal story of human origins. As the Captain recognizes, "We seem to have gone back in the course of a night from a state of advanced civilization to a primitive condition of society" (22): they become primal humans at the beginning of their inevitable march from pre-history to a state of civilization. Yet, as the Captain also says, the colonists still possess the "intelligence belonging to a state of advancement" (22). The wagon then signals the colonists' double position at the beginning and end of history. They are representative humans and exemplary Britons, demonstrating in their former capacity "what the unassisted labour of man can do" (22) and in their latter capacity what labor assisted by capital permits.

This familiar imperial *topos* in which Britons stand in for the universally human and write the archetypal human story lays out a correspondingly abject role for the cultural Others of the story, the Bushmen. In the first chapter Martineau hypothesizes that "their short stature and clumsy form" (4) might not be "sufficient proof that they are of an inferior race" (4) and argues that it "seems probable that if Europeans were driven from their homes into the mountains, and exposed to the hardships of a savage life, they would become stunted in their forms, barbarous in their habits" (4). In fact, "Life in the Wilds" disproves every one of these hypotheses. These Europeans *are* driven from their homes and exposed to hardships; instead of succumbing to barbarism, they recreate civilization. The Bushmen, premodern humans, should be able to exemplify "what the unassisted labour of man can do"; instead, these "savages," thieving and slaughtering, prove to be of an "inferior race." Though Martineau does raise the possibility that the colonists who have hunted the indigenous people like "wild beasts" (4) may be partly responsible for the Bushmen's savagery, the logic of the story has in effect already taken the issue out of play. Despite favorable conditions conducive to the Bushmen's emergence as civilized beings—South Africa offers a bounty of "pure and wholesome" air and "fertile" soils which "richly repay the toil of the farmer" (3)—the Bushmen failed to advance to the intermediate stage of agriculturalists even *before* the arrival of Europeans. The proof of their inferiority, the story implies, is written in the stage they made their own *on* their own.

On several counts, that failure is the crux of Martineau's systematic explanation of economics and of her piecemeal justification of colonialism. It underscores the importance of the colonists' double role as (primitive) humans and (civilized) Britons, for it appears either that the Bushmen have reneged on their representative function in the stadialist plot of history or that their function is to represent the possibility of failure. In either case, it allows the colonists to carry the entire burden of representing the progressive possibilities of human civilizations in a story that can now be seen to possess not one but two intertwined plots: the story reveals the socioeconomic principles that accompany the human rise to civilization in the guise of the colonists, but it also tells the tale of a people hypostatized at a primitive stage, whose only recourse under pressure is to degenerate. The Bushmen's failure derives from and makes newly coherent a discourse on race and colonial power. It is not merely that "Life in the Wilds" treats the indigenous inhabitants as if they actually are "savages" or "wild beasts" or *Bush*men. The story's most potent gambit is to refuse to grant them the legitimacy of being able to represent history—even the archaic stage of history!—and thus to prevent them from asserting any symbolic stake in the contest for control of South Africa.

Martineau's description of how economic principles evolve reproduces these ideologies of colonial power. As we have seen, South Africa was chosen as a location for the first story because Martineau wanted to examine the effect of "labour uncombined with Capital." In this bountiful country, Mr. Stone argues, "natural productions are in such plenty, that we know we have only to work" (29). It is an odd and telling comment. The Captain and Mr. Stone in their first discourse on political economy fantasize about an edenic environment so bounteous that it seems as if manna fell from the sky, and Mr. Stone in his effort to prove that there is "no wealth without labour" is forced to imagine that someone under these circumstances must at least have "troubled himself to hold back his head and open his mouth" (25). To argue that "we know we have only to work" is therefore a tautology—one could not otherwise survive anywhere—and only worth emphasizing in this case because the colonists actually need not work very hard to survive. Strangely—and

Mr. Stone is the first to admit it—South Africa's natural fecundity is a poor choice of venue for focusing on the demands and necessities of working hard.

Thinking about the colonists' labor in this way begins to unpack some of the dense ideological work that Mr. Stone's "we know we have only to work" accomplishes. It seems to grant the colonists title to the land on the foundational principle, derived from John Locke, that ownership accrues to individuals upon mixing their labor with the land. That which the colonists remove out of a state of nature becomes their property. Hard work secures the colonists' abstract claim over against the indigenous inhabitants' material presence. Nonetheless, in Martineau's construction of economic origins where even the act of tipping back one's head to eat manna from heaven must be construed as labor, the Bushmen by virtue of their very survival must also surely be construed as having labored on the land. Martineau's need to justify the colonists' rights to South Africa therefore directs her exercise of Lockean theory into a logical impasse, which the story solves by switching its emphasis from one explanatory system to another according to the varying imperatives of colonial logic. Justifying the presence of colonists whose only ethical claim to possession rests on the labor they mix with the land urges a universalized theory of labor: to assume otherwise is to have to posit a competing explanation for the Bushmen's original occupation of the territory. This interpretation of the settling of South Africa extends to the Bushmen, even if they are considered the most indolent of laborers. Yet a countervailing and wholly untheorized distinction between productive and nonproductive labor must also govern the story if the colonists' labor is to grant them property rights over the Bushmen's having mixed some sort of labor with the land immemorially and thus "possessed" the land first. Stages theory helps to close the gap in Martineau's logic in a sort of theoretical bait-and-switch. Indolently subsisting off the land's natural bounty for generations is marked as inadequate because all the Bushmen's labors to survive has not helped them acquire a more advanced stage of civilization. Their failure to enter the right kind of historical process circumvents the need to define why all their work to survive on the land must be construed as the wrong kind of labor.

Importantly, Mr. Stone's argument about working hard to secure the colony situates labor in relationship not to survival but to a concept of wealth. The first discourse on political economy in the story—entitled "What is Wealth?"—adopts a stance that seems wholly given over to a concept of use value. The colonists' tribulations prove that "money is not wealth" (22).[8] When Arnall, the erstwhile merchant, tries to buy the wagonload of goods from Cape Town at the end of the story with a "pretty large amount of gold coin" (112) he is refused, because at this stage in the development of the colony, the Captain says, people rank "according to the comparative utility of their labours" (112). Martineau employs the isolation of the community, in fact, to imagine pure use value. According to the Captain, the worth of the commodities arrayed before them is that "Your labour will be made easier, that is all" (113). Before Arnall's gold becomes valuable as a symbolic general equivalent the colony will have to progress through more stages: not only "more productions" (113) and more (money) capital, but for a time a system of barter: a "regular system of exchange . . . will be of the productions themselves for some time before we find it convenient to pay in coin" (113).

Yet Martineau's stadialism guarantees the eventual creation of a money economy. The Captain has no doubt that they will one day find it convenient to pay in coin (he advises Arnall to "Keep your coin . . . and take care of it" [113]). While "Life in the Wilds" seems to focus on a first cause—the principle of economic good that exists prior to exchange, which Mr. Stone anatomizes in terms of "no wealth without labour"—the nature of Martineau's stadialist analysis means that each term signifies only in relationship to an overarching plot of history that begins with labor and proceeds "through many stages to a perfect union with Capital." Labor is not self-identical, a concept that can be understood without reference to its consequences. Mr. Stone, for example, introduces the topic of labor by asking "what the real wealth of society consists of, and what the unassisted labour of man can do towards producing that wealth" (22), a formulation that makes it clear that Mr. Stone is conceiving of labor in terms of producing useful items rather than the amount of labor exerted. In the same vein, productive items are conceptualized in terms of wealth rather than survival—as what is "necessary, or useful, or agreeable to mankind" (23) rather than what will keep this colony alive through its crisis. Implicit here is one reason for the Bushmen's failure: an appropriate exercise of labor carries within it the assumption that such work will capitalize (on) the land by making it and its productions part of a "regular system of exchange"; as a corollary, labor performed outside the logic of a system of exchange cannot produce "wealth." This is one reason that the Bushmen's abjection can be explained quite precisely in terms of their failure to achieve agriculture, the stage of the civilizing process at which stable settlements begin to bring about property and market relations.

It is worth pausing at this juncture to look more closely at the fluid logic governing the crucial step from a "savage" mode of existence to a "regular system of exchange" by examining the seminal account upon which Martineau depends: John Locke's description in the *Second Treatise of Government* of the emergence of property, property rights, money, exchange, and civil society during the normal progression of societies from a state of nature to a liberal polity. Locke's problematic is the same as Martineau's: how to resolve the gap between the "first ages of the world" (32), characterized by a "commons" in which "every man should have as much as he could make use of" (32) because "there is land enough" (32), and the appearance of money and market economies, characterized by accumulation and unequal ownership of property. This process Locke presents, rhetorically, as a fait accompli: "And thus came in the use of money, some lasting thing that men might keep without spoiling, and that by mutual consent men would take in exchange for the truly useful, but perishable supports of life" (37). Much rides on this turn of the argument. The use of money allows exchange; exchange allows humans to access enduring value ("some lasting thing" that exists "without spoiling"); and, since the exchange of money can only happen by "mutual consent," money brings into being, or at least seems synonymous with, the emergence of a civil society. The rhetorical flourish of "And thus," however, represents as an inevitable consequence what could be seen as an especially problematic step in Locke's exposition. Money does not spoil; but why is spoilage even an issue if, as Locke has just argued, it would be foolish or dishonest for a man in a state of nature to "hoard up more than he could make use of" (37)—and if, in an abundant state of nature, one could simply replace whatever had spoiled? From this perspective, it would seem that money could only emerge in a state of nature if humans foolishly did what was *un*natural or if resources in a state of nature were in fact scant.

At this crux, borrowing from an already well-worn exercise in political economic discourse, Locke deploys an island idyll: "for supposing an island, separate from all possible commerce with the rest of the world, wherein there were but an hundred families, but there were sheep, horses, and cows, with other useful animals, wholesome fruits, and land enough for corn for a hundred thousand times as many, but nothing in the island, either because of its commonness, or perishableness, fit to supply the place of money; what reason could anyone have there to enlarge his possessions beyond the use of his family and a plentiful supply to its consumption" (37–38). "Supposing an island" satisfies several requirements for Locke's theory of humans living in a state of nature. It allows for self-sufficiency; it lacks anything "fit to supply the place of money"; it lacks commerce and processes of exchange; and (Locke overlooking for the moment the issue of spoilage) it has a "plentiful supply" for people to consume. It would therefore seem resistant to the development of property rights, for it would seem irrational ("what reason could anyone have") for anyone to "enlarge his possessions" beyond what is needed to survive.

Yet Locke's island-fable ends up by a sleight of hand proving the inevitable demise of a state of nature. It seems necessary to suppose an island because commerce—in possibility if not fact—already exists in the "rest of the world." Locke, moreover, has to specify that the island lacks anything "fit to supply the place of money" because the criterion for a fit material is nothing more than being "pleased with [the] colour" of something or being attracted to a "sparkling pebble or diamond" (37). Such a material being present, it would naturally be treated as money. Money, then, should not be thought of as the effect of a preceding sequence of causes ("And thus came in the use of money"). The desire to accumulate more than subsistence that, Locke says, bestows an enduring value on some materials—those that become "money"—must in fact exist *prior* to the "mutual consent" that is supposed to give money its value. Materials become valuable when they act as money, in short, but they would not be able to act as money unless a concept of money and value preceded the moment at which someone recognizes them to be valuable. The supposed difference of the island thus masks a tautology—a concept of money must exist in order for a concept of money to exist—and the "way how a man may fairly possess more land than he himself can use the product of" is less the question that needs to be "found out" than the factor that generates the inquiry. In Locke's rhetorical schema, the exemplary island state of nature defining the origin of the historical process that results in a civil society actually follows the "And thus" that introduces money. And rightly so. The island could not function as an origin if the economic steps that are supposed to come in later historical eras—the recognition of the value of some enduring or pretty materials, the desire to accumulate more than one can use, the advent of mutual consent, exchange, and commerce—did not already exist to define its status as the arche of the process. Imagining a fabulous isle into existence suggests that Locke writes the plot of polity backward: his historical knowledge of the fact of money generates the abstract concept of an orderly, linear progress from a state of nature to subsequent stages of sociality.

"Life in the Wilds" replicates, perhaps even more confusingly, this logic of multiple conceptions of historical order. Explicitly, the narrative of the colonists' resurgence inscribes onto history a linear logic: the colonists' step-by-step efforts to put together a functioning polity stand in for the stage-by-stage history of civilizations, so that the story structures itself around the linear and progressive advance of a people from a "primitive state" to (near) civilization, putting forward what would seem an unexceptionable account of how labor contrives to produce more and more wealth once the colonists (re-)discover the virtues of a division of labor and an efficient management of limited resources. But the story also insists that it is possible to grasp and formalize the entire linear structure of history—to see it as an abstract whole—only in retrospect by those who have achieved a vantage point at the end of the process. To aver otherwise would be to open up the possibility that humans who are merely caught up within the process (such as the Bushmen) might also be able to understand it. The same logic argues that the colonists must have achieved *the* ultimate stage of civilization. If they had not, the Britons as the culture of reference and representation would be in the same position as the Bushmen, locked into a process that they could not understand because they have not yet completed it. One narrative sign of this demand for closure might be in Martineau's decision to end the story before the colonists develop commerce and industry for themselves. There is no compelling need to inquire whether human evolution can progress beyond the stage of industry when the story seems to preempt the question by positioning the distribution of the wagonload of goods as the act that will follow the conclusion of the narrative. What comes next—the social felicity attending the unpacking of the goods—is already known and understood. That this is a rhetorical sleight of hand Martineau's own narrative implies: beyond the unpacking of the wagon must lie at least one more stage, the one that permits an industrial nation to evolve imperializing ambitions and send colonists to a place such as South Africa.[9]

The narrative mechanism that attempts to resolve the tension between linearity and retrospection in this story is a recursive structure which is already implicit in Martineau's strategy of positioning the colonists at the material end and symbolic beginning of history. Each step forward the colonists take iterates a stage of human history that has already passed, and whose passing has made it possible for the colonists to take it again. That iterative function centers Martineau's historical schema. History in fact seems knowable solely through its iterability. The historical process can only be replayed in its entirety by those whose ancestors have traversed its stages before: those ancestors having achieved civilization is what makes it possible for these colonists to represent the process that leads to it. Indeed, they can do nothing *but* represent it. One consequence of living at the end of the civilizing process, as the Captain recognizes when he notes that the colonists still possess the "intelligence belonging to a state of advancement," is that they cannot literally be primitive. They can only ever perform, or represent, primitiveness; what permits them to represent history is what prevents them from experiencing those early stages again in all their immediacy and fullness. Since the authentic candidates for primitive human life, the Bushmen, fail so miserably at representing the stage of primitiveness, one implication of the story is that between the failed Bushmen and the performing colonists there are no "true" primitives to be discovered in South Africa—a perspective that legitimates the intrusion of a colonial power into a territory that no longer need be respected as the cradle of a new, up-and-coming civilization.

The story's recursive structure becomes a powerful interpretive and ideological tool. For one thing, it appears to solve at a stroke many of the questions raised above about the puzzling origins of the socioeconomic forces Martineau examines. Since the plot of the story (purportedly) recapitulates the pattern of human history, and since the ability to represent history signifies a successful traversal of it, we need look no further than the act of telling the story for an explanation of why Europeans succeeded on the road to civilization or why the Bushmen failed. History vanishes into and becomes indistinguishable from acts of narration. "Life in the Wilds" answers the question of why Europeans succeeded in terms of *how*: every move the colonists take to put their community to rights dramatizes what early Europeans (purportedly) must already have done. Similarly, the narrative answers the question of why the Bushmen fail to utilize soil that would so "richly repay the toil of the farmer" dramatically: the first paragraphs of the story depict them as a marauding band assaulting the British colony, a tactic that explains their antipathy toward the economic securities of settlement and agriculturalism by merely narrating it. Once one accepts the validity of an imagination in which history is nothing but its representation, the story's iterative logic also helps to explicate Martineau's truncated account of history—an account, that is, which skips the question of which people(s) actually stand at the beginnings of the historical process and ends by sliding the fact of colonization behind the "final" stage of commerce and industry. In narrative terms these omissions appear not to exist. The British colonists govern the beginning of the narrative (and by implication the historical) process. And their presence ensures that the British colonization of South Africa opens the story as a key premise of the plot; far from appearing to require explanation, it is what establishes the structure that generates the explanation in the first place.

As these formulations begin to suggest, a perfectly circular logic underpins every event of the story. The Bushmen must have failed because the story depicts them failing; the colonists' European ancestors must have succeeded because the colonists succeed; colonization is the utopian end of history because these colonists prove successful. Indeed, one function and consequence of the iterative structure is that the colonists cannot possibly fail: as they battle to set their community back on its feet they are coming back, step by step, into possession of what they always already possess. Once more the story brilliantly weds Martineau's pedagogical requirements to an imperializing conception of historical order. There is no more doubt about whether the colonists will return to a state of civilization than there is about whether Britons are civilized. The narrative could not use them to exemplify economic development were those propositions not considered already true. The story therefore allows for no suspense in representing the colony's triumphant progress toward restoring civilization. Though unexpected events occur (one colonist dies from a snake bite, for example), the story must resolve in the colonists' favor: indeed, the fact that they have been chosen to represent history means that history *already has*. The story's iterative order therefore possesses one other important rhetorical function: since a homology cannot be constructed until the original and prior structure which it embodies is fully understood, the plot's unerring movement implies not only the inevitability of the colonial project but the certainty of unerring knowledge. Each is the reciprocal of the other. The colonists' exemplary iteration of history ensures that it is not possible to perceive history as a site of contest and question.

Nearly two centuries after "Life in the Wilds," *Survivor: Borneo* (2000; producer Mark Burnett), the first season of the fantastically popular *Survivor* franchise, neatly recalls key elements of Martineau's playbook.[10] "Marooned" in the wilderness (on an island in the South China Sea) and "wiping the slate clean," sixteen competitors must, as show host Jeff Probst's voiceover tells us in the first few seconds, "work together to build shelter, find food, and survive the island."[11] Like Martineau's colonists, the competitors will be "forced to band together" to "carve out a new existence." Absorbing details of camp construction—building shelters, making a fire, hunting for fish—occupy many passages of the first episodes. Rooted in the formulas of the Robinsonade, *Survivor*, like "Life in the Wilds," also rests comfortably on colonial paradigms. Scholars have pointed to the way *Survivor* "simulates nineteenth-century imperial adventure fiction" and "British colonial travel writing."[12] Episode 1, for example, opens with a brief clip of "sixteen Americans [on the] adventure of a lifetime" making their way across a precarious boardwalk at a "tiny Malaysian fishing village" while a gaggle of children—representing the villagers—look on. Paternalism quickly gives way to primitivism as, a few seconds of show time later, they paddle toward a "beautiful but dangerous" island. Ostensibly uninhabited, the island, like Martineau's empty savannah, reminds us of a key imperialist trope: land re-imagined as a slate wiped clean, prior inhabitants and claims to possession erased, and therefore open to colonization.

Scholars have argued that the political and economic significances of *Survivor* can in fact be understood most readily in the way it "frames itself as a natural, primal society."[13] The show sets out to normalize the logic of corporate capitalism in terms of what appears to be humans, under duress, expressing authentic human instincts: competition, a work ethic, "class-related hierarchies," and an "aggressive self-interest" underpinning a survival-of-the-fittest, snake-eat-rat, social Darwinism.[14] Simultaneously, the competitors participate in and uphold a social order characterized by consumerism and surveillance. Unashamed product placement—the prominent display of Probst's Visa card is one example—accompanies a covert and seamless embrace of a "highly mediated symbolic world" where the camera has become "part of the furniture" for the competitors.[15] Before its seemingly non-selective eye, the deprived contestants are shown naturally longing for the "commodities and luxuries of consumerism," while a violent history of colonialism is re-figured "not as one of violence and conquest, but of adventure, excitement, and a communion with nature."[16] Mystifying the effects of ideology, fantasy and play prove to be conduits for the "imperialistic gaze" and a capitalist logic whereby contestants begin in a state of equality and "end unequally, divided into victors and losers."[17] It is hardly surprising that Jean Baudrillard's work on "simulacra," where reality and history disappear into the hyperreal environment of media simulations, should have become the lynchpin of so many appraisals of the show.[18]

It would be in keeping with these critical assessments of the show's ideological commitments to corporate capitalism to read the show as a reverse Robinsonade. The opening of each episode intersperses brief clips of the contestants with a barely sketched story: "16 Castaways . . . Marooned . . . 39 Days . . . One Survivor." This rudimentary plot possesses at least two functions. It prepares us for a narrative that derives pleasure and suspense from most castaways *failing* to learn to survive. And it dovetails with another plot invoked early in each episode, which is to say the million dollars ("in cash," Probst always appends) rewarded to the sole survivor. To assume that the show organizes all its storylines around this central plot, the quest for one million dollars, means that this competition is always-already the only reality—the only game in town. The final episode [13] conforms to this logic by opening with the remaining competitors paying allegiance to the exigencies of that competition: "It's cutthroat time" (Sue); "I'm here for me and everybody else can kiss my ass" (Kelly); "we were in a position of power where we could get rid of anybody we wanted to" (Rudy); "Now it's all money" (Rudy).

The first season of *Survivor*—after which the show began to repeat and thus normalize its own codes—proves trickier to negotiate than this sort of approach suggests. The notion that the show uses primitivism, or even a simulated primitivism, to mystify its ideological messages is particularly flimsy. In Episode 1, for example, the quest of the Tagi tribe men for fire—and on the island "fire represents life," as Probst mechanically reminds the contestants—is played for laughs. After one fire-maker collapses from rubbing sticks together in comic exhaustion, Sean tells the camera that it would be nice to have fire so that they could sit around the campfire and sing songs. Fire comes to the Pagong tribe via B.B.'s bifocals (used as a burning glass) and 50 waterproof matches (won in the first immunity challenge), and to all contestants after the first Tribal Council, which ends with every participant carrying away a flaming torch. Later, the tougher "primitive" conditions endured by the competitors turn out to be some wet nights, bug bites, and a protracted diet of boiled rice. Throughout, the mechanics of the show are on display, both obviously—supplies parachuted in (Episode 4), camps visited by two Green Berets prior to one of the immunity challenges (Episode 6), a luxury yacht moored off the island (Episode 11)—and covertly, as when Sue's stingray-stung hand (Episode 12) seems to have been professionally dressed.

Even the show's neo-colonial paternalism, usually on conspicuous display regarding the inhabitants of Malaysia—highlighted by the egregious moment in episode 13 when the three surviving contestants walk through palm fronds waved by chanting "natives," as Probst calls them—falls apart during the peculiar scene where Probst takes Kelly to a "mysterious bar" as reward for winning an immunity challenge (Episode 12). Immersing viewers in an endlessly looping consumption of signs, we watch *Survivor* showing Kelly product-placing (drinking a popular light beer) while watching a clip of herself on the first episode of *Survivor*. But the camera also records a number of what appear to be Malaysians at the bar engaged in idle and unscripted activities. At stake here is not the provenance of the bar. In his book about the first season of *Survivor* Mark Burnett gives a fascinating (and very self-satisfied) account of how the production team constructed the bar and peopled it with a "small group of Malays who'd boated over" to assist the filming, who were "only vaguely aware of the castaways existence," and who were thus authentically indifferent to the bewildered visiting castaway.[19] They turn out to be locals *and* members of the production team; they are unscripted and, in accordance with the protocols of Reality TV, there to *represent* unscripted-ness. The point is that, under any circumstances, the spectacle of the people at the bar collides with, and exposes, representations of the Malaysian Other as children or as half-naked "natives" waving palm fronds or as altogether absent. *Survivor: Borneo* does not represent "the primitive" seamlessly. Its producers are not particularly worried about masking its simulations, nor concerned with consistency, nor self-consciously parodic.

In the same vein, the producers of the show offer a surprising amount of airtime to a variety of counter-narratives, especially as it moves toward a conclusion. As Colleen puts it brilliantly in Episode 11: "This is definitely what happens when you put a big chunk of cheese in a maze and let all the mice go at it, you know? And see who eats who and who scrambles on top of who and I don't want to be any part of it. It's . . . not a fun game, no" (Episode 11). "I've had a lot of moral issues" says Kelly (Episode 13) before the final Tribal Council, at which a number of contestants express their dismay about the show's encouragement of ugly, cutthroat behavior: "This island is pretty much full of only two things: snakes and rats" (Sue); "Sue was doing the backstabbing, the lying. . . . It disgusts me what she just did" (Gervase); "I couldn't have been ruthless" (Jenna); "The general sentiment in the jury box is that this contest has degenerated from a contest of who's the most deserving into a contest of who's least objectionable" (Sean). These reservations are carefully orchestrated. Certainly, they could be construed as an attempt on the part of the producers to provide a moral compass and thus mystify the show's exposition of cutthroat, snake-eat-rat capitalism. All the characters cited above are caught on camera at other times sabotaging these moral positions. Yet characters who wander from their own professed positions without seeming to be aware of it are particularly powerful guarantors of unscripted-ness. The astonishing success of *Survivor* did not emerge from its dramatization of a single, monologic narrative about US consumerism or a social Darwinist society in which people compete to end up "victors and losers," but from staging a number of provisional, ill-aligned, and even contradictory narratives, which opened a variety of spaces that viewers could occupy. It is plausible to think that many viewers might have derived most pleasure from *Borneo* by taking *Colleen* as its "victor."[20] Purely ideological readings miss the power of *Survivor* when they rely on a fantasy of the ideologically pure—upwards of 50 million viewers of the final episode mesmerized as one by the show's meretricious simulations.

A more complex interpretation of the show's dynamic cultural work can be derived from its evocation of a fabulous new society. Cast members do not merely participate in a Robinsonade (as castaways), nor merely in a reverse Robinsonade (as competitors). They are also "forced to work together to create a new society."[21] That emphasis on process—wiping the slate clean, working together, creating a new society—might convey viewers to a disappointing "neo-liberal utopia."[22] But in reducing *Survivor* to a fantastic representation of consumer capitalism, scholars have tended to overlook the role of the fantastic in representing political economic thought. One important context for *Survivor* is the very prominent tradition in political economic thought of imaginary, but paradigmatic, commonwealths. Island fables such as Thomas More's *Utopia* (1516), Francis Bacon's *New Atlantis* (1626), and James Harrington's *The Commonwealth of Oceana* (1656) provided influential models of how to stage an island as an imaginary commonwealth and thereby grasp the nature of human beings, good government, a wise management of resources, and the orderly development of civilized societies. Jean-Jacques Rousseau (1762) argued that language and society itself must have originated on islands, since "among men thus collected, and forced to live together, a common idiom must have started up much sooner, than among those who freely wandered through the forests of the mainland."[23] For John Locke, as we have seen, the act of "supposing an island" underwrites *the* crucial step in theorizing how property rights, money, and relations of exchange emerged from a state of nature to structure human societies anew.

Locke, in fact, helps to explain one of the oddest features of *Borneo*'s symbolic architecture, which is that the producers construct its overarching plot around a million-dollar prize but that the "new" social arrangements on the island refuse all forms of exchange. It has taken the franchise twenty years to introduce a currency (fire tokens in Season 40) with which contestants can trade goods. There would seem to be at least three reasons for this strategy. First, the show detaches its "new society" from a market economy to expose what Mark Burnett calls the "core essence of humanity." Like Locke's islanders attracted to a "sparkling pebble or diamond," island life stripped of all market accouterments seems to naturally develop social relations gravitating toward desire and acquisitiveness so that market society and the cutthroat competition it generates appears, like Locke's "And thus," as the necessary consequence of "natural" human characteristics. Second, a society without money or markets has to be supposed because everyone, like Locke, is aware that it cannot, because it does not, exist except in theory or on a fantasy island. Third, as a corollary of both points, the fantasy of creating a "new society" without markets implies a metanarrative: an explanation of how history "works" to construct a market society where none had existed.

In its broadest outlines, *Borneo* conforms to a classic stadialist narrative. The season begins with two tribes of hunter-gatherers and concludes with the emergence of market society as the winning contestant carries off the treasure chest of one million dollars, "cash" now acquiring a potent value as a visible and tangible sign of exchange. Instances of the stages Martineau meticulously retraces in "Life in the Wilds" frequently appear. Introduced to a state of nature, the castaways must discover what Mr. Stone tells Martineau's survivors: "we know we have only to work." Working together is Probst's first admonition to the castaways, hard work a constant refrain of the opening episodes as some of the contestants vie to make their work ethic count toward their survival. "We got a lot of lazy people if you want to know the truth. . . . You can't have lazy people," says B.B. (Episode 1). The show represents a division of labor, which political economic thought considered the crucial step societies employed to use resources more efficiently and thus accrue capital, in several ways. In the opening episodes castaways assign their energies to a variety of different survival tasks—shelter building, fishing, fetching water—which are then pooled for their survival. And before the "merge" (when the two reduced tribes become one), many immunity challenges depend on individual members of the two competing tribes performing different tasks, which are then combined to complete the challenge. Capital stock in the form of new technologies hasten the process. Dramatic changes come to the Tagi tribe upon acquiring a fishing spear and snorkel during an early challenge, since one castaway is now able to provide protein (fish) to supplement their rice diet.

The accumulating effects of labor reshape the "new society" the contestants are supposed to create on the island. Stages theory argued a division of labor, labor-saving technologies, and capital accumulation begins to put an end to the brutal physical labor required to survive amid primitive conditions. The more efficient use of resources under agriculture, for example, was held to introduce leisure and the first intensive pursuit of symbolic endeavors such as arts and religion. *Borneo* follows this logic closely. Early episodes concentrate on scenes of the castaways sweatily building shelters and hunting for fish or tapioca root. In later episodes, the show's attention shifts almost entirely to the contestants' competition for symbolic capital as voting strategies, alliances, games, and conversations about the competition itself occupy more and more airtime. Across the trajectory of the show, a fragmentary though still legible plot of polity appears. Two hunter-gatherer tribes in competition with each other gives way to one "tribe" emphasizing individuals in competition with each other. The symbolic plot of society-building concludes in tandem with the show. One million dollars changes hands, reinserting everyone (cast and production team) back into the exchange relations of market society and establishing that society as the telos of the historical order.

To this relatively conventional plot of people laboring to build a "new society" along classic stadial lines, *Borneo* introduces important amendments. Most obviously, the show collapses the stages of hunting-and-gathering and advanced market capitalism into each other and presents their narratives simultaneously. Before the castaways fight to get their raft to the island and construct their shelter, we know their off-island jobs and that there is a million dollar at stake. Episode 1 ends by displaying it in the form of a chest stuffed with bundles of money. Martineau's recursive narrative structure helps to understand some of the consequences of this interweaving. The settlers of "Life in the Wilds" were able to recreate a functioning polity because every step was ghosted by the entire sequence of steps their ancestors had already taken before them. Primitive conditions become Martineau's and the colonists' symbolic capital. *Survivor* merely makes that same process more evident. In one sense the contestants are working to build shelters so that, one day, they can reacquire the prerogatives of a market society. In another sense, on dramatic display from the first moments of the show, that day is already here. They are working two tasks at once: building shelters *and* working to win a million dollars.

The same recursive structure emerges from the dramatic and symbolic work accomplished by the crate of supplies rafted to the island in Episode 1, which the Tagi tribe break open within a few seconds of landing. Developing over several minutes of airtime, the scene features the new castaways excitedly naming various supplies—canned food, twine, a frying pan, kerosene, an axe—accompanied by cries of delight.[24] A comic discourse develops round the crate prior to its opening as the castaways joke about whether it contains Fritos, or a bathtub, or a blowtorch. Crate-opening also implies another technological marvel: the camera and its arts of electronic mediation, which invisibly participates in and relays the enchantment of discovery.[25] Like the wagonload of supplies arriving from Cape Town at the end of "Life in the Wilds," the crate implies, and structures, a plot of polity. Wagon and crate together circumvent the dramatic implausibility of having the settlers/castaways create a technologically advanced market society in a few weeks. They also speak to the inevitability of the metahistorical process. Manufacturing (steel axes, canned food) must supersede primitive conditions such as foraging for driftwood and food, and this "new society," given time, could not help but supersede the child-like social arrangements at the "tiny Malaysian fishing village" where the show begins, *because they already have*. These castaways, like Martineau's settlers, look back from the end of history, privileged to represent a natural and necessary evolution of human societies from the primitive to the civilized by virtue of being able to encompass the entire process. That process, importantly, includes electronic mediation. The manufactured goods in the crate could be found at the fishing village (and indeed in Martineau's time). The castaways' prerogative lies in knowing how to open the crate entertainingly before, and for, the governing eye of the camera. *Survivor* and "Life in the Wilds" speak to the story of how civilizations evolve not in terms of their characters' ability to live it but in terms of their ability to command representations of it.

What has changed across nearly two centuries is the claim these otherwise similar works make on truth. Martineau's goal for *Illustrations* was, she stated in her prospectus, to convey "as much truth as any set of propositions on the subject" by creating a "faithful history" rather than "works that pretend to be stories, and turn out to be catechisms."[26] As a "faithful history," "Life in the Wilds" hews rigorously to the abstract propositions formally stated by political economists, which Martineau held to be a truthful description of the metahistorical process and of the events it governs. Metahistory explains the shape and purpose of, and thereby legitimates, historical events such as the British colonization of South Africa, as well as "Life in the Wilds" itself to the extent that the story represents "history" accurately. *Survivor*, in contrast, sketches in a stadialist schema without attempting to describe or formalize its properties. None of the castaways step forward like Mr. Stone to understand or articulate the process within which they appear to be immersed. The show records exemplary events without articulating the broad narrative they are supposed to exemplify. The Tagi tribe, for instance, win the fishing spear and snorkel that enhances their lives in a challenge—and ridicule Sean's efforts to create a fishing rod (with which he catches nothing), even though it is the one serious attempt in the entire first season to construct a useful tool. The show recognizes the transformative, even revolutionary, consequences of adding to one's capital stock. But the tribes' capital stock increases *only* through game play. The castaways otherwise make no concerted effort to abide by the requirements of the stadial script.

Scholars are therefore not incorrect to emphasize the show's fervent embrace of simulacra. One implication, in line with Fredric Jameson's influential critique of a postmodern age that "has forgotten how to think historically" in embracing the logic of multinational, consumer capitalism, is that *Survivor* constructs a pastiche of a once-coherent philosophy of history.[27]

Propositions about history *and* metahistory vanish into entertaining but haphazard acts of representation, containing no more substance than Probst's risible attempts to invoke the island spirits or tell a local folktale. If so, the show's piecemeal stadialism invokes one specific relay in consumer capitalism's creation of a perpetual present: the late-nineteenth-century rise of the deliberately ahistorical discipline of neoclassical economics. Defining its purview solely as the science of exchange, economic thought in the twentieth century would simply assume the universality of the principles it now took for granted: methodological individualism, subjective and relative values, utility functions, rational economic behaviors, and (perfect) markets. Consigned to a vague premodernity were older classical economic ideas, such as historicist and holistic thinking, moral and ethical considerations about the good of the body politic, informal, non-mathematical narratives—and grand metanarratives such as the orderly progress of civilization. In *Survivor* "faithful history" becomes muddled story because stages theory no longer retains any *formal* explanatory power. The show articulates its economic values through the voices of the rational economic agent posited by neoclassicism: Kelly's "I'm here for me" and Rudy's "now it's all money." The rest is simulacra.

Even here, the fabulous island opens spaces that confuse economic paradigms both classical and neoclassical. *Borneo* does not abrogate its authority to represent history. But its disjointed plot of polity constitutes that authority through a variety of contradictory schemas, staging as no more than a persuasive fable Martineau's colonial presumption that those who have reached the end of the political and economic process can see, and represent in formal terms, how history resolves in their favor. If one plot direction leads to primitive "natives" waving palm fronds to salute TV heroes, another leads to a befuddled and fooled survivor being led to a fake bar peopled by authentically indifferent twenty-first-century locals. Allowing a multitude of partial and even bewildering stories to invade its overarching narratives is one way in which the show gestures toward its post-coloniality. If that means little more than social relations built upon simulacra, the show nonetheless seems unwilling to surrender to the notion that its contribution to the long political economic tradition of model island commonwealths is to stage an impeccable and remorseless neoclassical logic—that the island, removed from history and geopolitical considerations, is there to stage the infinite wants of the competitive individual struggling to win a million dollars in a snake-eat-rat world. *Borneo* fumbles toward the notion that the neoclassical paradigm requires a telos.

A case in point is the final Tribal Council (Episode 13) that ends the first groundbreaking season of *Survivor* and brings it to a triumphant ideological climax: the possessive individual reunited with market exchange, all mediated in a money-spinning finale before over 50 million viewers. As many scholars have noted, the show seems to present the sole victor as the beneficiary of wholly rational "cutthroat" behavior. It revels in the castaways' propensity to form alliances and then betray them—to employ the "language of the collective to solidify an individual position and then quickly eliminate the collective"[28]—with the show's piecemeal stadialism endorsing this narrative arc as the natural culmination of the historical process. But the finale also reintroduces a collective voice in the shape of the Tribal Jury, composed of the final seven castaways to be voted off the island. It is something of a dramatic masterstroke. The jury members dominate proceedings with their often-vituperative speeches, which precede a close and suspenseful 4–3 vote, but also work to represent a massive TV audience. The jury allows 50 million people with a variety of attitudes toward the show and toward the contestants to "climb on board." It is also something of an ideological counterstroke. Sean's innocent-sounding remark about the "general sentiment in the jury box" introduces fleetingly a "back story," a sense of off-stage dissent un-simulated enough to *not* make it into the show. It implies that the end of the show's symbolic narrative might allow for a different survivor: a barely imagined and largely unacknowledged collective composed of millions of castaway-viewers scattered throughout the world and held together, just, by their desire for communal judgment.

NOTES

1. Adam Smith, *The Wealth of Nations* (London: W. Strahan & T. Cadell, 1776; New York: Bantam Books, 2003), 23–24.
2. Smith, *Wealth*, 12, 25, 12.
3. Smith, *Wealth*, 355–56.
4. Henry Wood, *The Political Economy of Natural Law* (Boston: Lee and Shepard, 1894), 153. Wood's italics.
5. I depend in this chapter on Ronald L. Meek's exemplary discussion of stages theory in *Social Science and the Ignoble Savage* (Cambridge; New York: Cambridge University Press, 1976), 5–36.
6. See Cathy Boeckmann, *A Question of Character: Scientific Racism and the Genres of American Fiction, 1892–1912* (Tuscaloosa: University of Alabama Press, 2000) for an excellent discussion of pseudoscientific theories designed to buttress white supremacy in the late nineteenth century.
7. Harriet Martineau, *Illustrations of Political Economy* (London: Charles Fox, 1832; London: Warnes and Routledge, 1859), xii, xiv. Subsequent references to this work are cited parenthetically in the text.
8. Martineau works hard to establish the (ostensible) inutility of money. Stone argues: "Put a man with a bag of gold into an empty house, in England or anywhere

else, and he will starve in a week unless he is allowed to give his gold in exchange for what will supply his wants" (23).

9. As Elaine Freedgood neatly puts it, the settlers have an "irremovable intellectual capital." "Banishing Panic: Harriet Martineau and the Popularization of Political Economy," in *The New Economic Criticism*, eds. Martha Woodmansee and Mark Osteen (New York: Routledge, 1999), 216.

10. In its first season *Survivor* was watched by an average of 22 million people per episode. Between 50 and 120 million people watched the finale. The show has been credited with revolutionizing Reality TV. Since 2000 it has run for over 42 seasons (two per year).

11. I cite *Survivor: Borneo* by episode. The quotations, unless otherwise cited, are taken from the televised episodes and checked against the detailed transcription of what the characters say on the show's fandom site (survivor.fandom.com).

12. Jennifer Bowering Delisle, "Surviving American Cultural Imperialism: *Survivor* and Traditions of Nineteenth-Century Colonial Fiction," *The Journal of American Culture* 26, no. 1 (March 2003): 42, doi: 10.1111/1542–734x.00072; Laura Hubbard and Kathryn Mathers, "Surviving American Empire in Africa: the Anthropology of Reality Television," *International Journal of Cultural Studies* 7, no. 4 (December 2004): 445, doi.org/10.1177/1367877904047863.

13. Christopher J. Wright, *Tribal Warfare: Survivor and the Political Unconscious of Reality Television* (Lanham, MD: Lexington, 2006), 13.

14. Wright, *Tribal*, 13; Tony Tremblay, "Reading the 'Real' in *Survivor*: Unearthing the Republican Roots in Reality Narrative," *TOPIA: Canadian Journal of Cultural Studies* 9 (2003): 53, doi.org/10.3138/topia.9.47. Murray Keat explores Mark Burnett's own explanation of the show as a mode of social Darwinism in "Surviving *Survivor*: Reading Mark Burnett's Field Guide and De-naturalizing Social Darwinism as Entertainment," *Journal of American and Comparative Cultures* 24, no. 3 (2001): 43–54, www.proquest.com/scholarly-journals/surviving-survivor-reading-mark-burnetts-field/docview/200651117/se-2. Tremblay arrives at the same conclusion without invoking Burnett's own words: "In the narrative of Survivor, social-Darwinism is a first principle." Tremblay, "Reading," 53. I take the "snake eat rat" metaphor from the speech during the finale of Season 1 where Sue attempts to explain island politics in terms of animals in Nature preying on each other.

15. Tremblay, "Reading," 59.

16. Keat, "Surviving *Survivor*," 51; Delisle, "Surviving American Cultural Imperialism," 45.

17. Keat, "Surviving *Survivor*," 49; Tremblay, "Reading," 57. See Tremblay for a succinct account of how "ideology works through fantasy" and "gamesmanship and play work . . . to render incontestable the infrastructure that games and ideology share." Tremblay, "Reading," 57.

18. For readings secured by a Baudrillardian approach, see, among many others, Tremblay, "Reading the 'Real'"; Christopher J. Wright, "Welcome to the Jungle of the Real: Simulation, Commoditization, and *Survivor*," *The Journal of American Culture* 29, no. 2 (June 2006): 170–82.

19. Mark Burnett, with Martin Dugard, *Survivor: The Ultimate Game* (New York: TV Books, 2000), 200–201.

20. Polls indicating that Colleen was the most popular member of the cast suggests that many people did.

21. Jeff Probst's introductory remarks at the beginning of *Survivor: Australian Outback*, the second season.

22. Hubbard and Mathers, "Surviving American Empire," 442.

23. Rousseau, Jean-Jacques. "The Second Discourse: Discourse on the Origin and Foundations of Inequality Among Mankind," in *The Social Contract and The First and Second Discourses*, ed. Susan Dunn (New Haven: Yale University Press, 2002), 117–18.

24. The scene occupies about 3 minutes between 9 and 12 minutes into episode 1.

25. Seconds of airtime before opening the crate, however, the episode has shown contestants speaking directly to the camera.

26. Martineau, *Illustrations*, xii, xiii, xiii.

27. Fredric Jameson, *Postmodernism, or, the Cultural Logic of Late Capitalism* (Durham: Duke University Press, 1991), ix.

28. Mathers and Hubbard, "Surviving American Empire," 442.

Chapter Four

Challenging the Privilege of *Again*

Recursive Plots of Polity in Octavia Butler's Dawn *and Nalo Hopkinson's* Midnight Robber

When the alien Oankali awaken Lilith, their human captive, from her centuries-long sleep, the first words of Octavia Butler's *Dawn* (1987) lay stuttering claim to familiar models of beginning and becoming:

> Alive!
> Still alive.
> Alive . . . again.[1]

These words sketch in a process of psychic formation. Mere consciousness (Alive!) leads to an awareness of continuity (Still alive) and thence, with "Alive . . . again," to the emergence of rational self-consciousness coalescing around memory, which implies an ability to apprehend repeated events, which implies an ability to coordinate events across time. *Dawn*, the first volume of the *Lilith's Brood* trilogy, goes on to iterate Lilith's psychic journey in its account of rebuilt social relations.[2] Having saved a small number of humans from the self-inflicted nuclear catastrophe that destroyed much of the Earth, the Oankali Awaken individuals (Lilith is one) who are supposed to lead small groups of humans back to the now-restored planet. On a "small simulation of Earth" (201), a perfect simulacrum of a tropical island constructed on board the Oankali ship, Lilith's tribe of humans will seek to "begin again" (41). The *topos* of beginning again is marked still more strongly in Nalo Hopkinson's *Midnight Robber* (2000), which opens on Toussaint, a planet colonized by Caribbean peoples journeying out from Earth, and ends on New Half-Way Tree, Toussaint's prison planet, where exiles from Toussaint's diaspora struggle in the jungle to survive and rebuild. This novel too transports us to lands of simulacra. Granny Nanny, the novel's AI narrator, casts New Half-Way Tree as a doubled or "dub version of Touissant" in the way a "shadow is a dark version of the real thing, the dub side."[3]

Scholars frequently read Butler and Hopkinson together as two of the more powerful voices in an emerging tradition of Afrofuturist writing. That embrace of the future is necessarily complex. Practices of decolonial world-building manifested in imaginary future worlds, Cienna Davis observes, draw on "countermemories, unwritten folktales, oral traditions, wisdoms, and mythologies of distinctly African origins."[4] And so *Midnight Robber*'s Toussaint recalls Toussaint Louverture, one of the leaders of the eighteenth-century Haitian Revolution. The planet invokes the historical figure in response to Hopkinson's millennial moment (in 2000), shaped by traumatic histories and the current reality of global capitalism, but newly open to the rebellious energies of postcolonial and feminist discourses.[5] Butler too shapes a "futuristic defamiliarization" to show how bedrock "liberal humanist ideals . . . have already eroded under free-market capitalism, militaristic nationalism, and neoliberal corporate entities."[6] To the extent that much science fiction has been preoccupied with the adventure of the discovery and colonization of new worlds, these works might be said to reimagine the very genre that underwrites their power. As Eric Smith puts it (speaking of Hopkinson), they "radically appropriate and reconfigure the conceptual machinery of SF and the narrative utopia to address the particular . . . circumstances of postcoloniality and globalization."[7]

Lilith's Awakening helps us to understand the logic governing these important assessments of Butler's and Hopkinson's works. "Alive" and "Still alive" evoke an unthinking consciousness of a colonial past and the SF narrative paradigms consistent with it. Becoming alive to the force of *again* is to enter historicity in the sense of recognizing the coordination of events across time—for example, the way in which the structure of a postcolonial age might be understood in the context of colonial practices—and then, with that understanding, not to have to repeat them again. But *Dawn* and *Midnight Robber* also put into play historical *meta*narratives. Society rebuilding on the Oankali spaceship and on New Half-Way Tree follow a familiar stadial script. Survival, for example, foregrounds the importance of labor. Like Mr. Stone's "we know we have only to work" in "Life in the Wilds," or like Jeff Probst exhorting the castaways in *Survivor* to "work together," the survivors on the Oankali spaceship have "got to be able to work together" (145), and the exiles on New Half-Way Tree must "work hard or [be] dead" (135). Like "Life in the Wilds" and *Survivor*, too, the idea of working together functions as part of a broader plot of polity. Butler and Hopkinson locate their survival tales within the parameters of stages theory. This is not to say that they accept its principles uncritically. Both challenge—without refuting—the recursive structure that allow Martineau's and Burnett's survivors the privilege of re-living, and representing, the metahistorical process. And, crucially, they make prominent what Martineau and Burnett downplay: the concept of commonwealth.

To prepare Lilith's little band of humans for their return to the restored Amazon basin, the Oankali follow Locke in "supposing an island." They simulate a tropical island so perfectly, within a hold so vast, that few of the Awakened humans believe Lilith when she tells them they are not on Earth. The "training floor" (187) teaches the survivors to become hunter-gatherers, learning how to construct shelters out of forest materials (204), "gather forest foods" (212) such as bananas, papayas, and breadfruit (205), hunt for fish with spears (238), and make fish traps (241). Other pedagogies are at work. By learning how to "work together," the humans must re-learn sociality. In many respects the training floor functions like a disturbing dry run for *Survivor*. The procedure for choosing the islanders—as for all Survivor seasons—begins with psychological profiling (116–26).[8] Sociality on the island proceeds by way of shifting alliances. "Loyalties can change" (175), Lilith remarks, and by the end of the novel even her "core group" (150) turns against her. Individuals (Curt, Derrick, Peter) are removed from the island having failed their tests. And all humans perform their tasks under nonstop surveillance. Re-learning sociality, to both sets of survivors, means learning how to "work together" *for* relentlessly controlling invisible eyes (the camera, the Oankali). On board the Oankali ship, though, Reality TV becomes the disciplinary power Michel Foucault theorizes in terms of the panopticon.

The training floor teaches humans how to survive and how to accommodate a new regime of surveillance. Like "Life in the Wilds," it also enacts a familiar stadial model of history. Indeed, the Oankali deliberately script it. "Tools will come later" (199) Nikanj tells Lilith as the humans arrive on the island, ensuring that they "begin to feel what it's like to live here" (200) as hunter-gatherers. A "heavily laden breadnut tree" (206) even implies that the island recalls that paradise of abundance Locke imagines for humans in a state of nature. Though the trainees' time on the training floor turns out to be short, working together on the island sketches in later stages. The humans set about "planting their own crops" (205) as they look to the more productive agricultural practices that stage theory anticipates. And like "Life in the Wilds" and *Survivor*, manufactured tools, including "waterproof tarpaulins, machetes, axes, shovels, hoes, metal pots, rope" (202), are eventually given to the islanders. These tools represent the industrial age to which, Martineau and Burnett both intimate, the assiduous efforts of castaways to survive must surely lead, partly because that history, having been already lived, is already known, but also because it seems the rational expression of bedrock economic efficiencies. Tools *will* come later, to paraphrase Nikanj, because they have, and must.

Social relations on the training floor, however, upset this familiar recursive pattern. Having prevented a potential rape, Lilith proclaims that there will be "no back-to-the-Stone-Age caveman bullshit!" (178). But her attempt to preserve the sanctity of a primitivism-to-civilization narrative fails. From the beginning, the Awakened islanders follow not Locke's but Thomas Hobbes's appraisal of a state of nature—a "Warre of every man against every man."[9] The band of humans fails to create a civil society, the necessity of which both Locke and Hobbes acknowledge, though they structure it in different ways: Locke in terms of a body of neutral laws, Hobbes in terms of a powerful sovereign. The humans split inexorably into battling (and murderous) factions. The Oankali exclude Lilith, the sovereign leader of the training floor, from the group of humans returned to Earth, because "they would have killed you" (243). The final confrontation takes place with Lilith and the Oankali facing down a "Hot, smoky, dirty, angry" group of people standing in front of their ill-made shelter wielding "axes, machetes, and clubs" (226)—a tableau that reads like the reversion to the uncivil "Stone Age" social relations that Lilith fears.

But *Dawn* does not inscribe its problematic of history through its human characters inverting a stadial model, which is to say through an atavistic devolution. Stadialism functions normatively to produce non-normative results. Brief as it is, the replayed history of humankind on the training floor corroborates an expected pattern of increasingly complex social relations emerging around greater tool usage, more efficient use of resources, and accumulating capital stock. Lilith, for one, is residually aware that evolving social relations were supposed to have solved the conflicts of what she labels the Stone Age. The novel's imagined history, however, has human evolution culminating in nuclear holocaust. The dawn and end of human history are characterized by warring parties who focus on weapons as the most important tools. Superior technologies merely make violent "Stone Age" practices more efficient. When Lilith remarks on the stupidity of her small band of belligerent humans playing "Americans against the Russians. Again" (175), the novel accords her the privilege of understanding and representing the plot of history from the vantage point of its end. But the plot she represents is no longer linear. Humans in fact are not "beginning again" as hunter-gatherers on the Oankali ship so much as representing where the stadial process ends.

The logic of *Dawn* here can be illuminated by comparing it with the "The Dawn of Man," the famous opening scenes of Stanley Kubrick's *2001: A Space Odyssey* (1968). Here Kubrick shows the changes wrought among two groups of early primates by the acquisition of a weapon—or more precisely the dawning cognition, after encountering the alien artifact, that a bone can be wielded as a club. Wielding it decides the competition between the two groups for a scarce resource (water). And securing the scarce resource makes at least one profound change to the successful band of primates: it gives the group a leader, and the leader his power. Kubrick's symbolic narrative resolves when the whirling bone flung into the prehistoric air suddenly segues into a spaceship orbiting the Earth. The weapon-tool implies the application of rational thought to transforming the environment, economy, and social structure. It grants one group the capital (resources) it needs to sustain it, which in turn allows it, as capital accumulates, to foment other social, technological, and artistic innovations. The bone that commands the watering hole ultimately brings about command of space—and Johann Strauss's graceful waltz, which accompanies the appearance of the spaceship in Kubrick's movie.

The plot of polity that conjoins the two, Kubrick implies as the movie flashes from bone to spaceship, is too well known to require telling. Whatever we can infer from the millions of years that are supposed to have passed between, however, is clearly consonant with, and legitimated by, fundamental principles of political economy. Even before the alien monolith arrives, the movie shows, groups of early "Man" competed aggressively with each other because resources are scarce. The monolith merely adds intelligent direction to a preexisting, trans-species logic. It need not return for millions of years because after being granted intelligence primates will *necessarily* go on to develop tools (weapons) and higher technologies (spaceships, HAL) in pursuit of ever greater efficiencies and ever greater command over the natural world. This invisible narrative also implies, and rationalizes, a stage of colonial domination: the scenes at the watering hole demonstrate that if colonial powers aggressively acquire other territories, they are merely following the example of the first humans. In not bothering to relate this story Kubrick, like the narratives of "Life in the Wilds" and *Survivor*, mystifies the movie's (neo)colonial pedagogies: *2001* too allows those who stand at the end of history to represent what it takes to successfully negotiate the advance beyond primitivism. That the movie seems to anticipate a still later stage that humans must traverse does not wholly dispel this logic. It merely slides its familiar story of an advanced civilization teaching primitives what path to follow behind the inscrutable alien monolith, as if to give the story the imprimatur of a divine edict.

By *ending* its narrative with a group of warring, weapon-wielding primates, *Dawn* constructs an ironic stadialism. Stage theory turns out to be an accurate description of the shape of human history. Bone-clubs, fish-spears, axes, and machetes have in fact led humans toward increasingly efficient technologies, profound sociopolitical changes, and command of Earth's resources. Kubrick dramatizes it; and the band of humans on the Oankali ship seem inevitably to replay it. But the end of *Dawn* corrects—or, really, rigorously follows to the correct conclusion—the logic of "The Dawn of Man." Kubrick's tableau of angry, competitive, resource-hungry primates led by a weapon-wielding male Butler accepts as the true ground of human history, and as what brings about its end. Stage theory therefore mistakes its own logic. The political economic narrative of humans finding more efficient ways to compete for scarce resources leads to more efficient ways of competing and dominating. The weapon-tool in the hands of warring groups ramifies over time to "Americans against the Russians. Again." In this respect *Dawn* turns inside out the privilege Mr. Stone, Burnett's castaways, and even Kubrick's aliens derived from being able to know and represent the value of repetition. Repetition leads humans to disaster on the Oankali ship because of their ideological commitment to a mistaken narrative. Poignantly, Lilith is one of the main culprits. Her outrage at humans falling back into the Stone Age clings to a stadial narrative as if it were true.

Like Octavia Butler, Nalo Hopkinson invests heavily in the narrative and historical potentialities of *again*. Colonized by people from the Caribbean, themselves the progeny of Earth's era of colonization, Toussaint finds itself shadowed forth once more on New Half-Way Tree as a "dark version of the real thing, the dub side" (2), the "mirror planet of Toussaint" (2). Mirror reflections need not imply mere replication. As Michel Foucault shows in his magisterial introduction to the concept of heterotopia, a space of ex-centric otherness in which relations of power begin to be revealed, the mirror can bring about a productive double take. "I see myself there where I am not, in an unreal, virtual space," Foucault remarks; the mirror constitutes "a sort of shadow that gives my own visibility to myself." Heterotopia is a "placeless place"—an oxymoron, a doubled space that makes visible space-between, which in turn can make visible the architecture of cultural spaces that would otherwise remain unacknowledged. Acts of observation are implicated in this spacing: "I begin again to direct my eyes toward myself and to reconstitute myself there where I am."[10] The novel's idiom for these destabilizing double takes—this act of beginning again—is "dub." The "dub side" implies a shadowy doubling. It also invokes dub music, which, as Leif Sorensen explains, refers to the tendency of the Jamaican recording industry to produce records whose B, or dub, side, contained a "remix or version" of the A side in a way that "problematizes and fractures the original."[11] "To "turn it over," as Granny Nanny urges, is to see "it have a next side to the tale" (3). As New Half-Way Tree echoes Toussaint, and both planets remix Earth, Hopkinson introduces us to, so to speak, dub-topia, a problematic site emphasizing both newness (begin) and continuity (again).

In *Midnight Robber*, it is certainly possible to read dub-topia in terms of repressed doubles. New Half-Way Tree, for example, can be understood as the political unconscious of Touissant, a place where the Douen, exterminated on Toussaint in order to open the planet to human colonization, still exist to bear witness to the practices the colonizers no longer wish to bring to consciousness.[12] The mirror planets of *Midnight Robber* can be addressed still more pertinently in terms of Homi K. Bhabha's concept of the "unhomed," derived from the term that Sigmund Freud used to theorize the uncanny.[13] Freud's "unheimlich" refers to that literary space within which repressed traumas—that which should remain secret and unacknowledged—suddenly make their presence terrifyingly felt. For Bhabha, the "unhomed" of the postcolonial world evokes the traumas that global capitalism has sought, unsuccessfully, to repress: "postcolonial migration, the narratives of cultural and political diaspora, the major social displacements of peasant and aboriginal communities, the poetics of exile."[14] The "'new' internationalism," as Bhabha calls it, conveys an "estranging sense of the relocation of the home and the world—the unhomeliness—that is the condition of extra-territorial and cross-cultural initiations." To be "unhomed is not to be homeless," but to live at home in relationship to places that were once considered home.[15] That postcolonial "process of displacement and disjunction" functions like heterotopia to make the political and economic significances of global transnational spaces uncannily visible, conveyed in unsettling translations (unhomely/unheimlich) and barely articulable tropes (unhomely, "placeless place").[16]

Midnight Robber constructs Toussaint and New Half-Way Tree—and Earth, in relationship to them—as unhomely heterotopias. All three planets are subject to an estranging "poetics of exile." Transits across space—from Earth to Touissant via "nation ships" (18), from Toussaint to New Half-Way Tree via the "next side of a dimension veil" (2)—emphasize the unsettling potential of space-between. Hard labor on the mirror planet of New Half-Way Tree, for example, reveals how far Toussaint's touted reliance on high tech to keep its people comfortable—"Back-break ain't for people" (8), proclaims Antonio—forgets those who do labor and pay taxes. Antonio and Ione have several house servants (nurse, cook, gardener, wet nurse) to supplement the work of the AI. Toussaint from the perspective of New Half-Way Tree might therefore be considered a "bourgeois utopia," a dub version of Earth.[17] But neither Toussaint nor Earth fit neatly into static schemas. Toussaint, for one, does not merely replicate Earth. Ben the gardener notes that the Jonkanoo [carnival] hats on Toussaint, made in the image of the Marryshow Corporation's spaceships, rewrites what Tan-Tan reacts to as the "nasty story" (21) of the slave-ships crossing the Atlantic on Earth. The new hats represent "how black people make this crossing as free people this time" (21). Ben's utopian story can certainly be challenged. The appearance of the Douen on

New Half-Way Tree shakes loose the repressed memory of what happened to (a version of) them at the hands of the "free people" of Toussaint, who in turn ship their "lost people" (2) to New Half-Way Tree as captives. But Ben seems to miss the fact that the Jonkanoo hats from Earth, which Toussaint's hats dub/double, *also* commemorate the end of slavery. The irreducible difference Ben wants to claim for the "crossing . . . this time," in short, requires negotiation. It is pertinent to the era of the Middle Passage but not necessarily Hopkinson's postcolonial era. Telling stories in terms of time and space between suggests that relationships between Earth, Toussaint, and New Half-Way Tree might be read more richly as an ex-centric ensemble of mirrorings and remixings.

To "begin again" on Toussaint and New Half-Way Tree registers the dislocating force of the heterotopian moment. "Again" insists that there are prior instances; prior instances imply the existence of a coordinating schema, without which those instances would be reduced to mere random events. But "again" also implies the possibility of dubbing/doubling that schema and in the process exposing the shadowy coordinating logic that organizes events as "instances of" a broader plot. Societies beginning again on Toussaint and New Half-Way Tree realize these heterotopian imperatives in two ways. First, the novel inserts itself into, and remixes, the long tradition in political economic thought of imagining model societies built from the ground up on an island, or empty savannah, or the White House lawn—or, here, a new world and prison planet. Stage theory plays a prominent role in those models. But Hopkinson also plunges into history, recalling and dubbing the prominent place occupied by Caribbean islands in nineteenth-century political economic thought. *Midnight Robber* "turns over" the hegemonic narratives—the A-side, as it were—of political economy, showing what model-making might look like on the dub side. As befits its heterotopian play, the novel ends up putting forward a better understanding of how models of commonwealth might function in our postcolonial world.

In the nineteenth century, US and British commercial, political, and cultural interests in the Caribbean relentlessly invoked political economic thought to secure the kind of positional superiority Edward Said describes so well in his analysis of Orientalism. *Caribbeanism* granted observers from abroad the privilege Martineau's colonists assume: knowing from the vantage point of the end of history how plots of polity are supposed to unfold, they made island cultures representative of economic activity from the dawn of human civilization.[18] The substantive, disciplined economic knowledge US and British visitors claimed to bring with them—rational decision-making, intelligent industry, sound governance, a functioning civil society, and efficient markets—is absent or performed disastrously. Accounts of island life—Jamaica, where Hopkinson was born, came in for particular attention, we shall see—focused on primitive marketplaces. Commodities are "buyable at so ridiculously small a sum of money" or exchanged via barter amid a "Chatter, gabble, clatter," so that "One stands in the market square bewildered at first."[19] Incomprehensible transactions in inefficient markets were held to be a microcosm of broader economic systems. Colorful fictions about Caribbean pirates accompanied scathing remarks about piratical economies. Julia Ward Howe, writing of a trip to Cuba in 1860, remarks that the wrecking grounds of the Bahamas Banks had taken the place of banks since the only way to make money was off a "desirable wreck."[20] Bribery was *de rigueur*. Labor was either misdirected or nonexistent. Somnolence is the "normal condition of every body in waiting," wrote one visitor to Cuba in 1879; cab drivers are "actually asleep upon the tops of their coaches" near the wharf.[21] For illustrator and author Howard Pyle, visiting Jamaica some ten years later, Kingston's harbor drew the "commerce of the Western world to its wharves until it became one vast storehouse of wealth," but the island's markets now represent the "very essence of Jamaica life, picturesque, shiftless, dirty, aimlessly busy."[22]

Pyle's comment about a profound reversal in Jamaican economic life is part of a long-standing discourse in the nineteenth century. Forty years before Pyle, W. E. Sewell casts himself as an economically-savvy Crusoe in his travelogue "Cast-away in Jamaica" in order to excoriate Jamaica's misuse of its rich natural resources: "Such quantities of cocoas, pines, oranges, mangoes, granadillas, sapodilloes, and vegetables of all descriptions—comparatively valueless in Kingston, but worth a mint if they could be taken to a Northern market."[23] The island is now a "shattered hulk."[24] The root of this discourse was the emancipation of slaves in 1838 by Britain and the ensuing refusal of many now-free laborers to work the sugar plantations. The cause of Jamaica's "unprosperous condition," argued Oran (the pseudonym of F. N. Otis) in 1858, is that land-owners sold "little spots of soil" to the "newly-made freemen" after emancipation; and since the "wants of the negro were few and easily supplied, he was content, and could not be induced to work for a hire," preferring "days of idle ease."[25] Oran clearly has Thomas Carlyle's hyperbolically racist "Occasional Discourse on the Negro Question" (1849) in mind, a work of political economy that was much reprinted and discussed in the United States following its appearance in Britain, in part because Southerners seeking to justify the institution of slavery seized on its diatribe against emancipated slaves in Jamaica. Their "indolence," Carlyle declared, was responsible for ruined and abandoned sugar plantations.[26] His account of life in a climate where, he asserts, half an hour's labor a day suffices to subsist foreshadows Oran's: the "pumpkins [are] cheap as grass in those rich climates: while the sugar-crops rot round them uncut, because labor cannot be hired, so cheap are the pumpkins."[27]

To Carlyle, this is not a situation to celebrate. Declaring that the act of working underpins all value—not free market capitalism—Carlyle insists that Black freed laborers will have to be forced back into involuntary servitude in order for them to participate in such a basic, humanizing activity. They are too happy eating pig-food, "their beautiful muzzles up to the ears in pumpkins, imbibing sweet pulps and juices."[28] Carlyle's racist invective and Oran's more detached analysis obscure two important issues. First, since both writers aver that freed slaves are perfectly content to live by eating free pumpkins, the tragedy of Jamaica as a "shattered hulk" only makes its presence felt, and is only worth inveighing against, because it threatens the wealth of the British plantation owners. Second, "indolence," supposedly the cause of Jamaica's economic malaise, seems a perfectly logical economic response to the richness of an island where one can subsist without laboring or engaging in market relations. Oran and Carlyle here encounter the conundrum that, in various ways, engage both Mr. Stone in "Life in the Wilds" and John Locke. How do concepts of labor, exchange, and private property emerge from a state of nature abundant enough to make labor supernumerary, or reducible (as Mr. Stone says) to opening one's mouth to receive manna from heaven? Oran's and Carlyle's answers are versions of Martineau's analysis of stadialism. Because Jamaicans, in the wake of emancipation, are beginning *again* they are necessarily functioning with the full knowledge of how orderly economic systems, following established protocols, once generated a "vast storehouse of wealth." As Pyle suggests, corroborating Oran and Carlyle, Jamaicans are reverse-engineering a process that had already run its course. Like Martineau's Bushmen, they cannot be authentic representatives of a state of nature because the privileged observers (American and British writers) have always-already inserted them into history.

This powerful discourse making Jamaica and other Caribbean islands the epitome of "backwards" economic life—primitive, but also going backwards from more advanced stages of human civilization—urges us to read the political economic conditions of Hopkinson's mirror planets differently. Sentenced to "live out we days in hard labour" (127) on a planet where Tan-Tan first appears to us as a "strong, hard-back woman," her "two arms hard with muscle" (1), the unhomed of New Half-Way Tree offer a thoroughgoing challenge to a Caribbeanist discourse accusing freed laborers of utter laziness—but also to a history of slavery, forced labor, and unpaid labor. So, though in a more complicated way, does the "bourgeois" ease some critics find on Toussaint, contextualized by the muscular pedicab runner's argument to Antonio in the novel's early pages that "Honest work is for people" (8). But this is not a wholly trustworthy riposte to the people of Toussaint who ask of the pedicab runners "Why do hard labour when Marryshow had made that forever unnecessary?" (10). The narrator's reply, "But the Grande 'Nansi Web had said let them be" (10), emphasizes the importance not of hard work but of choice. On Toussaint, Granny Nanny unsettles nineteenth-century postures of consent: enslaved people who cannot choose whether to work or not, and, later, a racist discourse accusing free people of choosing not to work—they "could not be induced," as Oran puts it.

This complicated play with a long-standing political economic discourse on Caribbean nations extends into the novel's "carnival poetics" as Tan-Tan adopts the pose of, and in a sense becomes, the Midnight Robber, a popular character of Caribbean carnivals, whose "stream-of-consciousness speeches always told of escaping the horrors of slavery and making their way into brigandry as a way of surviving in the new and terrible white devil's land" (57).[29] Evolving as a parodic, and poignant, reversal of the role of plantation owners—the robbers who thieved labor and lives from those enslaved—the Midnight Robber's exaggerated rhetoric dubbed/doubled the owners' claims on civilized speech, their vast profits from the plantation system ironically symbolized by the small amounts of money freely given to the worthy performer. In Sweet Pone's town square, Tan-Tan's continues that centuries-old tradition. After her first speech, a "few of them flipped coins of copper and brass into her sack" (317); having defeated Janisette, "Carnival pounds and pennies rained on Tan-Tan's head" (327). These small sums of money are trivial in the context of Sweet Pone's market economy, about which the narrator reveals little. They are much more consequential in challenging plantation piracy *and* a Caribbeanist discourse emphasizing piracy and disorderly economies, capped by the anonymous man who makes sure Tan-Tan collects her hard-won earnings.

The novel's dub version of nineteenth-century discourses and practices is nowhere more evident than in the stadial narratives governing the political economy of the growing communities Toussaint's exiles set up on New Half-Way Tree. Like Martineau, Butler, *Survivor*, and *2001*, *Midnight Robber* presents across the arc of its plot a rapid-fire version of a familiar plot of polity. Technological advancements take us from a mortar and pestle and "wattle-and-daub cottages" (122) at Junjuh, the first settlement Antonio and Tan-Tan reach, to Iron Age technology—Tan-Tan's iron hunting knife—before her departure (for killing Antonio with it). A primitive car (261) and rifle (270) becomes a "bullet-shaped tank" advancing on "oiled treads" (318) prior to Tan-Tan's final showdown with Janisette. "Solar-powered texts" (304) appear at Sweet Pone. Stages of social organization follow suit. Antonio and Tan-Tan arrive on New Half-Way Tree in the bush where "business" (92) means barter and where Chichibud shows himself to be a "fine hunter" (117) after killing the mako jumbie bird. Antonio will "hunt for the both of you," Chichibud tells Tan-Tan. Hunting and gathering leads to Junjuh's rudimentary agriculture (small gardens and cornfields), which yield later to indentured servitude in the canefields at Begorrat (284), to money and swindles in Chigger Bite (251–53), and finally to the orderly "market" and "tradespeople" (304) at Sweet Pone where the people "looked content; thin and wiry from manual labour, but healthy" (304).

These plots of social and technological advance are accompanied by theoretical accounts of the emergence of civil societies. Chigger Bite, for example, operates by an emphatically Hobbesian set of social arrangements. Here, Alyosius tells Tan-Tan, it is "every man and woman for themself" (241). He continues, "say a next feller put him eye 'pon your goat for some nice goat curry for him dinner; well then you best watch your back" (241). At Junjuh, One-Eye extends Alyosius's tale of uncivil societies. When he arrived, One-Eye relates, "Junjuh Town was madness": "Everything you had, somebody else ready to take it from you. And take your life too, if them had them way" (127). One-Eye's answer to this Hobbesian state of nature is to enforce Hobbes's solution: along with Claude he claims a sovereign power to "enforce the rules" (127). Implicitly, Sweet Pone completes what looks to be a symbolic trajectory from Hobbes to Locke—from a "Warre of every man against every man" in Chigger Bite, to a (more) civil society governed by sovereign power at Junjuh, to an orderly civil society at Sweet Pone, where Tan-Tan, despite fearing at first that her pregnancy might make her an "easy target" (304), instead finds "people working hard to build a new life" (304).

At Sweet Pone, for the first time on New Half-Way Tree, Tan-Tan finds a true sense of community—she notes "how Melonhead said 'we'" (304) when speaking about the town—and of commonwealth. Structured by contract, not coercion, it appears to be the first community on New Half-Way Tree to have a market. It has even begun to institute a public sphere, in Jürgen Habermas's sense of a virtual space of debate and civic and self-improvement separated from centralized state authority. Sweet Pone has a "Palaver House" where "we . . . could meet people and talk" (304) and a small library. "No wonder people could develop skills here," marvels Tan-Tan, "they had books to teach them" (304). Having instituted secure markets, a hard-working commercial society, and a workable, non-coercive civil society, Sweet Pone therefore seems to mark the successful resolution of the classic stadial narrative. Its books are crucial. The town's advance arises not merely from what it learns of the slow accumulation of skills developed by humans over the centuries, but from the recognition of a coordinating plot of polity that reveals what learning those skills leads *to*, and therefore why they are worth repeating. In this respect, Sweet Pone's books perform a structural function similar to Mr. Stone's story of civilization in "Life in the Wilds," and even the castaways' knowledge of how to simulate reality perfectly in *Survivor*. In each case, the goal is not to learn a particular activity, but to master the skill of representing the overarching metanarrative that makes particular activities meaningful.

Midnight Robber, however, generates potentially dystopian counternarratives. One of them recapitulates the implication of *2001*'s "The Dawn of Man" that advanced weaponry, not technology in the abstract, is what underwrites escalating dominations of nature and other human beings. Within nine months—the gestation period of Tan-Tan's baby—the iron workers of Junjuh progress from an iron knife to a rifle, with which they kill two Douen (269–70), to a car "made of rusting sheets of iron" (261), and thence to a bullet-shaped tank "buffed to a reflective shine" and moving on "oiled treads" (318). The foundry workers have clearly pumped oil and rediscovered the art of making steel. "Nothing on all of New Half-Way Tree looked like it" (318), the narrator informs us. That situation will not last. Though humans believe the Douen "never thought to advance themselves any further" (139), Chichibud informs Tan-Tan "we preparing weself" (231) to avoid the fate of the Douen on Toussaint by establishing foundries to replicate human technologies, which may have to include "Guns. Bombs. Cars. Aeroplanes" (230). Perhaps more important, the Douen derive from humans a specific plot of "advance" built around competition for scarce resources. The pressure to build foundries arises from their ability to grasp the entirety of this metahistorical plot. They look back from the logical end of the process—an end that has already transpired in other times and places—to recognize the significance of this moment on New Half-Way Tree. *Midnight Robber* clearly holds open the bleak possibility that in the planet's future lies warfare or the Douen's extermination, as on its mirror planet, Toussaint.

Both plots of polity—one ending with Sweet Pone's solar panels and civil society, the other ending with a tank in its town square—have to be correlated with a third, represented by the AI, the "Grande Nanotech Sentient Interface" (10), or Granny 'Nansi, or Granny Nanny. Embarking on an eight-year quest through the dimension veils to relocate Tan-Tan, the AI's odyssey results in bringing Tubman, Tan-Tan's unborn child, back into the Nation Worlds. Accompanying Granny Nanny, Tan-Tan's house *eshu* reveals itself to have been the narrator all along. (In what follows I refer to Granny Nanny, taking the house *eshu* as her avatar or subroutine.) Completing the arc of the plot begun in the prologue, Granny Nanny and her electronic outrider are therefore positioned to resolve the novel's plot of polity. Occupying the end and—we realize on the last page—the beginning of the novel, the AI bookends the competing metanarratives colliding in the town square of Sweet Pone. Concluding the novel a few pages after the tank appears, the AI seems to represent a superseding stage of technological development. But the revelation of the narrator's identity shows that this stage was already in place. What reads like a linear narrative of people on New Half-Way Tree moving from primitive to sophisticated technologies turns out to have been a *retrospective*. Here Hopkinson seems to follow the classic plot of stage theory. Like Mr. Stone—and like the nineteenth-century European and US visitors who castigated what they considered the "backwards" economies of Caribbean islands—the AI possesses the privilege of *re*-telling a tale that can only be seen whole when its end is already known.

This potentially unsettling conjunction of Granny Nanny with a posture of colonial privilege has vexed scholarly approaches to *Midnight Robber*. Most readings privilege the mythopoeic dimensions of Granny 'Nansi, who "manages her society through an electronic web that incorporates ideologies and myths from traditional African, Caribbean, and both North and South American cultures."[30] Granny 'Nansi, for example, spins her Web of connections to Anansi spider-trickster stories circulating among West African, Caribbean, and African American peoples, to Spider Woman/Grandmother, wise guide and leader of the Hopis, and incorporating, via the house eshu, the Yoruban "trickster god Esu."[31] A "benevolent technological force," Granny Nanny's omniscience "makes her the moral and ethical safeguard of peace in the Nation Worlds."[32] But it is clearly possible—some have made this determination—to read Granny Nanny as the key component of a dystopia, aiding the Marryshow Corporation in its violent terraforming of Toussaint, instituting round-the-clock surveillance of the citizens of Toussaint (and of the other Nation Worlds [10]), and now finding a way to reach across to a new world to make an unborn child's "whole body" into "one living connection" (328) with the Web. Incorporating New Half-Way Tree into the Nation Worlds it surveils, the AI can represent the unrelenting incursion of a totalizing rationality into the "political unconscious" of New Half-Way Tree. If so, the novel shares surprising common ground with *Survivor*, the AI erasing all difference and all reality in the field of the corporate (Marryshow Corporation's) gaze. The midnight robbers of this novel, like the characters of Reality TV, end up having to recognize the hegemony of mediated lives in the corporate carnival of a postcolonial world.

These diametrically opposed responses to Granny Nanny illuminate the structural limits of the discourse on Hopkinson. This is particularly evident in the persistent attempts to find common ground. Belen Martin-Lucas, for example, argues that Toussaint is under "totalitarian control by the Grande Anansi Web" before admitting, uncomfortably, that those scholars who see Granny Nanny as a guardian of the community do uncover a "potential for subversion"—leaving unanswered the question of how such an entity could allow any sort of subversive spaces to exist when the entire logic of totalitarianism insists on closing them down.[33] Martin-Lucas also rightly notes, however, that those who foreground Granny Nanny's "role as protector and guardian of the community" are forced to acknowledge "some of [her] violent aspects."[34] Elizabeth Boyle negotiates this problem by situating the novel in conversation with *Earth's* eighteenth and nineteenth centuries, arguing brilliantly that the trope of the "vanishing 'black' body" found in narratives of the Middle Passage underwrites the moment when Tan-Tan and Antonio are shipped away from Toussaint, so that the AI's control over the Nation Worlds "mirror the historical exchange and revision of tropes between black Atlantic narratives."[35] Rooted in the same context—the "countermemories . . . latently present in Afrodiasporic subjectivity"—Cienna Davis reads the troubling aspects of Granny Nanny in terms of an Afrofuturist "critical utopia" where "optimistic social dreaming, grounded sociohistorical reflection, and critique can all occur simultaneously."[36]

However skillfully done, such approaches evade the issue Martin-Lucas tackles head on: that when the "Marryshow Corporation sink them Earth Engine Number 127 down into [Toussaint] like God entering he woman" (2) prior to the extermination of the Douen, Granny Nanny participates willingly in what the house eshu here plainly describes as a planetary rape.[37] The event grounding Toussaint's "optimistic social dreaming" makes the planet seem less "critical utopia" than a site of crisis. The novel ends, moreover, with New Half-Way Tree poised on the brink of repeating the same pattern of brutal events. To think of the novel's events merely in terms of Earth history—to read Tan-Tan's "vanishing 'black' body" only in terms of the nightmare of the slave trade—is to skirt the facts of the novel, which depicts *Afro-Caribbean* descendants masterminding the colonization of Toussaint and "vanishing" people to New Half-Way Tree. Reading Granny Nanny as beholden to her mythopoeic contexts *or* to corporate totalitarianism *or* to Earth history runs the risk of hypostatizing the novel. Trickster gods cannot cease being trickster gods; totalitarian entities cannot willingly cede power; Earth history (from the time frame of the novel) is over and done.

The logic of *Midnight Robber*'s mirror planets instead mandates an inquiry into how and why a process of violent colonization can begin again and then, if the arms race ramping up on New Half-Way Tree is any indication, yet again. Scholars have been loath to broach the obvious historicizing solution to this dilemma, which is to interpret the pattern of events on Toussaint and New Half-Way Tree as the direct consequence of the brutal colonization of Earth's Caribbean.[38] The colonized have learned from the colonizers how to colonize. That might, as Jessica Langer argues, grant the people of Toussaint the privilege of now "possessing agency," for they are "free this time."[39] But by defining agency and freedom in terms of the ability to commit genocide, such arguments come perilously close to justifying colonialism in accordance with a definition of power divorced from any sort of ethical consideration. Arguments that attempt to have it both ways at once—to see Toussaint as a site of "intense ambivalence," or a "single community" hosting a "colonial power and a historically dispossessed people"—merely defer the question of how Hopkinson is modeling the relationship between dispossession and power as one society gives way to another.[40]

Thought about dispassionately, Granny Nanny's participation in the violent events that make Toussaint "safe for people from the nation ships" (33) clearly presages the bleak extension of totalitarian power into New Half-Way Tree's once-rebellious communities. The problem with such an approach is that it seems wholly out of step with what most critics seem to take as an emotionally compelling reunification of the AI and one of the unhomed, the unborn Tubman.[41] The logical inference—that Granny Nanny actively changes over the course of the novel—has, in line with the mythopoeic/totalitarian axis of scholarly approaches, received remarkably little attention. Kate Perillo is one of the very few to argue that "in generating new forms of sentience and choosing to cross the dimensional veil of its own accord, the computer may be able to transgress some of its own limitations as a tool used for conquest" (14). The still more pertinent question is whether the AI continues to possess the same limitations. The novel begins with the house *eshu* detailing the violence and genocide of Granny Nanny's original role on Toussaint. But the prologue describes two beginnings. Once we have learned from the conclusion that the prologue is narrated by the AI, our retrospective view makes it possible to read the prologue as an account of her beginning (the terraforming of Toussaint) and of her *beginning again* to tell the same story. The AI who narrates the tale is the dub version of her own A side, the next side to her own tale.

To see the logic of this position, it helps to *metahistoricize* the novel—to think of it in terms of a political economic tradition given over to imagining model societies, and to modeling how societies might develop over time. Tan-Tan's time on New Half-Way Tree sketches in the rise of a primitive to a technologically advanced society, accompanied by the authoritative posture of a narrator who reveals the story from the vantage point of the final stage. Stadial narratives, we saw, secured that authority recursively. Narrators could not do otherwise than repeat the story of the metahistorical process that had granted them the perfect knowledge to tell the story in the first place. Nineteenth-century visitors to the Caribbean adopted exactly that pose. W. E. Sewell, for example, diagnosed Jamaicans' ills in terms of laziness, disorderly markets, and an inefficient use of resources because he, the sole "castaway" on the island, knew what more efficient labor and markets looked like. In structural terms, Granny Nanny performs the same role and claims the same privilege. As the prologue begins, she already knows how new forms of society will emerge on New Half-Way Tree. Camping in the bush will lead to a civic square; an iron knife will lead to a tank and library; and all such technological advances must lead to, because they already have led to, an AI.

And Granny Nanny commands the future too now that she has the calibration, via Tubman, to "seed" New Half-Way Tree.

Put this way, the AI represents Hopkinson's Hobbesian solution to a Hobbesian dilemma. At a moment when a "Warre of every man [and Douen] against every man" looms, the novel seems to accord Granny Nanny the sovereign power to make Toussaint's mirror planet also "safe for people." The crucial question *Midnight Robber* raises is whether Granny Nanny might choose to exercise her sovereign power differently than on Touissant—whether the privilege accruing to her as the interpreter of the metahistorical process might be transformed into the privilege of *not* repeating it. Scholars who see Granny Nanny as a benevolent force often point to her guiding principles. She has been "designed to be flexible, to tolerate a variety of human expression, even dissension, so long as it didn't upset the balance of the whole" (10), says Maka, Antonio's co-conspirator. But these principles are in fact consistent with removing the Douen from Toussaint—and therefore perhaps from New Half-Way Tree—on the ground that making planets "safe for people" is the first step toward instituting a more balanced and just *human* society.

The AI's prologue, however, puts forward a different concept of balance in terms of dub. Two issues in particular encourage us to think of Granny Nanny's taletelling as a B-side remixing of the A side, a mirror heterotopia. First, coming to the end of the novel allows a sudden recognition that the AI, an invisible shadow, has been doubling "the narrator" from the start. Re-reading the prologue with that information in mind is to dub our first experience. A new knowledge of unexpected spacings, for example, can be brought to bear. *This* Granny Nanny is re-telling a tale two hundred years after her earlier incarnation terraformed Toussaint, and eight years after the vanishing of Tan-Tan. Second, the space-between the A-side AI and her dub version signifies a remixing of the political economic logic that led to the terraforming of Toussaint. That action honored the zero-sum watering-hole logic of *2001*. The AI and the Marryshow Corporation must have thought of the planet as a scarce resource for which various parties (the humans and the Douen) would necessarily compete. Winning the competition for those resources is what leads to technological advance on Toussaint—or, in *2001*, to a spaceship in orbit with its symphonic accompaniment.

The AI's eight-year-long "fearsome journey" (328) through the dimension veils to re-home one person suggests a different approach: a superabundance of resources and a willingness to be profligate in using them. *Midnight Robber* here enacts a similar structure of phantasy and desire as (the later) *The Martian*. Like the entire planet Earth doing whatever it takes to rescue Mark Watney, Granny Nanny abandons all economic considerations in committing so many resources to finding one "kidnap" (327) victim. Unlike *The*

Martian, *Midnight Robber* situates its economic irrationality within specific historical contexts where "rational" economic strategies visited untold violence on Afro-Caribbean peoples. Granny Nanny's grand odyssey takes on particular poignancy in light of Tan-Tan's unhomed ancestors who were kidnapped away into slavery without a powerful guardian and guide to prevent it. Too, Granny Nanny neatly reverses nineteenth-century Caribbeanist discourses devoted to positioning the islanders as irrational economic agents who squander their vast natural resources and fail to monetize their freedom. Granny Nanny's plot of polity ends not with the terraforming of Toussaint but with a rescue mission by an irrational economic agent transforming one life into a resource worth sustaining. If there is hope for human-Douen relations on New Half-Way Tree, it rests on reading Granny Nanny as a dub version of Hobbes: a sovereign power committed to resisting the historical sovereign powers that constrained Afro-Caribbean lives, but who might use that resistance now to reconceive the "war of all against all" consonant with a political economy of competition, technological advance, capital accumulation, and uncivil societies. The novel's hope for the future lies in Granny Nanny realizing the possibilities of a wholly irrational political economy.

NOTES

1. Octavia Butler, *Dawn* (New York: Popular Library, 1987), 3. Subsequent references to this work are cited parenthetically in the text. Following Butler, I capitalize "Awaken" when referring to the Oankali rousing humans from hibernation.

2. The trilogy was originally named *Xenogenesis*.

3. Nalo Hopkinson, *Midnight Robber* (New York: Warner Books, 2000), 2. Subsequent references to this work are cited parenthetically in the text.

4. Cienna Davis, "Re-programming the Present: The Dynamism of Black Futurity in Nalo Hopkinson's *Midnight Robber*," in *Race and Utopian Desire in American Literature and Society*, eds. Patricia Ventura and Edward K. Chan (London: Palgrave Macmillan, 2019), 268.

5. To N.A. Pierce, *Midnight Robber* is a "saga of female empowerment." "At the Crossroads: Carnival, Hybridity, and Legendary Womanhood in Nalo Hopkinson's *Midnight Robber*," in *Bad Girls and Transgressive Women in Popular Television, Fiction, and Film*, eds. J. Chappell and M. Young (London: Palgrave Macmillan, 2017), 211.

6. Joe Heidenescher, "Problematizing Consent in the Posthuman Era: Octavia E. Butler's "Bloodchild" and "Amnesty," in *The Bloomsbury Handbook to Octavia E. Butler*, eds. Gregory J. Hampton and Kendra R. Parker (London: Bloomsbury Academic, 2020), 58.

7. Eric D. Smith, "'The Only Way Out is Through': Space, Narrative, and Utopia in Nalo Hopkinson's *Midnight Robber*," *Genre* 42, no. 1 (2009): 135, https://doi:10.1215/00166928–42–1–2–135.

8. As Mark Burnett describes in *Survivor: The Ultimate Game* (New York: TV Books, 2000), 10.

9. Thomas Hobbes, *Leviathan* (London: Andrew Crooke, 1651; Harmondsworth, UK: Penguin, 1985), 196.

10. Michel Foucault, "Heterotopia," trans Jay Miscowiec, n.p., web.mit.edu/allanmc/www/foucault1.pdf.

11. Leif Sorensen, "Dubwise into the Future: Versioning Modernity in Nalo Hopkinson." *African American Review* 47, no. 2–3 (Summer/Fall 2014): 268, https://www-jstor-org.ezproxy.neu.edu/stable/24589753. I depart from Sorensen's excellent essay in thinking of a dub mix as a trope of undecidability rather than a dialectic.

12. Bill Clemente, for example, argues that New Half-Way Tree offers a "submerged or repressed" history of Toussaint. "Tan-Tan's Exile and Odyssey in Nalo Hopkinson's *Midnight Robber*," *Foundation* 91 (2004): 152, Accession number 2004297217.

13. Homi Bhabha, *The Location of Culture* (New York: Routledge, 1994), 14–15.

14. Bhabha, *Location*, 7.

15. Bhabha, *Location*, 8, 13.

16. Bhabha, *Location*, 8.

17. Smith, "The Only Way Out," 158.

18. I analyze the model-island trope in political economic thought at greater length in *Kitchen Economics: Women's Regionalist Fiction and Political Economy* (Tuscaloosa: University of Alabama Press, 2020), 64–106.

19. Howard Pyle, "Jamaica, New and Old," *Harper's New Monthly Magazine* 80, no. 476 (January 1890): 178, Cornell University Library Making of America Collection.

20. Julia Ward Howe, *A Trip to Cuba* (Boston: Ticknor and Fields, 1860), 607.

21. Frank H. Taylor, "Street Scenes in Havana," *Harper's New Monthly Magazine* 58, no. 347 (April 1879): 683–84, Cornell University Library Making of America Collection.

22. Pyle, "Jamaica," 178.

23. W.E. Sewell, "Cast-away in Jamaica," *Harper's New Monthly Magazine* 22, no. 128 (January 1861): 176, Cornell University Library Making of America Collection.

24. Sewell, "Cast-away," 170.

25. Oran, "Tropical Journeyings en Route for California," *Harper's New Monthly Magazine* 16, no. 95 (April 1858): 579, Cornell University Library Making of America Collection.

26. Thomas Carlyle, "Occasional Discourse on the Negro Question," in *Carlyle's Complete Works* (Boston: Estes and Lauriat, 1885), 300.

27. Carlyle, "Occasional," 295.

28. Carlyle, "Occasional," 295.

29. Marlene D. Allen, "Tricksterism, Masquerades, and the Legacy of the African Diasporic Past in *Midnight Robber*," in *Afterimages of Slavery: Essays on*

Appearances in Recent American Films, Literature, Television, and Other Media, eds. Marlene D. Allen and Seretha D. Williams (Jefferson, NC: McFarland, 2012), 83.

30. Jillana Enteen, "'On the Receiving End of the Colonization': Nalo Hopkinson's 'Nansi Web," *Science Fiction Studies* 34, no. 2 (2007): 264, https://www.jstor.org/stable/4241525.

31. Allen, "Tricksterism," 77.

32. Davis, "Re-programming," 269–70, 271.

33. Belen Martin-Lucas, "Posthumanist Feminism and Interspecies Affect in Nalo Hopkinson's *Midnight Robber*," *Atlantis* 38, no. 2 (2017): 112, journals.msvu.ca/index.php/atlantis/article/view/5314/105–115%20PDF.

34. Martin-Lucas, "Posthumanist," 112.

35. Elizabeth Boyle, "Vanishing Bodies: 'Race' and Technology in Nalo Hopkinson's *Midnight Robber*," *African Identities* 7, no. 2 (2009): 178, doi.org/10.1080/14725840902808868.

36. Davis, "Re-programming," 268, 278.

37. Granny Nanny's planetary terraforming/rape has called forth a number of uneasy responses. For Elizabeth Boyle the AI "displays both female and male biological attributes" so that its "bonds of maternal love and cooperative behaviour" somehow resist its "hyper-masculine, imperialist structures." Boyle, "Vanishing," 181. For Kate Perillo, the AI's "admittedly coercive act also 'calls forth disorder'" to bring about a more dynamic society. Kate Perillo, "The Science-Fictional Caribbean: Technological Futurity in Nalo Hopkinson's *Midnight Robber* and Beyond," *Small Axe* 22, no. 2 (2018): 13, https://doi.org/10.1215/07990537-6985642.

38. Marlene Allen, for example, notes that "vestiges of the slave past from Earth still follow her black characters into the future." Allen, "Tricksterism," 76. Gina Wisker, speaking of Hopkinson's "A Habit of Waste," draws attention to "ways in which once-colonized people can be seen to internalize worldviews and behaviours that limit their development, stunt their identities." "Moving Beyond Waste to Celebration: The Postcolonial/Postfeminist Gothic of Nalo Hopkinson's A Habit of Waste," in *Postfeminist Gothic: Critical Interventions in Contemporary Culture*, eds. B. Brabon and S. Genz (London: Palgrave Macmillan, 2007), 114. Brecken Hancock also notes that the settlers of New Half-Way Tree "mimic the society of their home-world, and if things continue to develop in the same way, the cars and guns and bombs and airplanes will eventually do to New Half-Way Tree what they did to Toussaint." "New Half-Way Tree and the Second World: Themes of Nation and Colonization in Nalo Hopkinson's *Midnight Robber*," in *The Canadian Fantastic in Focus: New Perspectives*, ed. Allan Weiss (Jefferson, NC: McFarland, 2015), 100–01.

39. Jessica Langer, *Postcolonialism and Science Fiction* (London: Palgrave Macmillan, 2011), 66.

40. Langer, *Postcolonialism*, 65; Perillo, "Science-Fictional," 11.

41. I agree with Perillo that most scholars, "whether they otherwise celebrate or condemn Toussaintian society and its technology, see Tubman's character as a gesture toward a liberatory future for both planets. Perillo, "Science-Fictional," 13.

Chapter Five

"Should've Kept Better Care of Her"

The Political Economy of Joss Whedon's Firefly

Science-fiction universe-building typically incorporates histories of the interim, of the in-between: accounts of what has occurred, sometimes over minutes, sometimes millennia, to replace a recognizable historical moment on Earth with a new set of conditions pertaining to a projected future. As brief as they often are, such accounts fill several important functions. Miniature imaginary histories imply a structuring sense of how and why events unfold in time. And they reframe Earth history by way of a backward glance from the hypothetical future to which it is held to have given rise. Such accounts invite readers to think of themselves as being no longer situated in a fluid present, looking to a conjectured future. The retrospective view made possible by an imagined future instead defamiliarizes Earth history by virtue of it appearing to have become static. Octavia Butler's history of the in-between in *Dawn*, for example, takes us from an Earth history of warring superpowers during the Cold War to the imaginary conflagration that brings ruin to Earth, the arrival of the alien Oankali, and thence to Lilith's awakening on the Oankali ship a couple of centuries later. By locking the Cold War into a moment that never occurred—a nuclear apocalypse—the novel draws new attention to the conditions of what did occur. So, as Lilith gloomily watches her charges playing Americans against the Russians yet again on the Training Floor, the novel advances an endgame logic of hierarchy, competition, and destructive male violence we might otherwise be loath to impute to an era that ended with the Earth still intact.

The history of the interim in Joss Whedon's *Firefly* universe—fifteen TV episodes of *Firefly* (2002–2003) followed by the capstone movie *Serenity*

(2005)—focuses squarely on issues of political economy. Occupying little screentime, that history is nonetheless crucial to understanding a franchise whose popularity over the past two decades seems linked in no small measure to its relevance to an era beset by economic and environmental crises. Welcoming us to a new "'verse" composed of dozens of planets, hundreds of moons, and a variety of societies, the brief voiceover prologue to the TV shows inform us that Earth was "used up." The opening scene of *Serenity* adds some detail. Against a backdrop of generation ships fleeing what appear to be nuclear explosions on Earth, an Alliance teacher explains to her pupils that "Earth-that-was could no longer sustain our numbers, we were so many." She invokes Thomas Malthus's bleak calculus whereby a geometric increase in population will eventually overwhelm the slower (arithmetic) increase in people's ability to subsist from limited natural resources. Famine, plague, and war will be the "miserable" consequence, Malthus predicts. Such thinking had an important influence on studies sounding the alarm over environmental degradation after the Second World War. Paul R. and Anne Ehrlich, for example, describe a doomsday scenario of environmental collapse as the global population explodes in *The Population Bomb* (1968)—a book whose title supplies both the logic for the teacher's little history lesson and the iconography of the exploding planet accompanying it. Her encomium to the Alliance—"now everyone can enjoy the comforts and enlightenment of true civilization"—implies that the Alliance has solved Malthus's classic conundrum of political economy. Its utopian credentials are rooted in its economic probity.

That the teacher shamelessly miscasts an oppressive regime should not obscure her more salutary insight into the relationship between political economy and the prospects for "everyone" enjoying the benefits of civilization and enlightenment, a preoccupation of *Firefly* and a concern of political economic thought for centuries. Malthus merely followed long-standing principles of resource-management to their logical conclusion. If, as Adam Smith said, productive economies grow over time, accumulating capital stock, which in turn allows a more efficient consumption of resources capable of supporting a greater population, how could there not be an upper limit to resource usage or population increase? As we began to see in Chapter 2, the spiraling growth of capital and consumerism toward the end of the nineteenth century urged writers to probe such issues—until the rise of neoclassical theory allowed them to be ignored. In the last half century, the existential threat of climate change, population growth, overconsumption, and resource depletion has encouraged a broad coalition of economists to challenge the logic of capital accumulation anew, this time by promoting a closed or circular economy over ever-increasing production and consumption. The trope of the spaceship, which models so well the imperatives of a closed, finite system, has often figured in such discussions. These anxious discourses about the "used-up" planet we still call home help to contextualize *Firefly*'s concern with imagining various models of commonwealth—a concern that manifests in two distinct approaches across the trajectory of the show as *Serenity* privileges social capital over *Firefly*'s emphasis on physical capital.

Most approaches to *Firefly* emphasize its provocative mashup of science fiction and the Western. It is "*Stagecoach* in Space," replete with "narratives of the Western frontier."[1] Satirized though they may often be, the Western attributes of the *Firefly* universe rough out a contrast between the Alliance—the "Eastern" urban realm of wealth and excess—and the frontier ethic of Captain Malcolm Reynolds and his rugged crew aboard the ship Serenity. Government is there to "get in a man's way," Mal insists in the pilot, and his philosophy seems to extend to the ship's commercial activities. They drift around the frontier, drawn to "illegal salvage," as the Captain of the *Dortmunder* calls it in "Serenity: Part I," theft (of the medicine in "The Train Job"), and a variety of barely remunerative mercantile activities.[2] Meanwhile, the border planets and moons are home to autocrats such as Patience ("Serenity: Part II") and Rance Burgess ("Heart of Gold"), neo-slavery ("Jaynestown"), and poverty. As Sheriff Bourne says in "The Train Job," these are "tough times" on the border planets when it is "hard to find yourself work."[3] Still, what Matthew B. Hill describes as the show's fascination with "motion and mobility as a response to power" holds true for Serenity's commercial transactions.[4] Small-scale mercantilism transcends the corrupt attitude toward power on the rich inner planets, exemplified by the wealthy Atherton Wing on Persephone ("Shindig") and given a clearer anti-corporatist spin by the time *Serenity* moves toward holding the Alliance's Big Pharma responsible for the catastrophe on Miranda.

The "used-up" Earth in *Firefly*'s history of the interim suggests another more provocative context for Serenity's small-market mercantilism. In an early, famous essay of the environmental movement, economist Kenneth Boulding distinguished between the "cowboy economy," symbolic of the "reckless . . . exploitative" behavior characteristic of societies where resources are thought to be "illimitable," and the "spaceman economy," the closed economy of the future, in which the "earth has become a single spaceship, without unlimited reservoirs of anything," and in which throughput—the rate at which resources are used—must be "regarded as something to be minimized rather than maximized."[5] A "cowboy economy" evokes a frontier-fantasy whereby the exploitation of resources in one place leads to yet another frontier across which lie still more resources to be exploited. Boulding's point is that Earth does not contain illimitable space, no infinity of frontiers. Many other writers follow suit. In a metaphor addressed to the carrying capacity of Earth, Herman E. Daly observes that however efficiently one distributes the cargo of a ship, too much cargo will still sink it.[6] The central fact of the "scale of human activity relative to the biosphere" is that it has "grown too large," Herman E. Daly and John B. Cobb argue in their classic *For the Common Good* (1989).[7] Throughput has become unsustainable because natural resources are being exploited at an alarming rate and because waste sinks are already overloaded. Fears of a catastrophic collapse of the biosphere—that Whedon's "used-up" Earth of the past lies in our near future—are growing.

That reorientation toward thinking of economic activity within a closed system is in some ways consistent with economic logic. As economist Barbara Ward noted in her book *Spaceship Earth* (1966), imagining Earth as a "single spaceship" on a precarious voyage means we return to thinking of "rational behaviour [as] the condition of survival."[8] Ward and Boulding's work has been supported by later green economists challenging the fundamental orientation of neoclassical economics toward a science of markets, in which market behaviors define what it means to be a rational economic agent. They argue instead that a market system governed only by profits *counters* rational economic behavior by making it impossible to consider the social value of goods beyond value in exchange. "Modern economic thinking encourages us to price the world's natural resources incorrectly," for example, because it fails to price externalities into cost-benefit analyses of production.[9] The logic here is that the production of goods has hidden costs that are borne by others rather than by the producer. So the price of electricity from a coal plant represents coal and capital costs (the plant, replacing worn out machinery, distribution networks, and so on) but not the costs it passes on to others through pollution—harm to people's health, some of which can be quantified in terms of medical costs, and long-term harm to the biosphere, the effects of which are cumulative, unpredictable, and potentially catastrophic. Conversely, the opportunity costs of green energy, which are typically held to be greater than traditional forms of energy production, are defrayed by the benefits it bestows on people and the environment.

Though it is possible to think of pricing in externalities by using markets to reduce pollution through carbon taxes, cap-and-trade programs, and credits for using green energy, green economists tend to challenge the very logic of free-market capitalism. One avenue is to argue that human beings in fact "have limited wants and needs."[10] The possibility that humans are not driven by infinite wants underwrites a challenge to the neoclassical assumption that healthy economies must grow. Markets, if markets are to remain a necessary component of human economic life, would have to function without constantly expanding.[11] Green economists have instead increasingly argued in favor of *sufficiency* marked by a state of equilibrium between economic and ecological systems—a steady-state economy, as Herman Daly puts it—maintained by the lowest possible rates of throughput.[12] For people and nations characterized by overconsumption, a steady-state economy implies "degrowth" and the "end of progress."[13] A return to scarcity, while fostering new forms of sociality and subjectivity no longer transfixed by (over) consumption, may be the only way to avoid impending ecological collapse.[14] Here, the trope of the "single spaceship" is especially productive. Redirecting economics away from today's profits and toward the study of how to preserve a future in a closed system, the "spaceman economy" must focus on the "nature, extent, and quality . . . of the total capital stock," where capital stock means the total resources—resources, equipment, systems, and knowledge—that go toward producing new goods, conserving resources, and enhancing quality of life.

Firefly demonstrates a persistent allegiance to a "spaceman economy." Episode after episode draws attention to the effort it takes to keep Serenity, a single spaceship, on the move "without unlimited reservoirs of anything." Failing to sell the salvaged goods to Badger in "Serenity: Part I," for example, is what forces Mal to treat with the perilous Patience on the border moon Whitefall. They must sell this cargo, Mal explains, otherwise they are "dead in the water." After taking payment for the cargo and evading the Reavers, Wash observes that there is "just enough left in us to hit a fuel station." That ethos of using limited resources as efficiently as possible abounds. In the salvage scene early in the pilot, the crew is forced to "go to blackout" in an effort to evade the Alliance cruiser which sails past, an entire brightly lit city in space. "Shut it down—now—everything but the air," Mal tells Wash. Even the "crybaby"—the fake distress beacon Serenity uses to lure away the Alliance cruiser early in the pilot—looks to be a repurposed coffee can with "crybaby" written in ink and taped to the side. The imperatives of "making do" with a limited and difficult-to-replace capital stock—scavenging, salvaging, recycling, repurposing—are central to the show's ethos.

In this respect, the exemplary episode is "Out of Gas." In the dinner scene early in the episode we are told that the cake Kaylee bakes for Simon's birthday is "pretty much what we just had for dinner" because she "couldn't get ahold of no flour." When the catalyzer blows, leaving Serenity adrift without power, the crew is down to a couple of hours of air supply. The situation is of course a common *topos* in science fiction. It underwrites movies like *Apollo 13* (1995), *Gravity* (2013), the *Love, Death and Robots* (2019) animated short "Helping Hand," and *The Martian* (2015), among many others. The trope of Spaceship Earth is so compelling in part because of the ubiquity of such dramas. But it is worth thinking through the characteristics of the nearly "used up" spaceship as they apply to the *Firefly* universe. First, basic resources such as air, water, heat, and food are understood to be finite, and running out. Second, there is no way to regenerate enough resources from within a closed system without additional inputs of power. So the catalyzer that fixes Serenity's engine must come from another ship since Serenity carries no spare and cannot manufacture one. Third—and crucially for Boulding's argument about the importance of capital stock—there is no way to purchase any more of what is needed to survive. Invariably, and unsettlingly, markets cannot solve the problems of dead-in-the-water spaceships. "Out of Gas" approaches this *topos* in an unusual and revealing way. Mal thinks he has saved the ship by entering into a trade with the captain of the passing vessel. "I feel like maybe we can do business," says the other captain—before he and his crew turn out to be pirates. By episode's end, Mal gets the catalyzer and the other captain receives nothing in return. The promised trade is a sort of narrative bait and switch. It resists the *topos* long enough to mark still more clearly the return to its immutable logic: market interventions cannot solve the problem of diminishing resources in a closed system.

As Barbara Ward argues, the closed system of a "single spaceship" compels characters to obey the maximizing logic that is supposed to underwrite economic behavior: economic agents, faced with scarce resources, are supposed to act rationally and efficiently in their best interest. The Captain's solution to the crisis on board Serenity—sending away the two shuttles (with independent though brief reserves of air) with four crew each, while he remains behind to field any responses to their SOS—is aimed precisely at maximizing their chances by eking out their capital stock as long as possible. Modeling the conservation of resources as a condition of survival, "Out of Gas" therefore performs an important function in how we construe the economic principles of the Firefly universe. It underscores the imperatives of closed systems, favoring "crybaby" recycling over the enormous city-cruiser in the sky, small and sustainable commercial operations over the wealth of the Central planets, sustainability over waste. In the absence of markets, it also highlights the importance of use value. After the fire, there is literally no value in anything *but* oxygen; as Mark Watney finds on Mars, air has absolute (cardinal), not marginal (ordinal), value. Though Serenity's crew is constantly scrambling for "coin," as Mal puts it, the emphasis on use value in "Out of Gas" turns out to be a common refrain in *Firefly* episodes. In "The Train Job"—the first episode that actually aired, in 2002—Mal walks back the heist once he discovers the goods they stole for crime-lord Niska, contents unknown, are vital medicines bound for the sick people of Paradiso. That the cruiser's captain does not consider replacing the medicine suggests that its usefulness to the Alliance is not keeping the miners alive so much as keeping them beholden to the regime's pharmaceutical provisions. The medicine exchanges for the miners' labor, not their health.[15] Though the medicine is worth a "tidy fortune on the black market," as the Alliance cruiser captain remarks, Mal not only returns the medicine and Niska's earnest money, but he also returns the medicine to its use value—to the miners' health. Most critics read this scene as a celebration of Mal's frontier code of honor. If so, it also honors an ecological imperative. It reads the preservation of capital stock as the one truly legitimate aspiration, overriding the bottom line of profit motives.

The "illegal salvage" operation taking place at the start of what was to have been the opening episode of *Firefly*, "Serenity: Part I," exemplifies the nature of the show's inquiry into political economic principles. That the *Dortmunder*'s captain writes off both the derelict vessel and its cargo—like the miners at Paradiso—testifies to the Alliance's economic malfeasance. Coming just a few minutes of airtime after the information about the "used-up" Earth, it also lays the groundwork for a broader critique of the Alliance's corporate attitude toward using up people, goods, and resources. The crew of Serenity, in contrast, spend the two pilot episodes putting stolen/wasted goods back into productive circulation. In Whedon's original schema, the return of medicine to Paradiso in "The Train Job" consolidates what viewers would have already gleaned from the pilot: that the crew focuses on the utility of goods. The meanings of the derelict's cargo, however, follow a quite different symbolic itinerary than that of Paradiso's medicine. "The Train Job" defers the revelation of what the crew has stolen in such a way as to shock Mal ("son of a bitch!" he exclaims) along with the viewers. In "Serenity: Part I," Mal, the crew, and their potential buyers (Badger and Patience) know that the bars are "genuine A-Grade foodstuffs" packed with "protein, vitamins, and immunization supplements," capable of feeding a family for a month. But the episode goes out of its way to mislead viewers about the true nature of the derelict's cargo, which, at first sight, looks to be gold bullion marked with a government stamp. Patience even refers to it as "treasure" before the true nature of the bars is revealed—when she bites into it—more than an hour of airtime later.

That delayed disclosure has several important effects. It revises our estimation of the original responses to the "illegal salvage." We now see that the Alliance captain was passing up valuable food, but also that the episode has tricked us for an hour into taking an Alliance-eye view, as it were, of Serenity, in which Mal's crew no less than the Alliance are concerned with the bottom line—gold. Revealing that the gold bars are foodstuffs shows that we have been misled: value operates variably across this universe. The Alliance spaceship, a vast city in space, does not pause to recover cargo, whether gold or food, because it operates on the assumption that it possesses illimitable resources. In Boulding's terms, it represents a "cowboy economy." But foodstuffs, not gold, are "treasure" on a border planet so empty that Patience is "running this little world" alone and nutrient bars are at a premium. Put another way, whoever lives on Whitefall cannot eat gold. This is not to deny that the bars have value in exchange. Serenity requires Patience's "two hundred in platinum" for the goods to keep flying. Nonetheless, the border planet of Whitefall represents what the Alliance cruiser does not: a "spaceship economy" in which the utility of goods outweighs their value in exchange.

But the symbolic transposition of foodstuffs for gold is still more consequential in light of gold's long history as the representative and guarantor of the very concept of value. For Locke, we saw in Chapter 3, the "use of money," cornerstone of a civil society, emerged at the moment when a man wanted to trade food for a "piece of metal, pleased by its color." It was therefore easy to imagine gold as being not merely a measure or sign of value but as a material that when stumbled on accidentally in a society without money would be instantly recognizable as an "object of universal desire," the arche of intrinsic value. And since everyone would instantly recognize it, in all countries at all times, it would have, as one late-nineteenth-century gold advocate put it, "universal purchasing power."[16] Gold could therefore also be considered the arche of systems of exchange. As Martineau's first discourse on political economy concerning the true nature of wealth demonstrates, however, conditions of extreme abundance or scarcity could problematize the significance of gold. Locke's dwellers in a state of nature need no mechanism for exchange because food is perfectly abundant. Similarly, the Captain in "Life in the Wilds" wishes that the "people in England, who think that wealth consists in gold, and silver, and bank notes, would come here, and see how much their money is worth in our settlement."[17] The answer for the settlers, their capital stock wiped out, is nothing. Scarcity on the veldt therefore puts pressure on the notion that gold has "universal purchasing power." The first cause of wealth, Martineau argues, is labor and the subsistence that labor produces—though the Captain urges the erstwhile merchant to hold on to his gold since it will become valuable again once markets are instituted, as stage theory predicts must happen to any society requiring more efficient methods of exchange.

One and a half centuries later green economists marshaled similar-sounding arguments to focus attention on the problem of market capitalism and the short-term pursuit of profit in an era of ever-scarcer resources. Extending the "spaceship" logic pioneered by Boulding and Ward, Buckminster Fuller in "Operating Manual for Spaceship Earth" (1969) considers the long-term effects of pollution in terms of the shipwreck of a gold-laden rich man who finds that he "can't extend his life with that sort of wealth" because gold cannot be eaten.[18] True wealth, Fuller argues, is our "organized capability to cope effectively with the environment in sustaining our healthy regeneration."[19] Fuller and other green economists here are rooted in Martineau's political economic logic. In an isolated region—the veldt in Martineau's case, the Earth in Fuller's—true wealth inheres in labor and capital stock. Gold is worthless in comparison to foodstuffs. But green economics follows this logic to wholly different conclusions. Martineau's settlers expect that they will repeat the path already laid out for them into a realm of capital accumulation, markets, and the more complex social relations attending them. Green economics instead looks to market capitalism and its privileging of gold (i.e., profits) over resources as the cause of crises to come—dwindling resources and increasing damage to the environment. Just as Martineau's settlers cannot buy their subsistence, markets today cannot buy a new biosphere.

The most compelling historical locus for discourses about gold is late-nineteenth-century US populism, which shares some intellectual ground with green economics and underwrites many aspects of Whedon's project. Populism was rooted in the Farmers' Alliance, which in 1892 drew together a loose coalition of Western mining interests and southern and mid-western agricultural associations to form the People's Party. Supporting Democrat William Jennings Bryan's run for the presidency in 1896, it began to fracture after William McKinley's victory. The Populist alliance assailed what in the nineteenth century took the place of Whedon's Alliance: the entrenched interests of finance capitalists controlling markets from the urban centers of the North-East, "ruthless corporations and trusts" that exercised monopoly power over the mechanisms of trade and commerce, and "banking, railroad, and other 'interests' that unduly influenced the political process."[20] Populists also blamed the "tight-money 'goldbug' policies of the financial establishment for unemployment, low farm prices, and growing indebtedness."[21] In many respects gold was populism's discursive center. Hard-working farmers were "the helpless victim[s] . . . of the tyrannical power of gold" on the premise that a small amount of gold specie allowed it to be hoarded by North-Eastern money powers.[22] "Holders of gold, by making money scarce or plenty at will, become masters of the situation," lamented one writer in *The Arena*, a populist journal.[23] The official policy of the Populists therefore became "free silver" in hopes that backing currency with silver as well as gold (i.e., bimetallism) would loosen the grip of North-Eastern financial centers. Silver "was the money of the people," as one writer said—"the other, of the rich."[24]

Gold was therefore accounted the mechanism used by late-nineteenth-century money powers to subject farmers and other laborers to "legalized robbery." It also symbolized a broader crisis of value. As William Jennings Bryan put it in his famous "cross of gold" speech, the "idle holders of idle capital" concentrated wealth unproductively in the hands of a few.[25] Populism sought to return the nation to what it considered the true producers of value—those who worked in the fields in particular—but also to the bedrock political economic principle that capital represented the stored-up potential of labor. Financiers in short were not merely robbing a class of people but actively thwarting the potential of capital, which functions best when accumulating, growing, and circulating to the benefit of the entire commonwealth. Silver would help to free that capital by putting it into the pockets of the country's real laborers. At the same time, many populists argued, the value of an inflated currency would be pinned to real agricultural production, thus collating capital with capital stock. To rephrase one argument: if a dollar buys a bushel of wheat, then a bushel of wheat buys the dollar; to inflate the money supply so that a bushel of wheat costs two dollars places more money in the pockets of farmers but leaves the original bushel of wheat unchanged. Wheat, not money, becomes the arbiter of value. The food unit therefore should be the standard upon which the currency system rests since food is the "sole common denominator of commodities; it is that which creates values, alone permits values, and by its own scarcity destroys values."[26] Despite many differences between late-nineteenth-century populism and late-twentieth-century green movements—silverite proclivities are one, favoring the expansion of (money) capital another—they share a decided anti-corporatist emphasis and the presumption that value must be grounded in environmental conditions, resources, and produce, not price points in the market. As Fuller shows, gold continues to be of great symbolic value to environmental analysis because it exemplifies how value in a closed system can be so badly misconstrued.

The salvage scene that begins *Firefly* maps in important respects onto Populist thought. It helps us to understand why the Alliance cruiser looks like a vast city—Wall Street in space—and why the cruiser is so indifferent to the "gold" bars sitting inertly on the derelict transport. Gold in bank vaults populists understood as "idle capital," which buttressed the power of finance capitalism precisely by *not* allowing capital to fulfil its full potential in the commonwealth. Because capital wished to be free and therefore productive, financiers were forced to hoard capital (gold) to maintain control over the system. What the cruiser captain calls "illegal salvage" thus plays a similar role to Populist calls to make silver into legal specie. Just as freeing silver was supposed to liberate the full power of capital, the crew of Serenity frees the stored-up potential of "treasure," which is worth so much more than when legally, but unproductively, hoarded on the derelict. Mal and the crew are not just salvaging goods: they are extending the power of capital to numbers of people who would otherwise go without its transformative power. They are also realizing the stored-up value of the gold bars in terms of nutritious food. The exchanges on Whitefall—gold bars for money, and gold transmuted into food—are not just to make "coin," nor just to add market value to an unproductive cargo, nor just to make a market of edible goods benefitting real people. It is also, like the exemplary bushel of wheat, to realize the value of "gold" bars in terms of the "Grade A foodstuffs" which, we suddenly see on Whitefall, *they have been all along*. One function of the gold/foodstuffs trick is to deny that the value of the bars ever was rooted in an inert metal—but also to demonstrate how easily one might be transfixed by a false measure of value. Indeed, the first season ends in "Objects in Space" with a similar trick, persuading us for a moment, as the disembodied voice of River speaks through Serenity, that the inert metal has come alive.

Firefly/*Serenity*'s orientation toward populism is perhaps on clearest display in its mercantile endeavors, which provides the economic rationale for what Mal conceives of as Serenity's main task—to "keep flying"—and generates a broad and important discourse on resource-distribution. For Populist writers, what caused widespread poverty and labor agitation in the United States was not a failure to produce enough wealth but the fact that its "mountains of wealth . . . poured into the coffers of the idle and affluent."[27] Since a "nation's prosperity does not lie so much in the amount of its wealth as in a just distribution of that wealth among those who have produced it," the solution to economic ills was not to force hardworking laborers to produce more but to distribute produce more fairly.[28] For Populists the railroad became the most prominent symbol of the corrupting influence of North-Eastern money powers. Colluding to raise transport charges rather than competing with each other, the railroad companies became a de facto monopoly, its owners "baron robbers who control the highways of commerce."[29] The network that was charged with facilitating the movement of goods from fields to markets instead placed its "relentless, remorseless and unyielding grasp . . . upon every avenue of trade and commerce."[30]

In *Firefly*, one function of Serenity's peregrinations is to highlight the Alliance's relentless grasp on this world's commerce. The episode that features a railroad, "The Train Job," is exemplary. Returning the medicine to the people of Paradiso following the heist does not merely restore it to its use value. Mal's actions underscore the Alliance's refusal to send another shipment, which puts on display its absolute control over the railroad, the towns it serves, and the goods it distributes. Mal offers a version of the Populist critique of monopoly power to Sheriff Bourne in Paradiso: "That sounds like the Alliance," he says sarcastically, "Unite the planets under one rule." That the mines at Paradiso will presumably become *less* prosperous as miners succumb to Bowden's disease reproduces the Populists' point about the railroad. Monopoly control over the "highways of commerce" grants a few "baron robbers" control over the wealth farmers produce—but at the expense of the nation's prosperity. As journalist Henry Demarest Lloyd put it in the aptly titled *Wealth Against Commonwealth* (1894), monopoly powers "assert the right, for their private profit, to regulate the consumption of the people of the necessaries of life," driving up profits by controlling distribution and limiting supply, but in the process wrecking the "true law of business," which is that "all must pursue the interest of all."[31]

"Shindig" extends this political economic rationale. At the beginning of the episode, Badger draws attention to the "conundrum" that Warrick Harrow, one of Persephone's richest men, will not trust him with some "property he wants to sell off-planet, to fetch a higher price." Mal quickly grasps a more important conundrum of political economy: Harrow turns to smugglers to offload his herd of cattle because the "local powers won't let him sell off-world." In one of the best (and few) essays to take on Whedon's concept of political economy in *Firefly*, Mercedes Lackey is correct to argue that smuggling goods is a form of collusion with the Alliance. The crew of Serenity, after all, helps Harrow reap a much higher profit from selling his cattle to the "backwater" border planet of Jiangyin (described in the next episode, "Safe"). But Populist thought helps us to add important nuances to this argument. First, carrying the goods off-world maximizes utility and profits for everyone involved. Jiangyin gets the cattle that can thrive on its self-described "Prairie Paradise"; Serenity makes money; Badger gets a cut from brokering the deal; and Harrow makes a greater profit even with Serenity's transportation costs factored in. Second, as a corollary, "smuggling" follows clear political economic principles. Cattle have more utility on Jiangyin than on Persephone; hence the higher price. But the higher price can only be realized because of competition, which *increases* the total amount of capital in play by breaking the attempt of the "local powers" on Persephone to monopolize trade. Third, again as a corollary, Harrow's actions recognize the illogic of the Alliance's attempts to control commerce. Whatever economic benefits the Alliance might have reaped from a legal sale of cattle on Persephone would surely have been greater had it been possible for Harrow to sell his cattle legally off-world. The same logic applies to healthy miners at Paradiso—and, indeed, to millions of people on Miranda. Smuggling—and withholding medicine, and genocide—is a sign that Alliance attempts to control the distribution of goods is ultimately counter-productive for their own bottom line.

The episodes of *Firefly* present a compelling political economic counterweight to the nightmare of a "used-up" Earth in the show's history of the interim. Life on the ship Serenity confronts the Alliance's fantasy of super-abundant resources—dozens of planets and hundreds of moons—with a version of "Spaceship Earth" emphasizing utility and sustainability. *Firefly* underscores creative recycling (the crybaby, even dead bodies that transform Serenity into what looks like a Reaver ship), the intrinsic value of food, air and energy, and a staunch challenge to control over the means of production and distribution networks by the Alliance and the Blue Sun corporation. It is enough that they are "still flying," as Mal says at very end of the pilot. But the show also values what it takes to keep flying, which is rooted in a careful and judicious use of capital stock: air, food, fuel. Those intricate connections between Serenity the ship and the concept of Spaceship Earth resonate with the show's history of the interim. "Should've kept better care of her," Kaylee laments when the power goes off in "Out of Gas." That jibes with Mal's "one purpose," which is, he tells Simon early in the movie, to "keep this boat in the air." Serenity represents what must happen if the Firefly 'verse is not one day to be "used up" like "Earth-that-was." And it represents what must happen if our "spaceship Earth" is not to become a real prequel to the show's imagined history—Earth-that-was in the show, Earth-that-still-is during the airing of the show.

The movie *Serenity*, however, rounds out the *Firefly* 'verse with a counter-narrative: an economic model associated not with the preservation of capital stock nor even the movement of material goods but with the production of symbolic capital. To be sure, *Serenity* begins in a familiar place. Losing their primary buffer panel on entry to a planet, Mal says to Kaylee "you told me the entry couplings would hold for another week." "That was 6 months ago, cap'n," Kaylee replies, reminding us of the ship's chronic capital stock maintenance issues stretching back to the disaster of "Out of Gas." But this passing reference proves to be the last. The ideological vector shifts toward Mr. Universe and a signal beamed to every screen in the 'verse. Whedon's shift to screen culture certainly makes *Serenity* into a potent critique of "corporate control and globalization" exercised through the "commercial structure of TV production."[32] A Blue Sun commercial at the beginning of the movie, for example, exemplifies the Alliance's fetish of surveillance and control. But Mal's broadcast uses the same technology to amplify and "globalize" the evidence of the Alliance's genocide on Miranda. Nominally his broadcast is tied to physical infrastructure. But that one site reaches out to the entire 'verse, overriding any physical obstacle the Alliance tries to place in its way, bypassing problems like blown catalyzers and missing buffer panels. As Mr. Universe puts it, "Can't stop the signal, Mal . . . I go everywhere." We seem to return here to the "illimitable" spaces of the "cowboy economy" via a new electronically mediated economy using virtually no resources.

The historical contexts informing this shift in emphasis from scarce capital stock to unlimited capital expenditures, where value begins to inhere in money-capital rather than material goods and resources, are also rooted in the late nineteenth century. In the last three decades of the century the rise of consumer society shifted economists' attention from thinking that "scarcity was a relation of productive forces to the earth" to thinking of it as a function of the mind, a "consequence of the insatiability of human desires."[33] Abandoning the presumption that "market relations were anchored in something more solid" such as the "labor and tools and materials required to produce them," neoclassical economics "unmoored the subjective process of buying and selling from the objective cost of what was being bought and sold. The value of anything was simply what people were willing to pay for it."[34] New concepts of humans as creatures of infinite wants required reconceiving the nature and function of capital. Capital under a regime of *limitless* accumulation put great pressure on classical interpretations, which assumed that the build-up of capital over time gradually decreased or stabilized. Many late-nineteenth-century writers began to challenge the notion that capital accumulation could or should have a limit. William Graham Sumner, for example, argued that capital can no longer be thought of in terms of a finite "common stock"; "human energy stored or accumulated" in the form of skill, knowledge, technology, social organization, and money generates "millions more of wealth, many-fold greater" than the investment.[35] George Gunton too insisted that there is "no limit" to human desire, for the "more it gets, the more it wants; the more it does, the more it aspires to do."[36] Society benefits economically from the ever-increasing consumption deriving from an "enlarged market" and the spiraling capital production it allows.[37]

Along the same lines, Henry George proposed in the influential *Progress and Poverty* (1879) that "wealth is greatest where population is densest" because the "more minute becomes the subdivision of labor, the greater the economies of production and distribution."[38] The efficiencies accruing to the division of labor among people who live near each other will lead eventually to great cities—the "type of modern growth"—where a highly developed infrastructure and the benefits of rapid intellectual exchange accrue an escalating value.[39] Cities become an ever more concentrated source of social capital because "invention and improvement [are] constantly adding to the efficiency of labor"—and "we can assign no limits to the progress of invention."[40] But at least two major problems appear in George's analysis. One, which he addresses everywhere, is that concentrated capital allows massive social inequities: cities generate untold wealth while allowing a few property-holders to siphon off most of it in rent. George's solution—a single tax aimed at distributing the rent from land to all citizens—is the main argument of *Progress and Poverty*. The other, which George barely acknowledges, is that humans participating in the limitless increase of social capital, once situated within a rational distribution of wealth, will want to restrain unlimited desire. Just as people at a feast with more than enough to eat will be constrained by the limits of their appetite, so, George argues, it is natural that "they should not be greedy of wealth" if that wealth is justly distributed.[41] Conceiving of society as a healthy organism constrained by a limited appetite ensures that increases in social capital will not take a corresponding toll on physical capital. George seems to acknowledge inadvertently that his economic theory, being fundamentally rooted in population pressure on land, might still have to confront Malthusian principles once the global population doubles—or quadruples.

George's assumption that increasing knowledge eventuating in new technologies might replace worn out capital stock and diminishing physical resources is common today. Boulding grants advancing knowledge an important function in the spaceman economy: "any technological change which results in the maintenance of a given stock total with a lessened throughput . . . is clearly a gain."[42] Grander claims have been made. The ITER Tokamak, for example, currently under construction in France, hopes to make nuclear fusion commercially viable by around 2025—an accomplishment that would by providing endless amounts of clean energy solve the world's energy and climate crises at a stroke. George's principles are perhaps realized most compellingly—because the technology already exists—in claims that new communications technologies will "fundamentally alter relationships of power in society" by blowing "apart all the monopolies, hierarchies, pyramids, and power grids of established industrial societies."[43] Jeremy Rifkin's solution for the specter of a "used-up" planet is to highlight the role of knowledge and information amplified "many-fold greater," as Sumner put it, through electronic media. He envisions that the "coming together of the Communications Internet with the fledgling Energy Internet and Logistics Internet in a seamless twenty-first-century intelligent infrastructure—the Internet of Things" will, by rationalizing the production of energy and goods, bring their marginal cost down to near zero.[44] New integrated global networks will create a revolution in economic principles since they will bring about "entirely new way of organizing economic life in an age characterized by abundance rather than scarcity."[45] And they will create new forms of radical democracy—indeed, the "democracy of networks will be contagious and impossible to quarantine"—characterized by a "Collaborative Commons" in which the internet will facilitate problem-solving on a global scale.[46]

In using Mr. Universe's unstoppable signal to put out the recording of what happened on Miranda, the end of *Serenity* follows this new economic logic by embracing the astonishing power of electronically mediated social capital. Mal's battle against the Alliance begins with interplanetary war, the glimpse of the battle of Serenity valley afforded us in the TV pilot depicting an immense outpouring and destruction of human and physical capital. He ends it with a podcast. Though the Alliance may not be overthrown—the Operative calls the fallout an "uproar," Mal says it will not be long before the 'verse "falls back asleep"—the effects of the recording are incalculable. The signal circumvents what now appears to be Serenity's overreliance on capital stock in the TV episodes—a crybaby coffee can, a broken catalyzer, a herd of cattle in the hold. It also circumvents Alliance power as embodied in the cruiser that sails past the derelict early in "Serenity: Part I," a vast city in space showcasing George's vision of how to out-maneuver Malthusian imperatives by way of ever-more concentrated human capital. By the end of *Serenity*, the Alliance cruiser turns out to be locked into Earth's nineteenth century. It has no power against the "signal." In fact, it reproduces George's inability to imagine an economy freed from the exigencies of land and land-based economic systems. George thought spatially in terms of population density, resource usage, and differential land values. The massive infrastructure that supports the Alliance cruiser's disciplining of civilian populations also requires a spatially organized view of authority. Value pertains to whether one lives on the Central planets or on the border planets or moons.

Mal's signal overrides the Alliance's emphasis on land, physical capital, and value coordinated with space. It ignores distinctions between sites that are supposed to represent massive concentrations of capital (the Core planets) and those that are resource-rich but capital-poor (the Rim). The result is a collaborative commons, which is a 'verse suddenly organized around forms of radical democracy in which, because knowledge is distributed impartially and instantaneously, everyone has the chance to participate equally in its outcomes. Once the recording gets out "there's a universe of folk that are gonna know" what happened on Miranda, Mal says; "They're gonna see it." Widespread "protests, riots" are one consequence, the Operative reveals, along with "cries for a recall of the entire Parliament"—an important addendum since those cries are aimed precisely at structures of centered power. The signal, in short, epitomizes the virtues of a zero marginal cost society. It requires a relatively tiny amount of infrastructure, costs virtually nothing, reaches everyone, and creates potentially vast changes. Capital reaches an extraordinary concentration, achieving George's vision but denying his premise that land produces wealth. It also challenges George's premise that, once sated, the human and social organism will simply stop wanting more. With Mr. Universe's broadcast technology in his hands, Mal, as he says, simply wishes to reach everyone in the universe.

George, Boulding, and Rifkin frame the problem of *Firefly*'s relevance to our own economic situation neatly: Can increasing social capital on a closed spaceship make up for ever-degrading capital stocks? Whedon's analysis seems to change over the trajectory of the show. Following the transposition of foodstuffs for "gold" in the pilot, many of the TV episodes adopt a populist rhetoric that aligns neatly with Boulding's focus on "capital stock" rather than "capital" in the pursuit of environmentally sustainable systems. *Serenity*, a few years later, shifts its emphasis to symbolic capital, replacing cattle, air, and fuel with virtual signs, knowledge, and information. Two factors, however, militate against accepting an "Internet of Things" as the endpoint of *Firefly*/*Serenity*'s political economy. One is that we never witness the "universe" of people who are supposed to have received the unstoppable signal. The Operative's increasing shock as Mal forces him to watch the Miranda recording stands in for that absent community on the grounds that if the *Operative* can be so transformed by the experience then we need have no doubt about everyone else in the 'verse. But the collective—the community on whose behalf Mal struggles—seems imaginable in the abstract but unrepresentable in fact. The virtual community remains wholly virtual, unlike the crew of "Out of Gas," whose emotional responses to the crisis are powerfully dramatized. The second factor is that the very last moments of *Serenity* return us to the ship taking off for a 'verse of dozens of planets and hundreds of moons—along with a panel that whirls away and will presumably need to be replaced. In walking back what appears to be a logical movement from capital stock to symbolic capital as the show unfolds from TV to the movie screen, the *Firefly* 'verse seems to end by putting countervailing economic principles toward inconclusive, even incoherent, outcomes. One sees that Whedon has chosen riveting characters and dramatic scenes over trying to represent the circulation of symbolic capital. We should note that this strategy is also discursively appropriate to "Earth-that-was"—that is to say, to Earth-that-is—to the hesitations, confusions, debates, and barely articulated anxieties marking this historical moment as a spaceship economy approaches, whether we want it or not.

NOTES

1. Fred Erisman, "*Stagecoach* in Space: The Legacy of *Firefly*," *Extrapolation* 47, no. 2 (2006), www.proquest.com/scholarly-journals/stagecoach-space-legacy-firefly/docview/234918195/se-2; Garrett LeCoq, "'Let's be Bad Guys': (Re)Visualizing (In) Justice on the Western Frontier in Joss Whedon's *Firefly/Serenity*," *Annual Review of Interdisciplinary Justice Research* 5 (2016): 99, canlii.ca/t/t9kw.

2. I take quotations from the *Firefly* episode scripts collected on firefly2002.weebly.com/scripts.html. These are organized by episode; there are no page numbers.

3. Taken from the fan-based script, n.p., www.myths.com/pub/tv/firefly/script-train-job.html.

4. Matthew B. Hill, "'I Am a Leaf on the Wind': Cultural Trauma and Mobility in Joss Whedon's *Firefly*," *Extrapolation* 50, no. 3 (Fall 2009): 501, www.proquest.com/scholarly-journals/i-am-leaf-on-wind-cultual-trauma-mobility-joss/docview/234919122/se-2.

5. Kenneth E. Boulding, "The Economics of the Coming Spaceship Earth," 1966: 7–8, arachnid.biosci.utexas.edu/courses/THOC/Readings/Boulding_SpaceshipEarth.pdf.

6. Cited in Frank Fischer and Maarten A. Hajer, *Living with Nature: Environmental Politics as Cultural Discourse* (Oxford: Oxford University Press, 1999), 40.

7. John B. Cobb and Herman E. Daly, *For the Common Good: Redirecting the Economy Toward Community, The Environment, and a Sustainable Future* (Boston: Beacon Press, 1989), 2.

8. Barbara Ward, *Spaceship Earth* (New York: Columbia University Press, 1966), 15.

9. Graeme P. Maxton, *The End of Progress: How Modern Economics Has Failed Us* (New York: John Wiley, 2011), 17.

10. Wolfgang Hoeschele, *The Economics of Abundance: A Political Economy of Freedom, Equity, and Sustainability* (Farnham, UK: Gower, 2010), 1.

11. Alan Gilpin broaches this argument in *Environmental Economics: A Critical Overview* (New York: John Wiley, 2000), 93.

12. Herman Daly, *Toward a Steady-State Economy* (San Francisco: W.H. Freeman, 1973).

13. I take the term from Maxton's *The End of Progress*.

14. The phrase "return to scarcity" is taken from H. C. Coombs's well-known *The Return of Scarcity: Strategies for an Economic Future* (Cambridge: Cambridge University Press, 1990).

15. As Jocelyn Sakal Froese and Laura Buzzard note, the Alliance operates under a neoliberal metric in which "bodies are valued only as sources of profit." "'I Mean for us to Live. The Alliance Won't Have That': New Frontierism and Biopower in *Firefly/Serenity*," *Slayage*, 13, no. 2 (Summer 2015): n.p., ISSN: 1546–9212.

16. David Wells, *Robinson Crusoe's Money* (New York: Harper, 1876), 40.

17. Harriet Martineau, *Illustrations of Political Economy* (1832; reprint London: Warnes and Routledge, 1859), 23.

18. Buckminster Fuller, *Operating Manual for Spaceship Earth*, 1969: 27, designsciencelab.com/resources/OperatingManual_BF.pdf.

19. Fuller, *Operating Manual*, 27.

20. Charles Postel, *The Populist Vision* (Oxford: Oxford University Press, 2007), 5.

21. Postel, *Populist Vision*, 5.

22. Leonidas L. Polk, leader of the Farmers' Alliance and a founder of the Populist Party, quoted in Gretchen Ritter, *Greenbacks and Goldbugs: The Antimonopoly Tradition and the Politics of Finance in America* (Cambridge: Cambridge University Press, 1997), 180.

23. John Davis, "The Money Question," *Arena* 5 (April 1892): 545, archive.org/details/ArenaMagazine-Volume05/page/n567/mode/2up.

24. W.H. Harvey, *Coin's Financial School* (Chicago: Coin, 1894), 8–9.

25. William Jennings Bryan, Speech to the Democratic National Convention, July 9, 1896, n.p., www.americanrhetoric.com/speeches/williamjenningsbryan1896dnc.htm.

26. Miles M. Dawson, "The True Basis of Currency," *The Arena*, 6 (1892): 91, books.google.com/books?id=hCdNAQAAMAAJ&pg=PA84&source=gbs_toc_r&cad=3#v=onepage&q&f=false.

27. Sarah E. V. Emery, *Seven Financial Conspiracies Which Have Enslaved the American People* (1887; reprint Westport, CN: Hyperion, 1975), 7.

28. Emery, *Seven*, 8.

29. N. B. Ashby, *The Riddle of the Sphinx* (Iowa: Industrial Publishing, 1890), 35.

30. W. Scott Morgan, *The History of the Wheel and Alliance and the Impending Revolution* (Hardy, Arkansas: W. Scott Morgan, 1889; Madison: University of Wisconsin, 2008), 16.

31. Henry D. Lloyd, *Wealth Against Commonwealth* (New York: Harper and Brothers, 1894; Englewood Cliffs, NJ: Prentice-Hall, 1963), 1, 160.

32. Erin Giannini, "'It Doesn't Mean What You Think': River Tam as Embodied Culture Jam." *Slayage* 13, no. 2 (Summer 2015): n.p., www.academia.edu/14061880/_It_Doesn_t_Mean_What_You_Think_River_Tam_as_Embodied_Culture_Jam.

33. Regenia Gagnier, *The Insatiability of Human Wants: Economics and Aesthetics in Market Society* (Chicago: University of Chicago Press, 2000), 4.

34. Jeffrey Sklansky, *The Soul's Economy: Market Society and Selfhood in American Thought, 1820-1920* (Chapel Hill: University of North Carolina Press, 2002), 9.

35. William Graham Sumner, *What Social Classes Owe to Each Other* (1883; reprint New Haven: Yale University Press, 1934), 38.

36. George Gunton, *Principles of Social Economics* (New York: G.P. Putnams, 1891), 439

37. Gunton, *Principles*, 78.

38. George, *Progress*, 45.

39. George, Progress, 75.

40. George, *Progress*, 48.

41. George, *Progress*, 75.

42. Boulding, "Spaceship," 8.

43. Darin Barney, *Prometheus Wired: the Hope for Democracy in the Age of Network Technology* (Chicago: University of Chicago Press, 2000), 19.

44. Jeremy Rifkin, "The Rise of Anti-Capitalism," *The New York Times*, March 15, 2014, www.nytimes.com/2014/03/16/opinion/sunday/the-rise-of-anti-capitalism.html11.

45. Rifkin, "Rise of Anti-Capitalism," n.p.

46. Barney, *Prometheus*, 19; Rifkin, "Rise of Anti-Capitalism," n.p.

Chapter Six

Feast Fables

The Bioeconomics of Turkeys and Roast Beast

"We must eat to live," writes US poet laureate Joy Harjo in her poem "Perhaps the World Ends Here." She has in mind sustenance for the body but also cultural life, the life of communities, which, the poem avers, commences at the most mundane of sites: "The world begins at a kitchen table" (1.1). As Harjo recognizes in the poem, food can represent an astonishing variety of cultural phenomena. An "entire semiotic system of political, cultural, and social significations" emerges from food practices.[1] Food is associated with important political and spiritual practices; it constructs and perpetuates gender roles; it is central to family and communal life and important rites of passage; it signifies and perpetuates important traditions; it establishes national and ethnic characteristics—and differences. In a consumer society, argues Carole Counihan, a host of "class, race, ethnic, and gender boundaries are maintained by eating differences."[2] Food can also represent the economic practices of a body politic. As Catherine Gallagher puts it in her discussion of "bioeconomics," "issues of bodily well-being and of economic circulation are frequently articulated both through and against each other."[3] Metaphors of eating and drinking have been used to describe characteristics of the body politic for millennia. Socrates was the first to raise the question that Harjo wittily invokes: do we eat to live or live to eat? Is the point of existence to subsist or to enjoy? Is the point of socioeconomic organization to provide subsistence or surplus? What then is the ideal shape of the body, or of the body politic?

Historically, one common vector for bioeconomic reasoning has been the fable. Fables such as Aesop's "The Belly and the Members" can, as Annabel Patterson argues in *Fables of Power* (1991), possess substantial political content and work to deconstruct hegemonic representations of the polity. Her "historicized poetics of the fable" shows that its form provided a symbolic discourse that was deployed in a variety of ways from the Renaissance to the nineteenth century as a "medium of political analysis and communication, especially in the form of a communication from or on behalf of the politically powerless."[4] Aesop's fable about the "Belly and the Members," for example, has the hands, mouth, and teeth rebelling against the belly until it "consented to take its proper share of the work." Finding that they begin to lose energy, the members end up realizing that "even the Belly in its dull quiet way was doing necessary work for the Body, and that all must work together or the Body will go to pieces."[5] The fable, Patterson notes, provided a "symbol of the distribution of wealth in the body politic."[6] Though it seemed to favor the claims of centralized power (the Belly), however indolent or ungrateful it might appear, it could also be used to affirm the demands made by the rebellious members. In the twenty-first century, for example, it would be possible to read the Belly as the mass of United States' consumers over against members such as the laborers in Amazon warehouses—"fulfilment centers"—who are forced to work manically against the clock to "fill" the belly. Fables are malleable and incorporative, responsive to changing socioeconomic circumstances.

Classical political economy also incorporated bioeconomic strategies, persistently invoking narratives about food production and distribution to explain its economic principles. Bioeconomic thinking underpins, for example, Henry George's narrative of developing civilizations, which begins, as we saw in Chapter 1, with the isolated human body forced inefficiently to perform every task for itself. But the end of his narrative imagines an ideal economy supporting a body politic in terms of the healthy appetites and satisfactions of the body. The "social organism," for example, "secretes . . . the necessary amount of capital just as the human organism in a healthy condition secretes the requisite fat"; "Accumulated wealth seems to play just about such a part in relation to the social organism as accumulated nutriment does to the physical organism."[7] Though for George there is no theoretical limit to capital growth, accumulation nevertheless obeys a principle of homeostasis: the body "in a healthy condition" would not want, or be able, to consume to excess. George and Harjo similarly employ the human body to metaphorize constraints on consumption and on the body politic that might be presumed to support it.

Today's mainstream economics, oriented toward mathematical modeling, avoids such overt metaphorizing. Perhaps a faint echo exists in the important concept of Purchasing Power Parity, which depends on the metaphor of a basket of goods whose comparative value can be assessed in different locales. Today's popular narratives, however, relentlessly employ food to represent the status of the body politic: its health, wealth, or otherwise.

Animated animal movies, today's beast fables, are an excellent example. So are feast fables. Feasts assemble a diverse array of people around food in such a manner as to publicly stage acts of production, distribution, and consumption; how food arrives at the table, who gets to eat first, and who presides, all speak to the specific socioeconomic arrangements governing everyday social relations. I begin with two well known, even iconic, illustrations of Thanksgiving—Thomas Nast's "Uncle Sam's Thanksgiving Dinner" (1869) and Norman Rockwell's "Freedom from Want" (1943)—both of which pose so well the political economic implications of the feast fable. I then consider several late-nineteenth-century Thanksgiving stories, which were so popular as to constitute an entire genre, and then forward to some versions of the Grinch franchise, which shifts the Thanksgiving iconographic tradition to Christmas. I conclude with an account of Joy Harjo's "Perhaps the World Ends Here," a "giving thanks" poem that recuperates a long discourse of feast fables while reminding us of what those fables overlook.

Thomas Nast's famous depiction of "Uncle Sam's Thanksgiving Dinner," published to celebrate Thanksgiving in 1869, serves as one touchstone for this long and complex discourse.[8] At a large Thanksgiving table, surrounded by portraits of George Washington, Abraham Lincoln, and Ulysses S. Grant, statues representing liberty and justice, and under a large painting pronouncing "Welcome," Uncle Sam stand at the head of the table carving a fine turkey. Flanking him are a diverse population of races and ethnicities, many engaged in lively conversation. A Radical Republican, Nast uses the Thanksgiving table to advocate for equality among the members of a polyglot nation. The cartoon no doubt strikes a delicate balance between offering a place at the table to a variety of people and overwriting history. In representing a Native American sitting to the left of Uncle Sam, for example, Nast seems to elide a history of conflict and expropriation of lands that was still proceeding apace under the symbolic aegis of—Uncle Sam.

Nonetheless, compositionally the cartoon sets out to represent an idealized United States *and* an abstract body politic. The turkey symbolizing prosperity is more than large enough to feed the assembled multitude, which may be why no one is eyeing the food particularly hungrily; indeed, if the enormous turkey may be taken as the product of prior prosperity, there would be no reason for anyone to be hungry in the first place. The oval or perhaps (depending on perspective) circular table implies equitable seating arrangements and equal distribution; even Uncle Sam, in charge of the carving and thus the size of portions, is standing oddly off-center.[9] A fable of national prosperity and just distribution, Nast's cartoon speaks to the other works considered here. Representations of the family gathered around traditional foods—pies, puddings, and the ubiquitous turkey—constantly invoke an imaginary body politic situated within diverse economic relations and real or fabulous or politically persuasive histories. Turkeys (and roast beasts) function as a bioeconomic currency in representations of Thanksgiving and Christmas. Cooked, carved, distributed in appropriate amounts, and consumed, turkey flesh becomes a symbolic currency for adjudicating between various people's needs and wants, for assigning meaning and value to numerous social relations, and for exchanging them, in the sense of passing them round the table along with the platters of food so that the feasters at the table, and the readers or viewers along with them, come to a better understanding of status, gendered roles, social functions, and economic priorities.

Norman Rockwell's illustrations—notably hundreds of covers for the *Saturday Evening Post* over nearly five decades—lay claim as much as anyone's to conveying the cultural mainstream of America or, at least, Americana. Long derided as the classic purveyor of American sentiment and kitsch, commentators of late have begun to appraise a more complicated figure.[10] "As far as many Americans were concerned," writes one biographer Laura Claridge, he "exemplified the country's heartland; he was its 'everyman.'"[11] In another biography, Deborah Solomon argues that his subject was "American life . . . steeped in the we-the-people, communitarian ideals of America's founding in the eighteenth century."[12] Those credentials are on complex display in "Freedom from Want."[13] The painting illustrates one of President Theodore Roosevelt's Four Freedoms—freedom of speech and religion, freedom from want and fear—which he made the subject of a famous State of the Union address in 1941. By the time Rockwell illustrated all four Freedoms in consecutive weeks of 1943 for the *Saturday Evening Post*, the United States was at war. One would be hard pressed to find signs of this historical context in the painting itself. The horrors of the Second World War seem to have been scrupulously scrubbed away. A happy, garrulous family laughs around the Thanksgiving table while (presumably) Grandmother sets the turkey down on the spotless tablecloth ready for Grandfather to carve.[14] The family members are already seated in a pecking order that intimates various narratives about social function. The youngest member of the family, for example, has been placed on grandfather's right. Here she will be last served, likely, but is symbolically first in the sense that her position, sheltered as it were under Grandfather's wing, charges her with conveying into the far future whatever wisdom this Thanksgiving embodies, including, presumably, the fact that (grand)fathers get to carve. The enormous turkey itself seems designed to dispel any sense that unequal distributions—being served last, for example, or being served most—are of any consequence, for there is more than enough to go around in this family, and of course in the nation whose resources have gone to the breeding of such a fine bird.

No wonder then that Grandfather looks proudly on. All is clean—even Grandmother's apron. All is orderly: the carving utensils, the celery, and salt and pepper pots are precisely aligned; place settings are neatly laid; hair coiffed. And the old folks presiding at the head of the table connect this paean to all that is orderly and joyful to the deep past: they must have been born well back in the nineteenth century. They invoke the sort of old-fashioned Thanksgivings late-nineteenth-century writers so often represented, as if Rockwell is not merely concocting a well-scrubbed fable but also looking back to a time when a ready audience could be found for sentimental political fables of a sort that the Second World War was making lugubrious. Yet Rockwell's mythmaking is at its most subtle in pushing past glories determinedly into the present. The old folks are still very much alive. They dominate the table effortlessly. Grandmother should look proud: she is hefting, easily, what appears to be at least a twenty-five-pound turkey. Grandfather, standing behind her but rising slightly above her, framing her with his dark suit, seems to approve benevolently of her, her labor, and the turkey he has presumably purchased. And we note that their eyes are on the turkey, while only one family member (the third on the left) seems to notice them. With self-effacing pride, they refuse to coerce their family into recognizing the authority they clearly exercise. Its quality of having been already given is perhaps one reason the family seems so carefree.

The fact that the family does not even acknowledge the presence of the grandparents proves to be a brilliant strategic move on Rockwell's part because we, the viewers, cannot help but do so. The food on the table and the water glasses lead the eye in S-curves directly toward the triumvirate at the head of the table: Grandmother, grand turkey, and Grandfather, his dark suit a bold contrast with the airy white spaces in front of him (on the table) and behind him (the curtains). Placed squarely in the middle of the painting, the turkey embodies and completes the composition. The prominent curve of its back reappears in the pile of fruit, the curve of the casserole dish, the tops of the glasses and plates, the tops of the revelers' heads, and of course in the pyramidal structure that leads from the forward-tilted heads up to the cheerfully looming figure of Grandfather. To recognize the effect of this composition is to become aware of the open space in the foreground of the painting—and to see that it extends an invitation to the viewer to participate in the festivities. Stepping into it is to make the grandparents, the family, and its feast ours—all the more so because the cheeky upward glance from the person in the right corner suggests that we too are standing, that we too have some sort of presiding role. And we occupy that role, it is important to note, in the first instant we gaze at the painting. We can proceed to dissociate ourselves from the painting's meanings and values, but only after our gaze has placed us (invisibly) at the table and completed the painting's pyramidal structure by forming its base.

At least, we do so in the moment that we gaze at the painting—a fact that is crucial to the cultural work that open space performs. That space is open in perpetuity. We fill it temporarily; it opens up again as soon as we move on to feast our eyes on something else; it is infinitely flexible. But the painting necessarily constitutes this entity of viewers—this "we"—as a problematic. One can surely speak of "we" to the extent that all viewers slotting into that open space are likely to begin their visual inspection by focusing on the triumvirate at the head of the table; and numerous people could of course do so simultaneously while looking at the actual painting or a reproduction of it. But it is also important to imagine each individual viewer moving on to free the space for another. It can be filled by any *one*. If the painting's composition constitutes us as a group, the openness of that space also frees individuals to respond to the table differently. One does not have to participate, as the grandparents' downward glance already implies that they are not challenging or inviting or in any other way compelling us with regard to the nature of our involvement. We get to take charge of our viewing experience. This open space therefore takes on the very important function of creating an abstract body politic: the twelfth person at the table is symbolically anyone and everyone. Participating in this "us" is a decision we make because of compatible values and ideas, not on the basis of kinship. It is tempting to argue that Rockwell imagines social relations on the model of a (fabulously happy) family: "We" get to join it if we are lucky. But it is also possible to imagine the family opening out to, and welcoming—but also having to accept—a potentially infinite variety of viewers. From that perspective, the abstract body politic has no necessary preconceived boundaries or shape; it can be, and is, and continues to be, constituted differently in accordance with the ever-changing "bodies" of viewers who gaze at it.

This issue of whether the painting invites "us" to join the family, or whether the family open out to "us," is a crucial one. Because the family is so wholeheartedly White, it is important to ask whether the painting necessarily invokes a White body politic, presided over by a White patriarch who, however benevolent, nonetheless furnishes the feast and takes responsibility for the carving. There is some ambiguity here. Are viewers welcome to join because, and as long as, the body politic remains predominately White—non-Whites occupying at most one-twelfth of the places at the table? Or does a predominately White body politic need to open itself up to a broader variety of people—an uncountable number of potential viewers over against the eleven at the table? Still, these "others" are not materially represented on the canvas; they have a ghost-like presence at the table. This question becomes all the sharper when we consider the possibility that the empty place at the table could well be occupied by non-Americans. Since the turkey is indigenous to the Americas, and since it is associated so closely with Thanksgiving in the United States, its depiction here can take on political overtones: the family stands in for the nation, quietly offering an American gift of plenty (and joy) to other nations in a war-torn world. From that point of view, people in food-rationed Europe who, Rockwell himself noted, "sort of resented" this idyllic-seeming image of prosperity, somewhat missed the point: by virtue of its openness and by virtue of the non-coercive gazes of the people already at the table, the open place represents not fact but opportunity, not a path but a promise.[15] And that promise is not wholly one-sided, the logic of an open body politic suggests: if this is to be an "American family" of nations, then the American family will necessarily be constituted differently.

The steps "Freedom from Want" takes towards imagining a new American and global body politic are best understood bioeconomically, which is to say in terms of the huge turkey that dominates the painting compositionally and symbolically. An unassailable-seeming icon of plenty, the turkey articulates numerous values Rockwell associates with a potential commonwealth. It represents a generous investment of labor. Its size intimates the time it must have taken grandmother to roast it; the carefully laid table speaks to the time it must have taken to prepare an appropriate place to receive it; her apron, still on, shows her work is not yet done. It represents a problem of resource management: someone has thought carefully about how much turkey is necessary to feed eleven people (as well as a symbolic twelfth, or even an unknown number of "others"). It sets out to solve issues of resource distribution: the enormous size of the turkey guarantees that all will get an abundant share, though the multigenerational family gathered here also implies, as a corollary, that each person's share will depend on their size and age. It does not argue, that is, for a perfect equality of distribution; it argues for parity relative to need. And it represents a multitude of social relations. The fact that Grandmother cooks while Grandfather provides and carves—his right hand is curled close to the carving utensils in preparation—implies a gendered division of labor. Moreover, she holds the turkey directly over his stomach, so that the gift of abundance she offers to the family and to viewers is symbolized through her husband. Her ability to feed others seems to be premised on feeding him—and, indeed, on having fed him through the long years that must have preceded this moment. This is one *more* gesture of caring. His gentle framing of her body in the triangle at the head of the table extends to her a complementary sense of recognition for her dedication and hard work. His eyes are on the turkey—beautifully cooked, delivered on time—because it demonstrates what he must already know intimately from a very long experience of his wife's talents. He has no need to draw attention to the obvious.

Though there is no reason to think that Rockwell is invoking Aesop's "The Belly and the Members" directly, there are two ways in which recalling this fable helps to make sense of the body politic gathered around this turkey.

First, the turkey is not merely a sign of abundance (or overabundance, as commentators are fond of emphasizing); it appears as the nexus of numerous relationships. The belly—understood, for example, as Grandfather's provisions for his family—cannot go it alone. This is most obvious in the way the turkey signifies the combined and complementary talents of Grandfather and Grandmother: he provides, she cooks, he carves; she holds the turkey, his body compositionally holds hers; she looks proud of the sign of her work, he looks proud of it and her. The other family members laughing among themselves also of course have a role. They acknowledge Grandmother and Grandfather's labors of love by representing, in a certain sense, the work of, and the claim of, other members of the body (politic): the human need for freedom from want, understood here as physical, emotional, and social nurture. Second, these various narratives coalescing around the turkey about how to free people from want have to be construed, ultimately, as a fable. A bioeconomic account of human relations insists *that* wants can be satisfied (rather than, say, ignored or rationed). But that account stands in for, and erases, any economic understanding of *how*. How does this turkey get to the table in the first place? The lack of provenance in this Thanksgiving scene—the curtains are close drawn, so we cannot see outside—means that this could be any (lower) middle-class family anywhere in the United States. We cannot tell, therefore, whether the turkey was purchased or home-grown—and therefore whether its size speaks to Grandfather's purchasing power and to the enormous productive capacities of the free market, or whether it consecrates the enormously productive capacities of the "American soil" and the rural virtues of hard work and freeholding it implies. Though it sounds like an oxymoron, the painting seems hyperbolically disinclined to say. It portrays the turkey as an unambiguous sign of what "American" values can produce but seems equally intent upon refusing to grant those values any sort of economic or historical materiality. It represents a body politic without an economy.

Rockwell may of course be more interested in depicting a "timeless" myth of US munificence than working it out as a practical undertaking. But the time frames investing the painting's implied cultural narratives are not at all "timeless." It is clear, for example, that while Grandmother proffers a vision of future plenty to the viewer, the painting actually interprets freedom from want not as something to achieve but as something that has been achieved already. This is surely a strong implication of the happy scene around the table. Apart from the one person on the left who looks to be applauding the turkey's arrival, the family is more interested in cheerful conversation than in the appearance of the mouthwatering turkey. They cannot be that hungry; they do not, at least, "want" for turkey. The bioeconomic "story" of this turkey therefore speaks most convincingly of the history of past prosperity that led to this more-or-less want-free scene. The painting cannot recommend an economic system for the forties; but it can emphasize the success of American economic systems prior to that time, for *whatever they were* they produced this impressive turkey. That non-specific sense of the grand political economy of the past dovetails with, and allows us to re-signify, the painting's deliberate erasure of its provenance. The painting is clearly not *of* the nineteenth century—some of the family members sport forties' hairstyles. But if this turkey came from a store, then it is certainly permissible to think of it, and indeed the store it came from, as the result of a long chain of happy economic circumstances with roots in the sort of farm scenes late-nineteenth-century writers so frequently invoked, and which could in fact still lie outside the window.

The grandparents stand, literally and symbolically, as guarantors of the turkey's bioeconomic meanings. Grandfather's neatly combed hair and Sunday-best suit, Grandmother's clean apron and ready-for-the-kitchen short sleeves bear testimony to what must be decades of hard work, orderliness, and clean living. The painting clearly consecrates those values; and in some sense Rockwell sets them against the nightmare of the Second World War, though he depends on his viewers to restore a context he seems unable to include in the painting's iconography. One strong interpretive possibility here is that Rockwell cannot depict the terrors of his historical moment without damaging the significations the charming couple at the head of the table possess, which is to say that those significations are not so much "timeless" as "out of time"; they belong to a simpler era when this couple was young. More persuasive, if more subtle, is the sense in which the grandparents underwrite a plot of polity that is historical, rather than a nostalgic plunge after values that seem now to exist only in a sort of oneiric fable. The painting raises questions about whether the grandparents and the national values they represent are still valid, but not that they *were* valid. The present moment is in jeopardy, not the decades the couple have spent in hard work and nurture to have built such a happy family and secured such an impressive turkey. In that, no doubt, lies Rockwell's faith that the United States will in fact prevail. But it is worth thinking through the fact that this strategy also locks into place a specific account of history that has striking implications for the table's symbolic body politic. That body, we have seen, is at least arguably infinitely variable, for it is reconstituted over and over by diverse viewers who might want to join the revelers at their Thanksgiving feast. But it would appear that the United States has only one legitimate history. The grandparents' history—that unfolding of an ethic of hard work and orderliness by two White people, which has brought this table into being—is inalienable. That story has already been told; the twelfth space at the table could not exist without it. Put another way, it is possible that the revelers at the table would have to reconcile their lives with whoever occupies the empty space in the foreground of the painting; but whoever occupies that space will have to reconcile their histories with the one that the grandparents stand as the living embodiment of.

Rockwell's iconic turkey therefore speaks to the extent to which we, the viewers, need to participate in a process of exchange by placing his painted signs within cultural narratives and by actively imagining what has happened to bring the turkey to this table, and what will happen when the turkey gets passed around. There is, after all, something fundamentally ambiguous about signifying a household, a political economy, and a body politic in terms of a dead bird. Food still lifes have traditionally, perhaps inevitably, juxtaposed food in all its fresh-picked or fresh-killed abundance with death. Paint "stills" what it represents; and still lifes in turn often exploit that quality to invoke *omnia mors aequat*, the equality of all things under death. The depiction here of such a vibrant family arranged around such an enormous carcass makes it hard to resist the implication that the turkey recalls, even as it tries to negotiate away, scenes of massive slaughter. Otherwise banished so assiduously from the painting, those scenes find their way back in a flagrant *et in arcadia ego* display of delicious, but dead, flesh. It would therefore seem incumbent on viewers to narrativize "Freedom from Want"—to insert the dead bird into cultural narratives that unfold temporally—as the only way to prevent one from *mis*reading this turkey as the sign of a moribund economy and nation, and to misread Grandfather and Grandmother standing at the table as a somewhat jollier version of Andrew Wyeth's *American Gothic* (1930).

At mid-century, Rockwell was participating in what was already a long and extraordinarily popular genre. Thanksgiving stories were a staple production among popular fiction writers over the second half of the nineteenth century. Frequently they allowed writers to tap into—and impose a moral and often celebratory spin on—national conversations about politics in the spirit of Thomas Nast's Thanksgiving cartoon. Harriet Beecher Stowe built a story about a (failed) attempt to enslave a Black family into an extended Thanksgiving celebration in *Oldtown Folks* (1869); Rose Terry Cooke wrote "My Thanksgiving" in 1863 to rejoice in the return of a Union hero during the Civil War while trying to reach out to the Southern White women who would have no such cause to be thankful.[16] As "My Thanksgiving" shows, Thanksgiving scenes also typically celebrated and indeed consecrated conventional gender roles. In Louisa May Alcott's short story "An Old-fashioned Thanksgiving" (1882)—made into a Hallmark movie in 2008—seven Bassett children have humorous adventures and complete preparations for the "time-honored day" of Thanksgiving after Ma and Pa, having heard that Grandma is dying, are called away and then delayed by snow.[17] At the end Ma, Pa, and Grandma—alive and lively after all—return to find half a feast. Tilly, fourteen, has mistakenly put wormwood and catnip in the stuffing and her plum pudding is "hard as a cannon-ball" (24). The feast nonetheless manifests what the story defines as a true Thanksgiving spirit even more pertinent because, as Pa put it, there is "special cause to be thankful that the sorrow we expected was changed into joy" (35). If it falls to Pa to produce a moral and read the Bible, the story gives Tilly the opportunity to prepare for a "grand cooking-time" (22): it allows her to display the domestic duties that, the story shows, are the prerogative and soon-to-be expertise of girls. At the end of the day, sister Prue, invoking maternal authority, comments "Ma said we really did do surprisin' well for such young girls" (35); Aunt Cinthy concurs that the "dinner [is] a credit to you" (34). Alcott's Tilly of 1882 could well become the Grandmother of Rockwell's painting.

Like Rockwell's "Freedom from Want," Mary Wilkins Freeman's many Thanksgiving stories seem dedicated to placing turkeys squarely in the center as signifiers of culturally approved political and economic narratives. But Freeman's many stories for adults and children across several decades hide in plain sight some of the more unsettling implications of the body politic gathered around the body of the dead bird. Though her Thanksgiving stories typically close around relatively conventional familial, Christian, national, and historical meanings, they also hide turkeys, elide them, dis- and re-member them, double them, displace them with other foods, and bring them back in a new guise. The end of "A Tardy Thanksgiving," for example, has Mrs. Muzzy eating her Thanksgiving dinner—while seated on the floor in agony, her foot having been scalded by a kettle of boiling pork fat after deciding to do her "pig work" on Thanksgiving rather than eat turkey with her sister's family. The sign of the turkey in these stories is never static. In the unsettling implications of "A Thanksgiving Thief" and in particular the children's story "Thankful," Freeman comes close to deconstructing the cultural logic that makes the turkey such an effective sign of a coherent body politic.

In "A Thanksgiving Thief," published in the November (Thanksgiving) edition of the *Ladies' Home Journal* in 1892, Sophia Hurd has a kitchen "full of warm savory and spicy odors," plum pudding, cake, a "row of new pies," and a "great turkey"—and the prospect, we see, of an empty Thanksgiving, since, Scrooge-like, she has misplaced its spirit: she deliberately excludes everyone else from sharing her feast.[18] She is the real Thanksgiving thief. Not so much coldheartedly as comfortably unChristian—"I can't keep track of all the poor folks in town, an' I dun know as I'm called on to" (1), she says—Sophia experiences a change of heart after her one-time friend Sam Brightman breaks into her house the night before Thanksgiving to steal some food for himself and his "half-starved dependents" (2). After Sam faints from hunger, Sophia restores him with some chicken broth. That action also restores her to herself: an "expression came into her sharp, homely face which had never been there before," explains the narrator, the "look of a mother feeding a child, and with it a curious averted effect" (2) as, "shamefacedly," she starts to realize the extent and import of her own selfishness. The last scene of the story has Sophia bringing the five Brightmans back to her house to share her feast. What would have been a substitute Thanksgiving for one person is about to be made whole by the addition of a family to which she can serve as surrogate mother and grandmother. Alice Barker Stephens's illustration in the *Ladies' Home Journal* of the final scene, showing Sam walking arm in arm with Sophia while his wife and children walk behind, strongly supports this sense of surrogacy.

Though kinship provides the model for commonwealth, the story once more draws on the familiar *topos* that the Thanksgiving "family" must move beyond kinship and constitute itself by reciprocally "allowing" caring relations to develop. The Brightman family becoming "hers" is not construed as a possessive or paternalistic action in this extended symbolic "family" because they must accept her being "theirs." The beginnings of a social contract make themselves felt here. These newly constituted roles are substitutive, and necessarily so, since they permit symbolic Sophias to (grand)mother more than one family. But they are also prescriptive. Becoming the family's symbolic (grand)mother locks Sophia into a socially conventional role of selfless nurturing—a "mother feeding a child," for example. This sense that Sophia makes herself whole by adopting a conventional role is consistent with the most obvious explanation for why the Brightman-Hurd feast will be a *true* Thanksgiving, which is that the extended family becomes "one body" in the body of Christ. Sophia becomes a type of Mother Mary, feeding Sam the "child," setting her lamp on the stairs above him, and then interceding on behalf of the family; she satisfies Christ's injunction to feed and care for the poor; and by doing so Sophia has presumably begun to prepare her soul for the more ominous implications of Sam Brightman's nighttime thievery: "The day of the lord will come like a thief in the night" (1 Thessalonians 5:2). The "grosser food" (1) of turkeys and plum pudding thereby makes way for more refined spiritual nourishment; the "substitute" (grand)mother turns out to be a stand-in for the true Mother; and a spiritual contract, informing the social contract, coordinates the symbolic family.

Freeman openly puts forward the extended/adoptive Christian body as a solution to current political and economic debates. A "poor, old free-lance in the poverty and labor question," Sam Brightman's position while unconscious raises the issue about what to do with the body (politic) "huddled in a forlorn heap at the foot of the stairs" (2). *Which* abject body Sam represents is, however, pertinent to the story's political and narrative strategies. Freeman refrains from posing the question of "Labor" in the more familiar late-nineteenth century terms of class solidarities and a social struggle between Labor and Capital, workers and bosses. Sam and his family are more or less indigent; he and his wife struggle to find any work at all because, as Sophia explains in a long early diatribe, “Them Brightmans never had any faculty” (1). Moreover, despite Sophia’s reference to “all the poor folks in town,” there seems to be no class of Brightmans. Their uniqueness seems to shift the discussion away from labor and class relations to how a maternal (or grandmotherly) Christian body might legitimately or practically oversee a distribution of largesse to the indigent. In a sense, it takes politics out of the body politic altogether, or perhaps constructs a fable in which (Grandmother) Sophia’s newly awakened maternal instincts stand for the possibility of a loving, nurturing society that will somehow supersede the selfish concerns of the late nineteenth century.

Yet the spiritual focus of Freeman’s Thanksgiving fable does possess political economic underpinnings. The soul’s economy, in the story’s diagnosis, seems to function differently than the body’s, for the “natural craving of a lonely and self-centred soul” is “not merely a question of material need and supply” (1); the soul is not, it would seem, susceptible to economic analysis. But the story appraises the self-centered soul by way of its somatic inclinations, as Sophia’s household economy shows: while the Brightmans starve, she buys and prepares so much food that she confesses “It’s goin’ to be considerable for me to eat up all that great turkey, an’ them two chicken pies” (1). A nascent critique of neoclassical economics underwrites what seems to be a generic call for middle-class women with well-stocked larders to be generous, for Freeman distributes the concept of supply and demand between two economic paradigms. Making the *soul* the seat of craving, desire, and “infinite wants” frees the body to metaphorize easily satisfied *needs*. Her feast reverses the neoclassical paradigm of a consumer choosing how to allocate limited resources to infinite wants because the story reduces the earthly consumer to the very limited needs of a small stomach: for that purpose, relatively modest resources are more than enough. One chicken pie would have sufficed for Sophia; and a little leftover chicken broth is in fact enough to get Sam back on his feet. Put another way, the neoclassical paradigm begins with the consumer confronted by an infinitely large space of potentially purchasable commodities; Freeman’s begins with the easily filled space of the stomach, posing the economy of the body (politic) in terms of what one can eat rather than what one might want.

As Sophia’s opening remarks putting forth her economic philosophy make clear, this construction of the body politic allows the story to rewrite the concept of homo economicus. Her account of why she turned down Sam’s request to make some money cutting lumber in her woods obeys the logic of limited resources: “old Mr. Thomas will cut it cheaper, besides working faster” (1), she says, a decision based on the knowledge that her capital is not infinitely elastic. It would be better to maximize her profit by minimizing her capital outlay *because* she also wishes to purchase a “new stove, a new lamp, a new chamber set" (1), a carpet, a spring bed, and of course a Thanksgiving feast. The story's critique of this perfectly sound economic logic begins with her defense of her actions: given that there will always be rich and poor, she argues, "there ain't no way to help it that I can see, except by shiftin' the money to the other side; like the weights in balances, one side's got to be up an' tother down." That being the case, she continues, "I dun know why them that's up have any call to go down, if they can help it" (1). Sophia's explanation is threadbare—"balances" imply a mechanism for equalizing weights, not for shifting weight entirely from one side to the other. But it is in accord with what now seems to be the *illogic* of homo economicus driven by competing demands, for Sophia, as the feast shows, has accumulated more than enough capital already. Allowing Sam to cut her wood, as she does at the end, respects this second logic of diminished wants and more-than-sufficient resources: a body politic organized by the requirements of the stomach allows for the possibility that there might be resources in excess of requirements. With one's own needs assuaged, it would therefore seem rational to distribute any excess to those most in need.

Body (politics) in balance receive their most striking analysis in "Thankful" (1890), a children's story that reads, on the face of it, as little more than a well-worked "thou shalt not covet" moral fable. Submit Thompson gets her friend Sarah Adams to agree to swap Thankful, her beloved doll, for Submit's workbox if her family's turkey turns out to be heavier. Submit's "naughty covetousness" leads her to cheat: she loads old Revolutionary war bullets into their turkey to make it weigh more.[19] Having confessed their sins—betting on one side, cheating on the other—both girls are sent to their respective rooms without Thanksgiving dinner. Then mercy prevails and, amid the girls' tears and apologies to each other, they are brought down again to enjoy the feast. Sin leads to redemption; "thou shalt not covet" to "thou shalt love one another"; and Sarah and Submit discover on Thanksgiving what they have most to be thankful for—not a competition for material things represented by the weight of the two turkeys, not Thankful the doll, and not even Thanksgiving itself, but each other's friendship and love.

This predictably redemptive conclusion takes place, however, in a moral realm transformed by our gradual recognition of the patriarchal relations governing Thanksgiving. The two girls' uncharacteristic "spirit of rivalry" (42) speaks through a concatenation of male voices judging the weight of turkeys. When Submit first compares turkeys, Sarah immediately invokes her father: "Father said he'd weigh twenty pounds" (42). Her mother concurs: "I believe father said he'd weigh about twenty pounds" (45). Submit's father mentally weighs the Thompson family turkey ("Seventeen or eighteen pounds" [46]); son Thomas does the same for the Adams' turkey ("Their turkey weighs considerable more than ours" [47]). Younger son Jonas not only agrees ("Their turkey weighs twenty pounds" [47]) but seems to have the neighborhood's entire turkey-history at his fingertips: their (artificially weighted) turkey weighing in at twenty and a quarter pounds is, he emotes, "the biggest turkey that was ever raised in these parts" (48). The girls' rivalries are constructed in an ideological realm measured by men's "steelyards" (48) (balances)—a symbolic general equivalent for weighing, measuring, evaluating, and comparing bodies of various sizes.

Men also govern the scales of Justice in which Sarah and Submit are weighed and found wanting. "Father sent me up here 'cause it is sinful to—make bets" (51) says Sarah; Submit's father, says her grandmother, "isn't going to whip you this time" (51). Submit's grandfather's justice, however, is incomprehensible. Upon hearing of Submit's sin, her father immediately "turned to his father" (50), Grandfather Thompson, to whom everyone defers as the "recognized head of the house" (50); to his forbidding assessment of her conduct Submit murmurs agreement "although she did not know what he meant" (50). Very quietly, the story transforms male bodies and the ideological weights they impose into a vague terror. Submit "shrank" (50) from Grandfather Thompson's gaze even though he is "full of a grave dignity" (50); and Sarah edges closer to the wall when their "perfect giant among turkeys" (44) struts by "proudly" and "gobbled"—the feathered version of grandfather's unintelligible speech—for "she was rather afraid of him" (44). The feasts that await the two girls at the very end of the story are billed as a privilege to which they have been reintroduced. But the story has already thrust the grandfather and the grand turkey—the very bodies who feature so often in Thanksgiving representations as signs of plenitude, of continuity with the wisdom of the past, and of an orderly family structure—into Submit's and Sarah's unconscious as disturbing elements which the joy of feasting together with the family has to cover up.

It is crucial to the story's re-gendering of the scales of Justice, then, that just before the feasts begin the narrative shifts from unforgiving men to the merciful women who actually invite the girls back: Sarah's Aunt Rose and Submit's grandmother. Their appearance also oversees a shift from comparative measurement to equilibrium. The girls apologize to each other in almost exactly the same words. Aunt Rose's "beautiful smiling face" (52) matches grandmother's "fair old face . . . as gentle as the mercy that tempers justice" (51), and Aunt Rose promises to make a doll for Submit exactly like Thankful. By the end, the story's moral compass has begun to veer toward Mrs. Thompson's pragmatic home economy: "What difference does it make if one weighs a pound or two more than the other, if there is enough to go round?" (49). As offhand as it sounds, Mrs. Thompson's remark introduces a radically different concept of the body politic. Male schemas of measurement—weighing turkeys on an abstract scale to compare them, weighing girls' "sins" against abstract principles of justice, and perhaps the girls' own sudden obsession with comparing doll to workbox—imply a symbolic general equivalent and therefore some system of exchange. One could not legitimately compare different entities without a system of measurement independent of that which is to be compared; and one would not require such a system unless there was some purpose to correlating them in the first place. Bringing the size of the Thompson turkey-body (politic) into equilibrium with Thompson needs—a situation in which there is "enough to go round"—obviates independent systems of measurement. Thompson's home economics implies plenitude *and* an economy circumscribed by an upper limit that approaches at an ever-increasing rate, for the Thompson turkey, as Submit discovers, is already closing in on a record weight. The finale of the tale nonetheless steps back from abandoning exchange altogether: Sarah's Aunt Rose promises to make a doll for Submit. It is a generous exchange, to be sure, but one that implies a general equivalent—some way of determining the greater value of Sarah's doll (Thankful) over Submit's—and the fact that some structure of exchange outside the immediate family is advantageous.

"Thankful" therefore "loads" or overdetermines the patriarchal structure to which Submit and Sarah submit without quite oversetting it. As the girls "joyfully" (52) go "down to their Thanksgiving dinners" (52) in the last words of the story, they are drawn back, perhaps inevitably, to a table that reinstates grandfather and the grand turkey, for all the frisson of fear they bring, at the center of a powerful cultural tradition. What remains more resistant to compromise, because pushed more deeply into the subtexts of the story, is the symbolic career of the transformed turkey after Submit fills its crop with Revolutionary War bullets. Those bullets possess an unusually detailed history. Submit, we are told, comes from a "brave race" (46): while her great-grandfather fought in the Revolution, her great-grandmother, "guarding her home and children, had shot an Indian" (46). Submit makes her confession about cheating while looking at great-grandmother's musket: the "same spirit that had aimed it at the Indian possessed her" (50), we are told, and she "spoke out quite clearly" (50). The bullets therefore represent a grand republican spirit of courage, forthright honesty, and equality, which Submit first traduces, by constructing a false turkey-body (politic), and then reacquires as she channels her great-grandmother's grit and for the first time "talks turkey" (i.e., tells it honestly). Indeed, restoring the natural weight of the turkey makes *her* responsible for reclaiming a glorious republican history over against a male obsession with measuring and comparing bodies and telling history in terms of the "biggest."

But some diligent reconstructive work is needed to make a glorious republican history square with the story at the core of the Thompson mythology: great-grandmother shooting an "Indian" at the time of the Revolutionary

War, an event historically plausible but not easily scrutable given the story's Thanksgiving contexts. Making its representative "Indian" a would-be murderer and great-grandmother a killer, that is, threatens the mythos of amicable relations between settlers and Native Americans at the "first Thanksgiving." Whatever body politic this story imagines seated round the Thanksgiving table would seem to make room for none but Anglo-Americans; a hard-edged nativism replaces an embrace, however desultory, of the Native (American). And it is possible that the story might suggest to the young girls for whom it is written that, in the maturing subjectivity of a young girl, the privilege of Anglo-American ethnicity must not be confused with the disabling structures of gender. One might fear patriarchy without construing it as a question of racial and ethnic prerogative. Indeed, if a young reader is to admire Submit's belated pluck and come to some recognition that she too can "talk turkey" in the presence of male power, then great-grandmother's staunch defense of her family against the racial other must be valorized. We can take this a step further: the killing of the "Indian" would seem to displace subterranean fears of grand-male power (Grandfather, biggest turkey) onto a male body "other" enough to appear vulnerable and thus serve as the story's symbolic focus for female resistance. Nonetheless, Submit's transformation of the turkey does pose this conundrum: the turkey-carcass stuffed with Revolutionary War bullets and the "Indian" shot with lead double for each other. The enigma of "Thankful," unacknowledged except in metaphoric registers that seem far removed from the girls' moral struggles, is that this body politic actually does make room for the body of the "Indian" on the table through its association with the slaughtered turkey, the product of competition, associated with White-male judgment, guilt, and deception, hidden but in plain sight.

Perhaps because of an increasing awareness of that unpalatable historical body at Thanksgiving celebrations, the cultural space of the feast fable has come to be occupied by Christmas—and, in the United States, by Dr. Seuss's (Theodor Geisel's) book *How the Grinch Stole Christmas!* (1957) and the animated film version (1966, directed by Chuck Johnson) showcasing the extraordinary voices of Boris Karloff and Thurl Ravenscroft. By the 1970s, these works had already become iconic.[20] Its villain, the killjoy who sets out to steal the Whos' Christmas feast and presents, has become eponymous for anyone who would impugn a spirit of generosity. Its villain transformed has captivated generations of readers and viewers searching for spiritual significance during the most commercialized time of the year. The Grinch's dramatic change of heart, told with haiku-like brevity and precision, may have contributed to the peculiarly fluid and even contradictory way in which the Grinch fable has circulated through US culture. In their dedication to *Cash Flow for Dummies* (2011)—published during the Great Recession—John A. and Tage C. Tracy cite the Grinch in the context of small business owners whose pursuit of dreams (as Dr. Seuss puts it in his book) "means just a little bit more" than allowed by the "politicians and banksters" who have spent "too much time managing other peoples' hard-earned money and not enough time creating real value, wealth, and opportunity." In contrast, economist Richard B. Freeman's "Seussian Perspective" on the Great Recession notes the "uncanny resemblance" between the "snarly heartless cave-dwelling Grinch" and the "bankers, mortgage brokers, and Wall Street-dwelling financiers" who fleeced Americans—and whose wallets, but not hearts, grew once stimulus money started to come their way.[21] The "Whos in the US" continue to go without. As these two allegories of recessionary times imply, *Grinch*'s nonspecific locale, generalizable Whos, and fable-like plot of rapaciousness transformed is ideally suited to represent an array of US economic experiences.

What cultural space, then, does Whoville, that most fantastic of mountain hamlets, occupy? For Richard Freeman, the final feast at which the Grinch "HIMSELF!" contentedly *"carved the roast beast!"*—a communal act unthinkable to the Wall Street Grinches—is where "Seuss and economic reality part."[22] Yet the *Grinch*'s iconography always evokes political economic narratives. The plot, for example, sketches in a familiar trajectory of emerging sociality. The book's first images show the solitary Grinch posed sourly against the dark maw of his icy cave. As Thomas Hobbes would have predicted of someone in such a state of nature, this archaic cave-denizen gains resources by thieving from others. Refusing to exchange with neighbors, the Grinch is forced to be his own tailor (for his "Santy Claus" suit), musher (for the sled pulled by Max), and thief; unsurprisingly, he is poor, dwelling in a place furnished with little more than a mirror, loading "old empty sacks" onto a "ramshackle sleigh." The inhabitants of Who-ville, in contrast, clearly work together to attain a state of civilization, with religion, art (singing), and tables laden with food. They can also afford luxuries such as (in the film) "Christmas stuff / Like bingle balls and whofoo fluff," not to mention a "great big electro who-cardio flooks!"[23] If the moral of the story is that Christmas might "mean a little bit more" than commerce, the Whos in book and film certainly *have* more than the Grinch's austere anti-commercialism produces. The film takes huge delight in naming toys and fripperies—Gah-Ginkers, Trum-Tookers, fuzzels, wuzzels, and the like—but Seuss too includes a two-page spread illustrating the Who children hard at play with their multitudinous presents. One of the most diverting visual effects of both film and book—the gargantuan sacks poor Max has to drag back up the mountain—speaks to the massive number of toys Whoville can afford to accumulate. Thieving them, the film says, takes the Grinch till a "quarter of dawn."[24] So while both book and movie represent Whoville as a tiny hamlet entirely isolated among the mountains, it must exchange economically with an industrial society. In this sense the non-specific location of Whoville performs the same sort of symbolic function as the outward-facing seat in Rockwell's painting: anyone can imagine themselves trading with the Whos so long as they are committed to trading the "floof" that the Whos desire.

The Grinch's change of heart and return inspires the feast-scene that concludes the plot and helps Seuss dramatize the story's moral without turning to the "thousands of religious choices" he had earlier discarded. "Without making any statement whatever," Geisel recalls, "I showed the Grinch and the Whos together at the table."[25] Though the feast evokes a celebratory mass, it does in fact work to extend the economic parable of emerging sociality by way of a bioeconomic discourse governing a long history of feast-fables. Both book and film gesture toward this history by staging *two* feasts: the first remembered and pictured by the Grinch as he recoils from the "Noise! Noise! Noise! Noise!," the second the joyous finale as the Grinch, now incorporated into the community, participates in the festivities. The concluding scene therefore establishes an important iterative schema in the story. What motivates the Grinch's mischief is the sheer reproducibility of such feasts; his rage has grown out the "fifty-three years I've put up with" such celebrations. The Grinch's "first" communal feast is the second depicted in the story, the fifty-fourth in the Grinch's life, and not the last but the *latest* supper in a familiar *topos* of Thanksgiving/Christmas representations. "*Who*-roast-beast" might be "rare" but is wholly legible in its function as the key symbol of an imagined body politic gathered around the table.

Seuss's illustration of the first feast, spread over two pages, makes some provocative changes from Rockwell's and Nast's. The larger Who sitting at the far left of the table holding and sharpening the largest knife, roughly in the center of the composition, seems to occupy the prominent place usually reserved for the grandfather (or Uncle Sam). But the sweeping backward-S of the table decenters this symbolic role. A stack of teacups tottering on "grandfather's" left draw the eye one way; a slew of Whos engaged in various antics draws the eye the other. Moreover, there is no food on the table.[26] Cooks triumphantly march in from the left, but their platters are covered. Distilled from fifty-three years of the Grinch's anger the image might be, but it conveys most strongly the Whos' joyous anticipation. How *we* enter the scene is more complex. While the white space at the bottom of the right-hand page, like the open seat in Rockwell's painting, offers viewers an opportunity to join the merry feast, we hover over it as if from a bird's-eye view. And the feast is carnivalesque. There seems to be no place for the eye to rest or focus as we try to assimilate a page crammed with distracting, heterogeneous, even surreal information. One Who-child is dancing atop a chair. The plate that appears to hang over the head of the Who-baby standing precariously on a very high high-chair either lies half-off the table beyond or is being thrown into the air by the baby. To the left of the high-chair baby is an enigmatic depiction of—an embryo with a single spike of hair?! Almost every fork is different: one Who is holding a wrench, another pincer pliers, a third what looks like a gardening trowel. The red cloth of the table turns the corner at the bottom of the page and becomes chair coverings instead. Presiding over everything are the strangely drooping Dali-esque candelabra.

The final illustration in the book, which zooms in on the Grinch carving the roast beast, reverses the earlier depiction of a carnivalized feast. The Grinch, flanked by two respectful and orderly Whos smiling up at him—one adult, the other a child—now occupies center stage in a symmetrically posed scene. The Christmas wreath, hung asymmetrically to "grandfather's" right in the first feast, now circles the grandfatherly Grinch's head like a halo, making of the composition an elongated pyramid. It is a whimsical scene—the Grinch's jaunty "Santy Claus" hat pokes up into the halo, and one disembodied Who-hand creeps into view on the right-hand side—but not ironic, as the depiction of the beaming, almost ecstatic (his eyes are closed) Grinch suggests. The roast beast to which he addresses his carving skills sits on an impressive platter stacked high with what is clearly fruit and/or vegetables. The text in the large white space in front of the platter applauds the Grinch for carving the roast beast but also for reconstructing "HIMSELF . . . !"—finding his true self among other Whos. The illustration also lowers our viewpoint. Now that we appear to sit level with the Whos, respectfully a little below the Grinch, no longer unsettled by a bewildering avalanche of miscellaneous detail, we are "drawn in," as it were, to take our place at the table, our welcome assured by the fact that young and old are represented there. The final page thus accomplishes a great deal of cultural work. It composes an orderly scene, and it reenacts a conventional iconography that has long been put to the service of depicting the social order—though such scenes do not necessarily understand "the" social order in the same way.

The 1966 animated film version reverses the book's schema to achieve similar ends. In the first (remembered) feast scene the book's carnivalized feast is replaced by mechanical, even manic, eating, which we glimpse as we pan swiftly in on the three or four Whos sitting under the Christmas wreath. In the meantime, a surfeit of food constantly arrives at the table: Who pudding, Who roast beast, and a strawberry, delivered to Cindy Lou in a playful sequence by a succession of ever smaller Whos. It is the final scene that now fosters a sense of anticipation as the Whos wait for plates of roast beast to be passed down the table. Even Max, the first to be offered a plate, seems to be waiting politely for everyone to be served. Our viewpoint now reverses the earlier scene. It begins with a tight focus on the Grinch and then rapidly pans away up the table—this time relatively straight—revealing the Whos seated formally on both sides passing plates of roast beast to the left and right toward the furthest Who. This turns out to be the viewer, situated at the table behind a huge fruit arrangement, opposite the diminished figure of the Grinch. The fade out and subsequent ascension of the viewpoint up the mountain sides into the heavens, accompanied by the voice-over of the narration, implies the universality of the moment. Whoville and the story we have witnessed appear to have passed into myth.

Both book and film establish their attitude toward a rising tide of commercialism by calling on the iconic figure who, in the bioeconomic discourse of celebratory feasts, takes charge of the carving, the orderly distribution of food, and the social order. Each also establishes a different problematic. In the book, the shift from the carnivalism of the first feast to the Grinch's holding court over the roast beast in the second raises the question of what sort of society Whoville models. The first feast poses a puzzle: Does it represent the Grinch remembering the discordance of the typical Who feast, even though the second seems so sedate by comparison? Or is that discordance a projection of the Grinch's jaundiced imagination—*his* "noise," not the Whos'—playing over fifty-three years of Who celebrations? If the latter, then the stylized and pleasingly symmetrical final feast signals his self-restoration and a return, potentially, to the sedate affairs Who feasts might have been all along. But it seems plausible to argue that viewers might acclaim what seemed disturbingly wild to the unregenerate Grinch, preferring his anxious imagination to the relatively dull affair enacted on the final page. There is no doubt that the final page establishes a congenial, because conventional, model of commonwealth signaled by the huge roast beast under the command of the authoritative carver who will soon distribute food to everyone. The promise of the Grinch restored is underpinned by plenitude and an orderly transmission of resources. What Seuss's work leaves open is whether social order enacted under the sign of the roast beast fulfills the anticipatory desires of the first feast, or replaces its noisy carnivalism, or merely offers an alternative mode of celebrating that follows but does not supersede the first. If the latter, then the book accommodates at least one other model of commonwealth: one in which, because the food is not yet disclosed, and no one has claimed, apportioned, or distributed it, everyone present can anticipate, join, and celebrate in their own way.

In the 1966 animation, the first sybaritic feast, motivated by a surfeit of food, jibes with the far greater attention the film pays to consumer goods. Christmas may not come from a store, but the store certainly makes its presence felt in the film's loving descriptions of the Whos' "floof," upon which it capitalizes to signify the Grinch's crucial change of heart. The challenge the final brief feast scene makes to the discourse of feast-fabling is therefore surprising. This scene begins where the book ends: a closeup of the Grinch carving the roast beast. Thereafter the viewpoint zooms smoothly away from the Grinch. This universalizing gesture has unexpected consequences. First, the shot begins with the Grinch and ends by drawing attention to our act of viewing; the movie does not leave us entranced by the static, pyramidal composition of carver and roast beast. Second, it finds a dramatic correlative to the "we" the narrator evokes in voiceover as the film ends: "Christmas day will always be just as long as we have we." By passing down the plates holding roast beast, the Whos at the table make sure that the Who seated furthest from the carver—the viewer—gets fed first. But the scene fades out with the act of distribution still underway, so that our final glimpse of the Whos shows them *still passing plates*. The moment emphasizes resource distribution as an ongoing activity, a pleasurable and important labor to which each and every Who can commit. This shot is no more than a moment, glimpsed between the formalized image of the Grinch carving and the universalizing fade out. Like so many other feast fables, it gestures toward a representation of commonwealth while enacting the difficulty of trying to find a stable and enduring viewpoint from which to represent "we."

In Joy Harjo's "Perhaps the World Ends Here" readers are invited to join the "we" who "give thanks" at the table. It is therefore a thanksgiving, or giving-thanks, and in some sense a Thanksgiving, poem. Published in the collection *The Woman Who Fell from the Sky* (1994), the poem predates Harjo's accession to the Poet Laureate of the United States in 2019—as a member of the Mvskoke (Creek) nation, the first Native American poet to be so honored—but it is in line with the ceremonial and sometimes commemorative duties of that position. In an interview just after becoming Poet Laureate Harjo foresees that her role is "going to have a lot to do with Native Nations poets," adding, however, that this responsibility is consonant with "how we sing the American story, which involves all of the voices."[27] The simplicity of "We give thanks" speaks generally to a complex, one might even say thankless, poetic task: finding a space within which the fraught histories and ill-aligned aspirations of Native Nations and the United States can coexist, particularly at a time when "We need something to counter the hate speech, the divisiveness."[28] If this is "possible with poetry," then poetry must somehow negotiate an oxymoronic collision between "divisiveness" and an ever more doubtful conception of "we." "Perhaps the World Ends Here" seeks that space by invoking a history of feast-invitations, and the imagined body politic attending them, to which Freeman, Cooke, Alcott, Rockwell, Dr. Seuss, and so many more have in diverse ways contributed. Harjo defamiliarizes that discourse, in part because of her overdetermined presence at the table. Native Americans have always been accorded a special welcome in a US Thanksgiving imaginary by virtue of the fact that they underwrite a fable of amity and generosity between indigenous peoples and colonists. That fable, as the dead Native American in Mary Wilkins Freeman's "Thankful" goes some way toward demonstrating, has always masked an actual "history where centuries stack and bleed."[29]

Giving thanks in Harjo's poem need not be limited to Thanksgiving. In her attack on capitalist practices—or "cannibal economics"—Winona LaDuke (Anishinaabe) remarks "You're always grateful for those gifts" bestowed by nature and therefore "you always pray."[30] Nonetheless, Harjo does extend the discourse on feast fables in several important ways. First, giving thanks in Harjo's poem brings characters and readers to a kitchen table rather than the formal dining rooms typical of this genre, which emphasize the move *from* the kitchen. In Dr. Seuss's book and 1966 film, we witness cooks bringing platters and utensils from an unpictured kitchen to the happy throng at the first feast. The final feast in the latest addition to the Grinch franchise, *The Grinch* (2018; directed by Yarrow Cheney and Scott Mosier), allows us some glimpses of two cooks and the kitchen, which is now open to the dining room. Here, too, our perspective veers away from the kitchen as, first, the Grinch carries heavy platters of cake and cookies to the table and, second, Donna Who carries the roast beast to the Grinch sitting opposite the kitchen, so that the kitchen vanishes from our view. One implication of Harjo's poem is therefore to refigure the table of thanksgiving so that it shares space with a site traditionally the preserve of women. This is not to say that representations of feasts ignore the presence and labor of women—in Rockwell's painting it is the be-aproned Grandmother who cradles the turkey she has prepared; in the 2018 *The Grinch* the enormous cake and roast beast showcase Donna Who's work. But transferring food from the kitchen to the dining room would seem a condition of whatever broader symbolic meanings these feast fables attain. Women's labor becomes significant by virtue of *having contributed* to the benevolent gazes of Washington, Lincoln, and Columbia (Nast) and Grandfather (Rockwell); to generosity of spirit (Seuss); to an end to loneliness (*The Grinch*). Moving back to the kitchen table restores the labor of women, and with it numerous other functions: here one can "hide in the shadow of terror"; here we have "prepared our parents for burial," and "given birth"; here "Babies teethe"; here "chickens or dogs" are welcome to attend.

The whimsical notion of chickens pecking under rather than cooked and ceremoniously arranged on top of a table of thanksgiving suggests the difference of Harjo's approach to the issue of who gets represented at the table, and how. One of the pleasures of the poem is attending to the peripatetic meanings of "we." "We must eat to live" is an incontrovertible fact pertinent to all humans. "We chase chickens or dogs away from it" or "We have given birth on this table, and prepared our parents for burial here" is instead culture- and period-specific. In the twenty-first century, United States, dogs are probable table companions, chickens rarely, newborns and dead people almost never—though all would be more likely in the nineteenth century. So the table and the people and animals sitting at it take on different shapes depending on what sort of "we" our personal experience and cultural knowledge allow "us" to project. The imagined person who chases chickens away from the table is most likely not "we" in the twenty-first-century United States; conversely, the person who has experienced chasing live chickens away from a kitchen table will construct a "we" with a different relationship to a dead fowl on top of a table of thanksgiving. The poem never specifies the form, features, personal experiences, or cultural knowledge required to attend the feast—and never requires us to specify them. Our one and only collective experience is of *having to construct* a "we." In this respect the poem works as the inverse of the Rockwell painting or the Grinch feast scenes that open a space for us to participate in the festivities. To a certain extent such scenes are not complete until we join them; but the represented figures awaiting us give form and feature to the kind of collectivity that is possible, so that whatever "we" we imagine will have to include the people already seated at the table. "Perhaps the World Ends Here" represents no "we"; "we" exists only as a space to be created, a pronoun in search of readers willing to give it a referent, potential merely until someone bothers to give it life.

The shape of this potential "we" around the table of giving-thanks also has to reckon with a new and disturbing configuration of history. It is a table where "Wars have begun and ended. . . . It is a place to hide in the shadow of terror. A place to celebrate the terrible victory." In line with the poem's potentially apocalyptic, world-ending overtones, this table invokes the Cold War where citizens were told to hide under the table while facing what would almost certainly be the "last sweet bite" for human beings across the globe. Too, the table brings us to a "history where centuries stack and bleed," whether that history is of the Lakotas, which Harjo references in the interview mentioned above, or of some other history of dispossessed people in wars of conquest, resistance, or retaliation, in North America or elsewhere, a "terrible victory" because of the cost of the victory or because it occurs within the context of a long losing struggle. It is also an ironic reversal of what the Thanksgiving table in the United States typically does celebrate: it emphasizes the "terror" of those who were the victims of colonial victory. A "terrible victory" makes more explicit the vague imputation in "Thankful" that the act of weighting the turkey with Revolutionary Era bullets—one of which was used to kill a Native American—might gesture toward a less savory Thanksgiving history than the one the United States, and the story, otherwise favors. And it makes more explicit the odd crosscutting of dead turkeys and preparing parents for burial. If the dead body of the turkey (or roast beast) in feast fables symbolizes the ideals of a body politic—prosperity, largesse, equity in sharing and distribution for all races and ethnicities (Nast) and ages (Grinch/Cindy Lou), complementary labors (cooking, carving)—Harjo's ghost supper manifests a different sort of "still life." Giving thanks at Harjo's table must at least acknowledge the ghosts of the dead crowding around the table and what they too often symbolize: lands bloodily expropriated and carved up, and people being cut off from the prosperity those acts of dispossession have granted others.

NOTES

1. Mehta, Brinda J. "Culinary Diasporas: Identity and the Language of Food in Gisèle Pineau's *Un Papillon dans la Cité* and *L'Exil selon Julia.*" *International Journal of Francophone Studies* 8, 1 (2005): 24, DOI: 10.1386/ijfs.8.1.23/1.

2. Carole Counihan, *The Anthropology of Food and Body: Gender, Meaning, and Power* (Hove, UK: Psychology Press, 1999), 126.

3. Catherine Gallagher, *The Body Economic: Life, Death, and Sensation in Political Economy and the Victorian Novel* (Princeton: Princeton University Press, 2006), 46.

4. Annabel Patterson, *Fables of Power: Aesopian Writing and Political History* (Durham: Duke University Press, 1991), 43, 2.

5. Patterson, *Fables*, 2.

6. Patterson, *Fables*, 4.

7. Henry George, *Progress and Poverty* (1879; reprint London: Kegan Paul, 1883), 86, 149.

8. The cartoon appeared in *Harper's Weekly* 13, no. 673 (November 20, 1869): 745, archive.org/details/harpersweeklyv13bonn/page/745/mode/2up?q=720.

9. A ceremonial rotunda reminiscent of the structure topping the Capitol building in Washington D.C. dominates the center of the composition.

10. As does Richard Halpern, for example, in *Norman Rockwell: The Underside of Innocence* (Chicago: University of Chicago Press, 2006).

11. Laura Claridge, *Norman Rockwell: A Life* (New York: Modern Library, 2003), 2, 12.

12. Deborah Solomon, *American Mirror: The Life and Art of Norman Rockwell* (New York: Farrar, Straus and Giroux, 2013), 4.

13. Published in *The Saturday Evening Post*, March 6, 1943. The illustration can be found at www.nrm.org/2016/11/freedom-want-1943/.

14. Rockwell's model for "grandmother" was the family cook, and family and friends also sat for the painting. In my analysis I pursue what seems to me the obvious implication that the painting depicts a multi-generational family.

15. Quoted in Richard Halpern, *Norman Rockwell: the Underside of Innocence* (Chicago: University of Chicago Press, 2006), 72.

16. I perform extended analyses of Cooke's and Stowe's stories in *Kitchen Economics: Women's Regionalist Fiction and Political Economy* (Tuscaloosa: University of Alabama Press, 2020), 110–21.

17. Louisa May Alcott, "An Old-Fashioned Thanksgiving," *Aunt-Jo's Scrap-bag*, Vol 6 (Boston: Roberts Brothers, 1882; Project Gutenberg), 8. Subsequent reference to this story are cited parenthetically in the text.

18. "A Thanksgiving Thief," *Ladies' Home Journal* ix, no. 12 (November 1892): 1, commons.wikimedia.org/w/index.php?title=File:Ladies%27_Home_Journal_Vol. 9, No. 12 (November 1892). Subsequent references to this story are cited parenthetically in the text.

19. "Thankful," *Harper's Young People* XII, no. 578 (November 1890); reprint in *Feasts and Frolics: Special Stories for Special Days*, ed. Phyllis R. Fenner (New York: A.A. Knopf, 1975): 45, archive.org/details/feastsfrolicsspe00fenn/page/n11/mode/2up. Subsequent references to this story are cited parenthetically in the text.

20. As Thomas A. Burns noted in 1976: "Dr Seuss' *How the Grinch Stole Christmas*: Its Recent Acceptance into the American Popular Christmas Tradition," *New York Folklore* 2, no. 3 (Winter 1976), 8e6147e654cb7cc71a2684fd8a9474ec.pdf.

21. Richard B. Freeman, "What Happened to Shared Prosperity and Full Employment and How to Get Them Back: A Seussian Perspective," in *Reconnecting to Work: Policies to Mitigate Long-term Unemployment and Its Consequences*, ed. Lauren D. Appelbaum (Michigan: Upjohn Institute, 2012), ix.

22. Freeman, "What Happened," xi.

23. Quoted from the fandom wiki (no longer available). Another version describes it as an "Electro Who-Cardio Shluxe."

24. transcripts.thedealr.net/script.php/how-the-grinch-stole-christmas-1966-FhJ.

25. Quoted in Neil Morgan and Judith Giles Morgan, *Dr. Seuss & Mr. Geisel: A Biography* (New York: Random House, 1996), 157–58.

26. It is hard to tell whether the urn in the foreground holds fruit or flowers.

27. "An Interview with Joy Harjo, U.S. Poet Laureate," n.p., Poets.org., poets.org/text/interview-joy-harjo-us.poet.laureate?gclid=EAIaIQobChMIvMDDxuj58QIV0R6tBh2_jAHhEAAYASAAEgIMufD_BwE.

28. "The First Native American U.S. Poet Laureate on How Poetry Can Counter Hate," *Time*, August 22, 2019. time.com/5658443/joy-harjo-poet-interview/.

29. "An Interview with Joy Harjo," n.p.

30. Winona LaDuke, "Prophecy of the Seventh Fire: Choosing the Path that is Green," Schumacher Center for a New Economics, centerforneweconomics.org/publications/prophecy-of-the-seventh-fire-choosing-the-path-that-is-green/.

Chapter Seven

Yak Burgers and Black Tea

Consumption, Deprivation, and the Literature of Himalayan Adventure Travel

"Some people," notes journalist Hilary Howard of new trends in global tourism, "want a little more out of their vacation than a fruity drink served poolside."[1] Howard is writing here about adventure tourism: the "little more" her vacationers want is to canoe a crocodile infested river in Zambia, their object to spurn what Dean MacCannell anatomized as the alienating effects of mass consumer tourism.[2] Her comment also usefully frames recent debates about culinary tourism, which Lucy M. Long defines as the "intentional, exploratory participation in the foodways of another."[3] Culinary tourists or "food adventurers," like Zambian kayakers, seek authentic experience. They avoid the practice of sipping generic fruit drinks beside generic pools in favor of exploring authentic ethnic or national cuisines—an effort that may enhance their understanding of the cultural Other and simultaneously stretch their sense of self, as Long claims, or, as Lisa Heldke has argued, threaten a return to an acquisitive cultural colonialism in which the goal is to consume the lived experiences of another culture along with its traditional or uniquely exotic food.[4] The goals of adventure tourists and culinary tourists clearly overlap. When adventure travel company Abercrombie & Kent promises to have clients "Participate in a food-offering ceremony with Buddhist monks in Bangkok," for example, it taps into a market that both groups of tourists would recognize and that can be analyzed in terms of the cultural capital generated by singular and exclusive experiences, whether the focus is adventurous eating or adventuring "out of the box," or, as here, both together.[5] It is no surprise that, as Heldke observes, "food adventuring is frequently described as a quest, and the food adventurer as an explorer."[6]

Adventure and culinary tourism provide one context for understanding the economic significations of the (English language) adventure literature of the Himalayas, which for more than a century has produced compelling narratives of mountaineering, trekking, exploring, and self-exploration in the highest and remotest areas of the world. Such narratives typically refuse the imputation that its participants are tourists in MacCannell's sense of postmodern consumers of "primitive" cultures, peoples, events, and foods, beguiled by a market for the authenticity missing from their mundane, alienated existences. The "romantic and other countermodern yearnings that were central to much of early [nineteenth-century] mountaineering" in the Swiss Alps have only intensified in twentieth-century Himalayan adventure writing, which over time has expressed an ever more powerful critique of alienating, routinized bourgeois-capitalist lifestyles, of cultures of overconsumption.[7] Climbing, Jeff Achey proclaims, is a "rebel yell and a vision quest."[8] Expeditions to the Himalayas are commonly cast in that mold. Wade Brackenbury writes near the end of his adventure of having to go back to California, back to the "mundane world of schedules and appointments, of honking horns, congested traffic, pollution, and faces lined with stress."[9] In "those high, ancient ranges" of Tibet, however, "I could soar above and be free of the rules and drudgery that lashed out at me like the sting of birdshot" (209). Perhaps David Breashears puts it best: "Climbing Everest is about the deprivations, the challenge, the sheer physical beauty, the movement and rhythm. And it's partly about risk. You learn about yourself, about what happens when you abandon comfort and warmth and a daily routine, the tyranny of the urgent."[10] So, in *Savage Arena* (1982), Joe Tasker hopes that his expedition to climb K2 in the Karakorum region of Pakistan will help him forget his just-completed "package-tour climbing holiday" in the Swiss Alps, which have become "too civilised, too accessible," leaving him "empty and unfulfilled."[11] Abandoning curated package tours allows Tasker to be filled with the "catharsis of total involvement with a foreign culture" and "planning survival in a barren land"; it allows the exchange of "some narrow escapes" on Alpine peaks for truly enormous risk.[12]

"Barren land" is a crucial marker of authenticity. It displaces the geopolitical arena within which Tasker's struggle for survival takes place so that the Karakorum becomes a symbolic arena, a "savage arena," a place for primal experiences. And it gestures toward two of the most pronounced and enduring topoi of Himalayan adventure literature: a minimizing of exchange relations in realms that seem to eschew markets and money, and a concurrent emphasis on a bioeconomic discourse generating value and economic meaning through *deprivation*. These writers invariably confront a lack of, or an inability to consume, food and drink. In part this is because until recently Himalayan peoples depended almost entirely on subsistence farming, which left little extra for visitors, and in part because of logistical problems of supplying food at altitudes above permanent human settlement. As pressing are the physiological problems of surviving at high altitude. Jon Krakauer, arriving at Everest Base Camp above 18,000 feet, suddenly finds that "My appetite vanished and my digestive system, which required abundant oxygen to metabolize food, failed to make use of much of what I forced myself to eat; instead, my body began consuming itself for sustenance. My arms and legs gradually began to wither to sticklike proportions."[13]

The moment is archetypical in this genre. Krakauer arrives at a site that consumes *him*, where attempts to manage a vanishing appetite amid the physical sufferings experienced by the hungering and thirsting body meet an intensified desire to survive, to conquer the peak, to find self-fulfillment. In this respect, narratives of high-altitude adventure perform a similar cultural work to culinary tourism: they place the value and meaning of appetite under surveillance and under pressure; they mark food as the signifier of difference between authentic and fake, mass-produced, experience; and, by situating the careful consumption of food at the heart of the metaphorical significance of their enterprise, they offer sometimes explicit challenges to a culture of (over)consumption. They therefore offer what looks to be a direct riposte to the logic of the feast fable. Those challenges, we shall see, are articulated within, and as a prominent part of, a complex discourse on consumption. Too, as many scholars have argued about culinary tourism, the strategic moves enabling this critique are, in Edward Said's term, "orientalist": they are part of an archive of imaginative constructions of high Asia which depend on a "flexible *positional* superiority, which puts the Westerner in a whole series of possible relationships with the Orient without ever losing him the relative upper hand."[14]

English-language Himalayan adventure literature falls into two formations organized roughly around World War II. Though a few American and British individuals did traverse the high ranges of the Himalayas before the twentieth century—George Bogle's account of his expedition from India to Bhutan and then Tibet in the late eighteenth century is a notable example—the catalyst for the bulk of early twentieth-century narratives was Britain's bid to expand its imperial reach across the Himalayas by sending a military-backed "Mission" to Tibet in 1904.[15] Its goal was in part to ameliorate the threat of growing Russian influence over a region that shared a thousand-mile border with British India.[16] Under the command of Sir Francis Younghusband, a small army of soldiers backed by thousands of porters crossed from Sikkim into Tibet, fought their way to Lhasa, and strong-armed the Tibetan government into opening its borders to British trade. That foray laid the political groundwork for numerous British attempts to climb Mount Everest (from the North) from the early twenties to the outbreak of World War II. It also produced several consequential monographs by newspaper correspondents Edmund Candler and Perceval Landon, army doctor Lawrence Waddell, and Younghusband himself, which shaped a strategic formation linking "barren land" and the problem of food consumption to a nascent counter-modernism.

After World War II Himalayan adventure literature adopted a more obvious critique of consumerism. I trace here a number of twentieth-century accounts, but emphasize two mass-market works, Jon Krakauer's very well-known *Into Thin Air* (1997) and Wade Brackenbury's *Yak Butter and Black Tea* (1997), both of which engage these issues with a level of self-reflection often missing from narratives of Himalayan adventure. Krakauer's account of his ascent of Everest and of the 1996 Everest disaster reproduces the classic *topos* of the Himalayan mountaineering narrative, which begins with the trek to the mountain, relates adventures and obstacles overcome on the way (usually) to the top, and concludes with the trek out and aftermath. Brackenbury's quest to become (he thinks) the first Westerner to visit the "secret" Valley of the Drung in Tibet exemplifies another category of Himalayan adventure: self-exploration. The story juxtaposes his efforts to overcome difficult terrain and the roadblocks (quite literally) put up by the Chinese in their occupation of Tibet with his growing sense of self-discovery. Both works contain overt critiques of specific forms of Western overconsumption. And in both the trope of deprivation recalls the socioeconomic conditions—and the logic of the feast fable—to which the writers cannot help but return.

From the beginning, the 1904 Mission to Lhasa promoted its political, military, and imperialist aims through a rhetoric of adventure. In his Preface to *The Heart of a Continent* (1896), a narrative of his travels throughout Asia, Younghusband says that he writes for the kindred spirits who share his "love for adventure and seeking out the unknown," of which there must be many, since it is "not natural to an Englishman to sit at an office desk."[17] Younghusband refined those tropes in *India and Tibet* (1910), his long description and justification of the Mission. He celebrated the "very risk and romance and novelty of the task" and the "stir and thrill of an enterprise which would ever live in history" as the expedition plunged into the "unknown beyond the mighty snowy range which lay before us."[18] Waddell's Preface too describes his colorful adventures as he "tramped many hundreds of miles along the mountain tracks of the Tibetan frontier" before ever finding his way to the "mystic land beyond the Himalayas."[19] Younghusband and Waddell here reproduce a familiar array of imperial moves. Robert Dixon's description of the *topos* of nineteenth-century adventure fiction—a "group of English adventurers plans a journey into unexplored regions to revive their flagging spirits and fortunes"—is pertinent here.[20] An emotional affinity for "risk and romance" re-signifies the moves of an imperial authority in terms of a vague but potent counter-modernism—the excitement of leaving one's boring office desk behind—while enforcing the prerogative of the adventurer to observe, experience, record, and exert control over the "unknown."

The documenters of the Mission consolidated their high (altitude) imperial adventure through a substantial bioeconomic discourse produced in part by having to supply a military force for nearly a year in terrain that is "barren enough" to require the porterage over high mountain passes of "hundreds of tons of food and other stores daily from Calcutta."[21] Logistics preoccupy the expedition's writers. Since "each of the coolies [*sic*] and the transport animals eats up a great portion of his load as he goes on the way" there is "comparatively little left to deliver at Chumbi [just inside the Tibetan border] to keep the garrison there in food."[22] The advent of spring when "Crops were plentiful" helps to solve the problem of the Mission's long supply lines.[23] It also helps to articulate the purpose of the Mission, which was, Younghusband explains, to improve trade relations and place them "upon a basis more consonant with the usage of civilized nations."[24] Spring thrusts the British and Tibetans into mutually beneficial exchange relations. Establishing a "trade-mart" at Gyantse, for example, was one of the stated goals of the Mission.[25] The point all writers underscore, however, is that trade constitutes itself there naturally and spontaneously. Within a few days of the troops' arrival at their spring quarters, writes Waddell, the "almighty rupee began to work wonders amongst the people" so that local inhabitants "came flocking in scores to our camp, bringing in all kinds of things for sale."[26] A "large bazaar or market was formed immediately outside the gate of our post," where "thrifty housewives . . . drove a thriving trade" selling "grain and fodder" to the Mission's Commissariat and "ridiculously cheap" food and "curios" to "crowds of our soldiers and followers."[27] "Shopping in Gyantse," Landon writes, was an "almost daily amusement."[28]

Waddell's "bazaar or market" in fact describes a subtle shift from bazaar *to* market. Tibetans are held to be traders—the "Tibetan peasantry," writes Younghusband, were "especially eager to trade—no keener traders could be found."[29] But they misconceive value. Foodstuffs, which should be priced at a premium in this barren land, are "ridiculously cheap," while other sellers tout useless "curios." The arrival of the "almighty rupee" works several market-wonders. It supersedes the Tibetans' primitive "bartering" and "chaffering" so that they end up, Waddell notes, "supremely pleased, never having had so much money in their lives before."[30] The writers' emphasis on long supply routes here takes on a new function. The rupee that funds the movement of hundreds of tons of supplies also brings new consumers during the off season when Gyantse would otherwise be experiencing a "petty trade."[31] Miraculously—for the first time in its history—the town welcomes a spring market. The first days at Gyantse therefore reconfigure the logic of the trade agreement with Tibet. It is not that the British come to secure the agreement; the paper document merely rubberstamps a commerce with which the Tibetans have always agreed because they, like all humans, have a natural proclivity toward markets.

The surprise attack by the Tibetan army on the Gyantse post on May 5 and the seven-week siege that follows therefore has several consequences beyond justifying (to the British writers) the subsequent advance on Lhasa. Though after Gyantse the British troops are forced to obtain "large supplies of grain . . . from the monasteries and jongs [forts] on the road," they continue to model the benefits of trade.[32] The inhabitants of Lhasa allegedly find the British "extraordinary people" since they pay for the food they need, whereas "Tibetan soldiers forcibly take . . . as much food and clothing as they want without any payment."[33] The "action of the English in paying full prices, and even more than full prices, for the food-stuffs they requisitioned," Landon claims, was an "unexpected shock to the authorities in Lhasa," who had unscrupulously refused to fund the army fighting in its defense.[34] Wrecking a marketplace so conducive to the well-being of Tibetans allows these writers to quietly efface the military posture of the Mission—which has forcibly entered Tibet—and emphasize instead the "grinding tyranny of their own priests, the Lamas," who force soldiers to coerce food and clothing from their own people.[35] Landon's accusation that the lamas "trade upon" the ignorance of the populace puts the issue neatly: the lamas renege on the "usage of civilized nations" by suturing their moral turpitude to economic inefficiency.[36]

For the next century, Himalayan adventure literature utilized and reconfigured key elements from the 1904 Mission documents justifying the British invasion of Tibet. Younghusband's "love of adventure" inspired generations of Himalayan travelers to abandon offices, package-tour holidays, and a life of overconsumption. Like the Mission reports, later accounts also rely on a functional difference between the Western adventurer's experience of deprivation and the subsistence economies and foodways of the Himalayan regions. Yet the trope of deprivation is a mobile and complex one, capable of multiple configurations, as an early scene of *Into Thin Air* suggests. Describing a Sherpani taking orders from a group of American trekkers at the Khumbu Lodge in Namche Bazaar, the social and commercial hub of Sherpa life, it emphasizes, like the British Mission writers, the beneficial irruption of market life into Himalayan society:

> "We hungry," a ruddy-cheeked man announced to her in overly loud pidgin, miming the act of eating. "Want eat po-ta-toes. Yak bur-ger. Co-ca co-la. You have?"
>
> "Would you like to see the menu?" the sherpani replied in clear, sparkling English that carried a hint of a Canadian accent. "Our selection is actually quite

> large. And I believe there is still some freshly baked apple pie available, if that interests you, for dessert."
>
> The American trekker, unable to comprehend that this brown-skinned woman of the hills was addressing him in perfectly enunciated King's English, continued to employ his comical pidgin argot: "Men-u. Good, good. Yes, yes, we like see men-u." (54–55)

The trope of food consumption here accomplishes an immense amount of cultural work: it structures cultural attitudes and values, speaks to processes of historical change, articulates the ideologies of competing economic systems, and positions Krakauer as a critical observer among them. Neat comic reversals have the Sherpani speaking the King's English and offering apple pie while the American stupidly speaks the pidgin that has typically been reserved for the "native" in a long history of imperialist encounters. Indeed, it is the Sherpani who reads the situation correctly, anticipating when she says "Our selection is actually quite large" that the American will both underestimate the lodge's cooking and desire a variety of foods. It is she who first offers the menu, a concept that might be said to distinguish US-style consumption from a subsistence economy. Menus imply abundance—a stockpile of food well beyond the capacity of any individual human to consume. And they imply choice. Food offered menu-style is a cultural practice in which each act of selection evokes a multiplicity of other such potential acts—the choices that could have been made, and that could have been accommodated, before the decisive one.

To Krakauer, the Sherpani's embrace of the menu identifies Namche Bazaar as a kind of global borderlands, a site where a high-Asian embrace of economic transformation transforms the cultural narratives Americans tell themselves. Cultural difference is configured oddly here. Krakauer recognizes that no differences could be various enough for the trekker's all-consuming fantasy of Nepalese life, which hungers for American-style service (the menu) and American food (coca cola) in Nepal, American-style food expressed in Nepalese terms (yak burgers), and Nepalese food Americans understand (potatoes). Yet Namche Bazaar has become the home of apple pie, coca cola, and the menu. Transfixed by a reified notion of cultural otherness that no longer obtains, the trekker is ignorant of profound changes in Nepalese culture that have occurred along with an orientation to Western-style consumption. "Most of the people who live in this rugged country," according to Krakauer, "seem to have no desire to be severed from the modern world or the untidy flow of human progress" (58). In this neat parable of postcolonial hybridity, it is the American trekker who has much to learn from the Sherpani's embrace of a "modern world" exemplified by multilingual education, flexible business savvy, and by a "borderless world of flows . . . and the imminent unbundling of territorial sovereignty."[37] Krakauer's description of the Khumbu Lodge therefore seems to reverse the imperial paradigm so pronounced in the British accounts of Gyantse. The Sherpani is fully in charge of the transaction. Nor is the Lodge a "pop-up" bazaar: the logistics of supplying menu-style consumption imply sophisticated market arrangements.

Krakauer's strategy of arraying himself on the side of the Sherpani against the arrogant American trekker does, however, have unexpected consequences. It succeeds in articulating a hybrid American/Sherpani perspective that is progressive and critical of a voracious appetite and assumption of cultural superiority. Yet the values that Krakauer associates with the Sherpani—education, flexibility, a talent for assessing and catering to the needs of clients, an embrace of rapid cultural transformation and entrepreneurship, an acceptance of menu-style consumption, and "untidy" but real economic development—are central to a neoliberal capitalist understanding of its historical success as it has reinvented itself under the auspices of globalism. Appearing to reverse the colonial paradigm, the scene nonetheless affirms an Orientalist logic. Krakauer's critique of the trekker's appetite, ventriloquized through the Sherpani, evokes a socioeconomic regime that verifies what the British observers at Gyantse averred: the high Himalaya regions benefit from markets and market values, even if they are underpinned by, and perpetuate, the economic forces that allow the trekker and Krakauer to pay for this kind of adventure tourism in the first place.

Leaving Namche Bazaar for the still higher altitudes of Everest—for "thin air," as his title memorably puts it—allows Krakauer to strike a wholly new posture typical of postcolonial Himalayan adventure writers, who represent themselves as being dismissive of all markets. Climbers are chronically strapped for cash. It was "time to face up to an old problem," laments John Climaco en route to the Baltoro glacier: "money, or more specifically, the lack thereof." "If even one of our porters found out how broke we were," he adds, "no one from Baltistan would come and retrieve us and our gear."[38] Charles Houston's expedition to K2 faces the same problem when, having reached Base Camp, the team finds that "After paying off the porters [we were able] to muster . . . approximately eight cents, and this only after each individual had given up all his own funds to the expedition treasury."[39] As a correlative, these narratives frequently impugn their *workers* as money grubbing. "Everything for foreigners is at least double, if not triple," storms Sue Cobb on the way to Everest, adding "From our perspective, it's extortion—and infuriating."[40] Having paid their Balti porters before the end of the expedition to K2, Greg Child finds that the porters, incorrigibly, want more: the porters "sit atop boulders . . . staring down on us like vultures."[41] Tom Hornbein also describes problems with his team's sherpas wanting more money for carrying less: "Perhaps it is the big, fat, rich American image . . . but it is much like a labour union trying to put on the squeeze."[42]

Relative to the porters who carry food and gear, Hornbein's "image" of the rich American is accurate. Expeditions always meet their financial obligations. Climaco, who arrives at the main road to inform his porters "we were broke," simply proceeds to the bank in Skardu "for the porters' money," presumably through credit or money transfer.[43] Houston's response to his "sorry financial position" is to "put away the worry until tomorrow," since it seems "unimportant among the splendid peaks which surrounded us."[44] And rightly so. At the end of the book one of their high-altitude porters, Kairal Hidayat, exclaims "I shall go to America"; but it is Houston who boards the plane back to the States where some months of "furiously" writing and lecturing "pay our debts."[45] As part of an ensemble of moves designed to produce a rhetoric of high adventure unencumbered by logistics or money, these accounts try to minimize or negotiate away the implication of a massive power and wealth differential between American climbers and some of the poorest peoples in the world. Indeed, the exigencies of Himalayan economies allows those people—Cobb's extorters of American capital, Child's and Hornbein's unionized mob of intransigent workers—to represent the "tyranny of the urgent." Krakauer constructs a version of this position in his barely concealed contempt for rich socialite climber Sandy Pittman who must be virtually dragged up and down Everest short-roped to Sherpa Lopsang. On the face of it the story reverses the hierarchy of Western climber over Sherpa. But Pittman's ineptitude demonstrates that she is in fact no climber at all. Her antics on Everest contribute on the one hand toward an appreciation of real climbers (like Krakauer) who ascend the mountain under their own steam and on the other to a definition of the service-oriented role of the Sherpa, whose business on Everest is to assist his boss's, Rob Hall's, client.

It is Krakauer's arrival at Everest Base Camp, however, that signals the most compelling discursive reorientation as (post)colonial capitalist relations given way to a bioeconomic discourse centered on the vanishing appetite and a body that consumes itself. Following the 1904 Mission's obsession with supply routes—Younghusband himself noted that the "chain of supply" would be crucial to the endeavor of climbing Everest—the earliest accounts of Western expeditions to the Himalayan region recognize that the consumption of food is a complex problem to be negotiated and, with luck, managed.[46] Underconsumption appears as a constant peril and thus the "importance of correct feeding," as F. S. Smythe says in *Kamet Conquered* (1932), "can hardly be over-estimated."[47] Hugh Ruttledge draws attention to the problem of "incipient scurvy" because "Fresh vegetables can only be secured with great difficulty in Tibet, [and] fresh fruit is unknown," though Eric Shipton, having consulted a nutrition expert before the 1935 expedition to Everest and imported "dried vegetables from England" to supplement local fare, considers the problem solved in "inhabited parts of Tibet."[48] The reason that "correct feeding" obsessed early expeditions to the Himalayas and continues to bedevil climbers today is that appetite for food dwindles dramatically at high altitudes. Above 26,000 feet in what is often called, without exaggeration, the Death Zone, the body deteriorates even under conditions of rest. To the 1924 Everest expedition, food was "nauseating" above the North Col; "eating tends to make one vomit" agrees Shipton; "one of the difficulties of high climbing," says E. F. Norton, is that "it is impossible to force oneself to take enough food even to begin to make good the day's wastage of tissue."[49] Joe Tasker cites another example of one of the film makers on the 1980/81 winter expedition to Everest, Graham Robinson, who "could hardly eat any of the food" and who "seemed to shrink visibly before our eyes"; it is, Tasker explains, a "feature of living at altitude."[50] Life at Base Camp and up becomes a kind of parody of Western-style consumption: the body consumes itself and, in direct challenge to an ethos demanding the kind of self-gratification displayed by the trekker at the Khumbu Lodge, climbers must force themselves to eat anything at all.

Over the twentieth century, three perspectives have come to dominate the discourse on food consumption (or lack of it) on expeditions from the West. The first, as Krakauer's account of the hungry trekker intimates, proposes variety as a solution to chronic under-consumption. "Palates must be tickled with dainties," F. S. Smythe says, and inventories at one point the luxuries bestowed on them by their sponsors—"caviare, paté de foie gras, tinned gherkins, Christmas puddings, tinned mushrooms."[51] The 1933 Everest expedition, Shipton writes, had "every conceivable variety—half a dozen kinds of breakfast food, bacon, ham, beef, mutton, chicken, lobster, crab, salmon, herrings, cod-roes, asparagus, caviare, foie gras, smoked salmon, sausages, many kinds of cheese, a dozen varieties of biscuit," and more.[52] But these early, elegant adumbrations of menu-style consumption fail: Smythe admits that their luxurious food led to "ill health and upset stomachs," and Shipton finds that "one and all, we agreed that the food was wholly unsatisfying."[53] The problem, as Shipton sees it, is that the foods he lists are all tinned, and his solution is a different *kind* of variety, where tinned food is supplemented with "fresh, salted or dried food."[54] Yet all writers agree that at high altitudes no amount of variety can tempt the climber. J. B. L. Noel, a member of the 1924 expedition, states that during a period of four days and nights at 23,000 feet he "ate no meat at all, and enjoyed a diet of Swiss milk mixed with strawberry jam."[55] Other climbers at altitude under conditions of extreme exhaustion eat virtually nothing.

This dwindling desire for food correlates with a near-desperate craving for liquid—the one natural desire that is sharpened unbearably at high altitudes, for the large quantities required by climbers are virtually unobtainable given the limited amounts of fuel that can be transported for melting snow. The consequences can be devastating. "Without liquid we would deteriorate rapidly" realizes Joe Tasker, facing a multiday fuel-less descent of Dunagiri.[56] "Everything was so slow moving when we had no water," says Willi Bauer of the high camp on K2 in 1986, where during a storm four climbers died of oxygen and fluid deprivation.[57] Hermann Buhl's account of his epic solo ascent of Nanga Parbat is dominated by thirst, which he describes at one point as becoming a "torture of hell, driving me literally mad."[58] At altitude, however, profound exhaustion makes procuring any liquid an immense challenge. Narratives of high-altitude mountaineering are rife with descriptions of endless forced sessions of melting snow and brewing up tea. "Melting a saucepan full of snow for water and bringing it to the boil took so long," writes Shipton in neat testimony to the problem, "that people tended to delude themselves that they had eaten a hearty meal."[59] Even drinks that are imbibed, writes Francis Younghusband, are "not very comforting, for at these high altitudes water boils at so low a temperature that a really hot drink cannot be had. Nothing more than tepid tea or soup can be concocted."[60] Like food, however, water merely augments the period of survival at high altitude. The ambiguous nature of high-altitude consumption of foodstuffs is that desire must be managed—a desire for water must be repressed or strenuously accommodated, and a desire for crucial calories heightened—but only in a realm where life can be prolonged, not sustained.

The other two responses to chronic underconsumption are also responses to the crisis of an appetite invulnerable to variety. First, variety quickly comes to be rewritten in the guise of careful food management on what Sherry Ortner calls the "military model."[61] Accounts of British expeditions from the 1920s on follow the concerns of the Lhasa Mission by detailing the diets of climbers and porters, and the shipment of foodstuffs, with military precision. The "nucleus of each day's food," Ruttledge explains, was a "basic ration containing all necessary vitamins and calories," variety coming in the shape of "'Christmas boxes,' many of them containing special delicacies obtained largely from Messrs. Fortnum and Mason."[62] For a couple of decades after World War II, the military overtones on large expeditions continue to be explicit. (Brigadier) John Hunt's 1953 expedition to Everest chooses to pack food in "man-day units," a "system which is now widely used by armed forces operating in small groups in the field."[63] The founding principle of consumption here is not the menu but the ration: a principle of controlled variety carefully measured in terms of optimal calorie and vitamin counts and designed to manage the peril of underconsumption. These early military-style ventures into food management find their counterpart in latter-day exercises of what one might call "performance mountaineering," where individuals accomplish near superhuman feats of endurance. Benoit Chamoux, for instance, attributes his successful twenty-three-hour climb of K2 to a "special diet" that "spreads out the various foods, taking into account their 'profitability' as far as the body and effort are concerned."[64]

Food supply on these expeditions could therefore be read ultimately as an Orientalist celebration of Western-style management of "third world" conditions, and accounts of high-altitude mountaineering do tend to focus on the methodical process whereby ever-smaller amounts of food and other gear are transported up the mountain to a succession of high camps, which necessitates the supervision of teams of porters working to supply the climbers' needs. In this respect, these narratives tend to be covert celebrations of Western brains (management skills) and "native" brawn (the porters' and yaks' load-hauling capacities). "Ascending Everest," writes Krakauer, is a "long, tedious process, more like a mammoth construction project than climbing as I'd previously known it," before calling expedition leader Rob Hall a "quartermaster nonpareil" who "pored over reams of computer printouts detailing logistical minutiae: menus, spare parts, tools, medicines, communications hardware, load-hauling schedules, yak availability" (95).

Hall's menus, however, carry a subtly different semiotic function from the Sherpani's postcolonial marketplace at the Khumbu Lodge, for they are prepared at an altitude where variety *per se* has little effect on the appetite and Western climbers could subsist just as well, or just as poorly, on a daily diet of rice and dahl. Krakauer's description of Hall's task at Base Camp draws attention instead to his managing *function*. In that respect, Hall's role looks back to a very long line of famous expedition organizers—Charles Granville Bruce, John Hunt, Chris Bonington, to name a few—whose command over a vast infrastructure of organization carried neo-imperialist overtones insofar as they represented differences between Western models of organization and the lifestyles of the indigenous peoples.[65] If that difference is no longer absolute or impermeable, as Krakauer's anecdote about the Sherpani and the arrogant trekker demonstrates, it is still maintained by principles Rob Hall exemplifies. The Sherpani shows promise at menu management; Rob Hall is "nonpareil."

Yet life at Base Camp and above seems to run counter to the lure of any form of consumption: one simply *cannot* eat. This fact structures the third response to the disappearing appetite, which is to embrace it as the provenance and exemplification of the counter-modern significances of mountaineering. Abandoning the "tyranny of the urgent" means experiencing life (to quote some book titles) "on the edge," in "thin air," "without mercy," in a region where appetite often fails or cannot be satisfied; where no one is indulged; where the rhythm of life is stripped down to subsistence and mere survival; where one's own decisions count for everything; where serious risk attends any accomplishment; and where toughness and endurance, rather than the equipment carried, brings success. Tales of Himalayan climbing, writes Greg Child, evoke a "picture of a person being strained through a metaphysical sieve, separating each component of the inner being, shedding all but the components essential to survival, then forcing those vital remnants to function at the limit."[66] As if such extreme conditions strip away all immaterial cultural differences—so that US or British climbers can go, as Jeff Achey said, on vision quests—writers of high adventure frequently transform their narratives into testaments to the fortitude of the human spirit. Watching climber Ed Viesturs climb slowly upward on Everest, Breashears writes: "I became aware that it embodied the ancient struggle between man and nature, a struggle that illuminates and exemplifies our questing, adventurous nature."[67]

In that confrontation with nature, nothing expresses the transcendent human spirit so completely as subduing all natural cravings for food, and in particular the tendency toward over-consumption experienced in Western countries. Climbing high, as Breashears says, is "about the deprivations"; and privation turns out to have unexpectedly positive counter-modern significances. Hardships endured are necessary for a new appreciation of simple things, for example. Returning from a freezing day on the Northeast Ridge of K2 to be greeted with "steaming mugs of hot chocolate," Rick Ridgeway notes: "One of the lessons one learns from hard climbing is how satisfying something simple can be."[68] For Tom Hornbein the "tasting of hardship" on Everest is one reason for the "simplicity that strips the veneer off civilization and makes that which is meaningful easier to come by."[69] One interpretation of "that which is meaningful" is the visionary experience at which many climbers aim. Wilfred Noyce, high on Everest in 1953, for instance, asks at one point: "What for supper? There was sausage-meat . . . now unpalatable. I decided to stew it up in the soup. When it was half-cooked, a not unusual event occurred. The Primus ran out of fuel."[70] But this prosaic moment leads to sudden transcendence as Noyce looks at the spectacular scene and finds:

> Something here beyond me, outside me, 'far more deeply interfused' than my muddled brain could care to know, lent a magic to the air that made human effort meaningless. I was, for the moment, again near to Nirvana.
>
> Heartened . . . I went back to cook sausage-meat in soup.[71]

Hermann Buhl experiences a similar moment on Nanga Parbat when, despite his torturing thirst, he finds himself "on that spot, the target of my dreams, and I was the first human being since Creation's day to get there."[72] Bivouacking in a crevasse above 23,000 feet on Annapurna, having gone days without food or drink, Maurice Herzog "floated in a kind of peaceful happiness" as "Everything material about me seemed to have dropped away."[73]

Such moments adumbrate some of the deeper symbolic meanings of (non-)consumption among the high summits. High altitude mountaineering brings climbers face to face with elemental conditions virtually unobtainable in the West, whose inhabitants, buffered from authentic experience in their luxurious over-consumption and endlessly unfulfilled yearnings for gratification, can feel, as T. J. Jackson Lears writes of the psychological experience of consumer capitalism, profoundly unreal or "weightless."[74] If deprivation must be managed to accomplish climbing goals, it is also responsible for the counter-modern meanings of high-altitude mountaineering. High altitude brings Westerners to one of the few sites where hunger can be almost completely suppressed or transposed metonymically into an abstract appetite (for the summit, conquest, victory, or insight), where desperate cravings (for water) can be justified in terms of one's survival beyond the next few hours, and where all consumption can be defined in terms of assuaging elemental needs. Entering the spatial and temporal boundaries of the Death Zone underpins the intensity of the experience—its "realness" and substance. It is also, counterintuitively, to embrace the logic that motivates neoclassical economics. Like Watney on Mars, or Martineau's colonists, or the contestants of *Survivor*, these adventurers seem faced with an uncompromisable recognition of the "bottom line"—individual choice, utility maximization, and scarcity—though now expressed powerfully as a critique of consumption.

Entry into the Death Zone, however, begins to structure a counter-narrative, for it poses to the sojourner there a stark imperative: return to consumption, or die. High altitude deprivation restores the meaningfulness of consumption, making it a vital and consequential act in the face of incredible hardship. Joe Tasker, for instance, devotes two separate paragraphs to detailing the "snow mushes" he and Dick Renshaw devise on the descent from Dunagiri, mixing a little melted snow with "bits of oats among the dirt in the bottom of our rucksacks."[75] Moreover, most tales of survival among the high peaks end with ecstatic accounts of appetite regained in the company of fellow feasters. George Bell, returning with his companions to the valley near Askole (in northern Pakistan) after ten harrowing days pinned down in a storm on the Abruzzi ridge of K2, writes that "we made hogs of ourselves": "We stuffed ourselves with apricots, chickens, eggs, grapes, apples, pears, and cucumbers, for the fertile valley was yielding luxuries unknown to the grim regions beyond."[76] One lunch for Bell was composed of "ten hard-boiled eggs, two small chickens, and chuppatis."[77] Wilfrid Noyce speaks of his "strongest memory" of the trip out from Everest being their desire for food: "In order to satisfy our greed, it was necessary to plunder villages all along the way. . . . That night we had seven chickens, but most declared this not to be enough."[78] Peter Boardman, down from an ascent of Changabang, writes: "Unlimited food, unlimited brews—this was Heaven."[79] Reintroduced to the joys of consumption, these climbers foreshadow the trekker at the Khumbu Lodge in their voracity and demand for variety.

Yet if the counter-modern significations of high-altitude deprivation resist the hegemony of bourgeois ease and over-consumption, they also resist the chronic under-consumption Westerners see as typical of the Himalayan region. While George Bell devours his giant chicken and egg "lunch for the sahib," he takes a moment to notice that his "dandy wallahs"—the people carrying him because of his frostbitten feet—"were perhaps a bit depressed by seeing me eat with such gusto."[80] Appetite restored, Bell reverts to the kind of overtly colonialist assumptions that has J. B. L. Noel in 1927 commenting: "If they are happy, fit and well fed, these simple-minded people will work with the strength of giants."[81] Recent accounts usually try to rescind this more or less conscious sense of cultural superiority. Krakauer's later approbation of Hall's assessment that "we would have absolutely *no* chance of getting to the summit of Everest without [the] help" (68) of Sherpas suggests as much. But that "flexible *positional* superiority" of which Said speaks nonetheless emerges subtly in dozens of accounts of trekking and climbing in the Himalayas, which preserve counter-modern values within a deeper, though occluded, embrace of Western-style patterns of consumption. The agriculture-based subsistence economies of Nepal and Tibet play an important role here in allowing Western visitors to rewrite the meaning of the terrain.[82] "I have the universe all to myself," says Peter Matthiessen in his well-known *The Snow Leopard* (1978), standing elatedly atop a high pass in Nepal, waiting for his Sherpa porters to arrive.[83] Matthiessen codes that particular land grab in terms of his quest for enlightenment. But what he articulates in terms of transcendence, others embrace in a more mundane but subtler re-visioning of socioeconomic and geopolitical boundaries. Tom Hornbein, hiking through the heavily terraced foothills of Nepal, notes that: "For all the size, for all the intransigent power of the ice-encrusted wall to the north, wilderness, as western man defines it, did not exist . . . here man lived in continuous harmony with the land. . . . It was an enviable symbiosis."[84] It is also a crucial symbiosis for Hornbein's symbolic purposes, for if the Nepalese create farming communities and live in harmony with their landscape *here*, the "ice-encrusted wall to the north" represents the limits of their cultural reach even though that land lies within Nepal.[85] It is "beyond man's control," as Broughton Coburn says, and Greg Child, after pondering balances between man and nature, agrees: "Perhaps the reasons we were drawn to the mountains was precisely because they were not man's place at all."[86]

Krakauer's *Into Thin Air* likewise reconfigures the significations of the Nepalese landscape. As if to sunder his relationship to the kind of "enviable symbiosis" Hornbein and others saw in Nepal, Krakauer's descriptions of Nepal on the trek to Everest are determinedly pragmatic—they are, as it were, determinedly anti-counter-modern. "Early Western climbers," according to Krakauer, regarded the country as an "earthly paradise, a real-life Shangri-la" (57), and it is this romantic misapprehension that the scene in the Khumbu Lodge, which underscores the Nepaleses' determination to live in the untidy "modern world," is designed to puncture. Later, Krakauer sets the Sherpani's entrepreneurial ambitions against a different, more sweeping assessment of Nepal: "it wasn't wilderness, and hadn't been for hundreds of years," for "Every scrap of arable land had been terraced and planted with barley, bitter buckwheat, or potatoes" (52). Krakauer looks backward to the subsistence economy still visible in every acre of tilled ground, and forward to the economic restructurings that tourism makes possible. But both perspectives undergird the rhetorical force of "it wasn't wilderness." Like Hornbein's "wilderness . . . did not exist," Krakauer equates the geopolitical entity of Nepal with habitable land while freeing the terrain of the higher regions from the herders and farmers—whose country it in fact is—for a new set of meanings organized around the ostensibly noneconomic activities in which climbers participate on the mountain. Underconsumption in the mountains takes on a wholly different set of meanings than underconsumption in the foothills. It is this act of deterritorialization of Nepal (and Tibet or Pakistan in other accounts) that allows writers such as Breashears to read an "ancient struggle between man and nature" in the landscape—and to allow writers to make symbolic claims about the "human condition" in terms of Western climbers who, in their massive efforts to achieve the summit, undergo an apotheosis as the adventuring human spirit.[87]

The bioeconomic meanings of deprivation on the high peaks also lends itself to an ancillary discourse: visionary quests for self-fulfillment. In *The Snow Leopard*, the arduous trek to Shey, the Crystal Monastery, in the Dolpo region of Nepal, allows Matthiessen as spiritual seeker to escape "proliferation without joy, corrosive money rot."[88] He notes that at Tarakot, where the dregs of the local beer are given to the cattle, "nothing in this old economy is wasted."[89] A few days before arriving at Shey, the "new" consumerist economy the travelers take with them begins to crumble: the expedition is "so short of money . . . that we could not afford an extra porter" to carry "more canned food to vary our diet."[90] He continues: "The sausage, crackers, and coffee are all gone, and sugar, chocolate, tinned cheese, peanut butter, and sardines are nearly finished; we shall soon be down to a pallid regimen of bitter rice, coarse flour, lentils, onions, and a few potatoes, without butter."[91] Life under this "pallid regimen" at Shey Gompa "promises to be stringent." In fact, this paring-down of their goods sets the stage for a familiar scene at Shey. This "spare, silent place" affords a precise antidote to "proliferation without joy": cold so deep and long that Matthiessen finds himself "inclined to my Zen practice"; an austere breakfast of tea and porridge encouraging visionary insight, so that the "mountains all around me take on life; the Crystal Mountain moves."[92]

Published in the same year as *Into Thin Air*, Wade Brackenbury's *Yak Butter and Black Tea* follows *The Snow Leopard* in employing a bioeconomic discourse to shape a high-Himalayan vision quest. *Yak Butter* details the efforts of three Westerners, and ultimately Brackenbury alone, to reach the "secret" valley of the Drung people in Tibet—a journey made complex by the fact of the area having been closed to foreigners since the Chinese occupation of Tibet. Acts of food consumption play a central role in expressing cultural values and negotiating cultural differences. One symbolic resolution of the narrative, for instance, is Brackenbury's solo journey through difficult mountain passes to the Drung valley, when he, like so many mountaineers making a summit push before him, relies entirely on his own skills at survival and on the food and shelter he carries with him. And it is at this point, unsurprisingly, that implicit hints of a journey toward self-knowledge become obvious. He leaves for the high pass with dreams of "being pursued by a great black bird" (171) and finds the way to the Drung valley accompanied by a visionary reliving of scenes with his father.

This visionary experience is a momentary relief from Brackenbury's preoccupation with the brute materiality of subsistence. Several factors keep the issue of acquiring food in the foreground. First, Brackenbury explains, the "constant exertion, coupled with the high altitude, meant that I was burning a tremendous number of calories. . . . As a result, I was hungry all the time and found a large part of my thinking devoted to food" (120).[93] Second, though the travelers carry some dehydrated food for a planned final push through high mountain passes, they have to spend much of their time scrounging food from local villagers. Third, the party constantly confronts the problem of traveling within a subsistence economy: there is no surplus food available for purchase. After they complain when promised supplies fail to materialize, one villager tells them: "You just don't understand. . . . You're used to being able to buy what you want, but here there isn't much extra of anything. When you get some eggs from a family in the morning, those are the eggs that the family was going to eat that day" (77). Considering the constraints on consumption in a truly subsistence economy far from the usual trekking routes, the only possible trade, Brackenbury comes to realize, could be by barter.

In the end, however, the Westerners must depend, not on barter, but on a kind of anti-economy: that is, on the incredible generosity of the Tibetans. At virtually every stop, the travelers share the villagers' meals, relying on them to such an extent that their occasional payments of money or chiropractic adjustments seem increasingly at odds with the villagers' largesse—to whom the money in any case generally means little. In terms of the symbolic meanings of Brackenbury's journey, this redefinition of the possibilities of consuming food is surprisingly powerful. Importantly, it allows readers to activate the significance of the Drung creation myth that Brackenbury inserts as preface to the book, and which begins:

> A long time ago when the world was young, the land was covered with people. The forests were filled with the sounds of many kinds of animals, all good for food. The good soil produced more corn and vegetables and barley than all the people could eat, so there was plenty of everything for all and no reason for unhappiness. (xi)

In one sense, this legend of a land of plenty stands in stark contrast to the actual situation of the Tibetans, who, Brackenbury shows, barely endure their encounters with a precarious environment. Yet the Tibetans, according to Brackenbury, exemplify a noncommodified approach to consumption—they simply share whatever they have—which their visitors from a consumerist Shangri-la of plenty to the West find a compelling counter-modern alternative.

Just prior to his solo journey through the high pass, for example, Brackenbury spends the night with an old couple who, despite having no supplies beyond "a leather bag full of butter, and another with tsampa," and no implements beyond "one cooking pot [and] one tea kettle," take him "right in for tea and food. I shared my buckwheat bread, and they cooked me several ears of corn. Neither could speak any Chinese, but they jabbered away in Tibetan, seeming to care not at all that I couldn't respond. We laughed together and ate" (169). The by-now-familiar gestures toward the value of non-commodified consumption—the old couple have literally two utensils and three items of food in their "small shanty," yet the meal is joyful—accompany hints of a pre-lapsarian state. They communicate without language, and enjoy a magical communion (breaking bread, eating, and laughing together), for which the Tibetans produce food seemingly out of nowhere. To this ceremony Brackenbury contributes his bread (actually bread given to him by other Tibetans the day before.) Quiet as it is, the scene promotes an ethos of communal sharing to place against the lonely strife of the one that follows and underscores the continuing relevance of the Drung myth. The Tibetans preserve paradisal virtues in a terrain where there is barely enough of anything for anybody, as opposed to the West where there is plenty of everything for all and every reason for unhappiness. For Brackenbury, the lack of food for excess consumption is what makes Tibet the potential repository of symbolic values set against an ethos of endless over-consumption. It is precisely the kind of scene that Krakauer skewers in *Into Thin Air*: the Sherpani is more interested in entrepreneurship than in Shangri-la.

Yet in *Yak Butter* the travelers' journeys do not so much resolve as sharpen the questions the book poses about an appropriate relationship to consumption in high Asia. Though the travelers eschew the common expedition-approach to trekking and mountaineering in which all supplies are carefully managed and then carried by porters, and though their stated goal is to escape the destructive commodity capitalism of the West, their trek toward the Drung valley nonetheless subtly takes Western-style consumption as its governing assumption. For example, the travelers never abandon the "menu" approach to consumption. The travelers desire variety. "People had been bringing us food," Brackenbury states at one point, "but it was the wrong kind. We had enough walnuts and cucumbers for two months, but getting eggs, meat, potatoes, butter, and salt seemed to be about impossible" (69). And later, as they slip away from the Chinese authorities who have been holding them, Brackenbury, like so many expedition planners before him, takes the time to inventory their food supply: "We had six days' worth of freeze-dried dinners, thirty-six Power bars, ten pounds of powdered milk, around three and a half pounds of yak butter, six pounds of buckwheat noodles, seven pounds of rice, six packs of instant ramen noodles, about a pound of dried yak meat, five very small potatoes, a pound of tsampa, and nine pounds of canned meat" (119–20).

This demand for a "menu" of foods points toward the cultural difference that appears more insistently as the book progresses, which is that the Westerners, in contrast to the Tibetans, define their lifestyle in terms of choice. The shape of the entire adventure and narrative hinges on certain choices the travelers constantly discuss: whether to approach the Drung valley by way of villages or through high mountain passes; whether to avoid the authorities or try to enlist their help; whether, in the face of opposition, they will press on to the valley at all. Two of the adventurers choose to return; Brackenbury proceeds to the valley. That decision to choose the valley is crucial for him because, as he eventually makes clear, exercising choices signify a kind of spiritual awakening to the endless possibilities of the human spirit. When he decides to return to the States rather than wander alone in the mountains for instance, he "felt a great welling-up of joy, not because of the choice I had made to reject the fantasy—to go back and continue the life I had left—but because it *was* a choice" (209).

An earlier scene where Brackenbury buys corn flour from a villager for a ridiculously high price provides an important contrast. The villager needs money to buy medicine for his sick mother. The next day, Brackenbury returns and gives the man forty yuan for two sacks of flour, having to fight off five young children who "stared on in apprehension as they watched me try to trade what must have seemed to them a few scraps of paper for what was probably all the food in the house" (79). The ironies of the scene are multiple. The villager does have a choice; but it is a choice that pits vital medicine against all the food in the house rather than choice which is interpreted menu-style, where one selection should be as gratifying as another because accommodated within a context of abundance. Brackenbury, for his part, claims that he was forced to take the family's food because "we desperately needed more food" (78). Yet it is clear that at any time during the trip the Westerners could return to their own countries. Brackenbury's decision is "menu-based" in the sense that his efforts to prolong the adventure do not negate the possibility of returning to a consumer paradise—the fallback position whose allure can always be traced in the travelers' hunger for more food.

This prospect of rich Westerners depending on some of the poorest inhabitants of the globe for their fantasies of a pre-consumerist Shangri-La is an unpalatable one, and Brackenbury does reveal a gradually dawning shame for so disrupting the lives of the villagers. Having lied to one villager whose family provides him with a "large dinner of buckwheat bread and pork with . . . lots of butter tea" (167) and a parting gift of a "giant round loaf of buckwheat bread" (169)—the loaf he shares with the old couple the following night—Brackenbury writes: "I felt dirty as I walked away. I suddenly saw myself as I imagined they must see me—a selfish Westerner, coming suddenly into their quiet lives, then disappearing, leaving trouble behind and them to pick up the pieces" (168). It "seemed wrong," Brackenbury notes, "to lie to and endanger the villagers who freely shared food and helped us in so many ways" (169). This scene is crucial to the symbolic moves that follow. This recognition of selfishness, followed immediately by the communal supper with the old couple to which he contributes food, frames the solo journey to the Drung valley—the self-reliance and the (self-)discoveries he now achieves given new weight because they are dissociated from selfishness on the one hand, and enabled by noncommodified consumption on the other.

Consuming food in *Yak Butter* always carries these kinds of uneasy and shifting symbolic meanings. At its richest, the book avoids the rhetorical sleight of hand manifest in so many accounts of climbing in high Asia whereby a high-altitude suppression of appetite underpins counter-modern values. Brackenbury cannot afford the trope of meaningful non-consumption. He cannot afford the porters and the variety of food brought from the West; that is to say, he cannot afford the apparatus of food management that enables high-altitude mountaineering to proceed as if it were *not* dependent on a wholly different socioeconomic regime than the ones typifying the Himalayan region. Brackenbury's and his co-travelers' dependence on the Tibetan people places them in a perpetually changing relationship to all economic systems. They choose to step outside a capitalist economy and are forced in turn beyond the traditional farming/barter economic activities of the

Tibetans. Yet they remain in relation to those economies and to the cultural assumptions that accompany them. Like so many other twentieth-century accounts of adventure in high Asia, privation in Brackenbury's book signifies a deep ambivalence toward the consumerist Shangri-la of the West. To choose privation is to oppose an ethos of self-gratification. Yet the context of Brackenbury's choice returns him to menu-based consumption in its privileging of the very act of choosing. Unsurprisingly, for it repeats a theme that ends virtually every narrative of high adventure in the Himalayas, one of Brackenbury's first actions on returning to a consumer economy in the tourist town of Dali is to enter the Tibetan Freedom Restaurant, where he "order[s] four dinners" (221).

Down for a few days' rest from the west face of Changabang, Peter Boardman reflects that "Joe [Tasker] and I were here seeking a survival situation. We had been struggling for survival not because of force of circumstance, but because of a deliberate choice we had made. Our adventure was a pampered luxury that we could afford to enjoy, it was pure self-indulgence."[94] Few Himalayan adventure narratives reach this level of insight into a menu-style articulation of material and psychic economies: they erase that insight by strategically containing scenes of deprivation within countermodern discourses. In this *topos*, the constraints placed on eating signify in complex ways: they counter fears of living a self-indulgent existence committed to over-consumption; they return mountaineers to a primal scene where eating counts as a matter of survival; and in the aftermath of climbs they make overindulgence comprehensible as reparation for privations endured. The consequence is not so much to embrace an ethos of under-consumption as to impart meaning, value, and "weightiness" to the appetite once more. It is for this reason that narratives of deprivation—though more remarkable than descriptions of the subsistence economies of Nepal, Tibet, and Pakistan—need to be read as profoundly Orientalist. As Boardman's little meditation suggests, the posture of this form of Orientalism, a strange conflation of absolute deprivation and pampered self-indulgence, is intensely oxymoronic. But it is menu *style*, and all the more exemplary for placing an ultimate premium on the one choice that is nowhere on the "men-u" called for by Krakauer's ugly American tourist: to consume nothing at all.

NOTES

1. Hilary Howard, "Adventure Vacations that reach the Extreme" *New York Times*, May 4, 2008, Section TR, 2, www.nytimes.com/2008/05/04/travel/04COMadventure .html. This chapter is derived, in part, from an article published in *Food and Foodways* 18, no. 3 (July-September 2010), doi.org/10.1080/07409710.2010.504105.

2. Dean McCannell, *The Tourist: A New Theory of the Leisure Class* (New York: Schocken Books), 1976, 39.

3. Lucy M. Long, *Culinary Tourism* (Lexington: University of Kentucky Press, 2004), 21.

4. See Lisa M. Heldke, *Exotic Appetites: Ruminations of a Food Adventurer* (New York: Routledge, 2003).

5. Abercrombie & Kent website, 2010. No longer available. Similar sentiments can be found everywhere on the 2022 website, www.abercrombiekent.com/.

6. Heldke, *Exotic*, xxiii.

7. Sherry Ortner, *Life and Death on Mt. Everest* (Princeton: Princeton University Press, 1999), 47. For an entertaining narrative of the antimodern underpinnings of eighteenth and nineteenth century Alpinism in Switzerland, see Fergus Fleming, *Killing Dragons: The Conquest of the Alps* (New York: Grove, 2000), 11–12, 83–85.

8. Jeff Achey, "Power to the People?" *Climbing* 232 (July 2004), 10.

9. Wade Brackenbury, *Yak Butter and Black Tea: A Journey into Forbidden China* (Chapel Hill: Algonquin Books, 1997), 208. Subsequent page references to this work are cited parenthetically in the text.

10. Quoted in Broughton Coburn, *Everest: Mountain Without Mercy* (Willard: National Geographic Society, 1997), 36.

11. Joe Tasker, *Savage Arena* (London: Methuen, 1982), 127.

12. Tasker, *Savage*, 127. This particular expedition ends with the death of his friend in an avalanche; Tasker himself was to die on Everest before *Savage Arena* was published.

13. Jon Krakauer, *Into Thin Air* (New York: Doubleday, 1997), 88. Subsequent references to this work are cited parenthetically in the text.

14. Edward Said, *Orientalism: Western Conceptions of the Orient* (New York: Pantheon, 1978; London: Penguin, 1991), 7. I follow the lead here of Sherry Ortner, Reuben Ellis (*Vertical Margins: Mountaineering and the Landscapes of Neoimperialism* [2001]) and Peter L. Bayers (*Imperial Ascent: Mountaineering, Masculinity, and Empire* [2003]), the three scholars who have worked most interestingly on the neo-imperialist and orientalist underpinnings of Himalayan adventure literature.

15. The expedition actually left in December 1903 and returned in September 1904.

16. This reason was frequently cited by the instigators of the expedition to justify it.

17. Francis Younghusband, *The Heart of a Continent* (London: John Murray, 1896; New York: Charles Scribner's, 1904), viii, ix.

18. Francis Younghusband, *India and Tibet* (London: John Murray, 1910), 140, 142.

19. Laurence Austine Waddell, *Lhasa and its Mysteries* (New York: E.P. Dutton, 1905), v.

20. Robert Dixon, *Writing the Colonial Adventure* (Cambridge: Cambridge University Press, 1995), 62.

21. Edmund Candler, *The Unveiling of Lhasa* (London: Edward Arnold, 1905), 91; Waddell 61.

22. Waddell, *Lhasa*, 105.

23. Candler, *Unveiling*, 94.

24. Younghusband, *India*, 86.

25. See Younghusband, *India*, 86, 404. The continued existence of the trading post at Gyantse was written into the Tibet Treaty signed in Lhasa in September 1904.

26. Waddell, *Lhasa*, 206.

27. Waddell, *Lhasa*, 207.

28. Perceval Landon, *The Opening of Tibet* (New York: Doubleday, Page, 1905), 124.

29. Younghusband, Introduction to Landon, *Opening of Tibet*, xii.

30. Younghusband, *India*, 170; Landon, *Opening of Tibet*, 125; Waddell, *Lhasa*, 207.

31. Waddell, *Lhasa*, 212.

32. Candler, *Unveiling*, 94.

33. Waddell, *Lhasa*, 357.

34. Landon, *Opening of Tibet*, 155.

35. Waddell, *Lhasa*, 164.

36. Landon, *Opening of Tibet*, 113.

37. Richa Nagar, Victoria Lawson, Linda McDowell, and Susan Hanson, "Localizing Globalization: Feminist (Re)readings of the Subjects and Spaces of Globalization," *Economic Geography* 78, no. 3 (July 2002): 260, doi.org/10.1111/j.1944–8287.2002.tb00187.x.

38. John Climaco, "Dangerous Liaisons," in *Epic: Stories of Survival from the World's Highest* Peaks, ed. Clint Willis (New York: Thunder's Mouth Press, 1997), 64.

39. Charles S. Houston and Robert H. Bates, *K2: The Savage Mountain* (New York: McGraw-Hill, 1954; reprint North Salem, NY: The Adventure Library, 1994), 43.

40. Sue Cobb, *The Edge of Everest* (Harrisburg: Stackpole, 1989), 74.

41. Greg Child, *Thin Air: Encounters in the Himalayas*, (Seattle: The Mountaineers, 1998), 88.

42. Thomas F. Hornbein, *Everest: The West Ridge* (San Francisco: Sierra Club, 1965; Seattle: The Mountaineers, 2002), 85.

43. Climaco, "Dangerous," 75.

44. Houston and Bates, *K2*, 44.

45. Houston and Bates, *K2*, 156, 157.

46. Younghusband, *India*, 260.

47. Frank S. Smythe, *Kamet Conquered* (1932; reprint London: Hodder and Stoughton, 1947), 68–69.

48. Hugh Ruttledge, *Everest 1933* (1934; reprint London: Hodder and Stoughton, 1938),

44; Eric Shipton, *Upon That Mountain* (London: Hodder and Stoughton, 1943; London: Pan Books, 1956), 196.

49. Ruttledge, *Everest*, 43; Shipton, *Upon*, 134; E.F. Norton, *The Fight for Everest: 1924*. (London: Edward Arnold, 1925; Varanasi and Kathmandu: Pilgrims Publishing, 2002), 116.

50. Tasker, *Cruel Way* 86

51. Smythe, *Kamet*, 34; Frank S. Smythe, *The Kangchenjunga Adventure* (London: Gollancz, 1930), 69.

52. Shipton, *Upon*, 197.

53. Smythe, *Kangchenjunga*, 69; Shipton, *Upon*, 197.

54. Shipton, *Upon*, 197.
55. J.B.L. Noel, *Through Tibet to Everest* (London: Edward Arnold, 1927), 170.
56. Tasker, *Savage Arena,* 63.
57. Quoted in Jim Curran, Jim. *K2: Triumph and Tragedy* (Boston: Houghton Mifflin, 1987), 193.
58. Hermann Buhl, "Nanga Parbat . . . Solo," (1956) in *The Armchair Mountaineer*, eds. David Reuther and John Thorn (Birmingham: Menasha Ridge Press, 1989), 31.
59. Shipton, *Upon*, 129–30.
60. Francis Younghusband, *The Epic of Mount Everest* (1926; reprint London: Edward Arnold, 1942), 133.
61. Ortner, *Life and Death*, 47.
62. Ruttledge, *Everest*, 44.
63. John Hunt, *The Ascent of Everest* (London: Hodder and Stoughton, 1953), 263.
64. Curran, *K2: Triumph*, 203.
65. Reuben Ellis, speaking of the first British expeditions bringing bottled oxygen to Everest, remarks that the British interpreted the technology as a "display of national and racial superiority, a symbolic construct consistent with the many representations that Europeans have made to themselves of their imagined right to empire." *Vertical Margins*, 150.
66. Child, *Thin Air*, 17.
67. David Breashears, "Upward Progress," in *Himalayan Quest*, eds. Ed Viesturs and Peter Potterfield (Washington D. C. National Geographic, 2003), 16.
68. Rick Ridgeway, *The Last Step: The American Ascent of K2* (Seattle: The Mountaineers, 1980), 123.
69. Hornbein, *Everest*, 180.
70. Wilfred Noyce, *South Col: One Man's Adventure on the Ascent of Everest, 1953* (London: William Heinemann, 1954), 167.
71. Noyce, *South Col*, 168.
72. Buhl, "Nanga Parbat," 27.
73. Maurice Herzog, *Annapurna* (New York: E.P. Dutton, 1952; reprint Guilford: Lyons Press, 1997), 222–23.
74. T.J. Jackson Lears, *No Place of Grace: Antimodernism and the Transformation of American Culture, 1880–1920* (New York: Pantheon, 1981; Chicago: University of Chicago Press, 1994), 8.
75. Tasker, *Savage Arena*, 74.
76. George I. Bell, "Out from the Mountain," in Charles S. Houston and Robert H. Bates, *K2: The Savage Mountain* (1954; reprint New York: The Adventure Library, 1994), 153.
77. Bell, "Out," 153.
78. Noyce, *South Col*, 274.
79. Peter Boardman, *The Shining Mountain* (London: Hoddard and Stoughton, 1978), 102.
80. Bell, "Out," 153.
81. Noel, *Through Tibet*, 294–95.

82. My argument here parallels that of Peter Bayers, who argues that the British naming of Himalayan peaks "effectively usurped the mountains from the indigenous populations," and in particular that of Reuben Ellis, who notes that in John Noel's *Through Tibet to Everest* the "mountain, the site of exploration, is radically set apart from the experientially defined region of toil and desolation," for it possesses a "geography that is symbolically British." Bayers, *Imperial Ascent*, 6; Ellis, *Vertical Margins*, 146.

83. Peter Matthiessen, *The Snow Leopard* (London: Penguin, 1978), 279.

84. Hornbein, *Everest*, 45.

85.A similar strategy emerges in National Geographic's brief history of "The Sherpas" in *Everest: Mountain Without Mercy*, which is entitled "Herders, Farmers, Traders, and Lamas."

86. Coburn, *Everest*, 36; Child, *Thin Air*, 83.

87. A particularly interesting example here is Sue Cobb's account of the Wyoming Centennial Everest Expedition of 1988, whose members, seeking to climb Everest without Sherpas, call themselves the Cowboys, which Cobb tells us is meant to "represent the Wyoming—and American—spirit of independence, free enterprise, and love of challenge." *Edge of Everest*, 6. What Cobb says directly others hint. At the end of one grueling trek to Base Camp on the Baltoro glacier, Greg Child, dismissing the expedition's surly Balti porters and seeing them sprint off down the glacier in a gathering snowstorm, remarks, with some glee, "We are home, the Balti are not." Child, *Thin Air*, 167.

88. Matthiessen, *Snow Leopard,* 39.

89. Matthiessen, *Snow Leopard,* 114.

90. Matthiessen, *Snow Leopard,* 151.

91. Matthiessen, *Snow Leopard,* 151.

92. Matthiessen, *Snow Leopard,* 192, 198, 207.

93. Brackenbury's "high altitude" is still below the altitude at which mountaineers' appetites generally shut down completely.

94. Boardman, *Shining Mountain*, 107.

Chapter Eight

Histories, Hedgestories, Herdstories

Beast Fables and Paleo Polities in Recent Animated Movies

A fable can be understood as an entertaining fiction disconnected from anything we might construe as real. But, as we saw in the previous two chapters, fables can also carry potent political and economic meanings couched in an "organicist rhetoric" that associates the body and its processes with constructions of the body politic.[1] Aesop's fable "The Ants and the Grasshopper," for example, describes a "starving Grasshopper" begging food from Ants who are industriously laying away stores of grain for the winter.[2] Having been too busy making music to collect food, the Grasshopper receives this terse declaration from the unmoved Ants: "Making music, were you? Very well; now dance!" Aesop's talking animals (and sometimes inanimate objects) underscore familiar morals—a time to work and a time to play, in this case—but also frequently expound on issues of politics and economics. This fable, for example, adopts a bioeconomic idiom to examine core principles of economic productivity. It certainly emphasizes industriousness over idleness, and in a sense cooperation over self-interest, as the appropriate way to utilize resources—but only under conditions of scarcity. The Ants have worked all summer long to amass just enough grain for themselves. This commonwealth seems to comprise several groups surviving self-sufficiently, and separately, without surplus. The Ants therefore survive without capital. There is no steady accumulation year on year; nothing grows more than present needs. Stadial theory would deem it a primitive form of accumulation prior to mechanisms of exchange, which might begin to allow the exchange of music for grain, or indeed a society productive enough to allow grasshopper musicians to flourish. Today's market-focused economics would not recognize the fable as having anything to do with "economics" at all.

One contention of this chapter is that animated movies are the contemporary analogs of Aesop's fables, employing talking animals and their strangely defamiliarizing societies to articulate numerous moral, political, and economic issues. *Ice Age* and *Over the Hedge* can be understood as entertaining glosses on a fable such as "The Ants and The Grasshopper," for their enterprising ice age/woodland animals pose similar questions about resource management, the value of labor, and the problematic of exchange. I use the *Ice Age* franchise to pivot from beast fables to a broader discussion of the concept of Paleo polities, to which contemporary beast fables are frequently drawn as a touchstone illustration of commonwealth. By "Paleo" I am not thinking primarily of attempts to account for the actual living conditions of the Paleolithic Era, but a broad cultural fable linking animated movies such as *Ice Age* and *The Croods* to popular archeology to the Paleo diet. In fact, I borrow the abbreviation "Paleo" from the diet regime on the premise that the vast majority of its adherents "return" to the Paleolithic by purchasing food from the supermarket. The script of this cultural fable, like so many other fantastic returns to purported origins, addresses the arche of economics. It asks, in an era of destructive consumerism where humans might be held to be *contra naturam*: What are the principles of resource usage arising among animals and humans living in a State of Nature? Which lead, as liberal political theory predicts will happen, to a civil society? And how does the concept of a civil society jibe with economic principles enacted at the end of history, which is to say the Anthropocene of the twenty-first century? These abstract questions can be conjoined to an issue of enormous practical importance: contemporary efforts to rethink the global (mis)use of common-pool resources by resurrecting a workable model of the commons. Though rarely citing the Paleolithic, these discussions map onto Paleo animated movies, which so often return viewers to pre-capitalist and pre-property conceptions of space.

To be sure *Over the Hedge* has little to do, strictly speaking, with the Paleolithic. Yet it outlines a familiar discourse in which creatures employing what seem to be the primordial principles of resource-management in a pristine natural world help to launch a critique of the economic misdeeds of modernity. The talking beasts who confront—and accommodate—the consumerism of the Anthropocene allow *Hedge* to imagine alternatives to both premodern hoarding and excessive contemporary consumption in the interstices of a society seemingly devoted to the destruction of their foraging-space. Like *Hedge*, *Ice Age* and *The Croods* afford a critique of twenty-first-century capitalist exploitation by returning to fables of how "economics" functions in a pristine space without property boundaries or mechanisms of exchange. The first *Ice Age*—the only one to feature human characters—and the two *Croods* movies place their fables of origins within a fragmentary stadial schema. *Ice Age*'s plot arc shifts from a Hobbesian war of all against all (represented by the "pack" of saber-tooth tigers) to a Lockean civil society (the "Herd," as the animals eventually term themselves); a free-for-all to the rule of law; hoarding to exchange. Its history, or "herdstory," maps onto space: like most Paleo fables, it conceives of the Paleolithic in terms of a commons threatened by the passing of time. That is certainly the case in the most interesting contemporary example of Paleo fabling, *The Croods: A New Age*, which employs its vibrant comic art to evoke a counternarrative, a "tragedy of the commons" associated with the symbolic home of animation: Hollywood.

"We eat to live," says RJ (Bruce Willis), the raccoon hero of *Over the Hedge* (2006); "these guys [humans] live to eat" (20:37).[3] That familiar Socratic adage aptly characterizes a movie whose "family" of animals wake from hibernation to find that, while they slept, encroaching suburbs have shrunk their woodland home to nearly nothing. Beyond the surrounding hedge lies a terrifying world. Suburbia represents the terror of life subjected to unimaginably fast change: death on two wheels or four, development in the blink of an eye, laser-beam security systems. It is characterized by isolation and frustration; Gladys Sharp (Allison Janney), the villainous, SUV-driving president of the HOA, lives alone; street scenes show oddly anemic interactions. At one point we see a group of children sitting with their feet in the gutter, separately entranced by their phones. The murderous Dwayne arrives in his Verminator truck to add a regime of surveillance. Suburbia is also a terrain of simulacra: our first view of the new suburb is on an advertising billboard; our second, rows of ticky-tack houses all the same; our third, as Verne (Garry Shandling), the turtle hero, staggers out onto Glady's lawn, of animal statues and a living shrub trimmed to look like a guinea pig. Mechanical reproduction seems to be part of the suburban DNA. Our first glimpse of Gladys shows her haranguing neighbors for having their grass half a centimeter too long.

By contrast the woodland animals, who spend the movie breaking through hedges and walls, function with harmony and industry in their still-pristine sliver of forest. Verne emerges from his log to the beauty of nature restored, eliciting a "Wow!" (7:57) moment from him as he views the trees, lake, dragonflies, and a flower popping into existence. Verne's first act is to organize the animals to start storing up provisions for next winter, 274 days away; "It's spring," Verne announces to the sleeping animals—"that means, we gotta get to work!" (8:22). Another is to encourage them to do so in an ecologically sound manner: "I've got to go wee-wee," says Hammy (Steve Carell), the frantic squirrel, on awakening, and Verne admonishes him: "Oh, not in the lake we drink from" (8:15). Another is to distribute the berries remaining from hibernation, one to each animal. This gentle emphasis on the possibilities of working together and sharing resources underpins the animals' later concerted efforts to raid Gladys' house, guided by RJ, the insouciant raccoon, in his plan to restore a bear's food-hoard that he has stolen, then destroyed, in the first minutes of the movie. Such actions prompt Judith Halberstam to claim that this movie "offers more in the way of a vision of collective action than most independent films and critical theory put together," rising to a "cross-species alliance to destroy the colonizers [the suburban humans]" and "tear down the partition." Halberstam offers a provocative alliance between queerness, anti-colonial practices, and pre-capitalist sociality, all of which makes for a "strangely radical combination of socialist and anarchist notions."[4]

Halberstam is certainly correct about the movie's often savage critique of a culture of excessive and empty consumerism, waste, and what we might call, building on the hedge metaphor, "walled sociality." History has become, as it were, "hedgestory." The developers' hedge that Hammy says "never ends" (12:10) is echoed everywhere in the fences partitioning off the suburbanites' lots; that humans live behind them is revealed only when they get smashed by a dog who is chasing Verne. Gladys defends her property with laser beams on one side and her tank-like SUV on the other. The movie broadens the significance of those walls by running rock group The Clash's "Lost in the Supermarket" over the final credits. "We had a hedge back home in the suburbs/Over which I never could see," sing The Clash in this song about an alienating "long distance" suburban lifestyle of the "special offer" and saving "coupons from packets of tea." Such dwellers, the refrain tells us, are "all lost in the supermarket."[5] In the *Hedge* world supermarket food comes packaged in plastic, metal, and cardboard, stuffed into fridges, and then thrown out into metal bins. These bioeconomic disciplines evoke "hedgestories" on a macro level too. The movie's fences incorporate the logic of capitalist property rights buttressed in the political realm by border walls between nations (such as between the United States/Mexico), restrictions on the free movement of peoples (Brexit, Syrian migrants), gated communities, NIMBYism, and (in the United States) the racist ghettoizing logic of restrictive covenants.

These supermarket-loving surburbanites make a fetish of consumption. "For humans," RJ declares in his hilarious guide to the way humans eat, "enough is never enough" (21:34).[6] The human mouth is a "pie hole" (20:43). A family at prayer, RJ informs the woodland creatures, is worshipping its food. Taking the animals on a food-finding mission to Gladys's garden, RJ's first port of call is the tsunami of packaging material pouring from her three giant trash cans (21:42), amongst which is enough discarded food to feed them all. Hammy is soon ingesting processed cheese from a canister—and squirting it in streams from his nostrils. Waste byproducts spurting from cans becomes a running joke in *Hedge*. Vaporized by a speeding truck, the bear's mountain of packaged food turns into a litter of wrappers, his favorite

Spuddies a flattened tube of dust. Unsurprisingly, the movie unleashes an entire repertoire of scatological jokes. The humans have heaps of food, says RJ, trying to get the foragers to join him on the other side of the hedge, "food out the wazoo" (17:23); "whatever kind of food comes out of a wazoo," replies Verne scornfully, "I really don't think we're interested in eating" (17:27). When RJ opens a packet of chips the animals are blown away by a pressurized cloud of cheese derivatives, a scene neatly doubled by Stella the Skunk's (Wanda Sykes) later gaseous explosion.

The movie does not, however, rigorously enact the plot of an updated Aesop's fable whereby the animals play the part of industrious Ants and humans that of the wasteful Grasshopper. The animals emulate Aesop's Ants precisely insofar as their labor functions in endless cycles. The previous year they must have worked industriously for 274 days to obtain a survival margin of precisely nine berries; this year Verne tries setting them to work before they are even awake. Next year would be the same—had the subdivision not decimated the forest, making it impossible for them to gather enough food. But the broader issue is that their subsistence economy makes survival precarious under the best of circumstances. "Oh boy—this is what I was afraid of" (9:14), says Verne, picking up the last berries in the log, for they are "nine berries away from starvation" (10:29). The economic logic governing *Hedge*'s fabling therefore allows a differently inflected reading of Aesop's fable. Ants (and animals) labor so much not to represent the value of being industrious; they labor so much to survive because, under conditions of subsistence, their lack of capital confines them all to endless cycles of storing up food, consuming it, and then laboring again to store up food. If 274 days of labor in between periods of hibernation equals nine surplus berries, there simply is no Aesopian "time to play." Verne's ecologically sound warning to Hammy not to pee in the lake they drink from has another implication: to fall sick for a week means starvation.

Hedge in fact deploys Aesop's fable in reverse. The animals' industry signifies the risks associated with a subsistence economy: to work for 274 days now, with the forest mostly gone, would be a waste of time. For their part, humans do not equate with Aesop's Grasshopper. The Grasshopper wastes time, producing nothing; humans waste huge quantities of an excessive production, which is sufficient to feed the humans, woodland animals, and bear. *Hedge* therefore skews the moral axis of Aesop's fable toward the dimension of time and history. It constructs a schema of economic development along stadial lines. Humans no longer subsist. A world in which an entire subdivision can be built in six months, food comes "out the wazoo," and fridges and vending machines appear magically stuffed with food, represents a later, and much more productive, stage of economic and technological development. In the time-honored logic of stadial theory, that stage must be marked by massive capital investment, freeing humans from the onerous labor of foraging for food.[7]

The movie's stadial structure has profound consequences for the capacities of *Hedge*'s fabling. Aesop's fable allows both Ants and Grasshopper to represent human moral characteristics—a time to work and a time to play, or industry over indolence—by constructing a timeless space within which foraging for food is the only means of subsistence. To begin with, *Hedge* follows suit: the woodland animals in their foraging, gathering, and subsisting can represent human life as it once was. But they cannot represent humans as they are because the era of the Anthropocene signals the end of the animals' foraging grounds. Their lives are no longer timeless, but time-bound and space-bound. Our first view of the new subdivision is of mechanical rows of streets and houses disappearing toward a dim horizon. The map RJ produces to prove to the animals that their sliver of woodland home is slated for development shows no end to the subdivision (16:43). It occupies all visible space. RJ's map therefore charts the end of the animals' lifestyle and economic relationship to the resources once at their disposal. Verne's "wow moment" is destined to be the last. That embrace of historical change poses a profound dilemma for the movie to negotiate. How, after their immensely satisfying victory over Gladys and Dwayne, will the animals survive now that most of their habitat is gone, the rest is about to vanish, and there appears to be no possibility of relocation?

The movie makes three significant moves toward resolving this dilemma.[8] The first is to have the *bear* carry the symbolic weight of the humans' alienating lifestyle. RJ's loss of and attempt to replace Vincent's (Nick Nolte) hoard of packaged food generates the entire plot of the movie. The hoard itself underwrites the movie's satire of excess and emptiness. Remembering his lost tube of Spuddies calls forth from Vincent a mechanical repetition of its ad jingle—when it comes to Spuddies "enough just isn't enough" (5:17)—that reminds us of the deluge of identical houses and packages, and indeed of the hoard itself, which RJ has been tasked with reproducing down to the last item. And RJ's final showdown with the bear underwrites *Hedge*'s moral compass. Betraying RJ's friends to return the bear's food is, Vincent says, the "most vicious, deceitful, self-serving thing I've ever seen; you keep this up, you're gonna end up just like me, having everything you ever wanted" (1:04:52). That the bear speaks here for the movie's humans—their excessive consumerism, proprietary individualism, extreme self-interest, and inclination toward vicious behavior—is shown by the denouement: he ends up caged with the human villains, Gladys and Dwayne, in a hole in the ground. Vincent returns the movie to the world of the Aesopian fable, where talking beasts represent human (im)morality. The problem is that the bear can represent the human threat to the animals, and to the ecology that sustains them, only if we ignore the fact that the humans, by decimating the wilderness, also threaten the bear. Vincent, in short, exposes the unsettling core logic of the movie's fabling, which is caught between having a beast denote timeless human values, and acknowledging a history of evolving human sociality in which the time and space of beasts is coming to an end.

The more potent option the movie makes available is the new vector toward entrepreneurship that RJ brings to the woodland. Having displaced Verne as leader of the "family," RJ quickly marshals the other animals in a newly efficient and creative division of labor as they scavenge for food. Heather the possum (Avril Lavigne) "plays dead" while others raid the human's food; during the assault on Gladys' kitchen, Hammy walks a fishing line to avoid the laser beams in the garden while Stella distracts the house cat with her furry charms, and so on. RJ, moreover, makes the work of foraging fun. Though the movie concludes by harnessing RJ's risk-taking to Verne's vision of collective prosperity, even Verne realizes that RJ's verve and vision is a necessary antidote to his profound conservatism. The movie celebrates the mythos of twenty-first-century global capitalism: an efficient division of labor, creative leadership, an entrepreneurial imagination and, as shown by one of the movie's wittiest scenes when Hammy drinks a "Mach 6" energy drink to set things right by outpacing the speed of light, a lightning fast and fluid response to a challenging world. The movie's final joke about Hammy finding his nuts should not obscure its gesture toward a more serious economic statement: natural talent plus a sugar high out of a can solves the problem of Gladys/Dwayne/Vincent *and* gets the log filled with acorns in less than a second.

As part of this creative accommodation of contemporary economic principles, RJ also introduces into the movie a tilt toward what I called in Chapter 7 "menu-style consumption." The original DVD begins with a menu of choices set up to look like snack-packages in a vending machine, a witty echo of the first scene of the actual movie where RJ tries desperately to retrieve a packet of "It's Nacho Cheese!! (Get Yer Own Bag)" (0:33) from such a machine. Clicking on a button to make the "Play Movie" or "Scene Selection" package fall forward emphasizes the viewer's ability to choose a particular experience, structuring attitudes toward the clashing modes of consumption found in the movie proper: the unproductive hoarding of mountains of nutrition-poor food on one side of the hedge, and on the other, the unproductive lack of choice that has Hammy, on Verne's recommendation, nibbling on bits of undigestible bark. Streaming the movie nowadays exercises essentially the same privilege: for example, we choose to watch *Over the Hedge* over against the multitude of other simultaneously available animated movies we might stream instead. The movie holds out that privilege to the foragers. Watching the spectacle of the "De-Pelter Turbo" deal with the movie's villains, the young porcupines roast marshmallows in the heat while RJ nukes a bag of microwaveable popcorn (1:12:42). Hammy's final warp-speed plot-resolution has him filling the log with acorns—but also gives him time to eat a chocolate chip cookie. As Verne says and as the vending machine implies, many of the choices the human world makes available are junk; but the movie holds out the promise that the animals' life will be better when they have a choice of chips, hotdogs, marshmallows, popcorn, and energy drinks to put alongside the acorns, berries, and bark.

Entrepreneurial skills and the availability of multiple choices offer the animals a plausible future should their last patch of forest be developed. Relying on the abundance of the human world to survive, they could plausibly live on as scavengers rather than foragers, *in* rather than over the hedge. This third interpretive option is aligned with a substantial body of theoretical work, notably Gilles Deleuze and Félix Guattari's "nomadology," which conceptualizes assaults on the structures of the State apparatus in terms of "deterritorialization." The nomad's capacity to pass beyond fixed points—to conceive of dwellings "in terms of the trajectory that is forever mobilizing them," so that points become relays and stable space becomes virtual—broadens to include Deleuze and Guattari's own beast fable: rats and other "vermin," to use Gladys' term for the woodland animals, are nomads *par excellence* given their propensity for living in between human constructions of space, and for passing with ease through, under, over, and beyond human barriers and boundaries.[9] "Vermin" are thus one symbolic vector for what Deleuze and Guattari term the "war machine"—creative social or intellectual formations that are "formally distinct from all State apparatuses or their equivalents, which are instead what structure centralized societies."[10] Once the animals unleash their war machine in their assault on Glady's garden they prove to be a truly formidable force, out-foxing laser beams and the DePelter Turbo, that technological marvel Dwayne thinks of as the last word in garden-boundary security systems. The animals quite literally deterritorialize Gladys' property, turning the garden into a huge pit.

That the woodland animals breach, and may have to survive within the interstices of, the humans' structured, walled, and violently defended properties may thus be taken as compensation for the probable loss of the entire woodland. Indeed, from Deleuze and Guattari's perspective the sanctity of a pristine forest surrounded by a high hedge within which creatures can forage in their age-old manner *should* be abandoned. Its loss burnishes their nomadic credentials, turning them into what Deleuze and Guattari celebrate as an "ambulant people of relayers, rather than a model society."[11] Reminding us of the animals' radical redesign of a body politic that can run variously on acorns, energy drinks, and Spuddies—food traditional and new, healthy and junk, foraged and scavenged for in an ever-changing, ever-renewing smorgasbord of options—this approach dovetails neatly with the new entrepreneurial spirit RJ instils in the woodland band. The problem, once more, is Vincent the bear. Unlike the other woodland creatures who do not (despite the movie's premise) truly hibernate, bears do require a stable space in which to hibernate for a significant portion of the year. Hibernating animals and those who are otherwise confined to a specific habitat therefore expose the limits of *Hedge*'s, and indeed Deleuze and Guattari's, fabling. As a fabulous space of entrepreneurship and creative nomadism, *Hedge* succeeds in keeping alive alternatives to the alienating subdivision. But one is hard pressed to imagine this as a convenient answer to the movie's uncompromising sense that the dwindling forest represents a *real-life* threat to animals and ecologies, so that Vincent is a bear as well as a bear that stands for humans. Current research has showed that "iconic species" are losing habitat to rats and pigeons; some environmentalists argue that the earth in the wake of widespread eco-catastrophe will support little more than vermin.[12] In that case, Deleuze and Guattari's vision of human resistance will transform into a terrifying truth about global ecologies. It is to head off such possibilities that other contemporary representations of early foragers—popular archeology, Paleo diet advocates, and the *Ice Age* and *The Croods* movie franchises in particular—attempt to recoup the commons.

At a revelatory moment in *Seahenge* (2000)—a lively account of the archeological digs leading to the discovery of an early Bronze Age wooden "henge" on a Norfolk (UK) beach—popular archeologist Francis Pryor condenses his erudition and decades of archeological experience into what can only be construed as an extravagant fiction.[13] Contemplating the evidence discovered at a grave site, Pryor writes, "I can imagine" a funeral procession that includes "two men, possibly brothers" (141) followed by two sisters who, breaking a bowl of honey to attract bees and wasps, subsequently faint from a multitude of stings.[14] The next day, recovered, the sisters become the "most honoured guests at the family feast" (141–42). Written in the declarative voice, the narrative is supposed to address what Pryor considers the "ultimate challenge" of deciphering a "lost world of myth and ideology" (136) from a few excavated fragments, since reconstructing the cultural, spiritual, or economic meanings Bronze Age people attributed to their actions is like "trying to dig wisps of smoke" (136). Three factors guide his nebulous excavation of the past. First, the narrative must fit the uncovered evidence: shards of pottery, the position of skeletons, a fox skull buried upside down, and so forth. Second, Pryor consults the "literature of anthropology," arguing back from the written records of more recent societies to understand how rites of passage thousands of years ago might have, for example, "required the removal of the people involved from the main body of society" (139). The collapse and removal of the bee-stung sisters preparatory to their ceremonial reappearance at next day's family feast is presumably prompted by this logic.

Third, Pryor frames his story to pique the interest of a mass public—a concern the book often articulates.[15] At one point he describes a non-academic lecture at which, fearing he was boring his audience, he asks to great approval if anyone would "care to hear what it was like actually to find the site" (286) of a long wooden causeway, a "prehistoric religious site every bit as remarkable" (285) as Seahenge. One woman even stands to applaud the idea. The lecture "had at last come alive" (287), remarks Pryor; now everyone listens with "rapt attention" (292). The ensuing ten pages describe an orderly sequence of slides interspersed with a visceral plunge into an almost primordial scene as Pryor digs with his bare hands for ancient wooden posts in a freezing and "horrible . . . mess of slub and muck" (289). Gradually what appear to be random fragments of wood resolve into a wooden causeway, a bridge across the fen, and a bridge from the Bronze Age to the twenty-first century—all of which is mapped onto yet another story of the billion-year "rise of human civilization" as shaped wooden posts, signs of primordial human order, begin to appear in a line out of the "deep muck" (289). Pryor's "big discovery" (289) is also about public interfaces. In this self-consciously self-reflexive account, it is not exactly that the lecture audience provides a model of how to listen. Rather it reminds us that we come to this book as *yet another* enrapt audience. One other discovery that the tale of Pryor's discovery allows, then, is the deep public interest in representations of paleo polities, particularly when it allows comfortably situated middle-class audiences to grapple with what appear to be primal matters. For Pryor and other popularizers of the deep past the point of archeology is to build on the abiding fascination of mass audiences with the arche: the first principle of human societies, the traces of which are still visible and recuperable in today's landscapes.

Animated movies such as the *Ice Age* and *Croods* franchises follow this logic. So does the popular Paleo (or "Stone Age" or "Caveman") diet, which seeks to reintroduce twenty-first century humans to the primordial foods and lifestyles that (supposedly) sustained their ancestors. Though both Pryor and Paleo proponents distinguish between the Paleolithic and the Neolithic and Bronze/Iron Ages—for the latter, the Neolithic agricultural revolution is precisely where the human diet starts to go wrong—"paleo" today functions more broadly as part of a counter-modern discourse. As Chelsea Leiper argues in one of the few illuminating articles on the Paleo phenomenon, Paleo diets are part of a broader turn toward "rewilding" strategies, products of the "ecological anxiety and desperation that characterizes environmental politics in the Anthropocene, where ameliorating relations with nature and the non-human is increasingly seen as critical to human health and survival."[16] The Paleo body, in short, becomes a "new frontier for an ecological ethic of health and sustainability" and a "microcosm for interrogating the politics that go along with it."[17] Those politics are not limited to ecological concerns. The Paleo diet, like movies of the "Stone Age," and like Pryor's fanciful funeral procession, presents an archeological imaginary, a paleo body (politic) charged with excavating the present and imagining alternatives to what all perceive as our contemporary "gutted" body politic.

From our standpoint, Pryor argues, it is impossible to represent the deep past in an "*accurate* or *truthful* manner" (133). But more-or-less fictional representations of the past certainly elucidate the socioeconomic truths of twenty-first-century modernity. Visiting Peterborough to research future digs, Pryor is aghast at how the old city was "swept away—today we would say 'redeveloped,' because it sounds nicer" (21); "Money doesn't talk, it swears," he adds, quoting Bob Dylan. Throughout the book, the drama of discovery is framed by the drama of a race against time, for "Modern development was ripping the old landscape apart. Fields were vanishing, to be replaced by factories and warehouses. . . . Trees were being felled, hedges grubbed up and the rough wayside verges, rich in wildflowers and diverse grasses, were being carefully sculpted into yet another characterless 'landscaped' mown suburban streetscape" (40). In Cambridgeshire, the Great Henge at Maxey has "disappeared into a gravel quarry" (174). Pryor envisages a time "When Southern England is eventually covered by sprawling estates of identical houses" 136). The "wholesale draining of wetlands" across Europe has been "cataclysmic" (190), both for archeology (for water preserves many remnants of the past) and the economy: "Vast sums of European, government and private money were poured into land drainage schemes, to produce fields which would grow mountains of grain, butter and meat that nobody could eat" (191). Nearer to hand, drainage has depleted the "complex world, or series of worlds" (42) of the once-wet Fens of Eastern England, now a "vast growing-bag" (42) of monoculture, which once yielded to the "discerning hunter, fisherman or farmer abundance in a variety of forms" (42) because they inherited a "wealth of experience handed down from previous generations" and acknowledged that "human beings were just a single, small element in a far larger Creation" (42). Now "we and our immediate predecessors have drained the heart, soul, and guts" (41–42) out of it.

Traces of the Neolithic and Bronze Age landscape, sometimes visible on aerial photos and recuperable during digs, lead Pryor over a period of decades toward the mapping of a ritual landscape in eastern England—a landscape imbued with religious significance, symbolically oriented toward, and honoring, the water, the earth, and the cycle of the seasons, a place that offered "abundance in a variety of forms" to the experienced and discerning people who celebrated it, a place that at its edges was somehow "closer to the next world" (140). If one point of the funeral procession is thus to imagine the societies that no longer exist because later societies have superseded them, another is to function as a potent counter-memory. Its imagined participants, held within a loving family and community, and sharing a meaningful symbolic landscape with bees, wasps, stags, and foxes, are guides to the living relationships that in modern times no longer exist not because they have been superseded but because money-that-swears has demolished them. In one sense the funeral is "just a fiction"; in another it is *the* fiction modernity most requires since it represents what modernity lacks: an authentic body politic, one with "heart, soul, and guts." Pryor's archeology orchestrates an array of ironic reversals. The dead and buried Neolithic landscape turns out to contain more life than the "gutted," de-sacralized landscape of factories, warehouses, identical houses, and monocrop agriculture that sits atop it. Archeology takes the place of the funeral procession, seeming to be the last guide left to the "next world." The real funeral, Pryor seems to be saying, is ours.

Paleo diet regimes concur. Loren Cordain, a prominent Paleo advocate, argues that humans are genetically "Stone Agers living in the Space Age," the "chronic diseases of civilization" having resulted from abandoning the dietary prescriptions responsible for human evolution for the two million years prior to the Neolithic agricultural revolution.[18] Ancient humans who "survived by hunting wild animals and fish and gathering wild fruits and vegetables" now depended on a small number of grains (such as rice or wheat), legumes, and tubers (such as potatoes).[19] For Paleo advocates, the solution is "hidden back in time."[20] In a quite literal sense, Paleo diets attempt to imagine, and retrieve for our present age, the Paleolithic gut—an ancient belly for new members of the body politic. As Staffan Lindeberg reflects, the basic premise of the Stone Age diet is that "human internal organs function best with the foods that have been available during human development."[21] To ignore that is to "clog our engines, make us fat, and cause disease and ill health."[22] Many books include variations on Robb Wolf's short autobiographical account of his foray into vegetarianism and the USDA's dietary recommendation, under which he became "gassy, bloated" and "started having really weird digestive problems," as well as developing a "monstrous sweet tooth."[23]

One consequence of the Paleo dietary recommendations is a usually scathing critique of today's marketplaces for food. "When we began to eat foods created in factories rather than grown on farms," argues Diane Sanfilippo, "we moved steadily away from health-promoting nutrition and toward building our bodies from synthetic, nutrient-poor foodlike substances."[24] The government, moreover, is "more likely to represent the interests of giant food corporations, which spend millions on lobbying and campaign contributions and whose hands are deep in our pockets."[25] Foods, says Walter Voegtlin, whose book *The Stone Age Diet* (1975) was foundational for the Paleo diet, are "canned, dehydrated, frozen, pasteurized, Fletcherized, fortified, ground, juiced, instantized, Osterized, precooked, prepackaged"—a "modern, highly scientific, yet faulty diet" so much at odds with a two-million year heritage of primal conditions that it has created "Civilization's King-Size stomach ache."[26] Like Pryor's view of the landscape, Paleo diet disciples generalize from a "gutted" body to the body politic that caused it. "Helped along by food companies' marketing," observes Sanfilippo, "as a nation, our waistlines grew and our internal, metabolic physiology became unbalanced."[27] "As a society," Robb Wolf says still more bleakly, "we have become so sick, weak, and broken, we accept the *abnormal* as normal."[28]

Pryor's popular archeology and Paleo diet regimes alike confront—or more often circumvent—a hidden problematic, which is to say the increasing erasure of productive space under conditions of modernity. For Pryor, modern development does more than rip up or cover over the "old landscape"; it affords no room for new ritual landscapes because the "sprawling estates of identical houses" soon to cover Southern England refuse to recognize any variation in, or prioritize any feature of, the landscape. With all difference erased, there can be no liminal space to draw people closer to the "next world." For premodern people, the ability to accord meaning to a ritual landscape and to find abundance relies on the ability to traverse a variety of spaces. In one sense, Paleo advocates concur: synthetic "foodlike substances" have taken the place for most people of the diverse foods humans once ate. Yet Paleo politics are fraught precisely because its core dietary component—meat—requires so much pasture to produce. It requires, in short, the extensive spaces Paleo- and Neolithic humans once had to roam. Voegtlin's *Stone Age Diet* recognizes the severity of the issue. Citing Malthus, he notes that our "island in space" is "nearing the saturation of our agricultural potential." A short-term solution lies in freeing up more land by reversing the "present trend toward suburbanization." But the long-term solution can only be to "*hold world population at its present figure*." Voegtlin's ugly recommendation—to favor "superior types of individuals" and encourage the "euthanasia of imperfect newborns"—may be one reason so few Paleo advocates are willing to address the global logistics of eating an ancestral diet, preferring to urge individual choice within an economy rich enough to support it.[29]

One exception is Loren Cordain who, in a brief appendix to *The Paleo Diet*, notes that the "starchy foods of the Agricultural Revolution are the world's cheap foods," which have "let our planet's population balloon to more than 6 billion."[30] "Without them," he argues, the "world could probably support one-tenth or less of our present population"—around 500 million.[31] Cordain's solution, which is a massive switch of agricultural land from growing grain to raising healthy, lean, high-quality cattle who graze outdoors all their lives, leaves unexamined the obvious consequence. Per gram, free-range beef may be more nutrient- and energy-intensive than grain—a claim Paleo proponents always make—but it cannot be more energy-intensive per acre farmed. Cordain's own statement about "cheap foods" shows that shifting production away from grain to cattle would necessitate a massive drop in available food resources—and therefore in the world's population.[32] The diet to which humans are genetically adapted, Cordain admits, has become the "elite food of wealthy, privileged countries."[33] Despite the animus against giant grocery stores "filled with aisle after aisle of packaged, processed 'foods'" in Paleo books, foraging in supermarkets for "readily available" organic foods suffices for most people who cannot achieve the "authenticity" of actually hunting and gathering their food.[34]

Paleo diets and popular archeology set out to restore a "gutted" landscape by imagining productive human behaviors within Paleo space. "Abundance in a variety of forms"—complex worlds, discerning hunter-gatherers, ritual landscapes, authentic eating—are all consistent with a world supporting "one-tenth or less of our present population." Leiper's move to place the Paleo diet within a broader twenty-first-century cultural emphasis on "rewilding" therefore makes a certain sense. The lively mammoths and saber-toothed cats of *Ice Age* and *The Croods* might be said to perform a playful version of the controversial 2005 proposal by Josh Donlan (et al.) to rewild vast tracts of North America by importing large mammals from Africa and Asia to replace the continent's extinct indigenous megafauna.[35] The elephant, threatened in its own habitats, would become the new mammoth or mastodon of the United States, helping to restore ancient ecologies. In *Ice Age* woolly mammoths still roam the earth, an entertaining counterpoint to such proposals.

It is, however, more appropriate to think of these movies in terms of *recommoning*, drawing on Garrett Hardin's "The Tragedy of the Commons" (1968), which transfers attention from the "wilds" to a primordial economic situation: the (ir)rational decision-making processes that guide the way humans utilize available resources in "a pasture open to all." His analysis proceeds to the "conclusion reached by each and every rational herdsman sharing a commons," which is to keep maximizing profits by adding more animals until the pasture, overgrazed, is ruined.[36] Hardin's work is a foundational essay of environmental economics. It advances a critique of pollution under capitalism. The automobile industry, for example, finds it rational, because profitable, to produce more and more vehicles despite the increasingly polluted air that everyone has to breathe. His key example, though, following Malthus, is the "misery of overpopulation."[37] Hardin argues that whatever good accrues to each family with the addition of one more child puts ever-increasing pressures on the limited resources of a finite world. "Freedom to breed," Hardin concludes, "will bring ruin to all"; the ideal of the commons, in fact, is "justifiable only under conditions of low-population density."[38]

Paleo diets and Pryor's popular archeology accord with Hardin's logic of the commons. For Pryor, a nascent concept of property, marked by barrows in Neolithic times and drove lines in the Bronze Age, emerged in a landscape spacious enough to allow generations of discerning Neolithic hunters and fishers to utilize its resources while respecting the rights of others to the same land. Paleo diet principles are also consistent with Hardin's analysis of a global commons in the sense that humans would be best served by instituting a world-wide pasture open to a population of some 500 million, the ideal carrying capacity of the earth. Most Paleo advocates do not openly endorse Hardin's (or Voegtlin's and Cordain's) position; their foraging ground is usually thought of as the supermarket. But Paleo diet principles cannot be scaled up to a global population of six billion. Like Hardin, advocates essentially perceive a miserable global population ill-fed on "cheap foods" like grain and tubers. The one difference is that a relatively small population well-fed on a Paleo diet, the privilege of people living in rich-world economies with access to diverse supermarket foods, seems able to prosper amid a sea of ill health.

Nonetheless, popular representations of Paleo space hark back to a long-standing tradition in political economy of imagining a ground—an empty or nearly unpopulated "wilds," a "pasture open to all"—that will underwrite the logic of rational economic strategies when pressure comes to be placed on their resources. "Picture a pasture open to all" invites Hardin; "Supposing an island," says John Locke, trying to model how money, property rights, and a civil society might emerge out of a State of Nature; "let us imagine . . . an unbounded savannah," says Henry George, beginning an analysis of how the division of labor works to increase land values; "Take an apocryphal island in the ocean," says Walter Voegtlin, going on to recount how "Malthusian dynamics" increased the population until "people began to starve."[39] These stories of origins find new and often extraordinary articulations amid the fantastic Stone Age lands of recent animated movies. Like *Over the Hedge*, these movies look back to the likes of Locke, Martineau, and Hardin, employing an idiom of food and resource usage on a richly imagined commons to envisage first principles of human economic development. Bioeconomics meets stadialism amid animated arche-scapes. Their economic fabling also looks to contemporary debates about the fate of today's common-pool resources, the threat to which these movies offer an imaginative counterpoint.

The five movies and numerous shorts of the *Ice Age* (2002–2016) franchise concern the heartwarming relationships and adventures of a "herd" of diverse animals—including Manny the mammoth (Ray Romano), Diego the saber-toothed tiger (Denis Leary), and Sid the sloth (John Leguizamo)—as they fight to survive amid tectonic shifts, climate change, and asteroid strikes.[40] *Ice Age* (2002) constructs a tale of redemption: the animals seek to return a lost human baby to his own "herd," while Diego walks back his plan to lead the baby and mammoth toward his pack's ambush. But the movie begins with Scrat (Chris Wedge), the saber-toothed squirrel-rat, whose hilarious, epic escapades play out over this movie and the next four, and also feature in several separate animated shorts. Over the course of his career, Scrat cracks open an ice shelf, diverts a great flood, sinks the island of Scratlantis, sets in motion continental drift, utilizes a time machine, finds a spaceship, and helps create the solar system—among other remarkable feats. The plot device that generates such imaginative mayhem is Scrat's obsession with acquiring and hoarding acorns. *Ice Age* begins with Scrat's quest to bury his acorn in a glacier, an inhospitable landscape of hard ice. Managing to crack the entire glacier apart on his fourth or fifth attempt, he dodges a hail of ice daggers and colliding ice walls, and survives a precipitous plunge into the valley, acorn intact—only to be (temporarily) squashed by a mammoth. This salute to the topoi of classic animal cartoons—a single-minded pursuit of some goal inspiring impossible misadventures followed by impossible resurrections followed by the renewal of said pursuit—is replayed with endlessly creative variations in subsequent scenes. At movie's end Scrat washes up on a desert island (twenty thousand years later, having been frozen in an ice cube!) and unleashes a volcano by trying to hammer a coconut into the hard ground.

As funny, manic, and fantastic as it is, Scrat's acorn-obsession contributes to the movies' quiet representation of evolving socioeconomic structures. Scrat's comic misadventures are organized around a logic of capital-hoarding in a primordial state of nature. The acorn is essentially inert. As the hard-ice opening sequence (and hard-ground concluding sequence) of *Ice Age* predicts, the acorn is never going to get planted or grow or stay safely hoarded. It never serves as food. Nor is there ever a market for acorns. Only once does Scrat contemplate exchange when, charmed by the wily Scratte in *Ice Age 3*, he almost hands over his acorn in return, presumably, for romance. Subsequent events show that his original hoarding instinct was the right one. Within moments Scratte—who turns out to be a *flying* saber-toothed squirrel-rat—soars off with the acorn, leaving Scrat to plunge to his (temporary) heart-shaped doom.[41] A later scene in *Ice Age 3* shows the hen-pecked Scrat moving furniture around to suit Scratte's domestic whims; but he is soon lured away from his chores by an acorn that Scratte, regaining possession of, predictably tries to hammer into the hard ground. In the next seconds, the acorn ping-pongs frantically between the two of them as they battle for control. Scratte and Scrat, in short, are constitutionally unable to exchange, share, gift, barter, or contract for the acorn, which has neither exchange value nor, in the sense that its value as food gets perpetually deferred, use value.

Consequently, there seems to be no way for the squirrel-rats to move forward into a civil society. Until its conclusion the first *Ice Age* movie concurs, organizing much of its dramatic and comic material around a Hobbesian "warre of every man against every man" in a state of "meer Nature," for "where there is no Common-wealth, there is no Propriety [i.e., right of ownership]; all men having Right to all things."[42] The acorn itself is up for grabs. Sid, looking for a meal, comes across it and pops it in his mouth—only to have Scrat wrestle him for possession. Other scenes in the first movie consolidate this sense of a primal battle for basic resources. Sid meets Manny, and begs his protection, after snaffling the single dandelion that two rhinos are about to make part of their "fresh salad." Later, looking for food for their young human charge, the "herd" battles dozens of dodos for three melons, which represents their "private stockpile" (28:39) of sustenance against the "billion billion years" (28:44) they think the coming ice age will last. A semi-logic backs their determination to defend their hoard: "If you weren't smart enough to plan ahead, then doom on you!" (28:51) the dodo chief tells Manny. Living up to their status as a byword for extinction-level events, the dodos in the next few minutes manage to wipe out themselves, and two of the three melons, by plunging into boiling steam vents and stepping off cliffs. A more serious ignorance of economic principles underwrites their comic fate. To make a tiny capital stock last their flock for more than one meal, the dodos need to have planted the melons—or to enter into exchange. As it is, their determination to go to war behind their trained band of "tae-kwon-dodos" (29:04) leads to an inevitable Hobbesian demise: lives that are "brutish, and short."

These comic interludes contribute to the movie's broader narrative arc of economic evolution, which is organized quite powerfully around the herd's visit to a cave of paintings (48:20) depicting Paleolithic animals and predators after their prey. It is the one moment where "herdstory" jibes painfully with history—the human-overkill hypothesis, for example, holding out the possibility that humans were in great part responsible for the Quaternary extinction of megafauna such as mammoths (and saber-tooths). For a few seconds Manny's shocked gaze impels the depiction of a tranquil family of mammoths into feverish animation, showing them being slaughtered by highly coordinated and adept bands of spear- and rock-throwing humans. The moment recalls a traumatized personal- and species-memory and probably shows why he has become a loner, though starting a family, as Sid artlessly tells him, is what "mammoths are supposed to do" (49:24). The scene uncovers for a moment a potential crisis in the movie: Manny returns the child to humans who are collectively responsible for the demise of individual (and perhaps one day all) mammoths. But they are "responsible" in a Hobbesian world where humans are only doing what they are supposed to do: compete violently for limited resources. The movie deals with the dilemma in two main ways. First, like *Hedge* shifting responsibility for empty consumerism to Vincent the bear, it transfers the fact of human predation—historically, humans did eat mammoth meat—to the pack of saber-toothed cats. The final action in the cave of paintings shows *Diego* turning away in self-loathing, since he is supposed to lead Manny and the child to the pack.

The second and more complicated avenue is to employ the human child as a token of—and the symbolic currency of—a potential civil society. Having attacked the humans, pack-leader Soto's task for Diego is to make the child signify in the same way as the acorn, dandelion, and melon: a mere alienable resource in a world without "Propriety," where all creatures have "Right to all things." The point in having Manny and Sid defend the child so strenuously is to underscore a shift to a socioeconomic model run by inalienable laws. The movie articulates those laws in terms of "the herd." Having saved Diego from falling into lava, Manny tells his amazed companion: "that's what you do in a herd, you look out for each other" (55:49). It is a crude and perhaps sentimentalized restatement of the concern of liberal political economists with how civil societies operate. The more pertinent question, which the movie dramatizes more subtly, is what rules govern the formation of, and exchanges between, packs and herds. The saber-pack, ruled by the megalomaniac Soto ("That baby is mine!"), owes allegiance to none other than itself and to Nature "red in tooth and claw." While waiting to ambush the mammoth, one tiger's (Zeke's) sanguinary fantasy has him slicing "its hindquarters into sections" to put the "white meat in one pile, and the dark meat in another," before continuing on to the "extremely juicy" shoulders (56:32). Blood, butchery, and betrayal are the prerogative of the saber-toothed predators, it seems, not the small band of humans, whom the sabers attack and scatter in one of the movie's first scenes, and certainly not the Herd with its disparate members and decentered structure. The moment when Diego turns guiltily away from the cave painting of the mammoth represents a symbolic transfer from the pack to the Herd, for he clearly begins to acknowledge the impropriety of treating Manny and the child as so much meat to which any creature has a right.

But the capstone of the movie is the final, emotionally powerful encounter between the child's father and Manny at Glacier Pass (1:09:09), where Manny wrestles away the human's spear before returning his child. Before departing with the child, however, the father hands the baby *back* to Sid and Manny once more for them to say goodbye. This exchange is crucial because it recognizes laws beyond the "propriety" of having a child brought up by its own species (something *Ice Age: Dawn of the Dinosaurs* also emphasizes when it begins with Sid trying to make his three T-Rex "children" fit in with Pleistocene mammals, with predictably disastrous results). The extra exchange recognizes a new understanding of nonviolent exchange among disparate groups, instigated by Manny's removal of the spear and then underscored by the father's faith that his child's rescuers would return the child a *second time*, though "naturally" wild animals would not. The father's faith therefore lies in the dawning recognition that exchange can be governed by consistent principles of equity and nonviolence. The fabulous encounter at Glacier Pass encapsulates an entire history of liberal political economy. The exchange of a child between two disparate groups (humans and Herd) at the end of a movie impelled dramatically by various kinds of war and plunder implies an evolutionary shift from social childhood to adulthood: "natural" or genetically constituted "packs" engaged in a war of all against all yield ultimately to nonviolent exchange between social groupings organized in multiple forms, the outcome of which is entirely to the common good. The child is restored; spear-wielding humans do not attack the mammoth.

Historically situated, *Ice Age*'s beast fable must be considered perilous nonsense. Human hunter-gatherers extending their territorial reach across the globe were probably responsible in some measure for the extinction of mammoths, saber-tooths, and many other Pleistocene megafauna. Sid's chatter as the movie's cheerful closing music sounds—"This whole ice age thing's getting old. You know what I could go for? Global warming" (1:13:26)—puts us uneasily in mind of another set of actual and probable extinctions. For the skeptical viewer, the final moments of *Ice Age* collapse the deep past and the present into a pretty, and cruel, fantasy of civil relationships between human and animal: the movie replaces extinct animals with their simulacra and shrinks a human population that has burgeoned across the millennia into the Anthropocene to a small and relatively meek band of hunters. But this would be to see the movie as no more than a phantasmatic and inert representation. As fable, and as the kind of model political economists have traditionally engaged to elucidate the arche of economic practices, it entails another set of possibilities. The passing back and forth of the baby at Glacier Pass is a reminder of a *potential* rapprochement between human and animal—a civil society based on nonmarket exchange and mutual respect—which the movie, appearing at the start of the new millennium (in 2002), represents as an emotional and moral imperative at a global crossing place, a crossroads, for all Earth's species, including *homo sapiens*.

The scene that most fully orients Glacier Pass as a fable for the twenty-first century, and not as a phantasmatic attempt to picture an authentic Paleolithic habitus, is the cave of paintings. The illustration of the mammoth family records two points of origin for *homo sapiens*. Based on actual cave paintings from Lascaux, the illustration recalls the first known human acts to represent the animal world. Manny's mammoth brain adds what the artist seems to have elided: that the cute mammoth family also depicts a Paleolithic food source, as they cringe under a hail of spears. Viewers might mourn this moment in various ways—because it represents real rather than cartoon violence, because humans probably helped mammoths on the path to extinction, or even because (for Paleo diet advocates) humans are no longer able to secure the food ideally suited to them by hunting mammoths. But these few seconds of screen time, which open up historical matters *Ice Age* does not anywhere else confront, certainly expose the scene at Glacier pass as an ironic fantasy, or at least draw attention to the "herdstory" ideological heavy-lifting it has to do in order to make that memory fade.

If Manny's historical insight is to see himself and his putative family as food-source, however, his technic is animation. He makes the animals and humans move in a rather primitive, herky-jerky way—this is animation mammoth-style after all—but it is his imagination in conjunction with the movie's animators that brings alive the inert images on the cave wall. The movie, in short, positions Manny's imaginative act at the end of eons of human techniques and technologies for representing the world, which have shifted from inert images on a cave wall to the sort of astonishingly mobile, hyperreal representations of the world possible with CGI. And CGI as it interfaces with Manny's mind seems capable of representing an entirely different version of reality than the cave-painters' inert images. That collusion is graphically demonstrated in a long moment of bonding between Manny and the human child—and through it, presumably, the children watching the movie—after Manny caresses the painting of the baby mammoth (50:54). Suddenly the child's hand appears beside Manny's trunk; the mammoth, returning the child's gaze, draws him up; at which point the child embraces Manny's trunk. In the diegesis of the movie, the child may be construed as embracing Manny as his surrogate father or offering himself as a surrogate child, and/or assuring him that he will become a mammoth-father (as he does in the third movie), and/or assuring him that the child, when grown, will not participate in hunting mammoths. In the movie's symbolic register, the trunk/hand juxtaposition must be seen as a pointed departure from the handprints or stencils appearing next to painted animals in Paleolithic caves. Whatever this represented—an attempt to bring hunted animals ritualistically under human control via sympathetic magic, or something else entirely—the movie categorically positions the human child's embrace of Manny as a promise of nonviolent future relationships. That promise, Manny's animation reveals, no longer pertains to mammoths. It can only be realized, and kept, in the twenty-first century and understood more generally and abstractly as an embrace of *future* productive exchanges between animal and human. The scene at Glacier Pass sets the seal on a promise made in the caves; but it is realizable only in the twenty-first century's world of animation.

The images on the cave walls are commensurable with the movie's acorn, melon, and dandelion in the sense that they all represent Paleolithic resource-management as inert. Hoarding the acorn and melon blocks their potential as capital stock; the illustration of the mammoth family disguises its true meaning (i.e., as a human food source); Scrat splats comically against a painted image of an acorn on the cave wall when he tries to grab it; the saber-pack's bloodthirsty attempt to corner the market in meat invokes a Hobbesian nightmare. But the Paleolithic becomes productive when subjected to the new technic of animation. Acorns, so to speak, refuse to be hoarded. The plot *always* puts Scrat's acorns into play; they must change hands if not be placed in exchange. The pack must never turn the Herd into so much meat. Scenes depicting outrageously silly or brutal attempts to hoard resources in the Paleolithic are precisely what inspires the dazzling, virtuoso mostly comic sequences of the movie. Put another way, twenty-first century "herdstories" depend on representing the Paleolithic as a time when resources are recognized, hoarded, fought over, and consequently not utilized properly, so that animating the deep past thrusts productivity toward change and exchange in extravagant sign systems. But this does not imply *market* exchange in a simple sense. Passing the baby back and forth between Herd and human in the cave and on Glacier Pass circumvents monetary exchange, while, of course, transforming stories about the deep past (and extinct species) into profit for Blue Sky Studios. Nonetheless, such scenes sketch in a different logic for how to make resources productive by monetizing the Paleolithic landscape and its now-extinct animals precisely as *simulacra.* If the emotional impact of the Glacier Pass encounter must be realized in some sense as Blue Sky's profit, then it also puts market-exchange to the service of transforming today's most common market transactions involving animals, which is to say using them as sources for food and clothing. Herdstory—the trunk/hand episode, the child's loving embrace of the mammoth, and the civil double-exchange at the Pass—implies not only that extinct animals were animated in the making of this movie, but that animals generated in sign-systems can transform real meat markets.

At the end of *Ice Age*, the humans head one way off Glacier Pass while the Herd goes the other, eliding the question of how they might coexist in a Paleolithic landscape in which the only territorial boundaries seem to be natural ones. The *Ice Age* franchise imagines Paleo-space in several distinct ways. First, the movies' characters, including the humans of the first movie, are entirely nomadic; they compete for resources but maintain no property or even pack territory to protect from others. In *Meltdown*, the main threat to the Herd come from two long-frozen Mesozoic sea creatures, not from competing with the valley's other animals, despite the fact that all are struggling to make their way to the "ark" that will save them from a great flood. Second, common ground is often imagined as a *play*ground. In *Dawn of the Dinosaurs*, Sid introduces his dinosaur "children" to a children's playground; *Meltdown* opens with the animals frolicking in a water park replete with ice slides and pools. Third, the common space within which animals live is disrupted by a variety of inanimate threats. A wall of water is going to drown the playground in *Meltdown*, along with the whole happy valley as soon as an ice dam crumbles. At other times volcanoes erupt under the characters' feet and glaciers move around (*Ice Age*); geysers erupt randomly (*Meltdown*); tectonic plates shift and tsunamis come ashore (*Continental Drift*); asteroids strike (*Collision Course*); and so on. The franchise entertains the idea of a common space within which creatures live without property or territorial boundaries; but the terrain is too unstable, and the creatures moving through it too nomadic, to underpin any concept of a commons.

The Croods franchise (*The Croods* [2013] and *The Croods: A New Age* [2020]) constructs a much more convincing commons—and tragedy thereof. *The Croods* begins with the Crood family huddled in a cave. When they go out, says cave-daughter and main character Eep (Emma Stone), "we struggled to find food in a harsh and hostile world" (1:32) that has already killed all their human neighbors. Some of them have in fact become food for other predators. The comic idiom of the ensuing movie brings that hostile Paleo world vividly and entertainingly alive. The Croods' breakfast turns out to be a large egg guarded by a ferocious bird. The ensuing wild chase through a desert landscape—a mélange of Road Runner cartoons and *Mad Max* (1979)—has the family fighting off numerous marauding bands of creatures all trying to poach their prey. Half a dozen species have the egg in their possession before the Croods win out. Having shared the egg's contents, one last small drop falls to Grug (Nicolas Cage). "That's all right," says their stalwart father, "I ate last week" (9:04).

The first movie shares with *Ice Age* an emphasis on hunting for scarce resources in a land seemingly without order or stability. Continental drift drives them from their cave then threatens the entire country, which the Croods survive by crossing a chasm to their new "home" while their old world falls apart. As they travel, the landscape changes around them with the fantastic malleability of George Herriman's *Krazy Kat* cartoons: desert becomes tropical jungle becomes a mazy cave system becomes (in the last scene) seashore. Food is hard to come by, or changes hands, or keeps changing shape. In one scene what look like squashes become feral animals; in another, the Croods hunt the egg of a fanged bird, which proceeds to hunt them, before—struck by lightning—it falls from the sky as a gargantuan roast beast. The beginning of *A New Age*, featuring another rollicking chase in which the Croods are now the intended prey, picks up this sense of a dangerous and disorienting world as they search for what Eep calls a "perfect place to call home" (3:28). Grug chooses to camp in a desert-like place because "nothing has tried to kill us in the last ten minutes" (3:29). "So hungry" (6:41) moans Thunk (Clark Duke).

When Eep and Guy (Ryan Reynolds) get round to lighting the fire, says Grug sarcastically, "we'll eat a ration of dry twigs and bitter roots" (7:51).

The next few minutes of the movie transform the Croods' lives. Reaching the Bettermans' farm allows them to realize what seems to be their "perfect place," Eden in fact, replete with a high wall, an injunction not to eat of one particular fruit (the banana), and the superior Phil Betterman (Peter Dinklage) who has, he proudly claims, "turned a desert into an oasis" (59:00) in search of his Paleo paradise. And the farm introduces wholly new elements into the Crood movies. It glistens with almost incandescent tropical-island colors; it out-Disneys Disneyworld with its extraordinary treehouse, water features, and massive (water) wheel. The Bettermans have invented an elevator, a Rube Goldberg–like automatically igniting stove, a sauna, a flush toilet, and flip flops. Walls protect the farm from predators; trained woolly mammoths plough the fields in straight lines. A machine harvesting several huge eggs at a time provides an efficient counterpoint to the mad and barely productive chase that begins *The Croods*. There is more food than the Croods can possibly begin to eat, as the all-in eating binge that marks their entry suggests. "Lots of things are better here," observes Guy, "like not starving" (46:55). The farm, in fact, seems to satisfy the Croods' longing for a world where, in Guy's repeated mantra, "tomorrow will be better."

The Bettermans' farm places the franchise's representation of Paleo polities on an entirely new trajectory. It creates a near-perfect stadial arc. Paleo life prior to entering the farm walls has consisted of facing deprivation and near-starvation in perilous surroundings; everyone competes for resources in a state of nature conforming to Hobbesian principles of a war of all against all. The Bettermans' farm introduces the benefits that stadial theorists argued were supposed to accrue to agriculturalists. It maximizes production through an efficient use of land—a division of labor (mammoths to pull the plough) and perfectly straight plough lines—which leads to a surfeit of food, and therefore enough leisure time to invent labor-saving devices, and therefore time to relax. Grug wakes the first morning to find Ugga (Catherine Keener) and Gran (Cloris Leachman) floating in an azure pool with what look like Mai Tais. As Guy's awed "this is tomorrow!" (47:26) suggests, the farm in *New Age* also affords a variety of amusing satires on post-Paleo technologies. Thunk's obsession with looking at the world through a rectangular window encourages all manner of jokes about TVs, computer tablets, and, since he seems unable to apprehend the real world otherwise, a Baudrillardian landscape of simulacra. By the time we watch Thunk trying to watch the rescue mission through the portable frame he constructs, the episodes offer us a witty window onto our own acts of screen-watching.

The Bettermans also reach back to the origins of the liberal polity by enacting a new social technology: proprietary individualism. The Bettermans' unofficial motto is "privacy promotes individuality" (22:00); its material sign is the high wall they build around the farm to keep intruders out (and Dawn [Kelly Marie Tran] in). Welcoming Guy "home," the Bettermans, Paleo NIMBYS, are soon scheming to remove the Croods from their compound. "I don't know if cavepeople belong in a modern world" (25:20) laments Hope Betterman (Leslie Mann). Hope's insight is well taken. If the farm amusingly evokes Eden and the imperative not to eat the fruit of the Tree of Knowledge, it more provocatively articulates the disciplinary demands of the liberal state. Phil's raised finger admonishing caveman Grug not to eat bananas positions the banana as his property, that which the Croods must not alienate. The Croods are granted their stay in the treehouse on condition of accepting the logic of contracts: "Eh? Eh?" Phil says to Grug over two raised thumbs, cajoling him to agree (21:34). Built around walls, privacy, prohibition, and contract, the Bettermans's "modern world" incorporates the ideology of the liberal polity. And that, as *Over the Hedge* showed, is built around a model of "walled sociality."

Much of the humor in *A New Age*, and much of its satire of modernity, rests on introducing "cavepeople" into the Bettermans' modern world whereupon, like the animals in *Hedge*, they proceed to "struggle with the concept of walls" (25:16). Eep tries to climb the treehouse (rather than take the elevator) and then helps Dawn jump the farm walls to go adventuring for the day; Grug and Sandy (Randy Thorn) wreak havoc on the treehouse partitions. When Grug and Ugg eat all the bananas in the Bettermans' compound, their action destroys the concept of contract, ends the Bettermans' precarious détente with the Punch Monkeys, but also leads, eventually, to a differently configured Paleo polity. Hope, already infuriated by Phil retreating to his "man cave" to get away from her, finally realizes the benefits of the Croods' "sleep pile." One of her last acts in the movie is to pull down a section of the wall because it "really opens up the place" (1.26.52). By the end of the movie, the Bettermans have welcomed back the Croods, made neighbors of the Punch Monkeys and, at the dawn of human sociality, freed Dawn from her familial constraints. In one sense the end of *A New Age* returns twenty-first-century viewers to an idealized commons shared by two families of humans, Punch Monkeys, sloths, Chunky the saber-toothed cat, and Gran's Wigasus. Now the humans set out to learn the monkey's language while leaning over, not behind, a fence. One might say that the farm has been transformed into Eden by virtue of allowing outsiders to enter. The end of history (the twenty-first century) would do well to learn from its dawn.

Like the cave paintings in *Ice Age*, the Bettermans' "new age" farm contains a surprisingly potent counternarrative: a tragedy of the commons that the Paleo paradise at the end of the movie cannot quite efface. In an odd twist, the movie's original Golden Age belongs to the humans' primate progenitors, the Punch Monkeys. "Many moons ago the world was a paradise" (37:21), translates Guy; here, the chieftain claims, the "water flowed freely," they had "art, politics, economics," and grew a surfeit of bananas. To be sure, their utopia is incomplete. Vertebrae and other bones festoon the gorgeous paradise we glimpse in Guy's pictured narrative; the visual corollary for "politics" shows two monkeys shrieking manically atop separate piles of bananas; "economics" shows two monkeys exchanging bananas, leaving one crestfallen at giving up his larger banana for a smaller; and a King Kong-like ape arrives at full moon to take massive bunches of bananas in tribute. The story, moreover, is relayed through Guy in the Punch Monkeys' "primitive language" (57:01) of slaps and punches, so one sees why Guy doggedly dwells on "good times" (58:16) rather than painfully revisiting the incongruous issue of the monster, as Phil and Grug want him to do. Nonetheless, the end of the story introduces us to the monkeys' un-ironized fall: a startlingly barren wasteland, no more bananas, and a very angry monster-ape. Then follows the plot-twist revelation that reconfigures the entire symbolic order of the movie: Phil has stolen the monkeys' water, which once flowed freely through their "paradise," by diverting it to his farm.

The effects of that action ramify through the entire movie. It impels the plot. The Bettermans' creation of their farm and its surrounding wall, the injunction on eating bananas, the Punch Monkeys' kidnapping of Grug, Phil, and Guy, and the Thunder Sisters' rescue mission are all linked to the fact that the waterless monkeys can no longer grow their own bananas to pacify the monstrous ape terrorizing them. The monkeys therefore enforce the "contract" with the Bettermans to supply bananas, at least until the Croods break it by eating every banana on the farm. The revelation of Phil's water diversion scheme also forces us to re-frame the significance of the Bettermans' farm. We see now that the high walls, among other issues, protect a stolen resource. But the implications of that water-theft can be glimpsed from the first moment we follow the awe-struck Croods, mouths agape, into Phil's "oasis," which functions for viewers who have become accustomed to the desiccated Paleo terrain rather like the moment Dorothy leaves gray-toned Kansas for technicolor Oz. The farm's iridescent colors, neatly ordered patterns, and turquoise "babbling brook" provide a moment of animation-sublime—it is hyper-animation, animation pushed beyond the threshold of what it seems possible for the medium to accomplish. But it clashes immediately with the ensuing scene showing the hungry Croods descending on the food in a mad, spinning bacchanalia, their wide-open mouths spilling neon plasticky goo. Here the colors are excessively garish, artificial, as if to evoke the candy house of Hansel and Gretel or the laments of Paleo diet advocates who read the agricultural revolution as the beginning of a ten-thousand-year decline toward today's synthetic factory foods. The Croods' gut seems similarly affected. "Am I sick?" (15:02) wonders Thunk after thoroughly stuffing himself with these food-like substances.

A scene in which food is so plentiful and so unappetizing as to leave the Croods lying in a dazed heap gestures toward its bioeconomic underpinnings as well as the unethical implications of Phil's actions. Like Hardin's rational actor on the commons, Phil maximizes his good at the expense of the entire tribe of Punch Monkeys who once counted on the common-pool resource of water. Enclosing the commons has a positive utility for the Bettermans in the shape of the wondrous farm. And this action is scalable because all humans follow Phil's lead. The Croods's first impulse on arriving at the farm is to eat as much as they possibly can, and they bring about the farm's demise by eating every single banana. In contrast, we might note, the Punch Monkeys' and the monster-ape's shaky but long-established compromise consists of *not* using up all the available resources. Phil's and the Croods' actions therefore map neatly onto Hardin's narrative. "Evolved people" making "tomorrow" happen lead to excessive acquisitions for those who have corralled the commons—for the farm grows too much for three people—and arid land and coercive relations for those outside. But the consequence, as Hardin predicted, is that ultimately humans follow rational economic logic toward ruin for all. The plentiful water that irrigates the farm's superabundance while driving the wheel of technology produces not healthy food but plastic goop, humans so stuffed they mistake the feeling for sickness, and an overdependence on walls.

The Croods: A New Age taps contemporary concerns in *our* age over water usage, water rights, and forthcoming fears of global water shortages during an era of climate change and burgeoning population growth. In California, for example, an era of extreme drought has coincided with a population increase from around 25 million in 1980 to 40 million in 2020, resulting in ongoing water conflicts between competing constituencies: farmers, city dwellers, river ecologies, fish populations, leisure industries, and so on. The movie also bears a more specific relationship to the historical water diversions that led to the creation of the real and symbolic home of animation—Hollywood—the "most exquisite invented garden in history."[43] Here Disney, which owns Pixar and 20th Century Animation, grew, as did Universal Studios, which has now acquired *The Croods* creator, DreamWorks Animation.[44] The rise of Hollywood was fueled by water taken from what was a common-pool resource. As Karen Piper has documented, a "monumental act of engineering" beginning in 1913 re-routed the Owens River to feed the growth of "the nation's most famous water seeker," Los Angeles, partly by using water wheels of the sort depicted at the Bettermans' farm.[45] A "never-ending supply of seemingly free water" from Owens Lake allowed the city to "dream" into being its "wealth, its lawns and gardens, its movies and studios." In the process it made of Owens Lake a "howling wasteland of toxic dust," decimated bird populations, cut Owens Valley farmers off from their water supply, and forced the city to confront a potential "environmental catastrophe" and "endlessly expensive remediation." "Perhaps," reflects Piper without much conviction, the "birds and the city can learn to co-exist" in what will have to be a managed commons.[46]

The Croods: A New Age stages a complicated version of Hollywood's vexed relationship to Southern California's scarcest resource. On the one hand, the final scene of the movie leaves (most of) the farm walls intact, the water unreturned, the beautiful water features undisturbed, placing the characters in what continues to look like a mixture of Disneyland/FarmVille/Oz. For those disposed to read ironically, it is a fable that attempts, and fails, to push into the far recesses of the movie the queasy memory of the neon-colored goo the farm produces, and therefore gestures toward LA's real-life Disneyland and the water diversions that caused, and continue to foster, a toxic waterless wasteland two hundred miles north. On the other, the final scene does animate the kind of reconciliation Piper urges between LA residents and Owens Lake birds in the shape of humans and Punch Monkeys coexisting in an "exquisite invented garden"—a moment of gorgeous hyper-animation enacting a promise of what "Hollywoodland" could be, rather than what it was or is. The final scene thus poses something of an interpretive dilemma. Is it a Disneyfied fantasyland covering over (and up) the historical eco-thefts that built Los Angeles, or a fable that, through Hollywood animation, re-animates the Hollywood ideal?

Put this way, the question is undecidable or decidable in too many different ways. The ending of *A New Age* can be profitably recontextualized, however, within current debates about how to assess, manage, and reimagine common pool resources. Hardin's analysis, following a Hobbesian logic, insisted that the commons must be policed. People must be coerced (as Hardin puts it) if the commons and the human species is to survive, for the economic laws currently in place to govern the management of common-pool resources are precisely those that guarantee its ultimate destruction. It is in the self-interest of each entity utilizing the commons to take more than a sustainable share. And laws allowing capitalist enterprises to maximize their profits in competition with others cannot simultaneously coerce them into refraining from polluting the commons of the air and water. Nobel Prize–winning economist Elinor Ostrom and others resist Hardin's call for a coercive power to govern the commons. Rejecting the notion that humans are in fact selfish economic actors, and observing that there have been many examples of people agreeing to manage commons sustainably over the long term—grazing rights to Swiss alpine meadows have been apportioned in this way for centuries, for example—Ostrom argues that it should be possible to reach an accord among concerned parties to respect common-pool resources without the coercive powers of private property or government being involved.[47]

At this point in time there would seem to be two major objections to Ostrom's position. One is that the crucial discussions aimed at protecting the world's common-pool resources have not in fact achieved their goals. As Greta Thunberg succinctly put it, the agreements surfacing from the major climate summit in 2021, COP26, are so much "blah blah blah"—empty rhetoric because there is no independent authority to guarantee the implementation of the agreements. In the United States, for example, a change in administration can cause them to be simply ignored, as happened in 2016 when the Trump administration withdrew from the Paris Accords. The other objection is that the world is running out of time to make considered decisions if, as many climate scientists predict, one effect of rising global temperatures is chaotic change. The threat to the commons here is not so much the way in which humans seize and use common-pool resources; it is that *whatever is left of the commons will become ungovernable*. In California, for example, recent predictions are that the snowpack in the Sierra Nevada, representing 30 percent of the state's water supply spread over the dry months, will disappear within twenty-five years. Increased vigilance in resource management may ameliorate what looks to be an impending water crisis—but only if one assumes that the *other* 70 percent will not be similarly impacted. The position that the commons can be preserved by agreement depends entirely on humans having enough time to reach the necessary accords.

The logic of Ostrom's position—and of COP26—recalls the kind of Paleo polity imagined in the Croods movies. Facing catastrophic change at the end of *The Croods*, the Croods merely cross a chasm to a beautiful new world, untouched by human hands or natural disaster. At the end of *A New Age*, the Croods and Bettermans go back to the farm at a time when there are still enough "tomorrows" to use the diverted water more wisely. As Guy and Eep coyly cross a bridge to their own house, an entire empty world awaits the "pack" that Ugg says the youngsters will naturally want to produce. The *Croods* movies therefore construct, and represent a longing for, a spacious commons with enough time to imagine alternative, productive uses, as well as scenarios in which threats to it can be cleverly finessed. From that perspective the movie's conclusion is not so much Disneyfied as structurally aligned with the politically palatable but empty ("blah blah blah") fable that "tomorrow" global powers will fend off eco-catastrophe. Put another way, the notion that the commons can be managed, restored, healed "tomorrow," or by 2030, or 2050—pushing into the realm of the unimaginable the prospect of imminent catastrophic change—is Paleo thinking. It reminds us too pertinently of the ending of *The Croods*. But at least *The Croods* is aware that its fantastic economics is a fable.

NOTES

1. Annabel Patterson, *Fables of Power: Aesopian Writing and Political History* (Durham: Duke University Press, 1991), 116.

2. Aesop, "The Ants and the Grasshopper," read.gov/aesop/052.html.

3. Approximate times in this and subsequent movies referred to in this chapter are cited parenthetically in the text.

4. Judith Halberstam, *The Queer Art of Failure* (Durham: Duke University Press, 2011), 19.

5. genius.com/The-clash-lost-in-the-supermarket-lyrics.

6. Here RJ uses the Spuddies ad jingle, which Vincent sings early in the movie, to characterize the human condition.

7. The only human laborer in the movie seems to be Dwayne the exterminator.

8. The map, incidentally, shows that Hammy's ability to fill the hollow trunk with acorns is not a viable long-term answer. Vincent, however, is taken off-map to the Rocky Mountains.

9. Gilles Deleuze, Félix Guattari, *Nomadology: The War Machine* (Seattle: Wormwood, 2010), 44. arl.human.cornell.edu/linked%20docs/Deleuze-Guattari_Nomadology.pdf.

10. Deleuze and Guattari, *Nomadology*, 13.

11. Deleuze and Guattari, *Nomadology*, 39.

12. See, for example, Helen Briggs, "Rats and Pigeons 'Replace Iconic Species,'" BBC report summarizing findings in the journal *PLOS Biology*, December 5, 2018, www.bbc.com/news/science-environment-46440396.

13. Apart from authoring many popular works, including the mammoth *The Making of the British Landscape* (2010; reprint Penguin, 2011), Pryor is also a member of BBC TV's celebrated *Time Team*.

14. Francis Pryor, *Seahenge* (London: Harper Perennial, 2001), 141. Subsequent references to this work are cited parenthetically in the text.

15. At one point, for example, Pryor notes that only a "fully qualified professional" (190) could understand today's field site reports.

16. Chelsea Leiper, "The Paleo Paradox: Re-Wilding as a Health Strategy Across Scales in the Anthropocene," *Geoforum* 105 (October 2019):129, doi.org/10.1016/j.geoforum.2019.05.015.

17. Leiper, "Paleo Paradox," 129.

18. Loren Cordain, *The Paleo Diet* (New York: John Wiley, 2001), 10, 11. Kenzie Swanhart in gives a partial list of terms for the Paleo diet: "primal, real food, clean eating, the caveman diet, and hunter-gatherer." *Paleo in 28* (Berkeley, CA: Sonoma Press, 2015), 16.

19. Cordain, *Paleo*, 9.

20. Cordain, *Paleo*, 9.

21. Staffan Lindeberg, *Food and Western Disease: Health and Nutrition from an Evolutionary Perspective* (Hoboken, NJ: Wiley-Blackwell, 2010), xii.

22. Cordain, *Paleo*, 10.

23. Robb Wolf, *The Paleo Solution: The Original Human Diet* (Las Vegas, NV: Victory Belt Publishing, 2010), 16.

24. Diane Sanfilippo, *Practical Paleo* (Las Vegas, NV: Victory Belt Publishing, 2012), 15.

25. Sanfilippo, *Practical Paleo*, 25.

26. Walter L. Voegtlin, *The Stone Age Diet* (New York: Vantage, 1975), 4, 4, vii.

27. Sanfilippo, *Practical Paleo*, 34.

28. Wolf, *Paleo Solution*, 11–12.

29. Voegtlin, *Stone Age*, 243, 247, 257.

30. Cordain, *Paleo*, 215.

31. Cordain, *Paleo*, 215.

32. It would also dramatically increase greenhouse-gas (GHG) emissions from methane: even now raising cattle for beef and milk causes 34% of the GHG emissions from all agricultural produce. "By cooking so many cows," says a writer in *The Economist* dryly, "humans are cooking themselves." "The Beef with Beef," *The Economist* 441, no. 9265 (October 2, 2021): 73.

33. Cordain, *Paleo*, 216.

34. Sanfilippo, *Practical Paleo*, 15; John Chatham, *Paleo for Beginners* (Emeryville, CA: Rockridge Press, 2013), 13.

35. A key document here is C. Josh Donlan et al, "Pleistocene Rewilding: An Optimistic Agenda for Twenty-First Century Conservation," *The American Naturalist* 168, no. 5 (November 2006), 660–81, doi-org.ezproxy.neu.edu/10.1086/508027.

36. Garrett Hardin, "The Tragedy of the Commons," *Science* 162, no. 3859 (Dec 13, 1968): 1244, www.hendrix.edu/uploadedFiles/Admission/GarrettHardinArticle.pdf.

37. Hardin, "Tragedy," 1248.

38. Hardin, "Tragedy," 1248.

39. Voegtlin, *Stone Age*, 242, 243.

40. A spin-off movie, *The Ice Age Adventures of Buck Wild*, was released in 2022.

41. His collision with the ground causes a heart-shaped plume of dust to arise.

42. Thomas Hobbes, *Leviathan* (Harmondsworth, UK: Penguin, 1985), 202.

43. Kevin Starr, *Material Dreams: Southern California Through the 1920s* (New York: Oxford University Press, 1996), 229.

44. Universal Studios was set up in Hollywood—what is now Universal City—in 1915; DreamWorks is headquartered in Glendale.

45. See Norris Hundley, Jr., *The Great Thirst: Californians and Water, 1770–1990s* (Berkeley: University of California Press, 1992), pages 123 and 125 for photographs of the water wheels.

46. Karen Piper, "Dreams, Dust and Birds: The Trashing of Owens Lake," *Places* (January 2011): 1, 10, doi.org/10.22269/110124.

47. A seminal work here is Elinor Ostrom, *Governing the Commons: The Evolution of Institutions for Collective Action* (Cambridge: Cambridge University Press, 1990).

Bibliography

Abercrombie & Kent. Accessed 2010. No longer available.

Achey, Jeff. "Power to the People?" *Climbing* 232 (July 2004), 10.

Aesop, "The Ants and the Grasshopper." read.gov/aesop/052.html.

Albertone, Manuela. *National Identity and the Agrarian Republic: The Transatlantic Commerce of Ideas between America and France (1750–1830)*. New York: Routledge, 2016.

Alcott, Louisa May. "An Old-Fashioned Thanksgiving." *Aunt-Jo's Scrap-bag*, Vol 6. Boston: Roberts Brothers, 1882. Reprint Project Gutenberg.

Allen, Marlene D. "Tricksterism, Masquerades, and the Legacy of the African Diasporic Past in *Midnight Robber*." In *Afterimages of Slavery: Essays on Appearances in Recent American Films, Literature, Television, and Other Media*, edited by Marlene D. Allen and Seretha D. Williams, 76–88. Jefferson, NC: McFarland, 2012.

Amariglio, Jack and David F. Ruccio. "The Transgressive Knowledge of 'Ersatz' Economics." In *What do Economists Know?: New Economics of Knowledge, New Knowledge of Economics*, edited by Robert F. Garnett, 19–36. New York: Routledge, 1999.

———. *Postmodern Moments in Modern Economics*. Princeton: Princeton University Press, 2003.

Anderson, Christopher Todd. "Post-Apocalyptic Nostalgia: *WALL-E*, Garbage, and American Ambivalence toward Manufactured Goods," *Literature Interpretation Theory* 23, no. 3 (2012): 267–82. https://doi.org/10.1080/10436928.2012.703598.

Appleby, Joyce, and Terence Ball, eds. *Thomas Jefferson: Political Writings*. New York: Cambridge University Press, 1999.

Arrow, Kenneth, Partha Dasgupta, Lawrence Goulder, Gretchen Daily, Paul Ehrlich, Geoffrey Heal, Simon Levin, Karl-Göran Mäler, et al. "Are We Consuming Too Much?" *Journal of Economic Perspectives* 18, no. 3 (Summer 2004): 147–72. doi: 10.1257/0895330042162377.

Ashby, N.B. *The Riddle of the Sphinx*. Iowa: Industrial Publishing, 1890.

Barker, Drucilla K., and Edith Kuiper, eds. *Toward a Feminist Philosophy of Economics*. New York: Routledge, 2003.

Barker, Drucilla K., and Susan F. Feiner. *Liberating Economics: Feminist Perspectives on Families, Work, and Globalization*. Ann Arbor: University of Michigan Press, 2004.

Barney, Darin. *Prometheus Wired: the Hope for Democracy in the Age of Network Technology*. Chicago: University of Chicago Press, 2000. ProQuest Ebook Central.

Bayers, Peter L. *Imperial Ascent: Mountaineering, Masculinity, and Empire*. Boulder: University Press of Colorado, 2003.

Bell, George I. "Out from the Mountain." *K2: The Savage Mountain*. Charles S. Houston and Robert H. Bates, 145–56. New York: McGraw-Hill, 1954. Reprint New York: The Adventure Library, 1994.

Bhabha, Homi K. *The Location of Culture*. New York: Routledge, 2004.

Blinder, Alan S. *After the Music Stopped: The Financial Crisis, The Response, and the Work Ahead*. New York: Penguin, 2013.

Boardman, Peter. *The Shining Mountain*. London: Hoddard and Stoughton, 1978.

Bose, Maria. "Immaterial Thoughts: Brand Value, Environmental Sustainability, and *Wall-E*." *Criticism* 59, no. 2 (2017): 247–77.doi.org/10.13110/criticism.59.2.0247.

Boulding, Kenneth E. "The Economics of the Coming Spaceship Earth." 1966. arachnid.biosci.utexas.edu/courses/THOC/Readings/Boulding_SpaceshipEarth.pdf.

Boyle, Elizabeth. "Vanishing Bodies: 'Race' and Technology in Nalo Hopkinson's *Midnight Robber*." *African Identities* 7, no. 2 (2009): 177–91. https://doi.org/10.1080/14725840902808868.

Brackenbury, Wade. *Yak Butter and Black Tea: A Journey into Forbidden China*. Chapel Hill: Algonquin Books, 1997.

Breashears, David. "Upward Progress." In *Himalayan Quest*, edited by Ed Viesturs with Peter Potterfield, 14–17. Washington D.C.: National Geographic, 2003.

Briggs, Helen. "Rats and Pigeons 'Replace Iconic Species.'" December 5, 2018. www.bbc.com/news/science-environment-46440396.

Brown, Laura. *Fables of Modernity: Literature and Culture in the English Eighteenth Century*. Ithaca: Cornell University Press, 2001.

Bryan William Jennings. Speech to the Democratic National Convention, July 9, 1896. www.americanrhetoric.com/speeches/williamjenningsbryan1896dnc.htm.

Buell, Lawrence. *Writing for an Endangered World: Literature, Culture, and Environment in the U.S. and Beyond*. Cambridge, Mass: Harvard University Press, 2001. ProQuest Ebook Central.

Buhl, Hermann. "Nanga Parbat . . . Solo." In *The Armchair Mountaineer*, edited by David Reuther and John Thorn, 20–33. Birmingham: Menasha Ridge Press, 1989.

Burnett, Mark, with Martin Dugard. *Survivor: The Ultimate Game*. New York: TV Books, 2000.

Burns, Thomas A. "Dr Seuss' *How the Grinch Stole Christmas!*: Its Recent Acceptance into the American Popular Christmas Tradition," *New York Folklore* 2, no. 3 (Winter 1976): 191. 8e6147e654cb7cc71a2684fd8a9474ec.pdf.

Burros, Marian, "Obamas to plant Vegetable Garden at White House." *New York Times*, March 20, 2009. www.nytimes.com/2009/03/20/dining/20garden.html.

Burwell, Jennifer. *Notes on Nowhere: Feminism, Utopian Logic, and Social Transformation*. Minneapolis: University of Minnesota Press, 1997.

Butler, Octavia. *Dawn*. New York: Popular Library, 1987.

Candler, Edmund. *The Unveiling of Lhasa*. London: Edward Arnold, 1905.

Caraway, Kylie, and Brett R. Caraway. "Representing Ecological Crises in Children's Media: An Analysis of The Lorax and Wall-E." *Environmental Communication* 14, no. 5 (2020): 686–97. https://doi.org/10.1080/17524032.2019.1710226.

Carey, Henry Charles. *Principles of Social Science*, Vol 1. Philadelphia: J.B. Lippincott, 1858.

Carlyle, Thomas. "Occasional Discourse on the Negro Question." In *Carlyle's Complete Works* (Boston: Estes and Lauriat, 1885).

Chatham, John. *Paleo for Beginners*. Emeryville, CA: Rockridge Press, 2013. Kindle.

Child, Greg. *Thin Air: Encounters in the Himalayas*. Seattle: The Mountaineers, 1998.

Claridge, Laura. *Norman Rockwell: A Life*. New York: Modern Library, 2003.

Clarke, John. "After Neo-Liberalism? Markets, States, and the Reinvention of Public Welfare." *Cultural Studies* 24, no. 3 (2010): 375–94. https://doi.org/10.1080/09502381003750310.

Clash, The. "Lost in the Supermarket." https://genius.com/The-clash-lost-in-the-supermarket- lyrics.

Cobb, John B. and Herman E. Daly. *For the Common Good: Redirecting the Economy Toward Community, The Environment, and a Sustainable Future*. Boston: Beacon Press, 1989.

Cobb, Sue. *The Edge of Everest: A Woman Challenges the Mountain*. Harrisburg, PA: Stackpole Books, 1989.

Clemente, Bill. "Tan-Tan's Exile and Odyssey in Nalo Hopkinson's *Midnight Robber*," *Foundation* 33, no. 91 (2004): 10–24. Accession Number 2004297217.

Climaco, John. "Dangerous Liaisons." In *Epic: Stories of Survival from the World's Highest* Peaks, edited by Clint Willis, 60–76. New York: Thunder's Mouth Press, 1997.

Coburn, Broughton. *Everest: Mountain Without Mercy*. Introduction Tim Cahill, Afterword David Breashears. Willard: National Geographic Society, 1997.

Cordain, Loren. *The Paleo Diet: Lose Weight and Get Healthy by Eating the Food You Were Designed to Eat*. New York: John Wiley, 2001. Kindle.

Crèvecoeur, Hector St. Jean de. *Letters from an American Farmer*. London: Davies and Davis, 1782. Reprint New York: Fox, Duffield, 1904. https://www.loc.gov/resource/lhbtn.00543/?sp=1&st=gallery.

Curran, Jim. *K2, Triumph and Tragedy*. Boston: Houghton Mifflin, 1987.

Cullenberg, Stephen, E., Jack Amariglio, and David F. Ruccio, eds. *Postmodernism, Economics and Knowledge*. New York: Routledge, 2001.

Davis, Cienna. "Re-programming the Present: The Dynamism of Black Futurity in Nalo Hopkinson's *Midnight Robber*." In *Race and Utopian Desire in American Literature and Society*, edited by Patricia Ventura and Edward K. Chan, 261–82. London: Palgrave Macmillan, 2019.

Davis, John. "The Money Question." *The Arena* 5 (April 1892): 543–55. https://archive.org/details/ArenaMagazine-Volume05/page/n567/mode/2up.

Dawson, Miles M. "The True Basis of Currency." *The Arena* 6 (January 1892): 84–93. https://books.google.com/books?id=hCdNAQAAMAAJ&pg=PA84&source=gbs_toc_r&cad=3#v=onepage&q&f=false.

Declaration of Occupy Wall Street. #OccupyWallStreet. September 29, 2011. www.nycga.net/resources/documents/declaration/.

Deleuze, Gilles, and Félix Guattari. *Nomadology: The War Machine*. Seattle: Wormwood, 2010. https://arl.human.cornell.edu/linked%20docs/Deleuze-Guattari_Nomadology.pdf.

Delisle, Jennifer Bowering. "Surviving American Cultural Imperialism: *Survivor* and Traditions of Nineteenth-Century Colonial Fiction." *The Journal of American Culture* 26, no. 1 (March 2003): 42–55. https://doi: 10.1111/1542–734x.00072.

Dixon, Robert. *Writing the Colonial Adventure*. Cambridge: Cambridge University Press, 1995.

Donlan, C. Josh, Joel Berger, Carl E. Bock, Jane H. Bock, David A. Burney, James A. Estes,

Dave Foreman, Paul S. Martin, et al. "Pleistocene Rewilding: An Optimistic Agenda for Twenty-First Century Conservation." *The American Naturalist* 168, no. 5 (November 2006): 660–81. https://doi-org.ezproxy.neu.edu/10.1086/508027.

Eagleton, Terry. "Brecht and Rhetoric." *New Literary History* 16, no. 3 (Spring 1985), 633–38. https://doi.org/10.2307/468845.

Eco, Umberto. "The Myth of Superman." *Diacritics* 2, no. 1 (Spring 1972): 14–22.

Elliott, Jane. *The Microeconomic Mode: Political Subjectivity in Contemporary Popular Aesthetics*. New York: Columbia University Press, 2018.

Ellis, Reuben. *Vertical Margins: Mountaineering and the Landscapes of Neoimperialism*. Madison: University of Wisconsin Press, 2001.

Emery, Sarah E. V. Emery, *Seven Financial Conspiracies Which Have Enslaved the American People*. 1887. Reprint Westport, CN: Hyperion, 1975.

Enteen, Jillana. "'On the Receiving End of the Colonization': Nalo Hopkinson's 'Nansi Web," *Science Fiction Studies* 34, no. 2 (July 2007): 262–82. https://www.jstor.org/stable/4241525.

Erisman, Fred. "*Stagecoach* in Space: The Legacy of *Firefly*," *Extrapolation* 47, no. 2 (2006): 249–58. https://www.proquest.com/scholarly-journals/stagecoach-space-legacy-firefly/docview/234918195/se-2.

Ewing, Jack. "How Climate Change Could Cause Financial Meltdown." *San Francisco Chronicle*, January 25, 2020: D3.

FarmVille Wiki: Beehive. https://farmvillecountryescape.fandom.com/wiki/Beehive.

FarmVille Wiki: Belted Cow. https://farmville.fandom.com/wiki/Belted_Cow.

FarmVille 2 Wiki: Levels. https://farmville2.fandom.com/wiki/Levels.

Feiner, Susan F. "A Portrait of *Homo Economicus* as A Young Man." In *The New Economic Criticism: Studies at the Intersection of Literature and Economics*, edited by Mark Osteen and Martha Woodmansee, 193–209. New York: Routledge 1999.

Financial Crisis Inquiry Commission. *The Financial Crisis Inquiry Report*. January 2011. https://fcic-static.law.stanford.edu/cdn_media/fcic-reports/fcic_final_report_full.pdf.

Fine, Ben. *Social Capital versus Social Theory: Political Economy and Social Science at the Turn of the Millenium.* New York: Routledge, 2001.

Fine, Ben, and Dimitris Milonakis. *From Economics to Freakonomics: The Shifting Boundary Between Economics and other Social Sciences.* New York: Routledge, 2009.

———. *From Political Economy to Economics: Method, the Social and the Historical in the Evolution of Economic Theory.* New York: Routledge, 2009.

Firefly scripts, https://firefly2002.weebly.com/scripts.html.

Fischer, Frank, and Maarten A. Hajer. *Living with Nature: Environmental Politics as Cultural* Discourse. Oxford: Oxford University Press, 1999.

Fleming, Fergus. *Killing Dragons: The Conquest of the Alps.* New York: Grove Press, 2000.

Foucault, Michel. "Heterotopia." Translated by Jay Miscowiec. https://web.mit.edu/allanmc/www/foucault1.pdf.

Freedgood, Elaine. "Banishing Panic: Harriet Martineau and the Popularization of Political Economy." In *The New Economic Criticism. Studies at the Intersection of Literature and Economics*, edited by Martha Woodmansee and Mark Osteen, 210–28. New York: Routledge, 1999.

Freeman, Mary Wilkins. "Thankful," *Harper's Young People* XII, no. 578 (November 1890). Reprint *Feasts and Frolics: Special Stories for Special Days*, edited by Phyllis R. Fenner. New York: A.A. Knopf, 1975.archive.org/details/feastsfrolicsspe00fenn/page/n11/mode/2up.

———. "A Thanksgiving Thief," *Ladies' Home Journal* IX, no. 12 (November 1892), 1–2. https://commons.wikimedia.org/w/index.php?title=File:Ladies%27_Home_Journal_Vol. 9, No.12 (November 1892).

Freeman, Richard B. "What Happened to Shared Prosperity and Full Employment and How to Get Them Back: A Seussian Perspective." In *Reconnecting to Work: Policies to Mitigate Long-term Unemployment and Its Consequences*, edited by Lauren D. Appelbaum, vii– xviii. Michigan: Upjohn Institute, 2012.

Friedman, Ted. "*FarmVille*: The Garden in the Machine." Dec 08, 2010: 1–4. https://www.academia.edu/12516321/Farmville_The_Garden_in_the_Machine.

Froese, Jocelyn Sakal, and Laura Buzzard. "'I Mean for us to Live. The Alliance Won't Have That': New Frontierism and Biopower in *Firefly/Serenity*." *Slayage* 13, no. 2 (Summer 2015), n.p. ISSN: 1546–9212.

Fuller, Buckminster Fuller, *Operating Manual for Spaceship Earth* (1969). https://designsciencelab.com/resources/OperatingManual_BF.pdf

Gagnier, Regenia. *The Insatiability of Human Wants: Economics and Aesthetics in Market Society*. Chicago: University of Chicago Press, 2000.

Gallagher, Catherine. *The Body Economic: Life, Death, and Sensation in Political Economy and the Victorian Novel*. Princeton: Princeton University Press, 2006.

Garnett, Robert F., ed. *What do Economists Know?: New Economics of Knowledge, New Knowledge of Economics*. New York: Routledge, 1999. ProQuest Ebook Central.

Gates, Kelly. "New Media Addiction," *Television and New Media* 10, no. 1 (2009): 58–59. https://doi.org/10.1177/1527476408325106.

George, Henry. *Progress and Poverty*. New York: Appleton, 1879. Reprint London: Kegan Paul, 1883.

Giannini, Erin. "'It Doesn't Mean What You Think': River Tam as Embodied Culture Jam." *Slayage* 13, no. 2 (Summer 2015), n.p. https://www.academia.edu/14061880/_It_Doesn_t_Mean_What_You_Think_River_Tam_as_Embodied_Culture_Jam.

Gilbert, Jeremy. *Common Ground: Democracy and Collectivity in an Age of Individualism*. London: Pluto Press, 2013. ProQuest Ebook Central.

Gilpin, Alan. *Environmental Economics: A Critical Overview*. New York: John Wiley, 2000.

Counihan, Carole. *The Anthropology of Food and Body: Gender, Meaning, and Power*. Hove, UK: Psychology Press, 1999.

Grapard, Ulla, Gillian Hewitson, eds. *Robinson Crusoe's Economic Man: A Construction and Deconstruction*. New York: Routledge, 2012.

Grusky, David B, Bruce Western, and Christopher Wimer, eds. *The Great Recession*. New York: Russell Sage Foundation, 2011.

Guardiola, Ivan G., Susan L. Murray, and Elizabeth A. Cudney. "Using Social Networking Game to Teach Operations Research and Management Science Fundamental Concepts." Proceedings of the ASEE Annual Conference and Exposition (2011, Vancouver, BC, Canada), American Society for Engineering Education (ASEE), June 2011. https://scholarsmine.mst.edu/engman_syseng_facwork/294/.

Halberstam, Judith. *The Queer Art of Failure*. Durham: Duke University Press, 2011.

Halpern, Richard. *Norman Rockwell: the Underside of Innocence*. Chicago: University of Chicago Press, 2006.

Hancock, Brecken. "New Half-Way Tree and the Second World: Themes of Nation and Colonization in Nalo Hopkinson's *Midnight Robber*." In *The Canadian Fantastic in Focus: New Perspectives*, edited by Allan Weiss, 95–105. Jefferson, NC: McFarland, 2015.

Hardin, Garrett. "The Tragedy of the Commons." *Science* 162, no. 3859 (December 13, 1968): 1243–48. https://www.hendrix.edu/uploadedFiles/Admission/GarrettHardinArticle.pdf.

Hardt, Michael, and Antonio Negri. *Commonwealth*. Cambridge, Mass: Belknap Press of Harvard University Press, 2009. ProQuest Ebook Central.

Harjo, Joy. "An Interview with Joy Harjo, U.S. Poet Laureate." Poets.org. https://poets.org/text/interview-joy-harjo-us.

———. "The First Native American U.S. Poet Laureate on How Poetry Can Counter Hate," *Time* August 22, 2019. https://time.com/5658443/joy-harjo-poet-interview/.

Harris-Lacewell, Melissa. "Michelle Obama's Garden." In "The Kitchen Table: Conversations Between Melissa Harris-Lacewell and Yolanda Pierce." princeton-profs.blogspot.com/2009/03/michelle-obamas-garden.html.

Harvey, W.H. *Coin's Financial School*. Chicago: Coin, 1894.

Heidenescher, Joe. "Problematizing Consent in the Posthuman Era: Octavia E. Butler's "Bloodchild" and "Amnesty." In *The Bloomsbury Handbook to Octavia*

E. Butler, edited by Gregory J. Hampton and Kendra R. Parker, 55–69. London: Bloomsbury Academic, 2020.

Heldke, Lisa M. *Exotic Appetites: Ruminations of a Food Adventurer*. New York: Routledge, 2003.

Herhuth, Eric. *Pixar and the Aesthetic Imagination: Animation, Storytelling, and Digital Culture*. Oakland, CA: University of California Press, 2017.

Herzog, Maurice. *Annapurna*. Translated Nea Morin and Janet Adam Smith. New York: E.P. Dutton, 1952. Reprint Guilford: Lyons Press, 1997.

Hewitt, Elizabeth. *Speculative Fictions: Explaining the Economy in the Early United* States. Oxford: Oxford University Press, 2020.

Hill Matthew B. "'I Am a Leaf on the Wind': Cultural Trauma and Mobility in Joss Whedon's *Firefly*," *Extrapolation* 50, no. 3 (Fall 2009): 484–511. https://www.proquest.com/scholarly-journals/i-am-leaf-on-wind-cultual-trauma-mobility-joss/docview/234919122/se-2.

Hobbes, Thomas. *Leviathan*. London: Andrew Crooke, 1651. Reprint Harmondsworth, UK: Penguin, 1985.

Hodgson, Geoffrey M. *How Economics Forgot History: The Problem of Historical Specificity in Social Science*. New York: Routledge, 2001.

Hoeschele, Wolfgang. *The Economics of Abundance: A Political Economy of Freedom, Equity, and Sustainability*. Farnham, UK: Gower, 2010.

Hornbein, Thomas F. *Everest: The West Ridge*. San Francisco, Sierra Club, 1965. Reprint Seattle: The Mountaineers, 2002.

Horwitz, Howard. *By the Law of Nature: Form and Value in Nineteenth-Century America*. New York: Oxford University Press, 1991.

Houston, Charles S., and Robert H. Bates. *K2: The Savage Mountain*. New York: McGraw-Hill, 1954. Reprint North Salem, NY: The Adventure Library, 1994.

Howard, Hilary. "Adventure Vacations that reach the Extreme." *New York Times*, May 4, 2008. https://www.nytimes.com/2008/05/04/travel/04COMadventure.html.

Howe, Julia Ward. *A Trip to Cuba*. Boston: Ticknor and Fields, 1860.

Hubbard, Laura, and Kathryn Mathers. "Surviving American Empire in Africa: the Anthropology of Reality Television." *International Journal of Cultural Studies* 7, no. 4 (2004): 441–59. https://doi.org/10.1177/1367877904047863.

Hundley, Jr., Norris. *The Great Thirst: Californians and Water, 1770–1990s*. Berkeley: University of California Press, 1992.

Hunt, John. *The Ascent of Everest*. London: Hodder and Stoughton, 1953.

Jameson, Fredric. *Signatures of the Visible*. New York: Routledge, 1990.

———. *Postmodernism, or, the Cultural Logic of Late Capitalism*. Durham: Duke University Press, 1991.

Jevons, William Stanley. *The Theory of Political Economy*. New York, Macmillan, 1871. Reprint New York: Kelley & Millman, 1957.

Johnson, Marianne. "'More Native than French': American Physiocrats and Their Political Economy." *History of Economic Ideas*, X, no. 1 (2002): 15–31. link.ezproxy.neu.edu/login?url=https://www.jstor.org/stable/23723148.

Johnson, Simon, and James Kwak. *13 Bankers: The Wall Street Takeover and the Next Financial Meltdown*. New York: Random House, 2010.

Keat, Murray. "Surviving *Survivor*: Reading Mark Burnett's Field Guide and De-naturalizing Social Darwinism as Entertainment." *Journal of American and Comparative Cultures* 24, no. 3 (2001): 43–54. www.proquest.com/scholarly-journals/surviving-survivor-reading-mark-burnetts-field/docview/200651117/se-2.

Kern, William S. "Robinson Crusoe and the Economists." In *Robinson Crusoe's Economic Man: A Construction and Deconstruction*, edited by Ulla Grapard and Gillian Hewitson, 62–74. New York: Routledge, 1999.

Klaver, Claudia C. *A/Moral Economics: Classical Political Economy and Cultural Authority in Nineteenth-Century England*. Columbus: Ohio State University Press, 2003.

Kohan, Eddie Gehman. *Obama Foodarama*. Blog.

Krakauer, Jon. *Into Thin Air*. New York: Doubleday, 1997.

LaDuke, Winona. "Prophecy of the Seventh Fire: Choosing the Path that is Green." Schumacher Center for a New Economics, https://centerforneweconomics.org/publications/prophecy-of-the-seventh-fire-choosing-the-path-that-is-green/.

Landon, Perceval. *The Opening of Tibet*. New York: Doubleday, Page, 1905.

Lawson, Tony. *Reorienting Economics*. New York: Routledge, 2003.

Lears, T. J. Jackson. *No Place of Grace: Antimodernism and the Transformation of American Culture, 1880–1920*. New York: Pantheon, 1981. Reprint Chicago: University of Chicago Press, 1994.

LeBel, Sabine. "Notes on Cool: The Temporal Politics of Friendly Monsters and the E-Waste Aesthetic." *NANO: New American Notes Online* 7 (June 2015): n.p. https://www.proquest.com/scholarly-journals/notes-on-cool-temporal-politics-friendly-monsters/docview/2326835642/se-2.

Lecoq, Garrett. "'Let's be Bad Guys': (Re)Visualizing (In)Justice on the Western Frontier in Joss Whedon's *Firefly/Serenity*." *Annual Review of Interdisciplinary Justice Research* 5 (2016): 98–124. canlii.ca/t/t9kw.

Leiper, Chelsea. "The Paleo Paradox: Re-Wilding as a Health Strategy Across Scales in the Anthropocene." *Geoforum* 105 (October 2019): 122–30. https://doi.org/10.1016/j.geoforum.2019.05.015.

Lewis, Michael. *The Big Short: Inside the Doomsday Machine*. New York: Norton, 2010.

Lewis, Chris, Noah Wardrip-Fruin, and Jim Whitehead. "Motivational Game Design Patterns of 'Ville Games," Proceedings of the International Conference on the Foundations of Digital Games," May 29, 2012: 172–79. https://dl.acm.org/doi/abs/10.1145/2282338.2282373.

Lindeberg, Staffan. *Food and Western Disease: Health and Nutrition from an Evolutionary Perspective*. Hoboken, NJ: Wiley-Blackwell, 2010. ProQuest Ebook Central.

Lloyd, Henry Demarest. *Wealth Against Commonwealth*. New York: Harper and Brothers, 1894. Reprint Englewood Cliffs, NJ: Prentice-Hall, 1963.

Long, Lucy M., ed. *Culinary Tourism*. Lexington: University of Kentucky Press, 2004.

Mid-America CropLife Association. "MACA Letter to White House about Organic Garden." March 31, 2009. https://www.croplife.com/crop-inputs/maca-letter-to-white-house-about-organic-garden/.

Madrick, Jeff. *Seven Bad Ideas: How Mainstream Economists Have Damaged America and the World.* New York: Alfred A. Knopf, 2014.

Marshall, Alfred. *Principles of Economics*. New York: Macmillan, 1891.

Martineau, Harriet. *Illustrations of Political Economy*. London: Charles Fox, 1832. Reprint London: Routledge, Warnes and Routledge, 1859.

Martin-Lucas, Belen. "Posthumanist Feminism and Interspecies Affect in Nalo Hopkinson's *Midnight Robber*." *Atlantis: Critical Studies in Gender, Culture, and Social Justice* 38, no. 2 (2017): 105–15. https://journals.msvu.ca/index.php/atlantis/article/view/5314/105-115%20PDF.

Matthiessen, Peter. *The Snow Leopard*. London: Penguin, 1978.

Maxton, Graeme P. *The End of Progress: How Modern Economics Has Failed Us*. New York: John Wiley, 2011.

McAfee, R. Preston, and Tracy R. Lewis. *Introduction to Economic Analysis*. Open Textbook Library, 2009.open.umn.edu/opentextbooks/textbooks/47.

McCannell, Dean. *The Tourist: A New Theory of the Leisure Class*. New York: Schocken Books, 1976.

McKenna, Erin. *The Task of Utopia. A Pragmatist and Feminist Perspective*. Oxford: Rowman and Littlefield, 2001.

McClanahan, Annie. *Dead Pledges: Debt, Crisis, and Twenty-First-Century Culture*. Stanford: Stanford University Press, 2017.

McDonald, Lawrence G, with Patrick Robinson. *A Colossal Failure of Common Sense: The Inside Story of the Collapse of Lehman Brothers*. New York: Crown Business, 2009. McNaughtan, Hugh. "Distinctive Consumption and Popular Anti-Consumerism: The Case of *Wall*E*." *Journal of Media & Cultural Studies* 26, no. 5 (June 2012): 753–66. https://doi.org/10.1080/10304312.2012.664116.

Meek, Ronald L. *Social Science and the Ignoble Savage*. Cambridge: Cambridge University Press, 1976.

———. *The Economics of Physiocracy: Essays and Translations*. London: George Allen and Unwin, 1962. Reprint New York: Routledge, 2003.

Mehta, Brinda J. "Culinary Diasporas: Identity and the Language of Food in Gisèle Pineau's *Un Papillon dans la Cité* and *L'Exil selon Julia*. *International Journal of Francophone Studies* 8, no. 1 (2005): 23–51. DOI: 10.1386/ijfs.8.1.23/1.

"Michelle Obama Digs Kitchen Garden at White House." *The Telegraph*, March 20, 2009. www.telegraph.co.uk/news/worldnews/michelle-obama/5023654/Michelle-Obama-digs-kitchen-garden-at-White-House.html.

"Michelle Obama's Organic Garden Angers US Farming Companies." *The Telegraph*, April 23, 2009. www.telegraph.co.uk/news/worldnews/michelle-obama/5204434/Michelle-Obamas-organic-garden-angers-US-farming-companies.html.

"Michelle Obama's Political Gardening," Green Hell Blog, March 20, 2009, n.p. greenhellblog.com/2009/03/20/michelle-obamas-political-gardening/.

Milgate, Murray, and Shannon C. Stimson. *After Adam Smith: A Century of Transformation in Politics and Political Economy*. Princeton: Princeton University Press, 2009.

Mill, John Stuart. *Principles of Political Economy*. London: John W. Parker, 1848. Reprint New York: Augustus M. Kelley, 1987.

Miller, Daniel, ed. *Acknowledging Consumption*. London: Taylor and Francis, 1995. ProQuest Ebook Central.

Morales, Angela, and Kyle Orland. *Farmville for Dummies*. Hoboken, NJ: Wiley, 2011.

Morgan, Neil, and Judith Giles Morgan. *Dr. Seuss & Mr. Geisel: A Biography*. New York: Random House, 1996.

Morgenson, Gretchen. "Slack Lifeline for Drowning Homeowners." *New York Times*, August 2, 2015: Sunday Business, 1, 5.

Morley, David. "Theories of Consumption in Media Studies." In *Acknowledging Consumption*, edited by Daniel Miller, 293–323. London: Taylor and Francis, 1995.

Mossner, Alexa von Weik. "Love in the Times of Ecocide: Environmental Trauma and Comic Relief in Andrew Stanton's *Wall-E*." In *Eco-Trauma Cinema*, edited by Anil Narine, 164–79. New York: Routledge, 2015.

Mulligan, Megan. "Michelle Obama to Create an Organic 'Victory' Garden at the White House," *The Guardian*, March 20, 2009.www.theguardian.com/world/2009/mar/20/michelle-obama-garden.

Murray, Robin L., and Joseph K. Heumann. *Ecology and Popular Film: Cinema on the Edge* Albany: SUNY Press, 2009.

Nagar, Richa, Victoria Lawson, Linda McDowell, and Susan Hanson. "Localizing Globalization: Feminist (Re)readings of the Subjects and Spaces of Globalization." *Economic Geography* 78, no. 3 (July 2002): 257–84. https://doi.org/10.1111/j.1944-8287.2002.tb00187.x.

Nelson, Julie A. *Feminism, Objectivity, and Economics*. New York: Routledge, 1996.

Nocera, Joe. "On Wall Street as on Main Street, a Problem of Denial." *New York Times*, September 16, 2008, A25.

Noel, J. B. L. *Through Tibet to Everest*. London: Edward Arnold, 1927.

Norton, E. F. *The Fight for Everest: 1924*. London: Edward Arnold, 1925. Reprint Varanasi and Kathmandu: Pilgrims Publishing, 2002.

Noyce, Wilfred. *South Col: One Man's Adventure on the Ascent of Everest, 1953*. London: William Heinemann, 1954.

Obama, Michelle. *American Grown: The Story of the White House Kitchen Garden and Gardens Across America*. New York: Crown, 2012.

"Obama: 'You're on Your Own' Economics Doesn't Work." *Real Clear Politics*, March 30, 2012.www.realclearpolitics.com/video/2012/03/30/obama_youre_on_your_own_economics_doesnt_work.html.

Oran. "Tropical Journeyings en Route for California," *Harper's New Monthly Magazine* 16, no. 95 (April 1858): 577–93. Cornell University Library Making of America Collection.

Ortner, Sherry. *Life and Death on Mt. Everest*. Princeton: Princeton University Press, 1999.

Paine, Thomas. *Common Sense*. Philadelphia: W. and T. Bradford, 1776. Reprint Project Gutenberg.www.gutenberg.org/ebooks/147.

Patterson, Annabel. *Fables of Power: Aesopian Writing and Political History*. Durham: Duke University Press, 1991.

Perillo, Kate. "The Science-Fictional Caribbean: Technological Futurity in Nalo Hopkinson's *Midnight Robber* and Beyond." *Small Axe* 22, no. 2 (July 2018): 1–17. https://doi.org/10.1215/07990537–6985642.

Pierce, N. A. "At the Crossroads: Carnival, Hybridity, and Legendary Womanhood in Nalo Hopkinson's *Midnight Robber*." In *Bad Girls and Transgressive Women in Popular Television, Fiction, and Film*, edited by J. Chappell and M. Young, 211–26. London: Palgrave Macmillan, 2017.

Piper, Karen. "Dreams, Dust and Birds: The Trashing of Owens Lake," *Places* (January 2011), 1–10. https://doi.org/10.22269/110124.

"Politics in Spades: Why the Obama Veg Patch Matters." *The Guardian*, March 23, 2009. www.guardian.co.uk/lifeandstyle/2009/mar/24/gardens-michelle-obama.

Postel, Charles. *The Populist Vision*. Oxford: Oxford University Press, 2007.

Power, Marilyn, Ellen Mutari, and Deborah M. Figart. "Beyond Markets: Wage Setting and the Methodology of Feminist Political Economy." In *Toward a Feminist Philosophy of Economics*, edited by Drucilla K. Barker and Edith Kuiper, 70–86. New York: Routledge, 2003.

Pryor, Francis. *Seahenge: A Quest for Life and Death in Bronze Age Britain*. London: Harper Perennial, 2001.

Pyle, Howard. "Jamaica, New and Old." *Harper's New Monthly Magazine* 80, no. 476 (January 1890): 169–86. Cornell University Library Making of America Collection.

Ricardo, David. *Principles of Political Economy and Taxation*. 1817. Reprint New York: Prometheus Books, 1996.

Ridgeway, Rick. *The Last Step: The American Ascent of K2*. Seattle: The Mountaineers, 1980.

Rifkin, Jeremy. "The Rise of Anti-Capitalism." *The New York Times*, March 15, 2014. https://www.nytimes.com/2014/03/16/opinion/sunday/the-rise-of-anti-capitalism.html11.

Ritter, Gretchen. *Greenbacks and Goldbugs: The Antimonopoly Tradition and the Politics of Finance in* America. Cambridge: Cambridge University Press, 1997.

Robbins, Lionel. *An Essay on the Nature and Significance of Economic Science*. 1932. Reprint London: Macmillan, 1945.

Rousseau, Jean-Jacques. "The Second Discourse: Discourse on the Origin and Foundations of Inequality Among Mankind." Amsterdam: Marc-Michel Rey, 1755; in *The Social Contract and The First and Second Discourses*, edited by Susan Dunn, 69–148. New Haven: Yale University Press, 2002. ProQuest Ebook Central.

Ruttledge, Hugh. *Everest 1933*. London: Hodder and Stoughton, 1934. Reprint London: Hodder and Stoughton, 1938.

Ruccio, David F. and Jack Amariglio, *Postmodern Moments in Modern Economics*. Princeton: Princeton University Press, 2003.

Ruccio, David F. *Economic Representations: Academic and Everyday.* New York: Routledge, 2008.
Said, Edward. *Orientalism: Western Conceptions of the Orient*. New York: Pantheon, 1978. Reprint London: Penguin, 1991.
Samuels, Warren J, and Stephen G. Medema. *A History of Economic Thought: A Reader*. New York: Routledge, 2013.
Samuelson, Paul A, and William D. Nordhaus. *Economics*. New York: McGraw-Hill, 1948. Reprint New York: McGraw-Hill, 2005.
Sanfilippo, Diane. *Practical Paleo*. Las Vegas, NV: Victory Belt Publishing, 2012. Kindle.
Scott Morgan, W. *The History of the Wheel and Alliance and the Impending Revolution*. Hardy, Arkansas: W. Scott Morgan, 1889. Reprint Madison: University of Wisconsin, 2008.
Seuss, Dr. [Theodore Geisel] *How the Grinch Stole Christmas!* New York: Random House, 1957.
———. Fandom Wiki. No longer available.
Sewell, W. E. "Cast-away in Jamaica," *Harper's New Monthly Magazine* 22, no. 128 (January 1861): 166–81. Cornell University Library Making of America Collection.
Shipton, Eric. *Upon That Mountain*. London: Hodder and Stoughton, 1943. Reprint London: Pan Books, 1956.
Sklansky, Jeffrey. *The Soul's Economy: Market Society and Selfhood in American Thought, 1820–1920*. Chapel Hill: University of North Carolina Press, 2002.
Smith, Adam. *The Wealth of Nations*. Introduction Alan B. Krueger. London: W. Strahan & T. Cadell, 1776. Reprint New York: Bantam, 2003.
Smith, Eric D. "'The Only Way Out is Through': Space, Narrative, and Utopia in Nalo Hopkinson's *Midnight Robber*." *Genre* 42, no. 1 (2009): 135–63. https://doi:10.1215/00166928-42-1-2-135.
Smith, Yves. *Econned: How Unenlightened Self Interest Undermined Democracy and Corrupted Capitalism*. New York: Palgrave Macmillan, 2010.
Smythe, Frank S. *The Kangchenjunga Adventure*. London: Gollancz, 1930.
———. *Kamet Conquered*. London: Hodder and Stoughton, 1932. Reprint London: Hodder and Stoughton, 1947.
Söbke, Heinrich. "Gaming a Non-Game? A Long Term (Self) Experiment about FarmVille." https://www.researchgate.net/profile/Heinrich-Soebke/publication/274373986.
Solomon, Deborah. *American Mirror: The Life and Art of Norman* Rockwell. New York: Farrar, Straus and Giroux, 2013.
Sorenson, Leif. "Dubwise into the Future: Versioning Modernity in Nalo Hopkinson." *African American Review* 47, no. 2–3 (Summer/Fall 2014): 267–83. https://www-jstor-org.ezproxy.neu.edu/stable/24589753.
Sorkin, Andrew Ross. *Too Big to Fail: The Inside Story of How Wall Street and Washington Fought to Save the Financial System from Crisis—and Themselves*. New York: Viking, 2009.
Staley, Charles E. *A History of Economic Thought from Aristotle to Arrow*. Oxford: Basil Blackwell, 1989.

Starr, Kevin. *Material Dreams: Southern California Through the 1920s*. New York: Oxford University Press, 1996.

Stewart, Gordon. *Journeys to Empire: Enlightenment, Imperialism, and the British Encounter with Tibet*. Cambridge: Cambridge University Press, 2009.

Stiglitz, Joseph E. *Freefall: America, Free Markets, and the Sinking of the World Economy*. New York: Norton, 2010.

Storey, John. *Culture and Power in Cultural Studies: The Politics of Signification* Edinburgh: Edinburgh University Press, 2010.

Strassmann, Diana. "Not a Free Market: The Rhetoric of Disciplinary Authority in Economics." In *Beyond Economic Man: Feminist Theory and Economics*, edited by Marianne A. Ferber and Julie A. Nelson, 54–68. Chicago: University of Chicago, 1993.

Strassmann, Diana, and Livia Polanyi, "The Economist as Storyteller: What the Texts Reveal." In *Out of the Margin: Feminist Perspectives on Economics*, edited by Susan Feiner, Edith Kuiper, Notburga Ott, Jolande Sap, Zafiris Tzannatos, 94–109. New York: Routledge, 1995.

Strychacz, Thomas. *Food and Foodways: Explorations in the History and Culture of Human Nourishment* 18, no. 3 (July–September 2010). https://doi.org/10.1080/07409710.2010.504105.

———. *Kitchen Economics: Women's Regionalist Fiction and Political Economy*. Tuscaloosa: University of Alabama Press, 2020.

Sumner, William Graham. *What Social Classes Owe to Each Other*. New York: Harper, 1883. Reprint New Haven: Yale University Press, 1934.

Sutherland, Lee-Ann. "The "Desk-Chair Countryside': Affect, Authenticity, and the Rural Idyll in a Farming Computer Game." *Journal of Rural Studies* 78 (August 2020): 350–63. https://doi.org/10.1016/j.jrurstud.2020.05.002.

Swanhart, Kenzie. *Paleo in 28*. Berkeley, CA: Sonoma Press, 2015. Kindle.

Tabb, William. *Reconstructing Political Economy: The Great Divide in Economic Thought*. New York: Routledge, 1999.

Tasker, Joe. *Savage Arena*. London: Methuen, 1982.

———. *Everest The Cruel Way*. London: Methuen, 1981.

Taylor, Frank H. "Street Scenes in Havana," *Harper's New Monthly Magazine* 58, no. 347 (April 1879), 682–88. Cornell University Library Making of America Collection.

Teltscher, Kate. *The High Road to China: George Bogle, the Panchen Lama, and the First British Expedition to Tibet*. London: Bloomsbury Press, 2006.

Terlutter, Ralf, and Michael L. Capella, "The Gamification of Advertising: Analysis and Research Directions of In-Game Advertising, Advergames, and Advertising in Social Network Games," *Journal of Advertising* 42, no. 2–3 (2013): 95–112. www.tandfonline.com/doi/abs/10.1080/00913367.2013.774610.

"The Beef with Beef." *The Economist* 441, no. 9265 (October 2, 2021): 73.

Thunberg, Greta. Speech at UN. Sept 23, 2019, n.p. https://www.npr.org/2019/09/23/763452863/transcript-greta-thunbergs-speech-at-the-u-n-climate-action-summit.

Tirole, Jean. *Economics for the Common Good*. Translated by Steven Rendall. Princeton: Princeton University Press, 2017.

Tremblay, Tony. "Reading the "Real" in *Survivor*: Unearthing the Republican Roots in Reality Narrative." *TOPIA: Canadian Journal of Cultural Studies* 9 (Spring 2003): 47–65. https://doi.org/10.3138/topia.9.47.

"Vegetable Garden will be Installed on White House Grounds." *Washington Post*, March 20, 2009. www.washingtonpost.com/wpdyn/content/article/2009/03/19/AR2009031902886.html.

Virgil, *Georgic IV*. Translated by A.S. Kline, 2001. https://www.poetryintranslation.com/PITBR/Latin/VirgilGeorgicsIV.php#anchor_Toc534524378.

Voegtlin, Walter L. *The Stone Age Diet*. New York: Vantage, 1975. Internet Archive. https://archive.org/details/The_Stone_Age_Diet/The%20Stone%20Age%20Diet/.

Waddell, Laurence Austine. *Lhasa and its Mysteries*. New York: E.P. Dutton, 1905.

Ward, Barbara. *Spaceship Earth*. New York: Columbia University Press, 1966.

Weir, Andy. *The Martian*. Self-published, 2011. Reprint New York: Crown, 2014.

Wells, David. *Robinson Crusoe's Money*. New York: Harper, 1876.

Wall Street's Bad Dream." *The Economist* 388 (September 18, 2008). www-economist-com.ezproxy.neu.edu/finance-and-economics/2008/09/18/wall-streets-bad-dream.

"What Went Wrong—Wall Street's Crisis." *The Economist* 386 (March 19, 2008). https://www-economist-com.ezproxy.neu.edu/briefing/2008/03/19/what-went-wrong.

"When the Rivers Run Dry; Economics Focus." *The Economist* 386 (March 8, 2008. https://www-economist-com.ezproxy.neu.edu/search?q=march+2008+when+the+rivers+run+dry.

White, Ben, and Eric Dash. "As Fears Grow, Wall St. Titans See Shares Fall." *New York Times*, September 18, 2008, A1, A33.

Whitley, David S. *The Idea of Nature in Disney Animation*. Aldershot, Hampshire, Burlington, VT; Ashgate, 2008.

Wisker, Gina. "Moving Beyond Waste to Celebration: The Postcolonial/Postfeminist Gothic of Nalo Hopkinson's A Habit of Waste." In *Postfeminist Gothic: Critical Interventions in Contemporary Culture*, edited by B. Brabon and S. Genz, 114–25. London: Palgrave Macmillan, 2007.

Wolf, Robb. *The Paleo Solution: The Original Human Diet*. Las Vegas, NV: Victory Belt Publishing, 2010. Kindle.

Woodmansee, Martha, and Mark Osteen, eds. *The New Economic Criticism: Studies at the Intersection of Literature and Economics*. New York: Routledge, 1999.

Wright, Christopher J. *Tribal Warfare: Survivor and the Political Unconscious of Reality Television*. Lanham, MD: Lexington, 2006.

Wulf, Andrea. "Politics in Spades: Why the Obama Veg Patch Matters." The Guardian, March 23, 2009. https://www.theguardian.com/lifeandstyle/2009/mar/24/gardens-michelle-Obama.

Yates, Michelle. "Labor as 'Nature,' Nature as Labor: 'Stay the Course' of Capitalism in *Wall- E*'s Edenic Recovery Narrative. *ISLE: Interdisciplinary Studies in Literature and Environment* 22, no. 3 (Summer 2015): 525–43. https://doi.org/10.1093/isle/isu124.

Younghusband, Sir Francis. *The Heart of a Continent*. London: John Murray, 1896. Reprint New York: Charles Scribner's, 1904.

———. *India and Tibet*. London: John Murray, 1910.
———. *The Epic of Mount Everest*. London: Edward Arnold, 1926. Reprint London: Edward Arnold, 1942.

Index

About the Author

Thomas Strychacz is the Frederick A. Rice Professor of English at Mills College at Northeastern University. *Economic Fables* is his fifth book. His first three books concerned modernist fiction and gender, particularly issues of masculinity. The fourth, *Kitchen Economics*, focused instead on women's regionalist fiction of the late nineteenth century, contextualizing it in terms of political economic thought. In some respects, this book is a sequel, though it transfers attention to popular culture and the possibilities it offers for challenging the failing theories and practices of contemporary neoclassical economic thought. Thomas Strychacz has taught at Mills College (now Mills College at Northeastern) for over thirty years.

www.ingramcontent.com/pod-product-compliance
Ingram Content Group UK Ltd.
Pitfield, Milton Keynes, MK11 3LW, UK
UKHW020840290926
15470UKWH00004B/1463

9 781793 633965